Nuclear Proliferation Today

Nuclear Proliferation Today

Leonard S. Spector

A Carnegie Endowment Book

Vintage Books
A Division of Random House
New York

A Vintage Original, October 1984

First Edition

Copyright © 1984 by the Carnegie Endowment for International Peace.
All rights reserved under International and Pan-American
Copyright Conventions. Published in the United States
by Random House, Inc., New York, and simultaneously
in Canada by Random House of Canada Limited, Toronto.

Library of Congress Cataloging in Publication Data

Spector, Leonard S.

Nuclear proliferation today.

"A Carnegie Endowment book."

"A Vintage original"—Verso t.p.

Includes index.

1. Nuclear weapons. I. Title.

U264.S63 1984   355.8′25119   84-19677

ISBN 0-394-72901-3 (pbk.)

Manufactured in the United States of America

Cover art by Jon Lomberg.

To Kristin

Contents

Foreword

With this volume, the Carnegie Endowment initi
ates a series of annual reports on the spread of nuclear
weapons. Through it, the Endowment hopes to stimu-
late greater public awareness of the dangers of proliferation and of the difficult foreign policy choices con-
fronting the United States as it works with others to try
to curb the spread of these extraordinarily destructive
arms. In addition, by providing detailed, up-to-date
information on the nuclear programs of the nations at
the nuclear weapons threshold, the Endowment seeks
to provide an easily used reference to encourage greater coverage and analysis of this important issue.

For the last decade or longer the progress of individual nations toward the acquisition of nuclear weapons
has been incremental and often ambiguous. With the
exception of India's 1974 nuclear test, for example,
there have been no dramatic demonstrations that
emerging nuclear states have acquired nuclear capabil-

ities or significantly expanded them. Coverage of the issue in the Western press, though considerable, gives prominence to only a handful of developments during any year; these are rarely analyzed with less newsworthy, but often highly revelatory, events. Moreover, coverage is usually episodic, focusing on particular events in particular countries, making it difficult to gain an appreciation of proliferation as a global phenomenon.

The Endowment's annual reports will provide a comprehensive, sharply defined picture of nuclear proliferation worldwide by drawing together the relevant data from the preceding year on the nuclear programs of the emerging nuclear nations. Major related developments in which these nations are not the central actors will also be incorporated. The annual report format will permit these and other key issues, such as the intensity of regional rivalries or the global pace of proliferation, to be examined over time so that trends can be identified and analyzed.

The United States and other governments seeking to curb proliferation must frequently choose between this long-term objective and other, apparently more pressing, foreign policy and economic goals; such trade-offs, though sometimes unavoidable, can have a cumulative impact on particular nations' nuclear capabilities or on international attitudes towards proliferation generally. Monitoring the status of proliferation in key nations annually will permit the effects of such incremental decision-making to be evaluated and better understood.

Regional tensions and rivalries appear to be the principal spurs to proliferation. Accordingly, this report is organized on this basis and much of its analysis focuses on regional issues. Other factors also have an important influence on the spread of nuclear weapons, however, including non-nuclear bilateral relations between the industrialized nations and the nuclear threshold countries, U.S.-Soviet relations, and international economics. Future reports will provide the opportunity for in-depth analysis of many of these aspects of the problem as well.

Nuclear Proliferation Today has been prepared by Leonard S. Spector, a Senior Associate at the Endowment, who has worked in the field of nuclear non-proliferation for nearly ten years, first at the Nuclear Regulatory Commission, and then on the staff of the Senate Energy and Nuclear Proliferation Subcommittee where he served as Chief Counsel from 1978 to 1980. While with the Subcommittee, Mr. Spector assisted in drafting the 1978 Nuclear Non-Proliferation Act, the basic law governing U.S. policy today. His writings on non-proliferation and related nuclear energy issues have appeared in various publications.

As always, Endowment sponsorship of this report implies a belief only in the importance of the subject and the credentials of the author. The views expressed are those of the author. Comments or inquiries are welcome and may be addressed to the Carnegie Endowment for International Peace, 11 Dupont Circle, NW, Washington, D.C., 20036.

Thomas L. Hughes
President
Carnegie Endowment
for International Peace

Acknowledgments

Although the name of a single individual appears as the author of this report, its completion would not have been possible without the contribution of many individuals and institutions.

The author is particularly indebted to Dr. Barry M. Blechman, who originated the idea of an annual review of nuclear proliferation and who assisted the author in obtaining continuing institutional support for *Nuclear Proliferation Today*. Dr. Blechman also served as Senior Editorial Advisor to the project, providing invaluable guidance and encouragement.

Nuclear Proliferation Today has been prepared under the auspices of the Carnegie Endowment for International Peace. The project is being sustained by a major grant from the Carnegie Corporation of New York, and additional funding has been provided by the Rockefeller Brothers Fund. The author greatly appreciates their support and also wishes to thank

Endowment president Thomas L. Hughes for his confidence in this project as an Endowment undertaking and for his ongoing counsel. Larry L. Fabian and Michael V. O'Hare of the Endowment have also greatly assisted the author with their thoughtful advice.

The Carnegie Endowment and the author wish to acknowledge and express their appreciation to the Roosevelt Center for American Policy Studies which provided initial support for this project.

The author would also like to thank Nan T. Kennelly, Susan Subak, and Renee M. Key for their major contributions to *Nuclear Proliferation Today*. Ms. Kennelly did an outstanding job in compiling and organizing research materials for the report; Ms. Subak provided invaluable assistance in readying the manuscript for publication and in managing the production phase of the project; and Ms. Key brought unusual skill and care to the difficult task of typing the manuscript and entering the hundreds of revisions as it progressed. The author owes a major debt to all of these individuals for the long hours they endured and their devotion to this effort. The author also wishes to recognize the considerable contributions of David Yang in preparing the footnotes for the manuscript and of Alan Crystal in providing editorial assistance. Susan C. Fisher copy edited the text with great proficiency and insight.

Nuclear Proliferation Today has been greatly aided by an informal group of advisors that assisted in reviewing the manuscript for accuracy and completeness. In addition to Dr. Blechman, the group included Dr. Joseph Nye, former deputy to the under secretary of state for security assistance; Dr. Albert Carnesale, academic dean, John F. Kennedy School of Government; Mr. Charles N. Van Doren, former assistant director of the Arms Control and Disarmament

Agency; and Mr. Myron Kratzer, former assistant secretary of state for oceans and international environmental and scientific affairs. The author greatly appreciates their contributions in enhancing the text's balance and comprehensiveness. The views contained in this report, however, are the author's, and the participation of these individuals does not necessarily constitute an endorsement on their part of specific statements or conclusions.

In addition, a number of other experts provided important assistance that the author would like to acknowledge. Warren H. Donnelly and Carol Eberhard of the Congressional Research Service were extremely helpful in making various research materials available; Paul Leventhal and John Buehl of the Nuclear Control Institute also provided assistance in this area. In addition, the author wishes to thank Leonard Weiss, Daniel Poneman, Ze'ev Schiff, Gerald Brubaker, Bertrand Barre, Hans Heyman, Lawrence Scheinman, and Thomas W. Graham for their contributions to the manuscript. Finally, the author also would like to express his appreciation to Endowment librarian Jane Lowenthal and her staff for their outstanding efforts to assist the project; to Rosemary Gwynn for her unfailing aid in arranging for its staffing needs; and to Sara Goodgame for the many times she provided backup assistance after hours and on weekends. Original maps for *Nuclear Proliferation Today* were prepared by Brad Wye.

Leonard S. Spector
Senior Associate
Carnegie Endowment for
International Peace

Chapter I:
Overview

The spread of nuclear weapons poses one of the greatest threats of our time and is among the most likely triggers of a future nuclear holocaust. It is sobering, for example, to reflect on how the superpowers might have responded if Israel had used nuclear weapons against Soviet-backed Egyptian forces in the 1973 Middle East War, a course Israel reportedly considered.

Even if nuclear cataclysm were avoided, the use of nuclear arms in a regional war could cause untold devastation. A handful of nuclear weapons could destroy any country in the Middle East as a national entity, cause hundreds of thousands of casualties in the densely populated cities of India or Pakistan, or, if used against the Persian Gulf oil fields, undermine the economies of the West.

The spread of nuclear arms also raises the risk that new nuclear weapon states may attempt to intimidate their non-nuclearized neighbors. Libya might well use nuclear arms to support its adventurism in Northern Africa, while South Africa's nuclear weapons capability may already be buttressing its efforts to impose a regional settlement on neighboring states. Even the major powers are vulnerable to such pressures: Argentina's possession of nuclear arms, for example, would certainly have entered into British calculations in responding to the invasion of the Falklands.

The spread of nuclear arms also increases the risk of their falling into the hands of dissident military elements or revolutionaries. Indeed, if the Shah's nuclear program had been perhaps five years more advanced, Iran's revolutionary government might today have the essentials for nuclear arms. The threat of nuclear terrorism is also growing. Boston, Orlando, Los Angeles, and Spokane have already been the target of apparently credible nuclear threats that later proved to be hoaxes. In the case of a genuine threat, national leaders would face agonizing choices. At the same time, the spread of nuclear weapons heightens the likelihood of conventional war, as governments become tempted to strike preemptively against the nuclear installations of potential adversaries. Israel took such a step in 1981, and some observers believe India may now be contemplating similar action.

Finally, the more nations that possess nuclear weapons, the greater the risk that such arms will be used accidentally or inadvertently. No nuclear command and control system can be fool-proof. The greater the number of such systems, the higher the probability of a failure.

For all these reasons, halting the spread of nuclear arms has been a long-standing priority for the United States and the international community. This volume records their successes and failures over the past year.

The Historical Setting

As of July 1984, five nations—the United States, the Soviet Union, Great Britain, France, and China—are known to possess nuclear weapons (i.e. atomic bombs) and even more powerful thermonuclear arms (i.e. hydrogen bombs).

These nations acquired such weapons by the late 1960s and have openly tested them and incorporated them into their military forces. But disturbing as these arsenals may be, relatively stable nuclear relationships have emerged among the five. In the late 1960s, however, a second wave of proliferation began, as less developed nations in tension-filled regions began to develop nuclear weapons capabilities.

Although it has never acknowledged possessing them, Israel is thought to have obtained such weapons secretly by 1968 and may now possess an arsenal of some twenty untested nuclear weapons (or their easily assembled components.) India detonated a single nuclear device in 1974 but has not conducted further tests nor, it is believed, manufactured nuclear weapons. South Africa is thought to have accumulated nuclear material for about fifteen nuclear devices beginning in the mid-1970s and may have built an undeclared nuclear arsenal. In view of developments between mid-1983 and mid-1984, it appears that Pakistan is now on the verge of acquiring a nuclear capability similar to these. Although it is not reported to have accumulated enough nuclear weapons material for a nuclear device, Pakistan may possibly have succeeded in producing a quantity of this material and is thought to have completed much of the remaining work needed to manufacture nuclear explosives.

Argentina, Brazil, Iraq, and Libya, although they lack the ability to manufacture atomic explosives, have all taken important steps at one time or another to develop such a capability.

Nuclear proliferation involving these nations—many of which have fought repeated wars with bordering states and have highly unstable governments—presents a host of new and unpredictable dangers to world peace. One need only recall Iraq's invasion of Iran and subsequent use of chemical weapons, and a recent Libyan threat to destroy U.S. nuclear depots in Europe to appreciate the uncertainties of military decision-making in the emerging nuclear states and the risks this might engender if nuclear weapons were present.

The International Non-Proliferation Regime

Manufacturing nuclear weapons is a daunting technological challenge. The most difficult obstacle is obtaining nuclear explosive material, either highly enriched uranium or plutonium. To obtain the former, natural uranium must be improved in an enrichment plant to weapons grade. Enrichment plants are particularly complex technologically, and the enriched uranium route to the bomb is generally considered the most difficult. Plutonium is produced in uranium fuel when it is used in a nuclear reactor. The used fuel must then be transferred to a reprocessing plant where it is dissolved in nitric acid and the plutonium extracted from other fuel constituents with which it is amalgamated. Building the necessary reactor and reprocessing installation also requires considerable technical skill. (See Appendix A.) Generally speaking, the nations arousing proliferation concern today have had to rely on assistance from the industrialized nations to build the facilities necessary to produce nuclear weapons material, although over the years a number of the nuclear threshold countries have developed considerable nuclear engineering and manufacturing capabilities of their own.

Not all nations with the ability to manufacture nuclear weapons have done so, for example, Canada, Sweden, Switzerland, Belgium, West Germany, and Japan. Over the years the United States has sponsored a number of important international initiatives aimed at reducing the motivations for nuclear weapons and limiting the spread of nuclear weapons capabilities.

Immediately after World War II, the U.S. proposed the Baruch plan to establish international control of all nuclear materials and facilities. When negotiations on this proposal foundered because certain aspects were unacceptable to the Soviet Union, the United States turned to a policy of secrecy in the hope that this would prevent other nations from developing nuclear arms. The Soviet Union's first test of an atomic bomb in 1949, and Great Britain's in 1952, made clear that secrecy alone would not halt proliferation.

Accordingly, in 1953 the United States inaugurated the Atoms for Peace program, offering to share peaceful nuclear technology with other nations if they would pledge to use U.S. equipment and material exclusively for peaceful purposes and to accept inspections for verifying their compliance. The United States subsequently signed agreements for nuclear cooperation with some thirty nations under this program.

In 1957 the United States was instrumental in establishing the International Atomic Energy Agency (IAEA), a U.N.-affiliated organization which now has more than one hundred members. The Agency's dual role is to promote the peaceful uses of nuclear energy and to implement a system of audits, physical inventories and inspections, known collectively as safeguards, to nuclear installations around the world to verify they are being used exclusively for peaceful purposes. The United States is also a chief sponsor of the 1968 Treaty on the Non-Proliferation of Nuclear Weapons, which some 121 non-nuclear-weapon states have now ratified, pledging not to manufacture nuclear weapons and to place all of their nuclear installations under the IAEA safeguards system. Argentina, Brazil, India, Israel, Pakistan, and South Africa have not ratified the treaty, however, and have important unsafeguarded nuclear installations that can be used to support nuclear weapons programs without violating any international undertaking.

Finally, in 1974 the United States brought together all of the principal nuclear-supplier nations to try to work out a common set of export control standards. The guidelines adopted by the group specified that IAEA safeguards would be applied to any exported nuclear material and equipment and that the suppliers would "exercise restraint" in making sales of enrichment and reprocessing facilities that, while ostensibly part of a recipient country's civilian nuclear program, could provide direct access to nuclear weapons material. Several individual supplier nations have adopted export policies that go beyond those adopted by the suppliers as a group. The 1978 U.S. Nuclear Non-Proliferation Act, for example, prohibits sales of nuclear reactors and fuel to nations that have not placed *all* of their nuclear installations under IAEA safeguards. (More details on the technological requirements for nuclear weapons and related international institutions and treaties may be found in the appendices).

How these various elements of the international non-proliferation regime operate in practice is explained in chapters dealing with the developments in specific countries. But valuable as this regime has been in slowing the spread of nuclear arms, it has not succeeded in halting the process, and the trend toward further proliferation is continuing.

Nuclear Proliferation Today

From mid-1983 to mid-1984, the period reviewed in this book, no new nation is known to have tested a nuclear device. It is possible, however, that one additional nation—Pakistan—may have acquired the capability for manufacturing nuclear weapons, a grave setback for efforts to curb the spread of these arms. This would mean that the line-up that has prevailed for nearly a decade—five full-fledged nuclear states and three ambiguous ones—may soon have to be recast to include a fourth in the ambiguous category. Moreover, the risk of further proliferation increased significantly over the twelve months ending July 1984, as several other nations near to, or just beyond, the nuclear weapons threshold took important steps to acquire or expand their capabilities to manufacture nuclear weapons and as pressures intensified on at least two such countries to pursue active nuclear weapons programs.

    South Asia. Pakistan has been seeking to develop nuclear weapons since 1972 but has lacked the capability to manufacture the necessary nuclear material.* In February 1984, however, Pakistan announced that it had mastered the uranium enrichment process, and in July, a senior Reagan administration official was quoted in the press as declaring that Pakistan had

---

* The developments summarized here are discussed in detail in the respective sections dealing with particular countries, along with detailed citations that will not be repeated. A glossary explaining key technical terms, such as "enrichment," is provided at the end of the book.

produced weapons grade uranium at its unsafeguarded Kahuta enrichment plant. Although other administration sources have questioned this report, U.S. officials have confirmed that Pakistan has continued clandestine efforts to design nuclear weapons and to obtain the equipment and materials needed to manufacture them. Indeed, in April 1984, the Reagan administration advised the Senate Foreign Relations Committee that the $3.2 billion U.S. military and economic aid program for Pakistan, initiated in 1981, would have to be terminated if (as proposed in pending legislation) it were made conditional on a Presidential finding that Pakistan was not engaging in such activities. Press accounts in June 1984 also disclosed that China has provided detailed information on the design of nuclear arms to Pakistan and was continuing to provide technical assistance for the Kahuta uranium enrichment facility. And in July, three Pakistani nationals were indicted in Houston, Texas, for attempting to smuggle electronic parts for nuclear weapons, themselves, out of the United States.

These developments indicate that one objective of the U.S. aid program, persuading Pakistan to forego continued development of nuclear arms by providing it with an alternative means for improving its security, has not been achieved. On the other hand, Pakistan has refrained from conducting a nuclear test and is not known to have violated the IAEA safeguards that cover a portion of its nuclear program, no doubt partly because of the threat that such action would trigger a U.S. aid cutoff.

How India may react to Pakistan's emerging nuclear capability is uncertain. New Delhi is reported to be maintaining a nuclear test site in a high state of readiness and will now be under increasing pressure to resume a nuclear explosives program in earnest after ten years of restraint. In addition, in mid-1983, India acquired a major new source of plutonium usable for nuclear weapons with the inauguration of its Madras I nuclear power plant, the first in India not subject to IAEA safeguards. By taking plutonium-bearing spent fuel from this reactor and extracting the plutonium at its Tarapur reprocessing plant, India could greatly increase its stock of nuclear weapons material that could be used in nuclear explosives without violating any international agreement.

Although it is still possible that an active nuclear arms race in South Asia may be averted, the risk of such a race appears to be dramatically increasing.

Latin America. Argentina announced in November 1983 that for five years it had been secretly building a plant capable of producing weapons-grade uranium in 1985—possibly enough for six weapons per year. The secrecy surrounding the plant, the fact that it is far larger than needed for Argentina's civilian nuclear energy program, and Argentina's refusal to place the facility under IAEA inspection strongly suggest that the installation was built to match Brazil's enrichment activities and to provide the basis for a future Argentine nuclear weapons capability.

It was hoped that with the inauguration of Raul Alfonsín in December 1983, Argentina's first democratically elected leader in over a decade, Argentina might slow development of some of the more provocative parts of its nuclear program or accept IAEA supervision of its currently unsafeguarded nuclear installations. By April 1984, however, the Alfonsín government had rejected both measures, and it appears that, for domestic political reasons, a major change of course in Argentina's nuclear program is not likely for some time.

Brazil, responding to Argentina's enrichment

breakthrough, has sharply stepped up its own nuclear research and development activities at its atomic research centers in São Paulo and São Jose dos Campos aimed at producing nuclear weapons material not subject to IAEA safeguards. Indeed, in a series of statements during late 1983 and early 1984, Brazilian military leaders made clear that the purpose of this effort was to give Brazil the capability to produce nuclear weapons by 1990, when a decision on whether to proceed with their manufacture would be made.

Argentina may yet shift to a less provocative nuclear policy, a step that would greatly reduce pressures in Brazil for the acquisition of such a capability; through mid-1984, however, the nuclear competition between the two Latin American powers appeared to be intensifying.

Middle East. The gravest new development in this region from the standpoint of nuclear proliferation may have been Iraq's use of another unconventional weapon—lethal chemical agents—in its war against Iran. The use of chemical agents directly violated the 1925 Geneva Protocol, which Iraq signed in 1931, casting doubt on its commitment to another arms control agreement it has ratified, the Nuclear Non-Proliferation Treaty, which prohibits the manufacture of nuclear weapons. Iraq's action also suggests that Iraq might have little compunction about using nuclear arms in its war against Iran if they were available.

Iraq's actual capability to manufacture nuclear arms was greatly set back by Israel's destruction of the Osirak research reactor in 1981. Nevertheless, in 1984 it was revealed that for several years Iraq had been seeking to purchase 34 kilograms of plutonium—enough for perhaps six nuclear weapons—through a 30-member Italian black market arms smuggling ring. Iraq also continues to hold 12.5 kilograms of highly enriched uranium fuel that France supplied for the now-destroyed reactor. This could be enough for a single nuclear weapon if carefully designed. Although the material is subject to continuing inspections by the IAEA, it could pose a near-term proliferation danger given Iraq's apparent readiness to violate its arms control pledges.

Also during 1984, Libya concluded an agreement for cooperation with Belgium to permit Libya's purchase of a specialized uranium processing plant—a plant for which Libya has no apparent need but which could possibly assist it in a future nuclear weapons development effort. In May 1984, it was revealed that Libya had provided Argentina with one hundred million dollars' worth of arms during the 1982 Falklands War. Some nine months after this transfer, a forty-five-member Argentinian delegation visited Tripoli to discuss increased Argentine nuclear and arms exports to Libya, suggesting the possibility of a nuclear quid pro quo for Tripoli's help during the Falklands crisis.

Israel has maintained its ambiguous nuclear posture while presumably continuing to build up its reported small nuclear arsenal, using plutonium produced in its reactor at Dimona. In addition, Israel began studies to select the site for a nuclear power plant. If, as it has done with its Dimona reactor, it refuses to place this facility under IAEA inspection, the plant could greatly increase Israel's capacity for producing plutonium for nuclear arms.

While no Middle East state thus passed a significant milestone in the pursuit of nuclear arms through mid-1984, pressures for further proliferation in the region remained strong.

Africa. South Africa may be substantially augmenting its store of weapons-usable highly enriched uranium. If reports are accurate that sometime between

1980 and 1982 Pretoria obtained significant quantities of low-enriched uranium not subject to international inspection from China, South Africa may be using this material as feedstock for its Valindaba pilot-scale enrichment plant; in principle, this step could allow Pretoria to triple the amount of highly enriched uranium usable for nuclear weapons produced in that installation.

Growing Constraints

However disturbing these developments, constraints on the spread of nuclear arms are also growing. The renunciation of nuclear weapons is slowly becoming a norm of international conduct, as seen in the increasing number of parties to the Non-Proliferation Treaty and the slow rate at which new nations are crossing the nuclear weapons threshold. The continued vitality of the IAEA and China's decisions to join that body and, reportedly, to require IAEA safeguards on all future nuclear exports, are also indications that the international non-proliferation regime is gaining strength.

The nuclear supplier nations are also exercising greater care than ever before in restricting exports that could aid additional nations to develop nuclear capabilities, as evidenced by a recent tightening of the suppliers' export control list and by France's refusal to supply compressors for a Brazilian uranium enrichment plant early in 1984—even though this facility is under international inspection. Furthermore, as seen in the recent decisions of all the Western nuclear supplier countries not to submit bids for the sale of a new nuclear power plant to Pakistan, the supplier nations appear for the first time to be prepared to impose joint nuclear trade sanctions against a non-nuclear-weapon nation that does not accept IAEA safeguards over its entire nuclear program. Previously, exports were considered acceptable by many suppliers as long as the specific facility in question was placed under safeguards.

The stepped-up non-proliferation activities of the United States since the mid-1970s have also meant that would-be proliferators have, in most cases, faced constant U.S. diplomatic pressure to halt their development of nuclear capabilities. U.S. threats to terminate nuclear cooperation and bilateral aid have also raised considerably the costs of "going nuclear."

While these factors have plainly not arrested the trend toward further proliferation, as the case of Pakistan so graphically illustrates, they appear to have reduced the attractiveness to emerging nuclear powers of the outright development of nuclear weapons—the model followed by the five declared nuclear weapon states. Instead, Pakistan may continue to follow the more ambiguous approach of Israel, South Africa, and (since 1974) India of acquiring a nuclear capability without overtly manufacturing weapons or conducting nuclear tests. This also may be the long-term goal of the nuclear activities in Argentina and Brazil that these nations have refused to place under international inspection.

While such indeterminate nuclear weapons capabilities may well present fewer overall risks than full-fledged programs under which nuclear arms are integrated into national military forces and can be used almost instantaneously, a world with six, or possibly more, de facto nuclear weapon states, which could count on having such arms in any protracted conflict, still poses serious dangers. And if more nations reach this level of nuclearization, there will be no guarantee that they will remain at this plateau or that still others will not be encouraged to follow their example. For these reasons, international efforts to curb the spread of nuclear weapons continue to aim at preventing nations from reaching even this stage of nuclear armament. As the events of the past year indicate, these efforts have met with only limited success.

* * *

The events of 1983-84 are analysed in detail in the chapters that follow on the eight emerging nuclear-weapon states—India, Pakistan, Israel, Libya, Iraq, Argentina, Brazil, and South Africa. Each includes detailed background information on the relevant nation's nuclear program so that the year's developments can be assessed in their historical context. A table detailing the nuclear installations in each of the eight nations and a map locating them appears at the end of each country section. A final chapter reviews important related events that took place outside the eight countries of greatest proliferation concern.

Chapter II:
Asia

Introduction

Pakistan and India may be poised on the brink of a major nuclear arms race. In the past year, U.S. officials reported that Pakistan may have produced nuclear weapons material not subject to non-proliferation restrictions and was continuing its program to design a nuclear bomb. Indeed, Pakistan, itself announced that it had mastered the technique for enriching uranium. Although the United States has threatened to cut off $3.2 billion in U.S. economic and military aid if Pakistan tests a nuclear explosive—and perhaps even if it assembles a complete nuclear device or violates IAEA safeguards to obtain weapons material—the United States may be prepared to tolerate Pakistan's acquiring all of the necessary components. With China rumored to have given Pakistan critical nuclear weapons design information that might make a test unnecessary, this "bomb in the basement" would look little different from a proven nuclear weapons arsenal, especially to Indian eyes.

India, meanwhile, which has held back from conducting further nuclear explosions since its May 1974 detonation, may be readying another test and now has both a small stockpile of nuclear-weapons-usable plutonium not subject to IAEA safeguards and operating facilities that could greatly increase the supply of this nuclear weapons material in the next several years. With Pakistan now virtually in possession of a nuclear weapons capability, India's leaders will perceive greater reason to restart the nation's nuclear explosives program and restore India's lead. The long-term outlook for continued Indian restraint appears unpromising: Prime Minister Indira Gandhi, who approved India's 1974 test, is already on record as stating that India would conduct further nuclear tests when they are "in the national interest." And, if further Indian tests are conducted, it is hard to imagine that Pakistani president Zia would hold back from a similar course.

Two other nations in Asia—South Korea and Taiwan—have initiated nuclear weapons programs in the past, but the possibility that they might acquire an operational capability in the near term appears less likely. In the mid-1970s, U.S. pressure caused both countries to terminate their weapons activities and agree not to build reprocessing facilities for separating weapons-usable plutonium from spent reactor fuel. Neither nation is now planning to build either such facilities or plants that could produce highly enriched uranium for weapons. Both nations are also parties to the Non-Proliferation Treaty.

Seoul initiated its nuclear weapons program in the early 1970s, apparently out of fear that the U.S. commitment to its defense was wavering.[1] Today, such fears have abated, and Seoul appears to accept U.S.

security guarantees—backed up by the deployment of U.S. troops in Korea armed with tactical nuclear weapons—as sufficient for its defense. Although tensions with North Korea intensified after a bomb planted by North Korean agents killed four members of the South Korean cabinet in October 1983, there have been no indications that Seoul is reconsidering its renunciation of nuclear weapons.

In Taiwan, confidence in U.S. ties may not be as strong.[2] While the United States has continued to supply it with defensive arms, the People's Republic of China is now applying increasing pressure to restrict such sales, and President Reagan's trip to China in April 1984, where he invoked Peking as a strategic counter to Moscow, demonstrated the growing importance to Washington of Sino-U.S. relations.

Taiwanese leaders plainly recognize that this may mean reduced U.S. military support for their island. Their strategy to provide for its security in light of these emerging trends has been to maximize U.S. aid, while developing its conventional arms industry, with particular emphasis on air defense capabilities; a nuclear deterrent is not known to be under consideration. Taiwanese president Chiang Ching-kuo told the German weekly *Der Spiegel* in May 1983 that his nation would not build atomic weapons, although he noted that Taiwan had the scientific and technological capability to do so.[3] Similarly, in November 1983, the Taiwanese press reported that Taiwan's cabinet, in a formal response to a question from a legislator, stated that "the government of the Republic of China under its established policy will never develop nuclear weapons . . . There is no reason to develop nuclear weapons to 'kill our own people.' However . . . the government has spared no effort to develop high technology defense industries in this country."[4] No evidence has emerged to contradict these declarations that Taiwan is not pursuing nuclear weapons at this time.

Finally, while Japan unquestionably has the capacity to produce nuclear weapons and is developing sizable reprocessing and enrichment capabilities, its history as the first victim of nuclear attack and the resulting strong domestic opposition to nuclear weapons exclude it as a proliferation threat at least for the present. It is conceivable, however, that were Korea or Taiwan to acquire such weapons, Japan might re-examine its stance.

India

Since demonstrating its ability to produce nuclear weapons in its May 18, 1974, nuclear test, India has refrained from conducting further nuclear tests or manufacturing nuclear weapons. India's nuclear weapons material production capability is growing rapidly, however, and its program for building intermediate-range missiles capable of delivering such weapons is progressing. Confronted with an emerging nuclear threat from Pakistan, India may perceive increasing reason to use this new potential for the overt development of nuclear arms.

I. Background

Early Developments. In 1948, a year after attaining its independence from Great Britain, India established an Atomic Energy Commission to advise government leaders on nuclear issues, oversee the training of Indian nuclear scientists, and survey India's potential uranium resources.[1] In 1954, the Department of Atomic Energy (DAE) was created to build and operate India's nuclear installations, and by the following year more than two hundred scientists were engaged in nuclear research and development at the DAE's Trombay Atomic Research Center. In a 1958 reorganization, the DAE was placed under the Atomic Energy Commission, which was given policy-making and budgetary authority over the entire Indian nuclear program, subject to approval by the prime minister.[2]

In 1956, India commissioned its first research reactor, Apsara, at the Trombay Center. The reactor was constructed indigenously and used medium-enriched uranium supplied by Britain.[3]

After two years of negotiations, India concluded arrangements in 1956 to obtain a large, forty-megawatt natural-uranium/heavy-water research reactor from Canada. The United States was to supply the heavy water for the facility, known as CIRUS (Canadian-Indian-Reactor-U.S.), which would later produce the plutonium for India's 1974 nuclear test. Under the terms of the agreements with Canada and the United States, New Delhi pledged to use the reactor, the heavy water, and any plutonium produced in the reactor exclusively for "peaceful purposes," but it did not accept bilateral or then-proposed international inspections on the plant to verify that it was adhering to this pledge.[4]

The reactor was completed in July 1960. Canada provided half the fuel for the reactor initially, with India gradually taking over an increasing share of the fuel supply, using uranium from Kerala State and a small fuel fabrication plant at the Trombay Center. A small West German-built heavy-water plant at Nangal was completed in 1962 to make up any heavy-water losses at the reactor.[5] Like CIRUS, none of these facilities was subject to safeguards.

India's opposition to international oversight of its nuclear program was not confined to the CIRUS agreements and its exclusion of the additional plants from external supervision. As early as 1954, Prime Minister Jawaharlal Nehru, in a speech to parliament had condemned the concept as it applied to nuclear raw materials and their production;[6] and at the Conference on the Statute of the International Atomic Energy Agency (IAEA), Homi Bhabha, head of the Indian Atomic Energy Commission, repeatedly sought to weaken provisions in the Agency's charter concerning the IAEA's oversight functions.[7] Bhabha was concerned particularly about proposed provisions in the statute that might have given the Agency the authority to determine the conditions under which nations could reprocess spent fuel to obtain plutonium or which would have required stocks of plutonium to be placed in Agency custody. India's stated reason for its opposition was that plutonium use was critical to India's long-term nuclear plan, established in 1954, which called for the development of plutonium-fueled breeder reactors that would irradiate thorium—an element India possessed in great abundance—to transmute it into uranium-233. This in turn could be used to fuel future nuclear power plants.[8] With plutonium playing such a central role in this long-term strategy, Bhabha objected to IAEA restrictions that would interfere unduly in the economic life of member states and abridge the "inalienable right of states to produce and hold the fissionable material [e.g., plutonium] required for their peaceful power programs."[9]

First Reprocessing Plant. India's nuclear energy plan also meant that reprocessing—the extraction of plutonium from spent reactor fuel—would be an integral part of the Indian nuclear program, and in 1958 plans were announced for construction of a pilot-scale reprocessing plant at the Trombay Atomic Research Center. The plant, with the capacity to handle thirty metric tons (1 metric ton = 2200 pounds) of spent fuel annually, was intended to extract plutonium from fuel irradiated in the CIRUS plant and two smaller research reactors at the site. This facility, too, was not subject to external safeguards of any kind. India received engineering assistance from an American firm, Vitro International, as well as from French engineering consultants. The plant began full-scale operations in 1966; plutonium extracted in it from the CIRUS reactor's spent fuel formed the core of the nuclear device detonated in 1974.[10]

At the time its construction began, however, the reprocessing plant may well have been intended exclusively as a means of advancing India's nuclear energy program. The United States and other advanced nations had touted reprocessing as an essential part of nuclear power programs, and during the mid-1950s both the United States and France declassified extensive information on reprocessing.[11] Moreover, between 1959 and 1965, the United States trained 271 foreign nationals, 58 of them Indian, in programs that included reprocessing and plutonium-handling, another indication of the prevailing view that reprocessing would play an important role in the development of civilian nuclear energy.[12]

It is well known that until his death in 1964, Prime Minister Nehru publicly opposed India's developing nuclear weapons. Throughout the 1950s, India sought to play an increasingly important role in international disarmament negotiations, and in 1954 it initiated a proposal for the suspension of nuclear tests by the nuclear weapon states which served as the catalyst for the eventual negotiation of a limited-test-ban treaty.[13]

On the other hand, India's policy of rejecting international safeguards and the early development of the unsafeguarded CIRUS reactor and the Trombay reprocessing plant were all orchestrated by the undisputed leader of India's nuclear establishment at the time, Homi Bhabha, who appears to have favored India's developing nuclear arms. Moreover, Prime Minister Nehru's approval of budgets for the construction of these plants suggests that Bhabha, with Nehru's knowledge, carefully steered India's nuclear policies throughout the 1950s and early 1960s toward development of the nuclear infrastructure that would give India a weapons option that could be exercised at a later time without violating any international commitments.[14] If this was indeed the underlying motivation behind the acquisition of the CIRUS reactor and development of the Trombay facility, India's nuclear leaders were considerably more farsighted about the military potential of these facilities than their American and Canadian counterparts, who actively aided both projects without insisting on ironclad nonproliferation controls.

Pressures for Nuclear Arms. In November 1962, Chinese forces decisively defeated the Indian army in a series of major border clashes in the Himalayas. This defeat, together with rumors that China might soon test a nuclear device, led a parliamentarian from the opposition Jan Sangh party to demand in March 1963 that the Nehru government develop nuclear weapons, the first time a major political party had taken such a stand publicly. Nehru, who had declared in 1961 that India would never develop nuclear weapons under any circumstances, flatly rejected the proposal.[15]

Nehru died in May 1964. In October, China conducted its first nuclear test. The event triggered an intense debate over India's nuclear posture, with strong support for the development of nuclear weapons coming not only from opposition parties, but also from important segments of Prime Minister Lal Bahadur Shastri's Congress party.[16] In a statement made immediately after the test, Indian Atomic Energy Commission chairman Bhabha declared that India could produce nuclear weapons in eighteen months if it wished to, and several days later he estimated that the cost of developing a stockpile of fifty atomic bombs and fifty two-megaton hydrogen bombs was well within India's means.[17] These statements were cited repeatedly by pro-bomb advocates, as Bhabha no doubt intended.

On November 24, 1964, Prime Minister Shastri, in what amounted to a major departure from his predecessor's unyielding public stance, stated that while his government continued to oppose the development of nuclear arms, this position should not be regarded as a permanent one: "I cannot say that the present policy is deep-rooted, that it cannot be set aside, that it can never be changed . . . an individual may have a static policy . . . but in the political field we cannot do so. Here situations alter, changes take place, and we have to mold our policies accordingly. If there is need to amend what we have said today, then we will say—all right let us go ahead and do so."[18] On November 27, Shastri appeared to go still further, stating in a parliamentary debate that he opposed nuclear weapons but supported the expansion of nuclear science for peaceful applications, including developing nuclear explosives, provided they were used for peaceful purposes, such as tunneling.[19] This was apparently the first public declaration by an Indian prime minister favoring the development of nuclear explosives for any purpose. Since peaceful nuclear explosives are essentially indistinguishable from nuclear weapons, except in the way they are used, Shastri in effect had opened the door to an Indian nuclear weapons option.

Also in late 1964, Prime Minister Shastri reportedly authorized Indian Atomic Energy Commission chairman Bhabha to develop the necessary technology for an Indian nuclear device—probably meaning designing a nuclear device and preparing its non-nuclear components—so that the lead time required to build an explosive could be reduced from eighteen to six months.[20]

Pressures on the Shastri government to develop nuclear weapons continued to intensify in 1965 as the Chinese conducted additional tests and threatened, during the Indo-Pakistani War of that year, to open a second front against India.[21] The withdrawal of U.S. military assistance following that conflict and China's testing of a nuclear-armed missile on October 27, 1966, raised calls for Indian nuclear weapons to a crescendo.[22] Shastri had died on January 10 of that year, however, and Bhabha was killed in a plane crash several weeks later. On taking power, India's new prime minister, Indira Gandhi, undertook a review of India's nuclear stance—according to one account halting the nuclear explosives development activities authorized by Shastri[23]—but refrained from declaring the course she would pursue, despite the gathering pressure for development of nuclear explosives. Not until 1970 did Indian government sources begin to hint that a nuclear explosives program was under way.

Mrs. Gandhi's nuclear explosives policy during the 1966-70 period is uncertain. She may have continued the apparent course of her predecessor of attempting to develop a nuclear explosives capability at the earliest feasible time but been unable to conduct a test before 1974 because India had not yet developed the necessary technological base. Through 1964, for example, the CIRUS reactor had run only intermittently, not achieving its potential plutonium production rate of nine kilograms (1 kilogram = 2.2 pounds) per year until after that date.[24] Similarly, the Trombay reprocessing plant was not inaugurated until 1966. Thus, for several years after Mrs. Gandhi took office, India apparently lacked sufficient plutonium to conduct a nuclear explosion.[25] The limited quantities of available plutonium would have also prevented Indian nuclear scientists from acquiring experience in handling the material and in studying the physics of nuclear explosives. One analyst has suggested that only after the construction of the plutonium-fueled Purnima reactor—which was authorized in 1968 and began operating in 1972—were Indian scientists able to obtain the experimental data necessary to construct explosives.[26]

Whatever the state of India's technical capabilities at the time, a number of political factors are also said to have prevented Mrs. Gandhi from approving a test. These included fears of harming negotiations with Canada for the purchase of two two-hundred-megawatt, natural-uranium/heavy-water nuclear power plants (Rajasthan I and II) to be constructed near Kota in Rajasthan and, possibly, concern that adverse U.S. reaction might hinder the completion of a pair of two-hundred-megawatt, low-enriched-uranium/light-water reactors being built with U.S. aid at Tarapur near Bombay under a 1963 cooperation agreement.[27]

In addition, 1965 to 1968 was the period of intensive negotiation on the Nuclear Non-Proliferation Treaty. A nuclear test at that time or immediately after the conclusion of the treaty, when the issue of proliferation was so much in the forefront of international diplomacy, would have provoked unusually sharp criticism. Moreover, a test would have undermined India's long-standing opposition in international forums to nuclear weapons, as well as its demand in negotiations on the Non-Proliferation Treaty that the treaty restrict the nuclear arsenals of the existing nuclear weapon states.

India refused to ratify the Non-Proliferation Treaty in 1968, claiming that it legitimized the primacy of the great powers by permitting them to retain their nuclear arms while freezing the non-nuclear-weapon countries in a state of permanent inferiority. In addition, India argued that the accord placed an unequal burden on the latter by requiring them to accept international safeguards on all their nuclear activities and precluding the development of peaceful nuclear explosives, which India asserted were essential for economic development.[28] By rejecting the treaty, a stance widely supported in India, Mrs. Gandhi also preserved the right to develop nuclear weapons and avoided the application of IAEA safeguards to the CIRUS reactor and the Trombay reprocessing plant.[29]

In 1970, the Department of Atomic Energy announced that India intended to develop the technology for underground nuclear explosions as well as the necessary technology to launch sizable space satellites.[30] In July 1971, India's intentions were made even more explicit when Mrs. Gandhi advised the parliament that India would conduct peaceful nuclear explosions. Her statement was followed in September by a formal announcement by Indian Atomic Energy Commission chairman Vikram Sarabhai at the fourth Atoms for Peace Conference that India had given top priority to the field of nuclear explosives engineering for peaceful purposes.[31]

By this time, the United States and Canada had become alarmed that India might be planning to use plutonium obtained from the CIRUS reactor for its nuclear explosives program. In November 1970, the United States had sent the Indian Atomic Energy Commission an aide-memoire stating that "the United States would consider it incompatible with existing United States-Indian agreements for American nuclear assistance to be employed in the development of peaceful nuclear explosive devices. Specifically, for example, the use for the development of peaceful nuclear explosive devices of plutonium produced therefrom would be considered by the United States a contravention of the terms under which American materials were made available." Referring to the terms of the 1956 Indo-U.S. contract for the sale of U.S. heavy water for the CIRUS plant, the memorandum went on to say that "the United States would not consider the use of plutonium produced in CIRUS for peaceful nuclear explosives intended for any purpose to be 'research into the use of atomic energy for peaceful purposes.' "[32] Although Indian nuclear officials informed their U.S. counterparts that they did not accept this reading of the 1956 Indo-U.S. contract, they conveyed the impression that peaceful nuclear explosives were being considered only as a potential long-term option, and U.S. efforts to intervene in the Indian nuclear explosives program apparently ceased.[33]

In October of the following year, Canadian prime minister Pierre Trudeau wrote to Mrs. Gandhi:

You will remember in our talks [of January 1971] I referred to the serious concern of the Canadian government regarding any further proliferation of nuclear explosive devices. The position of my government on nuclear explosions has been stated on a number of occasions. You will no doubt be well aware of it.

The use of Canadian supplied material, equipment and facilities in India, that is, at CIRUS, at Rajastan, or fissile material from these reactors for the development of a nuclear explosive device would inevitably call on our part for a reassessment of our nuclear cooperation arrangements with India.[34]

As in the case of the response to the U.S. aide-memoire, the Indian government rejected the Canadian interpretation. Mrs. Gandhi wrote in reply:

The obligations undertaken by our two governments are mutual and they cannot be unilaterally varied. In these circumstances it would not be necessary, in our view, to interpret these agreements in a particular way based on the development of a hypothetical contingency.[35]

Canada, too, apparently accepted these assurances without pursuing the matter further.

The decision to conduct an explosion appears to have been taken by 1972.[36] It is not known whether a specific event triggered Mrs. Gandhi's decision. In 1971, India had decisively defeated Pakistan in the war that resulted in East Pakistan's becoming the independent state of Bangladesh, effectively eliminating Pakistan as an Indian security concern. The U.S. "tilt" toward Pakistan during that conflict and the amelioration of Chinese-U.S. relations in 1971-72 may have raised doubts, however, about India's long-term security position, doubts that were offset only partially by the signing of the Treaty of Friendship and Assistance with the Soviet Union. A desire to demonstrate leadership in the Third World and to create a distraction from domestic political turmoil may also have played a role.[37] Another possibility is that the 1974 test was simply the culmination of long-standing plans to implement the Shastri decision of 1966, which had been postponed for largely extraneous political and technical reasons.[38]

The 1974 Test and Initial Reaction. At 8:05 a.m. on May 18, 1974, India detonated a nuclear device in the Rajasthan desert near the Pokharan Range with a reported yield of fifteen kilotons (1 kiloton = 1000 tons of TNT), in the same range as the Hiroshima bomb. The device may have required fifteen kilograms of plutonium, twice the minimum said to be necessary by the International Atomic Energy Agency and perhaps three times as much as is used in sophisticated devices of this yield.[39] The device is generally considered to have been too large and unwieldy to have been directly usable as a nuclear weapon.[40] Whatever its military implications, India characterized its test as a peaceful nuclear explosion intended to study the cratering and cracking effects on rocks.[41] This characterization would be crucial to India's legal argument that it had not violated its assurances to Canada and the United States that material from the CIRUS reactor would be used exclusively for "peaceful purposes."

Pakistan, which is believed to have begun an active nuclear weapons development program in 1972, reacted with alarm. Prime Minister Zulfikar Ali Bhutto called the event "a fateful development" that resulted in "a qualitative change in the relation between the two countries."[42] Bhutto declared that his country would be "no victim of nuclear blackmail," and his chief of staff vowed that if India developed a nuclear force, "we will have to beg or borrow to develop our own nuclear capability."[43]

Canada reacted sharply to the Indian test, its secretary for internal affairs stating that his government saw no distinction between peaceful nuclear explosions and those for military purposes.[44] Four days after the test, Canada suspended all assistance to India for the

Rajasthan II reactor and the Kota heavy-water plant, both then under construction. Although the Canadian-supplied Rajasthan I reactor, which had been operating since 1973, and Rajasthan II were both subject to IAEA safeguards, as were the two U.S.-supplied reactors at Tarapur, Canada made further cooperation conditional on New Delhi's placing all its nuclear activities—including the CIRUS plant and the Trombay reprocessing facility—under the IAEA system. After the failure of these discussions some two years later, Canada terminated all nuclear cooperation with India.[45]

U.S. reaction was considerably more ambivalent. State Department press guidance at the time merely stated that "the United States has always been against nuclear proliferation for the adverse impact it will have on world stability. That remains our position."[46] In June, the U.S. Atomic Energy Commission (AEC) permitted the export of a previously authorized shipment of nuclear fuel for the Tarapur reactors, apparently with the express authorization of Secretary of State Henry Kissinger.[47] The AEC, however, decided to withhold approval of further licenses temporarily while it sought assurances from India that plutonium produced from U.S. fuel in the Tarapur plants would not be used for nuclear explosives of any kind. The 1963 Indo-U.S. agreement for cooperation covering the reactors ruled out the use of plutonium produced in them for "atomic weapons or for research on or development of atomic weapons or for any other military purpose," but did not explicitly prohibit its use for peaceful nuclear explosives.[48] Throughout the summer of 1974, India refused to accept any limitation on its use of the Tarapur facilities that explicitly banned peaceful nuclear explosives; however, on September 17 it agreed that all plutonium produced in the Tarapur reactors would be "devoted exclusively to the needs of the Station"—meaning that India would use the plutonium only as an alternative fuel for the reactors—effectively ruling out the peaceful nuclear explosives option.[49]

U.S. officials were apparently less concerned over India's future use of plutonium from the CIRUS reactor. The United States had warned in its 1970 aide-memoire to India that it would consider India's use of plutonium from the reactor in nuclear explosives of any kind to be a violation of the 1956 contract for the supply of heavy water for that plant. But following the 1974 test, American officials appear to have made little effort to obtain India's agreement that plutonium from the CIRUS facility would not be used for future nuclear explosions. In effect, the United States turned a blind eye to the possibility of India's continued misuse of CIRUS-produced plutonium once Washington received further assurances concerning the Tarapur reactors. The U.S. suspension of fuel shipments for Tarapur was lifted on September 16.

Further evidence that the United States was not prepared to take a hard stand against India's nuclear explosives program was seen in the June 1974 decision of the U.S.-led consortium of Western industrial nations to increase economic assistance to India by $200 million.[50] Moreover, although an August 14, 1974, amendment to the International Development Association (IDA) Act directed American representatives to the board of the multinational development bank to "vote against any loan for the benefit of any country which develops any nuclear explosive device unless that country is or becomes" a party to the Non-Proliferation Treaty, U.S. officials did not implement this law effectively. The United States routinely voted against loans to India at the IDA until this requirement was lifted in 1977 but made no effort to gain the support of other IDA members, permitting itself to be outvoted on twenty-six occasions.[51]

One factor that undoubtedly tempered congressional reaction to the episode was that the Nixon and Ford administrations did not disclose that U.S. heavy water had remained continuously in the CIRUS reactor and had thus been used in producing the plutonium for India's nuclear test. Indeed, only as a result of congressional investigations was the fact finally made public in 1976.[52] The belief that India had violated the 1956 heavy-water sales contract—and that U.S. officials had been slow to reveal this fact to avert criticism of their lenient attitude toward the Indian test—were major spurs to the enactment of the 1978 Nuclear Non-Proliferation Act. The act greatly restricted the discretion of U.S. executive branch agencies in formulating U.S. non-proliferation policy and, among other changes in U.S. nuclear export practices, prohibited exports of nuclear reactors and fuel to any non-nuclear-weapon country, such as India, which did not accept international inspections of all its nuclear facilities by March 1980.

It also has been reported that some U.S. officials may actually have known of the Indian test in advance but took no steps to try to block it. According to a July 1974 statement by Senator Henry M. Jackson, India tried unsuccessfully to detonate a nuclear explosion in February 1974, three months before the Pokharan test. The Indian fizzle was apparently picked up by seismic detectors operated by the U.S. military, but Jackson claimed that U.S. authorities "made no attempt to get them [the Indian government] to stop" the later successful test. A U.S. Atomic Energy Commission spokesman denied his agency had knowledge of Indian preparation for any nuclear test; nor apparently was the Arms Control and Disarmament Agency aware of any such previous attempt.[53]

Pressures for Broadened Safeguards. In the years following the 1974 test, India's principal nuclear suppliers tried with only partial success to use their leverage to slow India's development of a nuclear explosives program and to put pressure on New Delhi to place an increasing portion, if not all, of its nuclear program under IAEA safeguards. Since safeguarded materials may not be used for nuclear explosives of any kind, the latter step would have ruled out India's conducting further tests or otherwise developing nuclear arms, unless it were prepared to accept the high diplomatic costs of violating the IAEA system.

By the mid-1970s, India was building a number of installations with the potential to augment substantially its existing unsafeguarded plutonium production capabilities—the CIRUS reactor and Trombay reprocessing plant—and thus its existing plutonium stockpile of perhaps fifty-five kilograms or less (enough for up to eleven carefully designed weapons).[54] The planned facilities included a new one-hundred-megawatt research reactor, the R-5, with more than double the plutonium output of CIRUS; several indigenously built nuclear power reactors (e.g., Madras I and Madras II) capable of producing far larger quantities of plutonium; and a large new reprocessing plant at Tarapur, three times larger than the Trombay plant, to extract plutonium from power reactor fuel, where safeguards would be applied only when fuel from safeguarded power plants—at the time, Tarapur I and II and Rajasthan I—was being processed.

Canada was the first to restrict nuclear sales to India because of concerns over safeguards coverage; it terminated all nuclear assistance to India in 1976, as noted above, after New Delhi refused to accept full-scope safeguards, which would have placed all of its nuclear activities under IAEA monitoring. The Soviet Union was next. Although Indian engineers were able to complete the Canadian-supplied Rajasthan II reactor independently in 1978, the reactor could not be operated because of a lack of heavy water.[55] Heavy water was also needed to make up for losses at the Rajasthan I reactor. When India tried to purchase the material from the Soviet Union in 1976, it was again confronted with a request that it accept expanded safeguards. Moscow apparently did not demand full-scope safeguards but insisted that New Delhi agree to particularly strong IAEA safeguards on the Rajasthan II reactor—which India had hoped to keep outside the IAEA system altogether—and apply these stronger IAEA measures to the Rajasthan I plant as well.[56]

India's acceptance of across-the-board safeguards also gradually became a condition for the export of U.S. fuel supplies for the Tarapur reactors. The issue was first raised in 1976 at hearings before the U.S. Nuclear Regulatory Commission, which, because of this and related questions over the possibility of India's reprocessing Tarapur spent fuel, temporarily withheld two pending export licenses for Tarapur low-enriched uranium fuel. Licenses were also delayed in 1978, in part because of controversy over the full-scope safeguards issue. In that year the Nuclear Non-Proliferation Act became law, which made acceptance of full-scope IAEA safeguards a condition for the receipt of U.S. nuclear fuel and reactor exports after March 1980. Although in mid-1980 the Carter administration chose to waive this provision so as to permit two additional fuel shipments to Tarapur despite New Delhi's refusal to meet this requirement, it became clear that subsequent shipments would be withheld because of mounting congressional opposition to India's stance.[57]

In early 1981, India advised the newly installed Reagan administration that it intended to terminate the 1963 Indo-U.S. agreement covering the Tarapur plants because of continuing delays in U.S. fuel shipments.[58] The impasse was not broken until July 1982 when Mrs. Gandhi, apparently seeking to improve relations with Washington, agreed to a modus vivendi under which France would supply fuel for the Tarapur plants in lieu of the United States, while all other terms and conditions of the 1963 Indo-U.S. accord remained intact. The arrangement thus allowed a termination of the U.S. fuel shipments to India as required by the 1978 act, but also ensured that IAEA safeguards and U.S. reprocessing approval rights would continue to apply to the plant. India was not, however, obliged to accept full-scope safeguards.[59]

Although India retained its right to conduct unsafeguarded activities despite the various nuclear export curtailments, the restrictions imposed a considerable economic penalty by severely slowing the Indian nuclear energy program.[60] They also provided a strong and continuing reminder of external opposition to India's development of nuclear explosives and undoubtedly contributed to India's decision to suspend testing as discussed below.

One additional goal of U.S. policy following the Pokharan test was to persuade India not to transfer its nuclear explosives know-how to other nations. India has apparently followed this course rejecting, for example, Libya's efforts in 1978 to obtain sensitive nuclear technology in exchange for assured supplies of oil. It is not known to what extent U.S. initiatives have contributed to India's adopting this stance.

Impact of the Pakistani Nuclear Program. India's objections to full-scope IAEA inspections appear to have been motivated principally by the desire to preserve the option of developing nuclear weapons in earnest, particularly as a counter to Pakistan's emerging nuclear capabilities. In 1973, Pakistan began negotiations with France for the construction of a large reprocessing facility, and although France largely abandoned the project in 1978, Pakistan continued to build this facility, as well as a smaller reprocessing unit adjacent to the Pakistan Institute of Nuclear Science and Technology. In 1978, Pakistan's secret effort to build a uranium enrichment plant with its potential for manufacturing weapons-grade uranium was disclosed. None of these facilities is currently subject to IAEA safeguards.[61]

Pakistan's emerging nuclear capabilities appear to have had a gradual but profound influence on Indian policy toward developing nuclear explosives, which underwent a series of changes after Mrs. Gandhi left office in 1977. Her successor, Moraji Desai, had been a long-time opponent of Indian acquisition of nuclear weapons; his public statements are reminiscent of Nehru's in their total rejection of nuclear arms. At the U.N. General Assembly in the summer of 1978, for example, Desai stated categorically that India would never test a nuclear explosive in the future, even for peaceful purposes.[62] Desai subsequently caused some confusion by stating that this did not mean India would not conduct nuclear "blasts," but reaffirmed his pledge not to build nuclear arms in June 1979, stating he accepted Pakistani president Zia's assurances that Pakistan was not developing atomic weapons.[63] Notwithstanding these pronouncements, the Desai government maintained India's refusal to accept international inspections on all of its nuclear installations, thereby retaining the option to pursue nuclear weapons at a later date.

Charan Singh, who served as prime minister after

Desai for a brief period beginning in July 1979, reversed Desai's declared nuclear explosives policy, stating as he took office that he intended to "keep our nuclear options open."[64] In August, he took these remarks a step farther and declared that India, in fact, would be prepared to develop nuclear weapons if Pakistan continued its quest for these arms. "We do not want to join the race to make a bomb," he said. "But, if Pakistan sticks to its plans to assemble a bomb, we will perhaps have to reconsider the whole question."[65]

By November, Indian defense minister, Chidambaram Subramaniam, reviewing India's defense strategy for the next decade, stated that India might soon be confronted with the "difficult decision" of building nuclear weapons as the result of Pakistani nuclear activities, the further spread of nuclear capabilities to additional nations, and the continued buildup of the superpowers' nuclear arsenals. Noting that India already faced a situation of "asymmetry" with regard to China, Subramaniam stated that "if Pakistan were to develop a nuclear arsenal, then a second situation of asymmetry to India's disadvantage will develop."[66] Indian commentators saw the speech as preparing the ground for a decision to develop Indian nuclear weapons, although it and Prime Minister Singh's earlier remarks may simply have been intended as a warning to Pakistan.[67]

Before Singh could bring any possible plans to life for rekindling India's nuclear explosives program, Indira Gandhi was returned to power. In an address to parliament on March 13, 1980, she, too, however, made clear that India intended to retain the option to develop nuclear weapons: "We must have our eyes and ears open . . . and must be in touch with the latest technology. We should not be caught napping. We remain committed to the use of atomic energy for peaceful purposes [but will] not hesitate from carrying out nuclear explosions . . . or whatever is necessary in the national interest."[68] A month later, Mrs. Gandhi underscored her interest in developing the military potential of India's nuclear program. Speaking to parliament, she declared there was no need for India to feel any sense of insecurity over Pakistan's attempts to produce highly enriched uranium, because India was also conducting enrichment experiments: "While we do not have all we would like to have in the defense sphere, we are trying to strengthen ourselves. So far as enrichment is concerned . . . we want to be ready. I do not think it would be proper to mention the details [of the experiments] publicly."[69]

Preparations for Second Test. By early 1981, as Pakistan's progress toward nuclear weapons continued unchecked, Prime Minister Gandhi may have decided to conduct a second test. In April 1981, as Mrs. Gandhi was advising parliament that India would respond "in an appropriate manner" to Pakistan's nuclear activities, U.S. intelligence sources were quoted as stating that India was preparing another test site near Pokharan.[70] These reported preparations coincided with a stream of articles in the Indian press by respected defense analysts and commentators, some with close ties to the government, calling for India's rapid development of nuclear arms.[71] Such overt pro-bomb advocacy, which had previously been limited to members of extreme Hindu nationalist parties, appeared to reflect a new level of support for an Indian nuclear weapons program.[72]

During the same period, Indian nuclear officials announced that the large Tarapur reprocessing plant would shortly begin extracting plutonium from the spent fuel of the Rajasthan I reactor. IAEA safeguards would be applied to the material—potentially enough for tens of atomic weapons—but U.S. observers remained concerned about its military potential.[73]

One spur to these developments may have been the Reagan administration's announcement that it intended to provide $3.2 billion in economic and military aid to Pakistan to buttress it against the threat of Soviet troops in Afghanistan.[74] At the time, U.S. law prohibited such aid to Pakistan because of its importation of uranium enrichment equipment.[75] Some Indian observers saw the administration's proposal—and subsequent congressional approval of it in late 1981—as a sign that the United States was prepared to tolerate Pakistan's continued progress towards nuclear weapons in order to advance the more highly prized foreign-policy objective of countering Soviet expansionism in Afghanistan.[76]

India has so far not tested a second nuclear device. One factor in this restraint may have been Washington's threat to invoke economic sanctions—specifically, refusal to extend new U.S. Export-Import Bank loans, possible reductions in bilateral aid, and opposition to multilateral financial institution lending to India. U.S. officials reportedly discussed imposition of such sanctions with their Indian counterparts during the first half of 1981 in response to India's threat to cancel the 1963 Tarapur agreement because of U.S. refusal to export fresh fuel for the reactor.[77]

The suspension of Export-Import Bank loans is required by U.S. law for any nation that terminates safeguards on U.S.-exported nuclear equipment or materials, a step India had threatened to take in conjunction with its annulment of the Indo-U.S. agreement. The same section of the Export-Import Bank Act, however, also provides for a suspension of new credits for any non-nuclear-weapons country that "detonates, after October 26, 1977, a nuclear explosive device," and this stricture would surely have been pointed out by U.S. officials in discussing the provision with their opposite numbers in New Delhi. U.S. officials may also have stressed another provision of U.S. law that required each American executive director of a multilateral financial institution to "consider in carrying out his duties" whether a borrower country has detonated a nuclear explosive device or refused to ratify the Non-Proliferation Treaty, or both.[78] The United States is also India's largest trading partner. All of these factors would have given Washington useful economic leverage in its attempts to persuade India to postpone further nuclear testing.[79]

Pressures to proceed with a second test seemed to subside in 1982, although official concern over Pakistan's nuclear intentions persisted. On March 2, Indian defense minister Venkataraman stated that Pakistan was continuing to build the plants needed for nuclear weapons and that India's "defense plans are prepared to meet contingencies arising from the adversary's capabilities."[80] This appeared to be a veiled reference to India's nuclear weapons program. In late 1982, however, U.S. intelligence officials were quoted as stating that India had developed a second plan for dealing with Pakistan's nuclear potential—a preemptive air strike to destroy Pakistan's reprocessing and enrichment plants, like that made by Israel against Iraq's research reactor outside Baghdad in June 1981.[81] The U.S. sources believed, however, that Prime Minister Gandhi had deferred the proposed raid out of fear that Pakistan might retaliate against Indian nuclear installations. Indian spokesmen vehemently denied the allegation and pointed out that India and Pakistan were in fact in the process of establishing a joint commission for the normalization of relations.[82]

Continuing Controversies: Safeguards and Reprocessing.
Despite New Delhi's agreement in mid-1982 to accept
France as a substitute for the United States as the nuclear fuel supplier for the Tarapur reactors, a fresh
controversy arose when France proposed that India
accept safeguards on French-supplied fuel that were
more stringent than those covering U.S. material under the 1963 Indo-U.S. agreement. France wanted
safeguards on the material to endure as long as the fuel
(or the plutonium produced in it during its use in the
Tarapur reactors) remained potentially useful for nuclear explosives—in effect, indefinitely. If India were
subsequently to use the produced plutonium as fuel in
a breeder reactor (which in principle can generate
more plutonium than is originally placed in it as fuel),
France wanted to ensure that this second-generation
plutonium would also be subject to IAEA inspection,
along with any subsequent generations of weapons-
usable material that might be produced.

The Soviet Union had insisted on such "perpetuity"
and "pursuit" clauses when it provided heavy water
for the Rajasthan I and II reactors, and the concepts
had been standard elements of IAEA safeguards
agreements since the mid-1970s. They were not explicitly included in the India-U.S.-IAEA agreement concerning Tarapur, however, an absence which India
claimed meant that safeguards on the plant and any
produced plutonium would expire in 1993, the termination date of the 1963 bilateral U.S.-India Tarapur
agreement.[83] The dispute has possible importance for
India's nuclear weapons capabilities because under the
Indian interpretation, which the United States has disputed, in 1993 New Delhi might consider itself free to
extract the seven hundred kilograms of plutonium in
the Tarapur spent fuel and use it to produce possibly
over one hundred nuclear weapons. Indeed, the Tara-

pur-produced plutonium represents India's largest source of the material, although, as noted below, India will shortly have access to considerable amounts of unsafeguarded plutonium from wholly indigenous facilities.[84]

After months of wrangling, France backed down and agreed that French-supplied fuel would be treated like that previously supplied by the United States, with a final decision on the duration of safeguards to be postponed for further negotiations.[85] For the moment, at least, India had again prevailed in its efforts to curb international oversight of its nuclear affairs.

A parallel controversy with the United States continued to fester through 1982 over India's right, now that the Tarapur reprocessing plant was ready to start operating, to reprocess existing stocks of Tarapur spent fuel (which both sides agreed were still under safeguards).[86] Since 1980, India had claimed that it had the right to extract plutonium from this material.[87] The 1963 Tarapur agreement stated (in Article II. E) that reprocessing of Tarapur spent fuel was permitted in Indian facilities "upon a joint determination of the Parties" that the safeguards provisions of the agreement could be effectively applied to the plant reprocessing the fuel; but India interpreted a 1968 letter from the U.S. Atomic Energy Commission as automatically granting U.S. approval once IAEA safeguards had been applied to the Tarapur reprocessing facility. The necessary IAEA formalities were completed in 1980. (Safeguards will be applied, however, only when spent fuel from safeguarded reactors is being processed.)

Washington claimed the 1968 letter did not amount to the necessary joint determination and continued to withhold permission for reprocessing the Tarapur spent fuel out of concern that any separated plutonium

India obtained would be readily usable in nuclear weapons if India chose to terminate its commitments to the IAEA. At the time, as noted earlier, India repeatedly threatened to annul the 1963 Tarapur agreement and withdraw the Tarapur spent fuel from safeguards which, it claimed, were required only because of the agreement's stipulations. Moreover, India claimed that in 1993, the expiration date of the Tarapur agreement, safeguards would no longer apply to the material.

The dispute over whether India could gain access to the plutonium in its largest stockpile of spent fuel has not been resolved. However, in November 1982, after a series of test runs, India began commercial operation of the Tarapur reprocessing facility, using spent fuel from another reactor, Rajasthan I. This material is under safeguards, which by virtue of the Soviet heavy-water agreement will last indefinitely. India plans to use the first 100 kilograms of plutonium in its fast breeder test reactor, which will require 54 kilograms of the material for its initial loading. Nonetheless, with an output of as much as 135 kilograms of plutonium per year—enough for more than twenty weapons annually, depending on the sophistication of their design—the start-up of the reprocessing plant meant India would shortly have access to enough nuclear weapons material for a sizable nuclear arsenal, albeit under strong legal restrictions, and that large quantities of unsafeguarded plutonium could be produced once India's unsafeguarded nuclear power plants came on line.

Indian Rocketry. As discussed more fully below, a principal obstacle to India's developing a nuclear force to match China's nuclear capabilities is India's lack of delivery systems able to strike China's major industrial and population centers. India's space program, however, has made slow but steady progress over the years and may eventually allow development of medium-range ballistic missiles.

India's 1970 long-term research and development plan called for the manufacture, at an unspecified future time, of "advanced rocket systems capable of putting 1,200 kilogram payloads into synchronous orbits," launch vehicles that could be readily converted into medium-range nuclear missiles.[88] In 1980 India launched its first satellite, weighing thirty kilograms, making it the sixth country to achieve that feat. Although the launch, which used a four-stage solid-fuel rocket, was described as a peaceful experiment, Satish Dhawhan, head of India's space research organization, declared that it demonstrated India's capability to develop nuclear missiles. "Any country which can place a satellite in orbit can develop an IRBM [intermediate-range ballistic missile]," he stated. Dhawhan also declared that liquid-fuel rockets capable of carrying up to 1300-pound payloads were planned.[89] U.S. analysts noted, however, that India was still far from developing a militarily useful nuclear missile.[90] According to one Western observer, the four-stage rocket is poorly suited to military uses since it is unreliable.

Although Indian scientists reported the successful testing of a new high-thrust rocket engine in early 1983, an Indian IRBM still appears to be an unlikely prospect before the 1990s.[91]

India as a Nuclear Importer and Exporter. In addition to its nuclear relations with the United States, the Soviet Union, and Canada, in 1969 India entered into an accord with France for assistance in the development of breeder reactors.[92] French aid under the agreement—especially the export of highly enriched uranium for the Indian fast-breeder test reactor—has slowed considerably, however, since the 1974 test.[93] French companies also participated with a Swiss firm in building the Baroda and Tuticorin heavy-water plants, while a German concern helped in the construction of the Talcher heavy-water facility.[94] Despite this foreign participation, the output of none of these plants is under IAEA safeguards, another example of India's reluctance to accept international supervision of its nuclear program.

India has also offered to help Iran complete a nuclear power plant begun under the shah and has exported zircaloy tubing to West Germany. In 1978, when India refused to provide Libya assistance related to nuclear explosives under their nuclear cooperation agreement, Libya terminated a one-million-ton-per-year oil supply contract with New Delhi.[95] In all, India has signed nuclear cooperation agreements with twenty-seven nations, seventeen of which were known to be in effect as of August 1980.[96]

II. Developments of the Past Year

Appointment of Senior Atomic Energy Aides.

In August 1983, Dr. Raja Ramanna was appointed chairman of the Indian Atomic Energy Commission, India's most senior policy-making post for nuclear affairs. In 1972, Ramanna had been placed in charge of preparing India's nuclear test, and supervised the team of scientists and engineers who designed and built the device and readied the Pokharan test site. If he was not the father of the Indian atomic bomb—Homi Bhabha may deserve that distinction—he appears, at least, to have been its midwife.[97]

In March 1984, Dr. P. K. Iyengat, believed to have designed the triggering mechanism for the Pokharan-test device and who subsequently received two awards for his contribution to the Pokharan "experiment," was appointed director of the Bhabha Atomic Research Center (formerly Trombay). The post is one of the most prestigious in India's nuclear hierarchy.[98]

Although Ramanna has a reputation as a hawk on nuclear matters, his public comments since taking office have focused on India's nuclear power and civilian research program, and it may be unwise to read too much into his and Iyengat's appointments.[99] Nonetheless, the elevation of figures so closely linked to India's nuclear explosives program indicates that Prime Minister Gandhi continues to hold this segment of India's nuclear establishment in high esteem. At the very least, the Ramanna and Iyengat appointments are not ones Mrs. Gandhi would have made if she had wished to underscore her pacific intentions in the nuclear field. Moreover, the two scientists' intimate knowledge of the military potential of India's nuclear program and their proven capabilities in realizing that potential, at least in part, invite speculation that Mrs. Gandhi may be moving towards developing nuclear weapons in earnest. Indeed, the appointments may have been a deliberate signal to Pakistan, and possibly the United States, that New Delhi would not stand idle if Pakistan continued its nuclear weapons program.

Spare Parts Controversy; Continued Test Preparations

In late June 1983, the *Washington Post*, quoting Reagan administration officials, reported that India was continuing its preparations for a second nuclear test.[100] The report, which gave few details of India's possible nuclear-explosives-related activities, arose in the context of yet another long-simmering Indo-U.S. controversy over the Tarapur reactors, this one concerning the supply of spare parts.

Export licenses for the needed equipment, pending since 1980, had been set aside while controversy swirled around the various Tarapur fuel shipments. In 1982, according to reports in the Indian press, U.S. officials had promised the components would be released as part of the deal to shift U.S. fuel supply obligations to France.[101] By mid-1983, however, the parts had still not been exported.

The reason, according to press reports, was that U.S. officials were aware of India's efforts in 1981 to prepare an additional nuclear test site in the Rajasthan desert. This meant that under U.S. law, nuclear exports could not be made to India unless it "took steps which in the President's judgment represent sufficient progress toward terminating such activities."[102] Although India had not conducted a test, it had kept the site in a state of readiness, not filling the excavations that had been prepared for the detonation. This appeared to indicate that a possible test was still under active consideration and prevented President Reagan from making the necessary finding to release the spare parts.

Under the circumstances, the only way the President could authorize the pending component licenses was to advise Congress that India was ineligible for exports under the 1978 act because of its test preparations and then to issue an outright waiver of the statutory prohibition. Given the intense congressional opposition to further nuclear trade with India and the outcry that had greeted the Reagan administration's arrangement with France the previous year to ensure continued fuel supplies for the Tarapur reactors, administration sources concluded that the granting of such a waiver was unthinkable politically. Moreover, the waiver would have been the first ever after a finding that a non-nuclear-weapon nation was engaged in nuclear-explosives-related activities, making it all the more embarrassing.[103]

The matter came to a head in July 1983, when Secretary of State George Shultz had promised the spare parts to India if no alternative suppliers could be found.[104] Congressional reaction was immediate and hostile.[105] By early 1984, non-binding resolutions condemning the proposed exports were enacted, and legislation proscribing nuclear component exports to all non-nuclear-weapon countries not accepting full-scope safeguards passed both houses of Congress.[106]

The political uproar appears to have led the Reagan administration to shelve the proposed exports, although efforts to assist India in obtaining some key parts from other suppliers for the now-obsolete Tarapur plants were partially successful.

The controversial exports could have a possible impact on India's nuclear weapons capabilities. At least one crucial component—a control-rod drive that will be necessary to govern the plant's operation when currently used equipment is no longer serviceable—is still needed and can only be obtained from the United States. Opponents of the sale argue that by withholding this critical item the United States may be able to force India to shut down the Tarapur reactors prematurely. Given India's repeated threats to reprocess Tarapur spent fuel and to end safeguards on this material and any extracted plutonium in 1993, they argue that to aid the facility's continued operation is to increase India's stocks of plutonium that will soon be

available for nuclear weapons. They would withhold
the components unless India agrees that Tarapur spent
fuel will not be reprocessed and that safeguards will be
maintained indefinitely.[107] (As described below, however, India will shortly have significant quantities of
unsafeguarded plutonium from indigenous sources,
which it could use for nuclear explosives without incurring the added displeasure that would surely follow
any use of U.S.-origin Tarapur fuel for this purpose.
This suggests that Tarapur plutonium, while potentially usable for nuclear arms, probably would not be
the first choice if other unrestricted sources were available.)

Administration spokesmen have argued that the
spare parts are needed to help ensure the Tarapur
plants' safe operation—a claim the critics dispute—
and should be allowed on humanitarian grounds. They
also argue that such a gesture is essential to improve
the atmosphere if negotiations on the reprocessing and
continuation of safeguards issues are to have any hope
of success.

For the time being, the impasse continues. Prime
Minister Gandhi has not taken the step of reprocessing
the Tarapur fuel in the face of U.S. objections, however, nor apparently has India proceeded any farther
toward a nuclear test.[108]

Major New Source of Unsafeguarded Plutonium

As noted earlier, one of the constraints on India's
developing a substantial nuclear weapons program has
been the limited quantity of plutonium available for
this purpose. By the time the Trombay reprocessing
plant was shut down in 1974, for example, India may
have had only fifty-five kilograms of plutonium available for nuclear explosives, possibly enough for up to

eleven well-designed weapons, but sufficient for only four weapons using the cruder design of the Pokharan test device.

The Tarapur reprocessing plant, which began full-scale operations in November 1982, has a maximum output of 135 to 150 kilograms of plutonium per year, although judging from experience at other such plants around the globe, it is unlikely to realize this potential.[109] The facility can process uranium oxide fuels from all of India's nuclear power plants, which now include Tarapur I and II, Rajasthan I and II, and the newly commissioned Madras I reactor, vastly multiplying New Delhi's nuclear weapons potential.

In comparison, the announced demands of India's nuclear energy program for plutonium—essentially to fuel the forty-two-megawatt Fast Breeder Test Reactor at Kalpakkam—are only for fifty-four kilograms, with reloads required at several-year intervals.[110] India is also completing the enlargement of its Trombay reprocessing plant to enable it to handle spent fuel from the soon-to-operate one hundred-megawatt R-5 research reactor and the CIRUS reactor. Estimates of the R-5's annual plutonium production capacity range from twenty-three to fifty kilograms, enough for one to ten nuclear weapons depending on the quality of their design. CIRUS can produce nine kilograms, enough for an additional weapon.[111] The R-5, CIRUS, and Trombay reprocessing plant are unsafeguarded.

Thus, within several years, India may have a plutonium production and extraction capability of more than 200 kilograms per year to meet an annual demand from India's nuclear energy and research program of perhaps 20 kilograms or less. Even if more conservative estimates of plutonium output are used, based on 50 percent of design capacity at the Tarapur reprocessing plant (67.5 kilograms per year) and lower estimates for the output of the R-5 (23 kilograms per year), nearly 100 kilograms of the material would be available—more than four times India's apparent needs and enough for six to twenty weapons annually.[112]

This pattern of apparently excessive plutonium-production capacity closely corresponds to that prevailing in the late 1960s when the Trombay reprocessing plant was extracting plutonium from CIRUS fuel for which there was no immediate need in terms of India's nuclear energy and research program.[113] At that time, it will be recalled, prime ministers Shastri and Gandhi were under pressure to respond to the Chinese nuclear weapons program. While the reprocessing activity was justified on the basis of India's long-term nuclear energy plan, in retrospect it is clear this was a cover for India's development of a nuclear explosives capability. Today, India faces a comparable external nuclear threat in Pakistan's unrelenting pursuit of nuclear arms. While Indian nuclear spokesmen continue to invoke the nation's long-term energy program as a rationale for its plutonium production capabilities, not all observers are likely to find the justification persuasive.[114]

This background is essential for understanding the significance of a development critically important to India's nuclear weapons capabilities, the start up of its fifth power reactor, Madras I, in late July of 1983.[115] The plant, located in Kalpakkam, is the first operational Indian reactor capable of producing significant amounts of plutonium whose use for nuclear weapons appears to be totally unrestricted by bilateral or IAEA limitations. India claims the entire Madras plant, its fuel, and its heavy water were all built or produced indigenously.[116] India has therefore not accepted IAEA safeguards on the installation nor made any pledges to the Agency or to any external supplier regarding its use. Even the CIRUS reactor, it may be noted, while not under IAEA inspections, was subject to "peaceful use" assurances given to Canada and the United States. While India interpreted these broadly as permitting the so-called peaceful nuclear explosion in 1974, India is not known to have built nuclear weapons, as such, with any of the plutonium produced in the reactor. Moreover, Canada's and later the United States' sharp reaction to what they perceived to be misuse of the material for explosives may have deterred Indian nuclear planners from the further use of the material for that purpose.

New Delhi appears to have gone to extraordinary lengths to keep the Madras reactor from coming under international inspection. The plant probably cost over $100 million, if not considerably more, and was apparently ready to start operation in early 1981 but sat idle for over two years because the 220 to 230 tons of heavy water needed in the reactor were not available. India repeatedly rejected the option of obtaining the material from the Soviet Union, because that would have required acceptance of IAEA safeguards, as the USSR had required in the case of the heavy water it supplied for the two Rajasthan reactors.[117]

Indeed, how India acquired the heavy water for the plant from domestic sources remains something of a mystery. Its four heavy-water production plants have been plagued with problems and have operated at only a fraction of their design capacity, so that by late 1981, only 40 of the 230 tons of heavy water needed for the Madras plant were on hand, and by September 1982, only 70. Apparently, India made up the difference partly by shifting heavy water earmarked for the R-5 and CIRUS research reactors in Trombay to Madras.[118] In addition, India appears to have taken diluted, but easily upgraded, heavy water that had leaked from the the Rajasthan reactors for use in Madras I. Although the Rajasthan plants are under safeguards, over the years India reportedly placed quantities of unsafeguarded heavy water in the Rajasthan facilities to make up for losses. India may have claimed that the degraded heavy water represented its share of the total inventory in the plants, leaving it free to remove the material without safeguards for use, after upgrading, in the Madras reactor. Although the withdrawn material inevitably contained Canadian and Soviet heavy water, with which Indian heavy water had been commingled, provisions in its agreements with the IAEA covering the imported material apparently permitted this arrangement.[119]

While no concrete evidence has emerged that India has employed this stratagem, the Indian press has reported that one hundred tons of heavy water, varying in purity from 3 percent to 30 percent, were shipped to Madras from Rajasthan in 1983.[120] It has also been reported that China may have supplied unsafeguarded heavy water to India, possibly for the plant.[121] Whatever the route, Madras I is today unsafeguarded and represents a potentially important source of material for a future Indian nuclear weapons program.[122]

III. Prospects for Nuclear Weapons in India

Notwithstanding rumors that India was on the brink of detonating another nuclear explosion in 1981 and that it has kept its nuclear test site in a state of readiness ever since, New Delhi has refrained from nuclear testing since 1974. Nor is there evidence that India has yet built nuclear weapons or deployed a nuclear force, however small.

On the other hand, it is possible that studies on "weaponizing" India's relatively crude 1974 device have been conducted, and as described in detail in the preceding section, India's unsafeguarded plutonium production capability is growing dramatically. This could allow India to build tens of nuclear weapons quickly if it chose this route to address a perceived nuclear threat from Pakistan. India's increasing capabilities in missile technology may also allow it to consider fielding a significant nuclear missile force possibly intended to counter China in perhaps another decade.

Judging from the Indian reaction to reports of Pakistan's emerging nuclear capabilities, a reaction that included not only widespread calls for India to develop a nuclear deterrent, but also the preparations for a second test and Mrs. Gandhi's declaration that India would conduct nuclear explosions if necessary "in the national interest," it seems evident that the pace and direction of any Indian nuclear weapons program will depend in significant part on developments in Pakistan. Were Pakistan, for example, to conduct a nuclear test, an Indian test series would seem an almost inevitable response, and some observers have suggested that India might "trump Pakistan's ace by detonating a hydrogen bomb."[123]

If Pakistan, because of U.S. pressure or for other reasons, refrains from testing a nuclear device, however, a more complicated situation would emerge. Pakistan's reported acquisition of nuclear weapons material, together with its reported actions to develop the non-nuclear components for nuclear weapons, will soon give it a de facto nuclear weapons capability that will roughly be on a par with India's. This may well be considered so provocative in New Delhi as to warrant renewed nuclear testing or deployment of a small, overt nuclear force as a means of reasserting India's nuclear superiority in the region. It is possible, however, especially given the trend towards normalization of relations between the two countries, that India may be willing to accept this situation without taking such action, since with its own unsafeguarded reactors and reprocessing plants it can match Pakistan's effort to accumulate nuclear weapons material and since it still has the nominal advantage of having conducted a test; at the same time, by following a course of restraint, the high political and economic costs of a nuclear arms race would be avoided.

It is difficult to predict which of these two courses New Delhi will follow now that Pakistan has moved significantly closer to obtaining nuclear weapons. As in 1981, domestic political pressure for an overt nuclear weapons program is likely to be strong, and as India begins to accumulate plutonium that is free from external non-proliferation restrictions, this option may appear temptingly close at hand. Moreover, suspicions of India's nuclear ambitions have been underscored by the recent promotion of two nuclear officials closely associated with India's 1974 test.

On the other hand, certain constraints may have been working to keep these pressures for nuclear weapons development in check.

The first restraint may be resources. It seems apparent that even before the 1974 test, Indian leaders had decided not to attempt to match China's nuclear capabilities in the near term, since this would have required massive expenditures for both nuclear material production facilities and ballistic missile development. Such outlays were beyond India's means.[124] In addition, the buildup of India's conventional forces after its defeat in 1962 may have been considered sufficient to meet any threat posed by future Chinese attacks. Indeed, as one thoughtful analysis has suggested, India's posture of developing a nuclear capability but not deploying a sizable nuclear force may have been intended more as a political response to China's nuclear capabilities than a military one.[125] As just noted, however, because of India's progress in obtaining nuclear weapons material, resource limitations will soon cease to be a barrier to development of a nuclear weapons program sufficient to address any perceived nuclear threat from Pakistan.[126]

A second constraint on India's nuclear posture has been international opposition to its developing nuclear explosives. This has grown over the years and has been accompanied by the termination of assistance for India's peaceful nuclear program, which has slowed that program considerably. In the wake of the 1974 Indian test, other international economic sanctions were also implemented, if halfheartedly in some cases, such as opposition to concessionary loans from the International Development Association and cuts in bilateral aid. In 1981, the United States is also said to have threatened further financial sanctions, including a cutoff of new Export-Import Bank lending, to avert India's abrogation of the 1963 Tarapur agreement and, possibly, to stop India's second nuclear test. In view of this history, New Delhi may fear that such sanctions would be applied more forcefully in the future if India were to develop a nuclear arsenal.

India has also been attempting for several years to build its ties to the West, and to the United States in particular. Prime Minister Gandhi's willingness to accept a compromise over the Tarapur fuel as a gesture of accommodation at the time of her 1982 visit to Washington has been cited as evidence of this new outlook. Efforts to improve relations with Washington and its allies would be jeopardized if India tested or deployed nuclear weapons, and such concerns have undoubtedly contributed to Mrs. Gandhi's decision to refrain from further testing for the time being.

Finally, slowly improving ties with Pakistan may temper New Delhi's response should Pakistan begin to produce nuclear weapons material in significant quantities. In September 1981, Pakistan offered to sign a nonaggression pact with India, and in January 1982, India responded by proposing that the two nations sign a treaty of peace and friendship. As a near-term measure, the two nations agreed to set up a joint commission for resolving specific bilateral disputes; it was formally established in December 1982. In November 1982, Pakistani president Zia stopped briefly in New Delhi en route to Malaysia and held talks with Mrs. Gandhi, an important step in the normalization of relations between the two countries. By early 1984, the joint commission was meeting with some regularity, and in March and May the foreign secretaries of the two nations held talks on a nonaggression pact, among other issues.[127] The status of these talks and other emerging ties between the two countries will undoubtedly influence New Delhi's perceptions as to whether Pakistani acquisition of a de facto nuclear weapons capability should be viewed more as a military challenge, necessitating reactivation of India's nuclear explosives program, or as a political statement of Pakistan's emergence from India's shadow, in which case a policy of continued restraint aimed at avoiding an active Indo-Pakistani nuclear arms race might be an acceptable alternative.

One additional option that may still remain open to Mrs. Gandhi is to deal with the Pakistani nuclear threat before Islamabad can amass significant quantities of nuclear weapons material by pre-emptively attacking the two facilities that may soon be able to produce this material—Pakistan's pilot-scale New Labs reprocessing plant and its uranium enrichment plant at Kahuta. Indeed, this is the only alternative, which, if implemented successfully, may allow India to maintain its nuclear monopoly on the subcontinent definitively, at least for the near term; it is also one that would quiet calls at home for development of nuclear weapons, a course that, to date, Mrs. Gandhi has apparently been unwilling to pursue. While reaction by the advanced nations, including the United States, might well be less harsh to an Indian pre-emptive raid than to a second nuclear test, Pakistani retaliation, possibly against Indian nuclear installations, would be likely. Indeed, the possiblity of war could not be ruled out, despite India's considerable superiority in conventional military forces.

Assuming a raid is not undertaken, New Delhi's policy has been to refrain from overt steps to develop nuclear arms (which could carry heavy diplomatic costs) but to complete and operate the facilities needed to manufacture nuclear weapons material—the R-5 reactor, Trombay reprocessing plant, Madras I reactor, and Tarapur reprocessing plant—and, reportedly, to ready a nuclear test site so as to shorten the time that would be needed to produce weapons should that decision be made later on. Whether India will respond to Pakistan's progress toward acquiring a "bomb in the basement" by revitalizing the Indian nuclear explosives program or by accepting a de facto nuclear-armed neighbor remains uncertain. Domestic political pressures to resume nuclear testing or develop nuclear arms are likely to be intense, however, and given New Delhi's apparent receptivity to this course, as seen by the preparatory steps already taken, these pressures may well tip the balance against continued restraint.

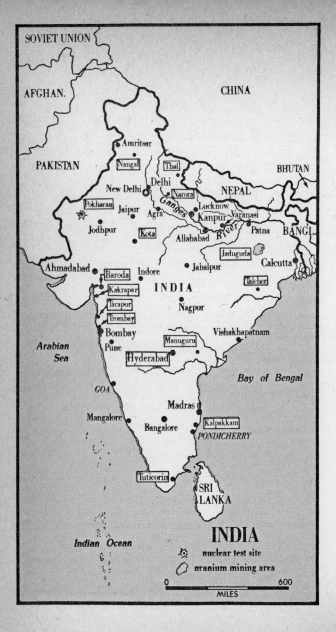

SOVIET UNION

AFGHAN.

CHINA

PAKISTAN

BHUTAN

NEPAL

BANGL.

Amritsar

Nangal

Thal

Delhi

New Delhi

Narora

Pokharan

Jaipur

Agra

Ganges

Lucknow

Varanasi

Kanpur

Jodhpur

Kota

Allahabad

River

Patna

Jaduguda

Ahmadabad

Indore

Jabalpur

Calcutta

Baroda

Kakrapar

INDIA

Talcher

Tarapur

Trombay

Nagpur

Bombay

Manuguru

Vishakhapatnam

Pune

Hyderabad

Arabian
Sea

Bay of Bengal

GOA

Madras

Mangalore

Kalpakkam

Bangalore

PONDICHERRY

Tuticorin

SRI
LANKA

Indian Ocean

INDIA

☼ nuclear test site

⬡ uranium mining area

0   600

MILES

64

India

Power Reactors/Operating or Under Construction

Tarapur I (light-water/low-enriched uranium, 200 MWe)
- supplier: General Electric (U.S.)
- start up: 1969
- fuel source: U.S.; France after 1982
- safeguards: yes

Tarapur II (light-water/low-enriched uranium, 200 MWe)
- supplier: General Electric (U.S.)
- start up: 1969
- fuel source: U.S.; France after 1982
- safeguards: yes

Rajasthan I, Kota (heavy-water/natural-uranium, 200 MWe)
- supplier: Canadian General Electric (Canada)
- start up: 1973[a]
- fuel source: Initial load, half Canadian Westinghouse, half Indian; subsequently all Indian.[a]
- heavy water: 130 metric tons from Canada and U.S.; 80 metric tons from USSR in 1973.[a]
- safeguards: yes

Rajasthan II, Kota (heavy-water/natural-uranium, 200 MWe)
- supplier: Larson and Toubro (India), following termination of Canadian assistance in 1976.
- start up: 1981
- fuel source: India
- heavy water: USSR,[a] India
- safeguards: yes

Madras I, Kalpakkam (heavy-water/natural-uranium, 220 MWe)
- supplier: Larson and Toubro (India)
- start up: 1983[b]
- fuel source: India
- heavy water: India; China (?)[c]
- safeguards: no

Madras II, Kalpakkam (heavy-water/natural-uranium, 220 MWe)
- supplier: Larson and Toubro (India)
- start up: 1985 (est.)[d]
- fuel source: India
- heavy water: India
- safeguards: no

Narora I (heavy-water/natural-uranium, 220 MWe)
- supplier: Richardson and Cruddas (India)
- start up: 1987 (est.)[e]
- fuel source: India
- heavy water: India
- safeguards: no

Narora II (heavy-water/natural-uranium, 220 MWe)
- supplier: Walchandnagar Industries Ltd. (India)
- start up: 1987 (est.)[e]
- fuel source: India
- heavy water: India
- safeguards: no

Kakrapar I (heavy-water/natural-uranium, 220 MWe)
- supplier: India
- start up: 1991 (est.)[e]
- fuel source: India
- heavy water: India
- safeguards: no

Kakrapar II (heavy-water/natural-uranium, 220 MWe)
- supplier: India
- start up: 1992 (est.)[e]
- fuel source: India
- heavy water: India
- safeguards: no

Uranium Resources/Active Mining Sites/Uranium Mills
- reasonably assured
  reserves: 42,500 metric tons[f]
- currently active site: Jaduguda[f]
- mills in operation: Jaduguda[f]

Uranium Purification (UO_2)
Hyderabad
- capacity: ?
- supplier: India
- start up: ?
- safeguards: partial (?)

Heavy Water
Nangal
- capacity: 14 metric tons per year[a]
- supplier: Linde Gmbolt (West Germany)[a]
- start up: 1962[a]
- safeguards: no

Baroda
- capacity: 67 metric tons per year[j]
- supplier: GELPRA (Swiss-French)[a]
- start up: 1977 (closed 1977-80; intermittant operation thereafter[k]
- safeguards: no

Tuticorin
- capacity: 71 metric tons per year[j]
- supplier: GELPRA (Swiss-French)[a]
- start up: 1978
- safeguards: no

Talcher
- capacity: 65 metric tons per year[a]
- supplier: Friedrich Unde Gmbolt (West Germany)[a]
- start up: 1979, but has operated at less than 10% capacity.[k]
- safeguards: no

Kota
- capacity: 100 metric tons per year[j]
- supplier: India, Canada (Canadian aid terminated 1974)[l]
- start up: 1984 (est.)[m]
- safeguards: no

Thal
- capacity: 110 metric tons per year[j]
- supplier: Rashtriya Chemicals and Fertilizers (India)[j]
- start up: 1986-87 (est.)[a]
- safeguards: no

Manuguru
- capacity: 185 metric tons[j]
- supplier: ?
- start up: 1987 (est.)[j]
- safeguards: no

Fuel Fabrication

Hyderabad
- capacity: sufficient for Rajasthan, Kalpakkam, Narora[g] and Tarapur[h]
- supplier: India
- start up: 1971[i]
- safeguards: partial (?)[i]

Reprocessing

Trombay
- capacity: 30 metric tons of spent fuel per year (CIRUS, R-5 fuel)[r]; being enlarged[a]
- supplier: India[s]
- start up: 1966; shut down, 1974; restart 1984 (?) (est.)[e]
- safeguards: no

Tarapur
- capacity: At 100 metric tons of spent fuel per year (currently for Rajasthan, potentially for Tarapur, Madras I, FBTR.[n]); 135-150 kg plutonium per year when at full capacity.[n]
- supplier: India
- start up: trial runs, 1979;[a] full scale operations, 1982[n]
- safeguards: partial (for Tarapur and Rajasthan reactor fuel only)

Kalpakkam
- capacity: 125 metric tons per year (for Kalpakkam, and fast breeder)[o]
- supplier: India
- start up: 1986 (est.)
- safeguards: no

Research Reactors

Apsara, Trombay (light-water/medium-enriched-uranium, 1 MWt)[p]
- supplier: India
- start up: 1956
- fuel source: United Kingdom
- safeguards: no

CIRUS, Trombay (heavy-water/natural-uranium, 40 MWt)[p]
- supplier: Canada
- start up: 1963[q]
- fuel source: Canada, then India
- heavy water: United States
- safeguards: no

Zerlina, Trombay (heavy-water/variable-fuel, 400 Wt)[p]
- supplier: India
- start up: 1961
- fuel source: India?
- safeguards: no

Purnima, Trombay (no moderator/plutonium, 10 MWt)[p]
- supplier: India
- start up: 1972
- fuel source: India
- safeguards: no

R-5, Trombay (heavy-water/natural-uranium, 100 MWt)[p]
- supplier: India
- start up: 1984 (est.)[e]
- fuel source: India
- safeguards: no

FBTR, Kalpakkam (fast breeder/plutonium & high-enriched uranium, 42 MWt)
- supplier: India, with French assistance[a]
- start up: 1984 (est.)[e]
- fuel source: India
- safeguards: no

Sources and Notes

a. David Hart, *Nuclear Power in India, A Comparative Analysis* (London: George Allen and Unwin, 1983), pp. 45-54.

b. "Sethna Present as Kalpakkam Reactor Goes Critical," *The Hindu*, reprinted in *Foreign Broadcast Information Service/Nuclear Proliferation and Development*, hereafter FBIS/NDP, August 3, 1983, p. 30.

c. Judith Miller, "U.S. Is Holding Up Peking Atom Talks," *New York Times*, September 19, 1982.

d. "Second Kalpakkam Unit Commissioning to be Delayed," *The Times of India*, reprinted in FBIS/NDP, March 18, 1984, p. 32.

e. *The Annual Report of the Department of Atomic Energy, 1982-1983*, pp. 5-8. As of mid-1984, Trombay reprocessing plant expansion is thought to be complete, but it is not known whether operations have begun.

f. Reasonably Assured Reserves at less than $130 per kilogram. OECD Nuclear Energy Agency and the International Atomic Energy Agency, *Uranium, Resources, Production and Demand* (Paris: OECD, 1982), pp. 186-187.

g. "Spokesman: Uranium Production to Double," *Delhi Domestic Service*, reprinted in Foreign Broadcast Information Service/Asia, August 8, 1982, p. E-1.

h. David Hart, *Nuclear Power in India*, p. 43.

i. According to the *Annual Report of the Department of Atomic Energy, 1982-1983*, Hyderabad started up in 1971, but according to David Hart, *Nuclear Power in India*, the facility started up between 1973 and 1975. Fuel fabrication line for Tarapur (light-water reactor) fuel is safeguarded. Line for natural-uranium/heavy-water reactor fuel apparently is not.

j. "DAE Official Writes on Heavy Water Production," *The Hindu Survey of Indian Industry*, reprinted in FBIS/NDP, April 9, 1984, pp. 18-20.

k. Pearl Marshall, "India's Desperate Push for Enough Indigenous Heavy Water to Commission," *Nucleonics Week*, May 27, 1982, p. 12.

l. "Problems in Production of Heavy Water Discussed," Jairam Ramesh, *The Times of India*, reprinted in FBIS/NDP, April 9, 1984, p. 11.

m. "AEC Chairman Describes Nuclear Energy Program," *The Hindu Survey of Indian Industry*, reprinted in FBIS/NDP, April 9, 1984, p. 14.

n. Milton Benjamin, "India Storing Arms Grade Plutonium," *The Washington Post*, February 20, 1983. India is currently reprocessing fuel from the safeguarded Rajasthan I reactor. India is barred by the United States from reprocessing spent fuel from the Tarapur reactors until at least 1993 under the 1963 Indo-U.S. agreement for nuclear cooperation and a follow-up agreement with France. India disputes this view, however.

o. "ISI Gives Details on Nuclear Reprocessing Plant," *ISI Diplomatic Information Service*, reprinted in FBIS/Asia, December 16, 1982, p. E-1.

p. Albert Wohlstetter, ed., *Swords From Plowshares* (Chicago: University of Chicago Press, 1979), p. 206.

q. Fully operational in 1963; started up in 1960.

r. David Hart, *Nuclear Power in India*, p. 54; but see, sixty metric tons per year, "ERDA: Fuel Reprocessing Capabilities, 1977," *Nuclear Proliferation Factbook*, Subcomm. on Int'l. Trade and Policy of the House Int'l. Relations Comm. and Subcomm. on Energy, Nuclear Proliferation and Federal Services, Senate Comm. on Governmental Affairs (Washington: Gov't. Print'g. Off., 1977), p. 200; one hundred metric tons per year, Wohlstetter, *Swords From Plowshares*, p. 214. Thirty metric ton figure selected because it is the most conservative and may best reflect actual operating experience.

s. India received engineering assistance from Vitro International (U.S.) and from French engineering consultants, Roberta Wohlstetter, *"The Buddha Smiles": Absent-minded Peaceful Aid and the Indian Bomb*, Monograph 3, Energy Research and Development Administration, Contract No. (49-1)-3747, April 30, 1977, p. 63.

Pakistan

Pakistan has been working actively to develop nuclear arms since at least 1972, and despite concerted (if belated) efforts by the United States and other advanced nuclear supplier nations, its program for building the facilities needed to manufacture nuclear weapons material is now close to fruition. Pakistan is also believed to have been working on the design of a nuclear weapon since at least 1981 (and probably for much longer) and in that year was said to be readying a nuclear test site. Although past predictions that Pakistan would soon have nuclear weapons have been disproven by events, the evidence available today suggests that Pakistan will shortly have all of the necessary elements within its grasp.

I. Background

Early Program. Pakistan's nuclear program began some seven years after India's, in 1955, when the Pakistan

Atomic Energy Committee was established. The committee's responsibilities included surveying the nation for uranium, establishing a nuclear research center, and providing advice on other nuclear issues. In 1956 the committee became the Pakistan Atomic Energy Commission, which arranged for the training of Pakistani nuclear scientists and engineers with outside assistance. Thirty-seven scientists were trained in the United States between 1955 and 1965.[1]

In 1965 Pakistan began operating its first research reactor, a five-megawatt, highly-enriched-uranium/ light-water facility supplied through the IAEA by the United States. The plant has been under IAEA safeguards and is not believed to have contributed to Pakistan's efforts to develop nuclear arms except for the training it has provided to native technicians. The reactor went into service some nine years after India's first research reactor (Apsara) and a year after India's second, the CIRUS plant, which produced the plutonium for India's 1974 test.

Pakistan's first nuclear power plant, known as KANUPP (for Karachi Nuclear Power Project), a 137-megawatt, natural-uranium/heavy-water reactor purchased from Canada, was completed in 1972. The United States supplied the heavy water for the facility, Canada supplied the fuel. It, too, is subject to IAEA inspections; but, as discussed below, many observers fear that plutonium produced in the reactor may ultimately contribute to Pakistani nuclear weapons.

Zulfikar Ali Bhutto was the chief architect of Pakistan's nuclear program. Between 1958 and 1971, the year he became prime minister, Bhutto held the posts of foreign minister, minister for fuel, power, and nuclear resources, and administrator in charge of atomic energy. In these various positions he supervised the negotiations to obtain Pakistan's research and power reactors, as well as the establishment of the Pakistan Institute of Nuclear Science and Technology (PINSTECH), Pakistan's principal nuclear research center. The facility included a British-designed reprocessing laboratory with an insignificant plutonium output, but useful for training Pakistani technicians in this sensitive field. Design of the lab was completed in 1971 and it was probably constructed shortly thereafter.[2]

As Bhutto revealed in 1978 in a testament written while he awaited execution, from the outset his objective was to make Pakistan into a nuclear power:

When I took charge of Pakistan's Atomic Energy Commission it was no more than a signboard of an office. It was only a name. Assiduously and with granite determination, I put my entire vitality behind the task of acquiring nuclear capability for my country . . . . A country does not have to be merely wealthy to possess nuclear capability. If that were the only requirement, every OPEC country would have nuclear capability. The essential pre-requisite is the infrastructure.

For this reason, I gave the highest priority to train thousands of nuclear scientists in foreign countries. Now we have the brainpower, we have the nuclear power plant in Karachi. All we needed was the nuclear reprocessing plant. Arrangements for the heavy water, the uranium and the fuel fabricating plant had been made. We were on the threshold of full nuclear capability when I left the Government to come to this death cell. We know that Israel and South Africa have full nuclear capability. The communist powers also possess it. Only the Islamic civilization was without it, but that position was about to change.[3]

As early as 1969, Bhutto had publicly declared his intentions. In his book *The Myth of Independence,* written four years after Pakistan's defeat in the 1965 Indo-Pakistani War and during a period when many

Indian leaders were calling for their nation to develop nuclear weapons, Bhutto wrote:

All wars of our age have become total wars . . . and it will have to be assumed that a war waged against Pakistan is capable of becoming a total war. It would be dangerous to plan for less and our plans should, therefore, include the nuclear deterrent . . . . India is unlikely to concede nuclear monopoly to others . . . . It appears that she is determined to proceed with her plans to detonate a nuclear bomb. If Pakistan restricts or suspends her nuclear programme, it would not only enable India to blackmail Pakistan with her nuclear advantage, but would impose a crippling limitation on the development of Pakistan's science and the technology . . . . Our problem, in its essence, is how to obtain such a weapon in time before the crisis begins.[4]

Such concerns undoubtedly contributed to Pakistan's refusal to ratify the 1968 Nuclear Non-Proliferation Treaty. In this, Pakistan followed India's lead. It left Pakistan free to develop nuclear arms without violating any international undertaking.

In 1971 India dealt Pakistan a crushing military defeat in a second war, resulting in the creation of the separate nation of Bangladesh from the area that previously had been East Pakistan. Zulfikar Ali Bhutto became prime minister of the now truncated Pakistani state in the west. Less then two months after taking office, Bhutto convened a group of Pakistan's top scientists in the city of Multan and announced that Pakistan would develop atomic weapons.[5] Bhutto also removed the head of the Pakistan Atomic Energy Commission, Ishrat Usmani, who reportedly opposed the development of nuclear arms, and appointed Munir Khan, a supporter of Pakistani nuclearization, to the post.

Reprocessing and Enrichment Plants. Over the next several years, Pakistan launched a number of initiatives aimed at developing nuclear arms. First, in 1973, shortly after the start-up of the Canadian-supplied KANUPP power reactor, Prime Minister Bhutto began negotiating with France for the purchase of a large reprocessing facility to be located at Chashma. The facility was to be a commercial-size plant capable of handling one hundred metric tons of spent nuclear fuel a year (1 metric ton = 2,200 pounds)—more than five times the annual output of the KANUPP reactor—and of producing perhaps one hundred and fifty kilograms of plutonium (1 kilogram = 2.2 pounds) annually, enough for possibly thirty nuclear weapons. The facility was far larger than could possibly be integrated economically into Pakistan's nuclear energy program;[6] its large annual capacity, however, would allow rapid processing of accumulated spent fuel from KANUPP to produce a stock of weapons-usable plutonium.

Before the negotiations on the plant were revealed publicly, Pakistan announced plans to construct a five-hundred-megawatt nuclear reactor near Chashma and a smaller nuclear desalinization plant, in what now appears to have been an attempt to justify the reprocessing facility. Subsequently, in its nuclear budget for 1975-76, Pakistan indicated an intention to build one nuclear power plant every two years from 1980 until the end of the century.[7] None of these plans has been realized, however, and only in 1983 did Pakistan issue bids for its first new power plant, as discussed below.

According to a January 1975 aide-memoire to the French ambassador in Islamabad, in October 1974—less than six months after India's nuclear test—the French firm Saint-Gobain Techniques Nouvelles (SGN) signed a detailed agreement for construction of the outsized reprocessing plant. SGN would be the principal engineer for the facility, furnish blueprints and some of the necessary hardware, aid Pakistan in purchasing other items through subcontractors, and help put the plant into operation.[8] The plant would cost some $60 million. French Atomic Energy Commission officials participated in the negotiations and had full knowledge of the project as it evolved. Given Bhutto's response to the Indian explosion, which he characterized as a "fateful development" that has "introduced a qualitative change in the situation prevalent in the Subcontinent," and the excessive capability of the reprocessing plant relative to Pakistan's nuclear energy program, the French could have been under few illusions that Pakistan intended to use the plant to advance its ability to develop nuclear arms.[9]

While negotiations on the plant at Chashma continued, Pakistan also began construction of a smaller, secret reprocessing facility adjacent to the Pakistan Institute of Nuclear Science and Technology near Rawalpindi. The facility, known as the New Labs, was built with the assistance of the Belgian firm Belgonucléaire and SGN, although the French government may not have been aware of SGN participation.[10] Reportedly, the plant was designed to produce between ten and twenty kilograms of plutonium annually, enough for two to four weapons.[11]

It appears that shortly after the Indian test, Pakistan launched a separate effort to acquire the capability for producing highly enriched uranium, the alternative material usable for nuclear weapons. The key to this secret endeavor was Dr. Abdul Qadir Khan, a Pakistani metallurgical engineer who was trained in Holland and Belgium between 1963 and 1972. From 1972 to 1975 Khan worked in the metallurgical section of a Dutch engineering firm, The Physical Dynamics Research Laboratory (FDO) whose parent company was playing a key role in an ultracentrifuge uranium enrichment plant then under construction in the town of Almelo in the Netherlands.[12] The Almelo facility was being built by the British-Dutch-West German consortium URENCO to produce low-enriched nuclear power plant fuel.

As a subsequent investigation by the Dutch government revealed, Khan gained access both to secret technical data concerning the plant's highly classified uranium enrichment process and to detailed lists of the equipment used in the facility, all of which he transferred to Pakistan.[13] Even before Khan had left his post in the Netherlands in 1975, Pakistani nuclear officials were using the information he had provided to begin purchasing key components for a Pakistani ultracentrifuge pilot plant to be built in the town of Sihala (a few miles southeast of Islamabad). Later, under Khan's direction, Pakistan initiated construction of an industrial-scale plant at nearby Kahuta with thousands of centrifuge units.

Islamic Ties. In the wake of Pakistan's defeat in the 1971 Bangladesh War, Prime Minister Bhutto worked assiduously to strengthen ties with other Muslim states to counterbalance India's new dominance of the Subcontinent. Bhutto took the lead in organizing the Islamic Conference, serving as its president until his death in 1979, and hosting the second Islamic summit in Lahore in 1974.[14]

As the wealth of the oil-producing Arab states skyrocketed in the early 1970s, Pakistan benefited economically from these ties, receiving hundreds of millions of dollars in economic aid, more than offsetting the increased cost of its oil imports and rivaling the amount of aid received from the Western Aid Pakistan Consortium.[15] In 1974-75, Pakistan was the second largest recipient of OPEC aid, and between 1973 and mid-1976 five Arab countries and Iran provided grants and loans worth nearly $1 billion.[16] Much of this aid was earmarked for arms purchases; at the same time, Pakistani nationals began to play an increasingly important role in the military establishments of the Arab states. According to one recent report:

Libya supported Pakistan by giving it $150 million in economic assistance and nearly $200 million for military purchases between 1975 and 1976. In return, Pakistan supplied military personnel under contract, particularly to the Libyan Air Force, where they were involved in the operation of MIG 21s, 23s, and perhaps some Mirage fighters. In addition, Abu Dhabi sponsored the largest of the arms deals financed with Arab money. It funded the direct purchase of 32 Mirage V's for the PAF [Pakistani Air Force] at a cost of $330 million and contracted for Pakistani crews to operate an additional 24 that were bought for the Abu Dhabi Air Force with the caveat that, in the case of an emergency, these too would be made available to PAF. The total cost of the deal was nearly $650 million.[17]

Bhutto's ties to Libyan leader Muammar el-Khadafi appear to have been particularly strong, and in 1973 the two nations are said to have cemented a relationship under which Libya agreed to finance Pakistan's acquisition of nuclear weapons.[18] As discussed below, Libya also transferred uranium not subject to IAEA monitoring to Pakistan. Although it has been widely speculated that in return for this aid Pakistan promised to provide complete nuclear weapons to Libya, the consensus in the U.S. intelligence community, according to knowledgeable officials, is that Pakistan never agreed to such a quid pro quo. During the 1970s, however, Libya is widely reported to have sought technical assistance to develop its own reprocessing or enrichment capability;[19] it is not unreasonable to surmise that Libya may have expected to receive such know-how in return for its contribution to Pakistan, particularly since at the time—as France and Belgium were demonstrating—international transfers of this kind were not considered contraband.

While these linkages between Pakistan and the Arab world may have helped underwrite the Pakistani nuclear program, they remain far short of a concerted Arab effort to obtain nuclear arms through the agency of Pakistan. All the same, Arab leaders may well have believed that the development of nuclear weapons by Pakistan, which was so strongly emphasizing its Muslim ties, would enhance the stature of the Muslim world generally and serve as a political counterweight to Israel's nuclear capability. This is probably the extent to which Pakistan's acquisition of nuclear weapons can be considered an "Islamic bomb," and it is in this context that Prime Minister Bhutto's comment, quoted earlier, that the "Islamic civilization" would shortly possess "full nuclear capability" should be interpreted.

Slowing the Chashma Reprocessing Plant. Following the Indian test of 1974, U.S. efforts to curb the spread of nuclear weapons gradually intensified. In the fall of 1974 the United States convened a secret meeting of the principal nuclear supplier nations in London in an effort to gain acceptance of a uniform set of nuclear export standards.[20] It also began to pressure Pakistan and then France to cancel the Chashma reprocessing plant sale. (At the time, Pakistan's separate programs for obtaining nuclear weapons material through the New Labs near PINSTECH and the Kahuta enrichment plant were apparently unknown to U.S. officials.)

Prime Minister Bhutto had indicated that he might consider abandoning, or at least postponing, the

Chashma reprocessing plant if the United States lifted the arms embargo that had been imposed against Pakistan in 1971 at the time of the Bangladesh War.[21] Out of increasing recognition of Pakistan's legitimate security concerns and, apparently, a desire to pursue this possible opening, the Ford administration lifted the arms embargo in February 1975.[22] It also maintained pressure on France to insist, at a minimum, that the facility be safeguarded, a step France adopted in 1975. France also insisted that any other reprocessing plant Pakistan might build over the next twenty years using the same basic process as the Chashma facility likewise be placed under International Atomic Energy Agency (IAEA) safeguards. The United States voted in favor of the French-Pakistani-IAEA agreement embodying these controls when it came before the IAEA Board of Governors in February 1976 and appeared prepared to go along with the sale on those terms.

At that point, however, the U.S. Congress intervened. Alarmed over the 1974 Indian test, West Germany's sale in 1975 of reprocessing and enrichment technology to Brazil, and the pending French reprocessing plant sales to Pakistan and to South Korea, it enacted the first of a series of major non-proliferation laws, the Symington amendment to the Foreign Assistance Act.[23] The amendment prohibited U.S. economic or military assistance to any nation importing enrichment or reprocessing technology unless the recipient accepted IAEA safeguards on all of its nuclear activities. In effect, the amendment meant that sales of U.S. military equipment to Pakistan would be available only on a cash basis and that all bilateral economic assistance would be terminated if the French reprocessing plant sale were consummated.

In the face of congressional opposition to the French sale, as well as sharp criticism from presidential candidate Jimmy Carter of the Ford administration's non-proliferation policies, Secretary of State Kissinger visited Pakistan in August in an attempt to persuade Bhutto to abandon the project.[24] As a further inducement, Kissinger offered Bhutto one hundred A-7 Corsair jet fighters, a transfer that would have greatly strengthened Pakistan's overall military capabilities. Nevertheless, Bhutto rejected the offer. Kissinger then flew to Paris where he attempted to persuade the French to cancel the sale, but French premier Jacques Chirac rejected Kissinger's request.

Chirac resigned shortly after this encounter, and President Valery Giscard d'Estaing took direct control of French nuclear export decision-making. In October, Giscard visited the United States and reportedly discussed overall nuclear export policy. On December 16, 1976, Paris declared it would discontinue further exports of reprocessing facilities until further notice.[25]

This policy did not directly affect the pre-existing sale to Pakistan, however, and through the spring of 1977, France planned to proceed with the next phase of the deal, the export of the cutting machine for chopping spent fuel into pieces at the "head end" of the Chashma plant. Only when American officials presented new evidence of Pakistan's intent to use the plant to aid its nuclear weapons program did France modify its position. Starting in June 1977, France began to delay performance under the sales contract while adding new conditions in the hopes that Pakistan would break off the agreement.[26] U.S. pressure on Pakistan continued as well. American military and economic assistance for Pakistan was terminated in September 1977 because of its continued pursuit of the French deal.[27]

Finally, in August 1978, France stopped performing under the contract.[28] Two months later, U.S. military and economic aid was restored. As late as December 1979, however, personnel working for SGN, the French firm responsible for building the Chashma plant, continued to assist Pakistan in various aspects of construction, while several French suppliers continued to export goods for the facility pursuant to Pakistani purchase orders. Even when this aid was stopped, apparently late in 1979, Pakistan continued efforts to build the plant by using blueprints and specifications previously obtained from France; little progress seems to have been made, however.[29] The ongoing activities at the Chashma site made it clear that President Zia ul-Haq, who deposed Bhutto in July 1977, intended to continue the nuclear policies of his predecessor.

By this time, virtually all overt nuclear aid to Pakistan had ceased, the Canadians having terminated spare parts and fresh fuel for the KANUPP facility in 1976 because of Pakistan's unwillingness to accept IAEA safeguards on all of its nuclear activities.[30]

While these intensive diplomatic efforts to block the completion of the Chashma reprocessing plant were being played out, Pakistan was also pursuing two alternative routes for obtaining nuclear weapons material: construction of an enrichment facility and completion of the New Labs pilot-scale reprocessing unit. Pakistan was critically dependent on purchases from the advanced Western nuclear supplier countries to build the first of these facilities and was able to obtain much of the equipment it needed both because these governments condoned some of the exports involved and because private-sector agents were often able to circumvent such export controls as the governments did apply. Pakistan has adamantly refused to place either plant under IAEA safeguards.

While little has been reported of the specific items obtained for the New Labs unit, Pakistan's purchasing effort for the Kahuta enrichment plant has been well documented. From the Swiss firm Vakuum Apparat Technik, Pakistan obtained high-vacuum valves needed to control flows of uranium hexafluoride gas in the plant; from the Swiss firm CORA Engineering, it bought an elaborate, specially designed and engineered gasification and solidification unit, so large that three Hercules C-130 transport planes were reportedly required to fly it to Pakistan; from the British firm Emerson Electric, it purchased over sixty high-frequency inverters for regulating the centrifuges; and from the Dutch firm Van Doorne Transmissie, it bought 6,500 specially hardened steel tubes for the centrifuges themselves.[31]

In each of these cases, the sales were arguably permissible under the joint standards adopted by the Nuclear Suppliers Group in 1976 because the items involved were not explicitly mentioned on the suppliers' "trigger list," the list of items whose export is prohibited unless special licenses are issued and the recipient country agrees to place the installation using them under IAEA safeguards. Although the Dutch government reportedly expressed concern at the sale of the hardened steel tubes—which was completed nevertheless—Swiss officials apparently made no effort to intervene in the sales by their domestic corporations. And only after a member of the British Parliament asked a question in the House of Commons about the Emerson Electric sale was the matter raised publicly in Great Britain.

Shortly afterwards, the United States began to focus on Pakistan's development of the Kahuta plant. The result was a major U.S. effort to revise the joint controls of the Nuclear Suppliers Group and, in the meantime, to persuade individual supplier countries to block the export of critical items for the facility. These efforts were only partially successful.

With the evidence now plain that it was seeking to import enrichment technology, Pakistan again became ineligible for U.S. assistance under the Symington amendment. In April 1979, after the failure of a special mission to Islamabad by Deputy Secretary of State Warren Christopher to persuade President Zia to cancel the Kahuta project, U.S. aid was terminated.[32] In May, Assistant Secretary of State Thomas R. Pickering, testifying before Congress, explained the basis for the Carter administration's concerns regarding the plant:

We believe uranium enrichment facilities or other sensitive nuclear facilities are not justified in terms of Pakistan's nuclear program which consists essentially of one research reactor, supplied by the United States, and one small heavy water power reactor supplied by Canada which does not require enriched uranium. We are concerned, therefore, that the Pakistan program is not peaceful but related to an effort to develop a nuclear explosive capability.[33]

Three months later, President Zia, in an address to the nation, responded to the U.S. aid cutoff, stating:

Our economic aid has been affected but we have absorbed its impact and the entire nation supports the government's stand because it is united on this issue . . . . We shall bear our vicissitudes ourselves. We shall lift our burden. We shall eat crumbs but we will not allow our national interest to be compromised in any manner whatsoever.[34]

President Zia's refusal to bow to the loss of U.S. aid was more than mere rhetoric. According to U.S. officials quoted in the press, foreign intelligence reports indicated that an underground nuclear test site was being prepared in southern Pakistan.[35]

The report of Pakistan's nuclear test site came

barely a week after a *New York Times* story that the United States was preparing to escalate its efforts to curb the Pakistani nuclear weapons program. Among the options being considered, the *Times* reported, were the sale of advanced F-16 aircraft to Pakistan, intensified economic sanctions such as restrictions on private American investment in the country and on grants by international lending institutions, and covert military operations to disable the Pakistani enrichment facility.[36]

The United States immediately denied that it intended to take paramilitary action against the Pakistani enrichment program, although press reports quoted government officials as acknowledging that the option had been considered and then rejected as "too dangerous and politically provocative."[37] Some U.S. officials, among them U.S. ambassador to Pakistan Arthur W. Hummel, Jr., apparently believed that the production of nuclear weapons by Pakistan was all but inevitable and that neither covert military action nor severe economic sanctions would turn it from its quest for such weapons.[38] Nevertheless, it appeared that the United States was quietly beginning to impose increased economic sanctions by taking a tough stand on the country's appeals for debt rescheduling.[39] For its part, Pakistan escalated the war of nerves in September by announcing that it intended to build the Chashma reprocessing plant on its own, despite the loss of French aid.[40]

In mid-October 1979, Pakistani foreign affairs advisor Agha Shahi held a series of talks in Washington with Secretary of State Cyrus Vance on a number of issues, including Pakistan's nuclear program.[41] Given the mounting U.S. pressure on Pakistan during the previous six months, including the termination of military and economic assistance, the apparent slowdown in multilateral lending, and the veiled threats of covert military action, it is possible that during these meetings the United States threatened serious consequences if Pakistan did not cease its pursuit of the bomb.[42]

Barely two months later, on December 25, 1979, Soviet troops invaded Afghanistan. Within weeks, U.S. policy towards Pakistan changed dramatically as the Carter administration urged it to accept a two-year, $400-million economic and military aid package. While the Carter administration initially intended to obtain a one-time emergency exemption from the Symington amendment barring Pakistan from any American aid because of its uranium enrichment activities, by February it had decided to seek an open-ended exemption that would allow assistance indefinitely.[43]

President Zia termed the Carter aid offer "peanuts" and instead sought a treaty with the United States formally guaranteeing Pakistan's security. During their visit to Islamabad in early February 1980, National Security Advisor Zbigniew Brzezinski and Deputy Secretary of State Warren Christopher, while downplaying the possibility of such a treaty, held open the prospect of increased aid. Reportedly, however, they carried instructions warning Zia that a Pakistani nuclear test would spell the end of any renewed U.S. assistance.[44]

Although Washington and Islamabad would dicker for the remainder of 1980 over the size and content of renewed U.S. aid and the quality of U.S. security guarantees, the Brzezinski-Christopher mission appeared to represent a turning point in U.S. policy toward Pakistan's acquisition of nuclear arms. Whereas prior to the Soviet invasion of Afghanistan, the Carter administration had been prepared to impose economic and military aid sanctions against Pakistan and to consider more severe measures to stop the Pakistani nuclear weapons effort in its tracks, the United States was now ready to maintain the flow of arms and aid even if Pakistan continued to advance its program, provided it did not *test* a nuclear device. Moreover, given Washington's goal of strengthening the Zia regime as a bulwark against Soviet expansionism, halting multilateral loans to Pakistan, a move which could threaten the stability of the Zia government, was also implicitly ruled out. This left technology transfer curbs as the principal tool for retarding Pakistan's ongoing efforts to develop nuclear arms. As discussed below, the Reagan administration adopted a similar stance.

Events during 1979 and 1980 demonstrated the difficulty of relying on nuclear-supplier country export controls alone. In November 1979, press reports stated that Pakistan had obtained as much as 100 metric tons of uranium concentrate (yellowcake) not subject to IAEA monitoring from Libya.[45] The material had originally been purchased by Libya from Niger and then re-exported to Pakistan, possibly along with material that Pakistan had itself purchased from Niger through normal, above-board channels. Under the terms of the Pakistan-Niger-IAEA safeguards agreement, all of Pakistan's direct purchases of yellowcake from Niger had to be listed with the IAEA and used only in safeguarded installations, such as the KANUPP power plant.[46]

To run its unsafeguarded uranium enrichment plant, however, Pakistan needed a source of yellowcake not subject to IAEA coverage. Such material would also be needed if Pakistan was considering the possibility of surreptitiously irradiating extra uranium fuel in the KANUPP reactor and subsequently reprocessing it, a stratagem that would appear increasingly credible, as discussed below.

From 1978 to 1980, Niger apparently made a number of sales to Libya believing that IAEA coverage was satisfactory because Libya was a party to the Non-Proliferation Treaty and therefore, presumably, obligated to ensure IAEA monitoring of all of its yellowcake imports. In fact, however, through 1980 Libya had not concluded the detailed safeguards agreement with the Agency required under the treaty, and thus the IAEA monitoring program was not in place during that period. This gap in coverage apparently permitted Libya to transship Niger-produced yellowcake to Pakistan without the Agency's being the wiser.[47] After the ruse was discovered by U.S. officials, Niger is said to have given the United States assurances that in the future, uranium shipments would be allowed only to countries where IAEA monitoring was actually in place.[48]

How much material may have been shipped to Pakistan by this means is not clear. In 1981 Niger's president Seyni Kountche stated that 450 tons of yellowcake had been sold to Libya and 60 to Pakistan directly; it is not known how much of the Libyan material may have been subsequently transferred to Pakistan.[49]

Another difficulty the United States confronted in implementing its program to stem the flow of equipment and technology to Pakistan was the lack of cooperation by some of the key western European nuclear suppliers. According to press accounts, French nuclear firms owned 54 percent of Niger's mining company Somair, which was responsible for the shipments to Libya, suggesting that the exports from Niger could not have been authorized without the knowledge of the French government.[50] More directly, during 1979 and 1980 it appeared that the Swiss government was knowingly permitting exports of sophisticated nuclear

technology to Pakistan despite U.S. objections.[51] The
Swiss government claimed that none of the exports in
question were explicitly prohibited by the Nuclear
Suppliers' Guidelines and that, accordingly, it lacked
the legal authority to stop the sales. At issue were two
items discussed above: the specially designed Swiss
high-vacuum valves to be used in Pakistan's enrichment plant to regulate the stream of uranium hexafluoride, and the CORA Engineering custom-made
system for converting uranium hexafluoride to a gas at
the beginning of the enrichment process and then con-
densing it into a solid after enrichment had taken
place.[52] As a means for pressuring Switzerland into
tightening its export control system, the United States
withheld approvals for the transfer of Swiss spent fuel,
which was accumulating at Swiss nuclear power plants,
to reprocessing facilities in France and Great Britain.[53]
By November, the Swiss had apparently gained the
agreement of several firms to reject new contracts with
Pakistan, although existing contracts were to be honored, and by the end of the year the Swiss government
had pledged to scrutinize far more closely and possibly
to ban any additional exports for the Pakistani enrichment program.[54]

Despite this apparent success in dealing with Switzerland, the United States was confronted during 1980
with additional evidence that Pakistan's clandestine
efforts to obtain nuclear technology were succeeding.
In September, Pakistan announced it had completed
the construction of a nuclear fuel fabrication plant to
supply the KANUPP reactor.[55] Canada had ceased
supplying fresh fuel for the plant in 1976 when it terminated all nuclear aid to Pakistan because of the latter's
refusal to accept safeguards on all of its nuclear activities. The inauguration of the complex fuel fabrication
facility almost certainly indicated that Pakistan had

been successful in obtaining significant outside aid. As discussed below, Pakistan's ability to manufacture its own fuel elements for the KANUPP reactor would make it increasingly difficult for the IAEA to safeguard the plant.

Barely three weeks later, the United States suffered what appeared to be yet another setback. According to U.S. intelligence experts, Pakistani technicians had nearly completed construction of the New Labs reprocessing plant.[56] The facility, about ten times smaller than the French-assisted plant at Chashma, was said to be capable of extracting ten to twenty kilograms of plutonium per year, enough for several nuclear weapons. While U.S. intelligence sources believed that the plant might be ready to operate in 1981, as of mid-1984 it appeared not to have been activated.[57]

One important limitation on the use of the secret reprocessing facility at New Labs was that Pakistan did not have access to a source of unsafeguarded, plutonium-bearing spent nuclear fuel. The exclusive source of such material was the safeguarded KANUPP reactor. Nevertheless, one U.S. source said, "I think we can be relatively certain that one way or another, the material they put through the reprocessing plant will come from the KANUPP reactor."[58] Despite U.S. discovery of the New Labs reprocessing facility, Islamabad succeeded in obtaining items needed for it from Belgonucléaire and the French firm, SGN.[59]

In December 1980, it became clear that the United States had not been completely successful even in curbing the flow of American technology for the Pakistani program. Early that month, Canada charged three men with illegally exporting to Pakistan electronic components that had been purchased in the United States. Prior to their arrest, the three had made at least five other shipments of similar electronic parts.[60] In June 1981, it was also revealed that Turkish companies had for over a year circumvented U.S. and European export controls by purchasing and then transshipping millions of dollars' worth of similar components to Pakistan.[61]

Finally, during this period Pakistan was also able to obtain a facility for converting yellowcake into uranium hexafluoride, a critically important installation to produce the feedstock for Pakistan's enrichment plant. The uranium hexafluoride facility had been illegally exported from Germany by the firm CES Kalthof GmbH of Freiburg, according to the West German government.[62] The export order was signed in 1977 and completed in 1980; reportedly the West German firm also assisted in testing the installation, located in Dera Ghazi Khan, after it was completed.[63]

Expanded U.S. Aid Offer. Shortly after taking office in 1981, the Reagan administration began negotiations with Pakistani president Zia for a U.S. economic and military aid program far larger than the one that had been proposed by President Carter.[64] By June, agreement had been reached on a six-year, $3.2-billion aid plan, including the sale of forty F-16 aircraft, the most advanced ever offered to Pakistan. Although the foremost purpose of the aid package was to demonstrate U.S. commitment to Pakistan as a way of counterbalancing the Soviet presence in neighboring Afghanistan, Under Secretary of State James L. Buckley stated that the military aid package also would advance U.S. non-proliferation policy:

Whatever their [Pakistan's] activities are, whatever the intentions or capabilities, the policies that we have followed in the last couple of years have obviously not slowed down or changed the direction of whatever it is they are doing in developing certain atomic research facilities and capabilities.

.We do believe that our best chance to influence the outcome, influence the future direction of what might be Pakistani intentions, is to help remove the very significant sense of insecurity that that nation suffers from today. We believe that if that real insecurity can be removed we will not only have a better chance to make sure that explosives are not detonated but also would be in the best position to use the argument of persuasion that this would not be in Pakistan's best interest.[65]

In urging the aid package, Buckley stated that Pakistan had pledged not to develop nuclear weapons:

I was assured by the ministers, I was assured by the President himself that it is not the intention of the Pakistani Government to develop nuclear weapons.[66]

Despite these assurances, Buckley acknowledged that Pakistan was, in fact, working towards developing a nuclear weapons capability and indicated that the Reagan administration, like its predecessor, was prepared to extend U.S. assistance, notwithstanding these activities:

Senator Glenn. Knowing what we know from our own intelligence sources and those of most other nations around the world that follow these nuclear matters, will the President of the United States be willing to state that it is his opinion that Pakistan is not in the process of developing nuclear weapons?

Mr. Buckley. One has to make the distinction between the nuclear option and nuclear weapons.

Senator Glenn. That is a big distinction, I agree . . .

* * *

Senator Glenn. Do you feel the President would now assure

us with the proposed arms package that in light of your conversation with General Zia, the President can send us a message and say he feels assured that Pakistan is not developing a nuclear explosives capability?

Mr. Buckley. There is, again, a distinction between developing a capability and utilizing a capability.[67]

In this hearing, however, and in other settings throughout 1981, administration aides made it clear that if Pakistan conducted a nuclear test, U.S. assistance would again be terminated, a restriction Congress firmly embedded in the legislation permitting the aid package to proceed.[68]

Even as Congress was reviewing the proposed aid package, new evidence of Pakistan's intentions emerged. In April, Senator Alan Cranston revealed that on the basis of information received from a number of executive branch sources, Pakistan was constructing a nuclear test site, a horizontal tunnel into a hillside in the Baluchistan mountains some forty miles from the Afghanistan border. Cranston noted that previous concerns about the site raised in August 1979 had waned, but that new construction in recent weeks justified renewed fears over Pakistani intentions.[69]

In June, the *Washington Post* quoted a State Department cable to the U.S. Embassy in Ankara as stating:

We have strong reason to believe that Pakistan is seeking to develop a nuclear explosives capability . . . We also have information that Pakistan is conducting a program for the design and development for the triggering package for nuclear explosive devices.[70]

In late September, reports surfaced that administration officials were investigating the possibility that

Pakistan had secretly removed plutonium-bearing spent fuel from the safeguarded KANUPP reactor. According to sources quoted in the report, a number of "anomalies" and "irregularities" had been detected, including a high rate of failure of surveillance equipment and problems in accounting for spent fuel.[71]

Finally, in October, U.S. customs officials arrested a retired Pakistani army colonel, said to be a close friend of Zia, as he was attempting to smuggle a large shipment of zirconium metal through Kennedy Airport in New York City.[72] Zirconium alloy is used to sheathe the uranium fuel used in the KANUPP reactor, and the material would have been needed to enable Pakistan to continue fabricating fuel elements for the reactor at its fuel fabrication plant in Chashma.

Notwithstanding these revelations, in late 1981 Congress enacted legislation removing the prohibition on economic and military assistance to Pakistan for six years and implementing the $3.2-billion aid program. However, an amendment tightened existing provisions requiring the termination of assistance in the event Pakistan conducted a nuclear test (or received or transferred nuclear weapons) by removing the President's authority to waive this prohibition.[73]

Possible Diversion. As noted above, in September 1981 U.S. aides were said to be concerned that Pakistan might have diverted spent fuel from the KANUPP plant. In October, IAEA director general Sigvard Eklund advised the Agency's Board of Governors that because Pakistan had acquired the capability to fabricate its own nuclear fuel, the Agency could no longer certify by means of the monitoring arrangements then in place at the facility that diversions at the KANUPP reactor had not occurred. Eklund called on the Pakistani government to permit a substantial upgrading of the IAEA's existing safeguards.[74] The IAEA finding was the first such determination in the the Agency's history.

Until the new fuel fabrication plant had begun operation in September 1980, the Agency had possessed complete knowledge of the amount of nuclear fuel available to be used in the KANUPP reactor, since it had all been imported from Canada and inventoried carefully. By adding up the amount of spent fuel at the reactor site and the amount of fresh fuel on hand, and then making allowance for material in use within the reactor (all of which the Agency checked by physical inspection) it had been able to verify that no material had been removed for military ends. With the completion of the Pakistani fuel fabrication plant at the Chashma atomic complex, however—which Pakistan refused to allow the IAEA to monitor—the possibility arose that Pakistan might secretly introduce additional, undeclared fuel elements into the reactor and remove them without advising the Agency. This would give Pakistan a source of plutonium-bearing spent fuel from which the plutonium could then be extracted for weapons in the New Labs reprocessing unit or the Chashma reprocessing plant, once either of these was completed.

Over the next year, negotiations on upgrading safeguards at the KANUPP site continued. In November 1982, Pakistan agreed to allow installation of most of the new equipment sought by the Agency.[75] Nevertheless, as of that date, IAEA safeguards remained insufficient to provide assurance that material was not being diverted, and it was not until March 1983 that the IAEA believed it was again in a position to safeguard the reactor properly.[76]

Thus, it is possible that from September 1980 until early 1983 Pakistan systematically diverted spent fuel from the KANUPP reactor. The reactor is said to have operated only intermittently through September 1982, however, and the Chashma fuel fabrication plant reportedly produced only trivial amounts of fresh reactor fuel.[77] During the entire period in question, moreover, IAEA safeguards, however imperfect, were being applied to the reactor and would have restricted Pakistan's use of some diversion routes. Given these factors, it seems unlikely that Pakistan could have secretly irradiated undeclared fuel in the reactor amounting to more than a fraction of the typical annual throughput of the facility. Since the reactor produces twenty-four kilograms of plutonium annually in its spent fuel under normal operating conditions—enough for three to four weapons—it seems improbable that Pakistan could have diverted spent fuel containing enough plutonium for more than one or two devices, if it diverted any material at all.[78]

Threatened Aid Cut for Reprocessing. Since both of Pakistan's reactors are under safeguards, Islamabad cannot produce plutonium-bearing spent fuel that is not subject to IAEA monitoring without violating the safeguards agreements covering the two plants. Moreover, none of Pakistan's spent fuel that is already under safeguards, or that will be produced under IAEA supervision, may be moved legally to another location unless safeguards are also applied there.[79] This means that if Pakistan began to process spent fuel in either of its unsafeguarded reprocessing plants (New Labs or Chashma), it would immediately be assumed that the material had been illegally produced in, or taken from, one of Pakistan's reactors, and thus that Pakistan had violated the IAEA regime. Although Pakistan may have already secretly produced spent fuel at KANUPP, no reprocessing is known to have taken place at either the New Labs or Chashma plants.

Apparently using a similar analysis of safeguards coverage in Pakistan, the Reagan administration had, by April 1982, significantly tightened the ground rules covering provision of U.S. aid, advising Pakistan that if it engaged in reprocessing, it would "seriously disturb" emerging U.S.-Pakistani ties and, by implication, jeopardize continued U.S. assistance.[80] Thus, the administration had declared that an action short of a nuclear test could trigger an aid cutoff, a tougher stance than that embodied in the Foreign Assistance Act. If Washington's threat succeeds in forestalling reprocessing, Pakistan would remain many time-consuming steps away from obtaining plutonium-based nuclear weapons. This would be a significant advance in reducing the proliferation risks posed by the Pakistani nuclear program.

II. Developments of the Past Year

Chashma Reactor Blocked.

Since at least 1981, Pakistan has been developing plans for the construction of a nine-hundred-megawatt nuclear power plant at Chashma.[81] With the global downturn in nuclear power plant orders, it has been widely assumed that France and West Germany, among other nuclear suppliers, would compete strenuously to obtain this order. (U.S. firms are precluded from making such a sale by the Nuclear Non-Proliferation Act, which prohibits exports of U.S. reactors to nations that refuse to accept IAEA safeguards on all of their nuclear installations.)

A major non-proliferation initiative of the Reagan administration has been to persuade other nuclear suppliers to refrain from entering into major new supply commitments with countries refusing full-scope safeguards.[82] Through mid-1983, it appeared uncertain whether France and West Germany, which had long opposed such an export condition, would follow the U.S. lead. Indeed, during a visit to Islamabad in March 1983, French foreign minister Claude Cheysson declared that France was prepared to sell Pakistan a large nuclear power reactor and explicitly stated that he did not agree with the United States' position that such sales should be withheld from nations having unsafeguarded facilities.[83]

Although Pakistan had agreed that the Chashma reactor would itself be safeguarded, the effect of a French sale would have been to re-legitimize nuclear trade with Pakistan and to remove one of the few sanctions imposed against it—denial of nuclear trade—for its continued pursuit of a nuclear weapons capability. Moreover, developing Pakistan's nuclear infrastructure even through a peaceful project would strengthen Pakistan's ability to pursue its military nuclear program through the training of skilled technicians, construction crews, and nuclear engineers.

Cheysson's statement notwithstanding, when the deadline for submission of bids on the Chashma facility came on July 31, 1983, no tenders had been submitted.[84] Pakistan thereafter postponed the final date for submitting bids until December 31, 1983. Again no bids were tendered, nor had any been through June 1984.[85]

The total boycott of the Chashma project by all the nuclear supplier nations, a significant economic and symbolic sanction, may represent an important milestone in U.S. efforts to establish a common front in curbing the spread of nuclear arms. During the 1970s, competition for nuclear sales had been an insurmountable obstacle to establishing a unified nuclear embargo against Argentina and Brazil as a means of pressuring them to adopt full-scope safeguards. Perhaps because

Pakistan's interest in nuclear weapons appears considerably more clear-cut than that of Argentina or Brazil, the nuclear suppliers were prepared to set aside their commercial interests in order to express their disapproval of Pakistan's nuclear ambitions. Another, less disinterested motive may have been that Pakistan's ability to pay for the facility was uncertain without massive credits, which none of the potential suppliers was prepared to offer.[86] Whatever the reason, the solid front presented by the nuclear suppliers appears to have been a quiet victory for Reagan administration diplomacy.[87]

Pursuit of Nuclear Weapons Capability.

In July 1984, a press report quoted an unnamed senior Reagan administration official as stating that Pakistan had produced weapons grade uranium at its Kahuta enrichment plant, thereby surmounting the final obstacle on its twelve-year quest for nuclear arms.[88] The conclusion was said to be based on documents obtained by U.S. authorities and radiation samples from the Kahuta area, although the latter were said not to be definitive. Other administration sources, however, disputed the press account, believing Pakistan had not made this breakthrough. Nonetheless, separate revelations of Pakistan's nuclear activities over the preceding year mean that Pakistan must now be considered on the verge of possessing the capability to produce nuclear weapons.

Enrichment Success Announced; Linked to Weapons. A strong indication that Pakistan might shortly produce highly enriched uranium came in February 1984, when Dr. Abdul Qadir Khan, head of Pakistan's uranium enrichment program, announced during an interview that "by the grace of God, Pakistan is now among the few countries in the world that can efficiently enrich uranium" and had "destroyed the monopoly forever" that the advanced nations had enjoyed in this field.[89] In an unusually explicit statement, linking this achievement to Pakistan's ability to manufacture nuclear weapons, Khan replied to the question "Can Pakistan make an atomic bomb?" as follows:

In brief, Pakistan has a proficient and patriotic team capable of performing the most difficult tasks. Forty years ago no one was familiar with the secrets of the atom bomb and education was not so widespread, but American scientists did the job. Today, 40 years later, we have ended their monopoly in this most difficult field of the enrichment of uranium in only 10 years. This job is undoubtedly not beyond our reach. India achieved this 10 years ago, although other countries definitely assisted it. We have the capacity to complete such a task. This is a political decision in which my colleagues and I have no concern except for the sake of the country's safety and security. Our honorable president had to make such a momentous decision and we were entrusted with this duty. We, my friends and I, will stake our lives but we will not disappoint the country and the nation, by the grace of God. In short, I wish to say that if India could accomplish such a feat 10 years ago, we are not so abnormal or mentally retarded that we cannot do this, and God willing, we will do it better as we have proved in the field of uranium enrichment.[90]

The following day, in a second interview, Khan again raised the issue of nuclear weapons, reportedly stating that an explosion was not necessary to gain a nuclear capability. If all the tests needed were done separately, he reportedly stated, they would amount to a successful nuclear explosion.[91]

In a press conference two weeks later, President Zia sought to temper the impression created by Khan's remarks. Zia stated, "Pakistan has acquired very modest research and development capability of uranium enrichment very successfully . . . for peaceful purposes."[92]

Khan's statements appeared to be part of a larger effort by the Zia government to publicize Pakistan's achievement in the enrichment field and to make Khan, who had stolen the plans for the Kahuta plant from the Netherlands in 1975 and subsequently supervised construction of the facility, into something of a national hero. Indeed, in mid-January the Kahuta plant was named the Abdul Qadir Khan Atomic Research Center in his honor.[93]

Khan's and Zia's comments were apparently intended to signify that Pakistan's efforts to master the process of enriching uranium had crossed an important threshold, although precisely how much progress had been made was not specified. In a June 1984 speech, however, Senator Alan Cranston indicated that Pakistan had completed construction of 1,000 centrifuge units at Kahuta—enough to produce fifteen kilograms of highly enriched uranium annually (possibly enough for one well-designed weapon)—and that it "is now enriching uranium." Cranston did not state the level of enrichment or the quantities involved.[94] If, as reported, Pakistan has produced highly enriched uranium, how much of this material it may possess had not been disclosed as of late July.

Chinese Assistance. Pakistan's efforts to obtain nuclear weapons have gone well beyond its production of highly enriched uranium. U.S. officials believe it has been actively working on nuclear weapons design problems and on the high-explosives triggering mechanism for atomic weapons.[95] Indeed, in July 1984, three Pakistanis were indicted in Houston, Texas, for attempting to ship electronic parts to Pakistan that are used in such mechanisms.[96]

The People's Republic of China is said to have helped Pakistan both in obtaining nuclear weapons material and in designing nuclear arms. Reports of such aid first surfaced in 1982 when James Malone, assistant secretary of state for oceans and international environmental and scientific affairs, stated that the United States was concerned about China's "relationship with Pakistan, which we're looking into now." Malone is reported to have said, further, that China had apparently supplied Pakistan with material "other than fuel-related items," which he declined to specify.[97] A month later, a separate press account stated that government officials were "disturbed by intelligence reports suggesting that China had helped Pakistan in trying to develop a capacity to enrich uranium for weapon use."[98] The implication was that China had given Pakistan technical information on the enrichment process.

In early 1983, a still more troubling report surfaced that China had provided Pakistan with sensitive information concerning the design of nuclear weapons themselves.[99] U.S. officials were quoted as stating that China may have confirmed for Pakistani technicians that a particular nuclear weapon design would work. A June 1984 report, however, indicated that China had actually given Pakistan the design for the weapon used in China's fourth nuclear test, a low-yield uranium device detonated in 1966.[100] If either report were true, it would mean that Pakistan could have confidence in its nuclear weapons without conducting a test, thus enabling it to avoid the termination of U.S. assistance. Indeed, this may have been the basis for Abdul Qadir Khan's statement in February 1984 that Pakistan could achieve a nuclear capability without a test. China denied that it had validated a Pakistani nuclear weapon design but has not replied to the other allegations.[101]

The possibility that China had aided the Pakistani nuclear weapons program caused the United States to delay talks with Peking in late 1982 on an agreement for cooperation in the fields of nuclear energy and research. By early 1984, however, U.S. concerns had apparently been put to rest by Chinese pledges not to aid other nations in acquiring nuclear arms. During President Reagan's trip to Peking in April, a U.S.-Chinese nuclear trade pact was initialed.[102]

In mid-June, however, the administration quietly announced it was not prepared to sign the accord. Sources said the administration wanted additional assurances concerning Peking's non-proliferation policies.[103] Whether information on new Chinese aid to Pakistan's nuclear program was the cause for this abrupt reversal or whether the administration had decided that the assurances it had received from China were insufficient in light of Peking's past conduct was not revealed. In either case, further Chinese aid for the Pakistani nuclear weapons program appeared to remain a serious possibility.

U.S. Reaction. As of late July 1984, it was not yet clear how the Reagan administration and the Congress would respond to the news of Paksitan's possible possession of nuclear weapons material.

Two votes in the Senate Foreign Relations Committee earlier in 1984, however, make clear that the administration and a number of key senators, concerned over Soviet expansion in the region, were prepared to continue economic and military aid to Pakistan even though they recognized it was steadily progressing toward acquiring nuclear arms.

On March 28, Senators John Glenn and Alan Cranston proposed an amendment to the 1984-85 foreign assistance authorization bill providing that U.S.

aid to Pakistan would be terminated unless the President certified that Pakistan did not possess a nuclear explosive device and was not acquiring technology, equipment, or material for manufacturing or detonating one. The Foreign Relations Committee passed the amendment unanimously.

Less than a week later, the Reagan administration notified committee members that it would be unable to make the certifications required by the amendment for the upcoming fiscal year and that, accordingly, U.S. aid to Pakistan (a six-year program begun in 1981 amounting to $3.2 billion) would have to be terminated on October 1 if the amendment were enacted. The committee then reopened consideration of the measure, and by a vote of eight to seven substituted an administration-backed alternative that no longer required the President to certify that Pakistan was not acquiring nuclear weapons, but only that Pakistan did not yet possess an actual nuclear explosive device.[104]

The administration's inability to make the certification required by the first version makes plain that it believed Pakistan continued to be working actively to develop nuclear weapons. Nevertheless, in order to provide a counter to the Soviet presence in Afghanistan, the administration and a majority of the committee fought to continue U.S. military and economic support for Pakistan. Included in the U.S. aid package, it may be noted, are forty F-16 fighter-bombers, among the most advanced in the U.S. arsenal, which are recognized, even by Reagan administration officials, to be the probable delivery vehicle for Pakistani atomic weapons.[105] As of late July 1984, twelve of the forty F-16's promised had been received by Pakistan.

Whether the new revelations of Pakistan's possible nuclear capabilities will lead to a reduction of U.S. aid or other sanctions remains to be seen. The U.S. response is likely to have an impact well beyond Pakistan, however, since other emerging nuclear states will see in it an indication of the costs they might incur for pursuing nuclear arms.

III. Prospects for Nuclear Weapons in Pakistan

If Pakistan has successfully produced highly enriched uranium, little would apparently stand in the way of its manufacturing nuclear arms except the time that would be needed to accumulate the necessary quantities of this material, perhaps a year, or so, using Senator Cranston's estimates. If this breakthrough has not yet taken place, Pakistan may nonetheless succeed in this endeavor in the near future. The arrest of three Pakistanis in June as they attempted to smuggle nonnuclear parts for nuclear-weapon-triggering mechanisms out of the United States leaves little doubt that General Zia has already made the decision to build such weapons.[106] Nor, to date, has there been evidence that the response of foreign nations to Pakistan's emerging nuclear capability has deterred its program to manufacture of nuclear arms.

A Pakistani nuclear test, however, does not seem likely for the moment. As noted earlier, in light of reported Chinese aid and Pakistan's years of weapons design work, a test may not be necessary for Pakistan to have confidence that its nuclear arms will work. Moreover, while the United States has tolerated Pakistan's incremental progress toward the nuclear threshold, the Reagan administration has stated that a test would jeopardize relations with Washington; in addition, under current law, it would mean the termination of U.S. aid.

New Delhi, too may be prepared to tolerate Pakistan's development of a de facto nuclear weapons capability without revitalizing India's nuclear explosives program. A Pakistani test, however, would be a direct challenge to India's current nuclear superiority and would almost certainly result in further Indian nuclear detonations or other steps to manufacture and deploy nuclear arms.

Similarly, Pakistani leaders may calculate that a nuclear test would unduly antagonize the Soviet Union. After the Soviet invasion of Afghanistan, General Zia's statements concerning Pakistan's nuclear potential are said to have become considerably more cautious, apparently out of fear of provoking a Soviet response.[107]

These various considerations also suggest that Pakistan will refrain from declaring it possesses nuclear arms. A declaration would seem unnecessary since Pakistan may soon be credited with possessing nuclear weapons even without an announcement. At the same time, a declaration could be viewed as a provocation and carry many of the adverse consequences of a test.

Fears of foreign reaction may also weigh against Pakistan's starting up its New Labs reprocessing plant. The facility, already well advanced in 1980 is now probably near completion. Indeed, in his June 21 speech, Senator Cranston stated that reprocessing had already taken place at the installation, an allegation subsequently denied by U.S. officials.[108] Since Pakistan lacks a source of unsafeguarded spent fuel, however, operation of either the New Labs reprocessing plant (or the Chashma plant should it ever be completed) would, as explained earlier, constitute a violation of IAEA safeguards. This would be an extremely serious breach of non-proliferation norms, which the Reagan administration has advised Pakistan might trigger a termination of U.S. aid, much the same as a nuclear test, and which might also be considered highly provocative by India and the Soviet Union. (In view of the considerable intelligence resources that America has apparently devoted to monitoring the Pakistani nuclear program, there is a fair likelihood that Pakistani use of either reprocessing plant in this fashion would be discovered.) Given the alternative of producing highly enriched uranium for weapons at Kahuta, which has raised fewer political difficulties since it would not entail violations of IAEA safeguards, it seems unlikely that Pakistan will activate the New Labs facility in the near term, even if it is completed.

* * *

The foregoing analysis suggests that the future course of the Pakistani nuclear weapons program will be influenced importantly by the response of the international community and especially of the United States, India, and the Soviet Union, to Pakistan's emerging nuclear capability. With the risk of a nuclear arms race in South Asia sharply increasing, and with other nations at or near the nuclear weapons threshold undoubtedly watching closely as they assess the costs and benefits of pursuing their own nuclear weapons programs, developments in the months ahead will have far-reaching implications for the future spread of nuclear weapons around the globe.

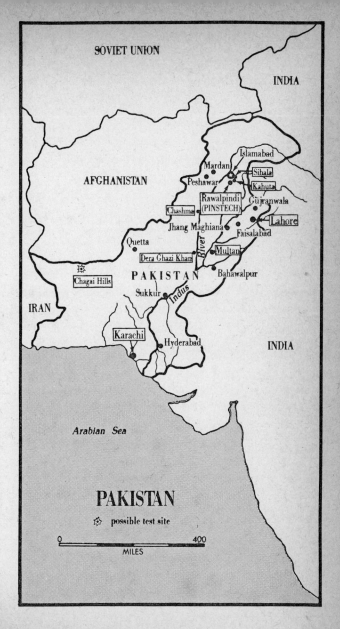

SOVIET UNION

INDIA

AFGHANISTAN

Islamabad

Mardan

Peshawar

Sihala

Kahuta

Rawalpindi
(PINSTECH)

Gujranwala

Chashma

Jhang Maghiana

Lahore

Faisalabad

Quetta

Dera Ghazi Khan

Multan

Chagai Hills

PAKISTAN

Bahawalpur

Sukkur

Indus

River

IRAN

Karachi

Hyderabad

INDIA

Arabian Sea

PAKISTAN

✿ possible test site

0   400

MILES

Pakistan

Power Reactors/Operating or Under Construction
KANUPP, Karachi (heavy-water/natural-uranium,125 MWe[a])
- supplier: Canadian General Electric (Canada)
- start up: 1972
- fuel source: Canada[b], also Pakistan after 1980
- heavy water: United States[c]
- safeguards: yes[d]

Uranium Resources/Active Mining Sites/Uranium Mills
- reasonably assured
  reserves: sufficient for Kahuta enrichment plant[e]
- currently active site: Dera Ghazi Khan
- mills in operation: Lahore[f]

UF$_6$ Conversion
- capacity: max. 218 metric tons of hexafluoride per year[g]
- supplier: CES Kalthof G.m.b.H. of Freiburg (West Germany)[h]
- start up: 1980[h]
- safeguards: no

Heavy Water
Multan
- capacity: 13 metric tons[c]
- supplier: Belgonucléaire (Belgium)[f](?)
- start up: 1980 (?)[f]
- safeguards: no

Karachi
- capacity: upgradation unit to serve KANUPP, quantity unknown[f]
- supplier: Canada (?)
- start up: 1976
- safeguards: (?)

Enrichment
Kahuta
- type: ultracentrifuge
- capacity: Currently 1,000 centrifuges; planned 2,000-3,000 (45 kg highly enriched uranium)[i]; some highly enriched uranium possibly produced[p]
- supplier: Vakuum Apparat Technik (Switzerland), CORA Engineering (Switzerland), Emerson Electric (Britain), Van Doorne Transmissie (Netherlands), Leybold Heraeus (West Germany), Aluminum Walzwerke (West Germany); items also obtained from U.S. and Canada; plans illegally obtained from URENCO.[r]
- start up: 1984 (partial)[j]
- safeguards: no

Sihala
- type: ultracentrifuge[f]
- capacity: experimental scale
- supplier: same as Kahuta (presumed)
- start up: prior to 1984 (presumed)
- safeguards: no

Uranium Purification (UO$_2$)

- capacity: sufficient to supply KANUPP reactor (presumed)
- supplier: ? (possibly associated with UF$_6$ plant)
- start up: 1980
- safeguards: no

Fuel Fabrication

Chashma

- capacity: sufficient fuel for KANUPP[c], (currently, probably less).
- supplier: Pakistan, plans from Canada[k]
- start up: 1980[j]
- safeguards: no

Reprocessing

Chashma

- capacity: 100 metric tons of spent fuel; 100 to 200 kg of plutonium per year[g]
- supplier: SGN (France)
- start up: France terminated this project in 1978; construction may be continuing.
- safeguards: uncertain; agreement between Pakistan, France, and IAEA provides for safeguards, but these provisions not yet in force.

New Labs, Rawalpindi

- capacity: capable of extracting 10 to 20 kg of plutonium per year[q]
- supplier: SGN (France), Belgonucléaire (Belgium)[g,m]
- start up: cold tests 1982; start up after 1984 (presumed).[n]
- safeguards: no (but might be subject to safeguards as a "replicated" plant under Pakistan-France-IAEA agreement covering Chashma, if safeguards under this agreement are implemented).

PINSTECH, Rawalpindi

- capacity: experimental scale[o]
- supplier: Pakistan (?); plans from Great Britain[o]
- start up: ?
- safeguards: no

Research Reactor

PARR, Rawalpindi (light-water/highly enriched uranium, 5 MWt)[a]

- supplier: United States[a] (through the IAEA)
- start up: 1965[a]
- fuel source: United States
- safeguards: yes[a]

Sources and Notes

a. International Atomic Energy Agency, *The Annual Report for 1981* (IAEA, 1982), pp. 73-76.

b. Canada terminated fuel in 1976 because of Pakistan's unwillingness to sign the Non-Proliferation Treaty; since 1980, plant has run partly on Pakistani-produced fuel and on remaining Canadian-supplied material.

c. David Hart, *Nuclear Power in India: A Comparative Analysis* (London: George Allen and Unwin), p. 133.

d. From September 1980 until March 1983, IAEA was unable to certify that no diversion of spent fuel occurred. Milton Benjamin, "Pakistan Backs Atomic Safeguards," *Washington Post* , November 17, 1982.

e. "Scientist Affirms Pakistan Capable of Uranium Enrichment, Weapons Production," *Nawa-I-Waqt* (Lahore), February 10, 1984, translated in Foreign Broadcast Information Service/Nuclear Proliferation and Development, hereafter FBIS/NDP, March 5, 1983, p. 36;

According to press reports in November 1979, Pakistan had obtained as much as 100 metric tons of uranium concentrate, or "yellowcake," not subject to International Atomic Energy Agency monitoring from Libya. The material had originally been purchased by Libya from Niger and then re-exported to Pakistan, possibly along with material that Pakistan had itself purchased from Niger through normal, above-board channels; John J. Fialka, "West Concerned by Signs of Libyan-Pakistan A-Effort," *Washington Star*, November 25, 1979.

f. P. B. Sinha and R. R. Subramanian, *Nuclear Pakistan* (New Delhi: Vision Books, 1980), pp. 35, 121.

g. Weissman and Krosney, *The Islamic Bomb* (New York: Times Books, 1981), p. 219, (UF_6); (pp. 80-84 New Labs); (p. 81, experimental reprocessing unit).

h. Weissman and Krosney, *The Islamic Bomb*, p. 219. John M. Geddes, "Bonn Says Firm Illegally Sent Pakistan Gear That Can Be Used for Atomic Bombs," *Wall Street Journal*, July 16, 1981.

i. Senator Alan Cranston, "Nuclear Proliferation and U.S. National Security Interests," *Congressional Record,* June 21, 1984, p. S 7901.

j. "Scientist Affirms," *Nawa-I-Waqt*, pp. 43-44.

k. "Nuclear Facilities in the Middle East," Department of State, submitted in *Hearings on the Israeli Air Strike,* June 18, 19, and 25, 1981, 97th Congress, 1st Session (Washington, D.C.: U.S. Government Printing Office, 1981), p. 40.

l. James Katz and Onkar Marwah, *Nuclear Power in Developing Countries* (Lexington: Lexington Books, 1982), p. 268.

m. According to Weissman and Krosney, *The Islamic Bomb,* France may not have been aware of SGN participation.

n. Cranston, "Nuclear Proliferation and U.S. National Security Interests." Cranston states facility has operated with radioactive material, but U.S. officials deny this. (Personal communication.)

o. Thomas W. Graham, "South Asian Nuclear Proliferation and National Security Chronology," Center for International Affairs, Massachusetts Institute of Technology, 1984, citing Weissman and Krosney, *The Islamic Bomb,* p. 81.

p. Russell Warren Howe, "Pakistanis Are Closer to Producing Nuclear Weapons," *Washington Times,* July 26, 1984.

q. Milton R. Benjamin, "Pakistan Building Secret Nuclear Plant," *Washington Post,* September 23, 1980.

r. See notes 31, 51-54, 60, 61, 70 and accompanying text and Weissman and Krosney, *The Islamic Bomb,* pp. 182-192.

Chapter III:
The Middle East

Introduction

Despite unrelenting turmoil in the Middle East, the danger of further nuclear proliferation in the region appears to have receded at least temporarily. Israel is thought to have already built some twenty nuclear weapons, or at least the easily assembled components for them. No other state in the Middle East, however, is likely to have both the motivation and the ability to match this achievement for at least ten years, if not longer.

Iraq and Libya have openly declared their interest in acquiring nuclear weapons, but at present this objective is beyond their reach. Libya's nuclear activities are extremely limited, and Iraq's expanding nuclear program was derailed when Israel destroyed its large research reactor in 1981, although Iraq reportedly has been seeking to purchase plutonium clandestinely in Italy.[1] Syria is a third country with a conceivable motive for acquiring nuclear weapons, but has shown little interest in such arms and completely lacks the resources needed for their manufacture.

Although Iran would presumably welcome a nuclear capability to tip the scales in the Iran-Iraq war and to help spread the Islamic revolution by intimidating nearby states, its civilian nuclear program, begun under the Shah, has made little progress. Mid-1984 reports attributed to West German intelligence sources that Iran was in the "final stages" of producing a nuclear bomb that could be ready in two years are generally regarded as erroneous.[2] A group of forty West German nuclear engineers did visit Iran in 1984, however, to review the possibility of restarting the construction of two uncompleted West German-supplied nuclear power plants at Boushahar.[3] One week later, the United States announced a complete ban on the supply of nuclear materials to Iran and called on other nuclear-supplier countries to follow suit.[4]

Egypt has announced a major nuclear-power program but is still reviewing bids for its first reactor. It is believed to have sought Chinese aid in developing nuclear arms during the 1960s[5] and is known to have used unconventional weapons—mustard gas and possibly other chemical agents—in 1967 when its troops were fighting in North Yemen.[6] Since concluding its peace treaty with Israel in 1979 and ratifying the Non-Proliferation Treaty in 1981, however, Egypt's nuclear intentions have appeared entirely peaceful.

However superior Israel's current nuclear capabilities may be compared to those of its adversaries, a number of factors will eventually erode its lead. Libya and Iraq have been building a corps of nuclear engineers and technicians for nearly a decade and, along with Syria, have been promised Soviet nuclear power plants that would significantly augment the Arab world's nuclear infrastructure, even if the facilities themselves were subject to strict non-proliferation controls. Iran's nuclear expertise grew rapidly until the Shah's overthrow, and Egypt's nuclear cadres will be expanded significantly as its nascent nuclear power program matures.

Further afield, Pakistan's nuclear weapons program, apparently financed in part by Libya, may soon bear fruit. While it is unlikely that the Pakistani nuclear program would pose a direct threat to Israel or that Pakistan would share its nuclear weapons with other states, given its increasingly visible Islamic orientation a Pakistani nuclear bomb could serve at least as a symbolic counterweight to Israel's capabilities.

Finally, Soviet nuclear forces must also be factored into the regional equation. During the 1973 Arab-Israeli war, there were reports that the Soviet Union had brought nuclear warheads to Egypt for possible use in Scud surface-to-surface missiles, in part as a deterrent against the small nuclear arsenal Israel reportedly possessed.[7] Although this putative event has never been confirmed, and may not have actually occurred, it foreshadows future dangers. With several thousand Soviet advisors now assisting Syria in operating an advanced air-defense system and overseeing deployment of one of the Soviet Union's most sophisticated short-range surface-to-surface missiles, the SS-21, Israeli planners considering the use of nuclear arms in any future war involving Syria would certainly have to weigh the risk of a Soviet nuclear response.

According to the available evidence, Israel, Libya, and Iraq have been the regional powers most active in seeking to develop nuclear weapons capabilities. Their efforts are the subject of this chapter. Pakistan's program is reviewed in the chapter on Asia.

Israel

Although the belief that Israel possesses nuclear arms is widespread, Israel has never claimed to have such weapons and no definitive proof that it has manufactured them, such as an acknowledged nuclear test, has come to light. Since the 1960s, Israeli leaders have maintained a posture of ambiguity regarding their nuclear intentions, repeating the formula that Israel will not be "the first to introduce nuclear weapons into the Middle East." Nonetheless, in 1981 former Israeli defense minister Moshe Dayan stated that Israel could produce nuclear weapons "in a short time." Indeed, the U.S. Central Intelligence Agency had concluded as early as 1968 that Israel had manufactured atomic bombs, and by 1976 the agency believed that Israel had developed from ten to twenty bombs of the size used on Hiroshima. While questions remain, today most observers accept the CIA view.

Israel's arsenal includes surface-to-surface missiles

and a variety of fighter-bombers capable of delivering nuclear weapons to targets throughout much of the Middle East. Still, most experts believe that Israel will not admit to its nuclear capabilities or use explicit nuclear threats in pursuit of its diplomatic and military objectives. Instead, Israel is likely to continue to view nuclear arms as weapons of last resort: a threat to be used only to deter enemies from those extreme military actions that might threaten Israel's very existence.

I. Background

The Israeli military's interest in nuclear matters dates back to Israel's first year of nationhood, 1948, when the Israeli Defense Ministry set up a Research and Planning Branch to explore uranium resources in the Negev desert. In 1949, nuclear research and development activities started up at the Weizmann Institute. By the early 1950s, Israel had invented a process for extracting uranium from phosphate ores and possessed a pilot plant for producing the heavy water necessary to operate nuclear reactors using natural, unenriched uranium. In 1952, Israel established an Atomic Energy Commission under the Israeli Defense Ministry.[1]

In 1955, the United States and Israel signed a nuclear cooperation agreement under which the United States agreed to supply Israel with a small, five-megawatt research reactor to train a number of Israeli nuclear engineers. The reactor, which began operating at Nahal Soreq in 1960, has been under International Atomic Energy Agency (IAEA) safeguards and does not appear to have contributed to Israel's nuclear weapons development program, although it is possible that nuclear technicians trained at the facility later participated in such efforts. A hot cell laboratory for reprocessing experiments built near Nahal Soreq with

British assistance and some U.S. equipment probably played a similar role.[2]

French Aid. In 1954 France and Israel announced that they had signed a nuclear cooperation agreement the year before, covering heavy water and uranium production. The agreement was revised in 1957 to permit greatly expanded French assistance;[3] but unlike Israel's nuclear agreement with the United States and the 1953 French accord, the details of the second agreement with France have been kept secret. Reportedly it covered four areas of vital importance to a possible Israeli nuclear weapons program.

First, France agreed to supply Israel with a large (twenty-four-megawatt) natural-uranium/heavy-water research reactor capable of producing one or two bombs' worth of plutonium annually in its spent fuel. The reactor was built at Dimona, in the northern Negev desert, and activated in late 1963 or early 1964.[4] Dimona's construction was kept secret, and no arrangements were made to verify that it would be used solely for peaceful purposes. Soon after the Israeli cabinet approved construction of the Dimona facility, six of the seven members of the Israeli Atomic Energy Commission resigned, apparently in protest over the decision by David Ben-Gurion's government to launch a nuclear weapons program.[5] Like construction of the plant itself, the resignations were kept secret from the public.

The second element of the deal, according to Francis Perrin, head of the French Atomic Energy Commission from 1951 to 1970, concerned the reprocessing of spent fuel to extract plutonium. The French government allowed a French corporation, Saint-Gobain (SGN), to supply Israel with blueprints for a reprocessing facility and turned a blind eye to subsequent collaboration.[6] France may also have agreed to take spent fuel from Dimona, reprocess it in France, and return the separated plutonium to Israel.

Third, France and Israel are also said to have cooperated in developing the Jericho surface-to-surface guided missile, a weapon that may be capable of carrying a nuclear warhead approximately 260 miles to targets throughout much of the Middle East.[7]

Finally, Israeli nuclear physicists may have helped France develop its atomic weapons, and France may have permitted Israeli scientists to observe the first French atomic bomb test in the Sahara on February 13, 1960.[8] One account, citing unnamed sources, states that France provided Israel with data from that test.[9] While the significance of the information transferred remains uncertain, Israel may have learned enough from its involvement in the French program to feel confident that it could successfully design a nuclear weapon without the need for a test of its own.[10]

U.S. Safeguards and Provisional Renunciation of Nuclear Arms. Israel maintained strict secrecy about Dimona's existence and, until a U.S. spy plane reportedly discovered it in late 1960, kept the United States completely in the dark about the plant. On learning of the plant, knowledgeable American officials immediately suspected that it was part of an Israeli nuclear weapons program, as is made clear in the following exchange between Secretary of State Christian A. Herter and Senator Bourke Hickenlooper in a January 6, 1961, secret session of the Senate Foreign Relations Committee:

Secretary Herter. There has been somewhat of a flurry in connection with the nuclear reactor in Israel. . . . It has been a disturbing element in the whole Middle East picture, largely because of the fact that this reactor apparently has been under construction for some time without anything public having been said about it. Certainly we had never been told about it, even though we have cooperated with Israel on the building of a small nuclear experimental reactor. The [deleted], indicate that it is considerably larger than any need for an experimental reactor in Israel, but the present statements of the Israeli Government are that this is still experimental, leading to a power reactor . . . .

Senator Hickenlooper. Mr. Secretary, I am not going to ask you to answer this question, but I am going to make a statement of my own. From whatever information I have had on this, which is some information I will say, I think the Israelis have just lied to us like horse thieves on this thing. They have completely distorted, misrepresented, and falsified the facts in the past. I think it is very serious, for things that we have done for them to have them perform in this manner in connection with this very definite production reactor facility which they have been secretly building, and which they have consistently, and with a completely straight face, denied to us they were building.[11]

These extraordinary efforts to hide the construction of the Dimona reactor and the unusual capabilities of the plant—which Senator Hickenlooper called a "production reactor," meaning a reactor designed specifically to produce plutonium—provide strong evidence that Israel intended to use it for a nuclear weapons program.

Under pressure from the Eisenhower administration, Prime Minister David Ben-Gurion went before the Israeli parliament on December 21, 1960, to acknowledge the existence of the reactor project and to declare that the Dimona plant would be used only for training, research, and other peaceful purposes.[12] In May 1961, Ben-Gurion agreed to permit U.S. scientists to visit the Dimona plant to verify how it was being used.[13]

Late in 1961, two of the six members of the Israeli

Atomic Energy Commission who had resigned secretly in 1957 to found the Committee for the De-nuclearization of the Israeli-Arab Conflict, a group that in April 1962 called for the establishment of a nuclear-weapons-free zone in the Middle East. Later that year, following a major internal debate, the Ben-Gurion government rejected a strategic doctrine that relied on nuclear weapons in favor of a conventional deterrent, but also rejected the idea of a Middle East nuclear-weapons-free zone until conventional disarmament in the region had been achieved, thus leaving the door open for nuclear arms development.[14] In the subsequent Knesset debate, the Israeli government articulated this provisional rejection of nuclear weapons with an ambiguous formula it would repeat over the years:

> There are no nuclear weapons in the Middle East and Israel will never be the first to introduce them. But Israel can be destroyed by conventional weapons and therefore the stress should be laid on conventional disarmament in the world and in the region.[15]

In 1963, Ben-Gurion resigned as prime minister and Levi Eshkol took his place. Eshkol reportedly had opposed Dimona's construction in 1957 when serving as Ben Gurion's finance minister,[16] and a number of his actions suggest that his opposition to Israel's developing nuclear arms became official Israeli policy during his tenure, which ended in 1969. Bowing to the wishes of the Johnson administration, for example, the Eshkol government agreed to permit annual U.S. inspections of the Dimona plant, which started up in late 1963 or early 1964, and also agreed to place certain limits on its use.[17] Similarly, in April 1966, Eshkol forced the resignation of the last of the original members of the Israeli Atomic Energy Commission (Ernst

Bergmann, a member of the pro-nuclear-weapons faction of Ben-Gurion's Labor party) and removed the commission from the Defense Ministry.[18]

On May 18, 1966, Eshkol stated in the Knesset the well-worn position of his predecessor that Israel would not be the Middle East's first nuclear power: "I have said before and I repeat here that Israel does not have nuclear weapons and that Israel will not be the first to introduce them into the region."[19]

Clandestine Program. Notwithstanding these denials, Eshkol continued to reject the idea of a Middle East nuclear-free zone.[20] More important, the Israeli defense establishment reportedly continued to pursue nuclear arms during this period by engaging in clandestine efforts to obtain the necessary nuclear materials.

As mentioned previously, there have been reports that under the 1957 French-Israeli nuclear understanding, France had agreed to reprocess fuel from Dimona in France and return the separated plutonium to Israel.[21] French and Israeli sources cited in one recent investigation agreed that a substantial amount of spent fuel had been sent to France to be reprocessed there; but while the French source claimed that enough plutonium for fifteen to twenty weapons had been returned to Israel, the Israeli source denied that any had been provided.[22] As of 1970, American officials believed that Israel had obtained fourteen kilograms of plutonium from France by 1967, enough for one or two weapons (1 kilogram = 2.2 pounds), in return for plutonium-bearing spent fuel from Dimona.[23]

Another possible clandestine source of nuclear weapons material during the mid-1960s was the United States. In 1966, the U.S. Atomic Energy Commission discovered that more than one hundred kilograms of highly enriched uranium that it had supplied to the Nuclear Materials and Equipment Corporation

(NUMEC) for processing between 1962 and 1965 had been lost.[24] By 1968, based on a range of circumstantial evidence, the U.S. Central Intelligence Agency concluded that the "most likely case" was that the "NUMEC material had been diverted and had been used by the Israelis in fabricating weapons."[25] The circumstantial evidence included the NUMEC president's extensive ties with the Israeli government, the company's contracts to supply nonmilitary nuclear items to an Israeli firm, and the extraordinarily lax security at the NUMEC facility. The agency also cited the fact that Israeli A-4 jets were practicing bombing runs of a type used only for nuclear arms and that soil samples taken from the Dimona area contained traces of highly enriched uranium that the CIA assumed came from the U.S. NUMEC plant.[26] Despite extensive U.S. government investigations of the incident, however, according to the Nuclear Regulatory Commission, no "concrete information concerning the final disposition or location of any material which may be missing from this facility" has emerged.[27]

The scope of the Israeli nuclear weapons program during this period thus remains uncertain. On the one hand, along with its activities at Nahal Soreq, Israel may, as it claimed, have merely operated the Dimona reactor at a level agreed upon with the United States and subject to U.S. inspections. On the other hand, Israel may have conducted in parallel with its other activities at Dimona and Nahal Soreq a clandestine weapons program that yielded enough nuclear weapons material for a number of atomic bombs.

Clandestine Program Expanded. Soon after the Six-Day War of June 1967, several figures known to favor Israel's development of nuclear arms returned to positions of political prominence, including Moshe Dayan, Shimon Peres, and Dr. Ernst Bergmann. According to several accounts, a decision was made in 1967 or 1968 to accelerate development of nuclear arms.[28]

The key component of the program was the reported construction of a reprocessing plant for extracting plutonium produced in Dimona's natural uranium fuel. The completion date of this plant, believed to be at the Dimona site, is not known. However, U.S. inspections, which ended in 1969, apparently did not uncover any reprocessing activities, and as late as July 1970 the United States reportedly believed that Israel lacked a reprocessing capability. During the 1970s, however, a number of sources, including the CIA, independently concluded that Israel was operating such a plant. Therefore, it is most likely that work on the facility began after the United States ended its inspections at Dimona in 1969.[29]

In order to produce plutonium for weapons clandestinely, Israel would first have to irradiate substantial quantities of uranium fuel in the Dimona reactor. Large-scale Israeli uranium purchases on the open market, however, might have raised suspicions.[30] Thus, in November 1968, Israel reportedly undertook a secret mission to acquire large amounts of processed uranium ore, or yellowcake. Using intermediaries, Israeli agents are said to have arranged to have two hundred tons of yellowcake shipped from Antwerp to Genoa and then to have orchestrated its "disappearance" while the material was in transit on the Mediterranean Sea.[31] In principle, several hundred kilograms of weapons quality plutonium could eventually be produced in Dimona from the material, enough for more than fifty weapons. By 1972, Israel was reportedly producing substantial quantities of yellowcake at a phosphoric-acid plant. Output at this and two other plants was expected to reach one hundred metric tons per year by 1981, more than enough to fuel Dimona.[32]

Changing U.S. Attitude. Israel provoked further suspicion in late 1968 during negotiations on the purchase of fifty U.S. Phantom F-4 fighter-bombers, when Israeli officials reportedly asked the Defense Department to equip a number of these planes with bomb racks specially wired for atomic weapons. The request was denied.[33]

During these negotiations, Israel also made clear that it would not sign the newly concluded Non-Proliferation Treaty, despite efforts by some U.S. officials to make it a condition for the F-4 sales. According to Paul Warnke, who, as Assistant Secretary of Defense, participated in these negotiations, "Israel categorically refused to accept this as a condition for the acquisition of the F-4 Phantoms. They said as a matter of national sovereignty they would not yield to that sort of pressure."[34] Israel also indicated it was not ruling out the production of nuclear weapons in the future by stating during those discussions that its pledge not to be the first power to "introduce" nuclear weapons into the Middle East meant only that it would not be the first to test such a device or to reveal its existence publicly.[35] Washington nevertheless approved the sale in October 1968.[36]

The F-4 negotiations may have marked a critical turning point in U.S.-Israeli nuclear relations. After 1960, the United States had made strong efforts to slow the military aspects of the Israeli nuclear program, insisting, for example, that the existence of the Dimona reactor be made public and that the United States be permitted to inspect it. However, U.S. resolve eventually weakened. By 1968, President Johnson is said to have known of the presumed Israeli diversion of highly enriched uranium from the NUMEC plant, and U.S. officials had also apparently concluded that Israel had diverted plutonium-bearing spent fuel from Dimona.[37] Nonetheless, the United States concluded the F-4 sale without securing any tighter controls over Israeli nuclear activities, indicating that Washington would take only limited measures, if any, to halt Israel's nuclear weapons program.

Indeed, U.S. efforts in this regard may well have weakened further during Richard Nixon's term in office. A National Security Decision Memorandum promulgated in February 1969, for example, reportedly directed U.S. officials not to participate in any effort to pressure hold-out nations to ratify the Non-Proliferation Treaty.[38]

Israel appears to have recognized this gradual change in U.S. attitudes: in 1969 it refused U.S. requests to ease restrictions on inspections at Dimona, and the inspections were terminated.[39]

Mounting Evidence of Israel's Nuclear Weapons—and U.S. Acquiescence. Throughout the 1970s, Israel's development of a nuclear weapons capability, and U.S. acquiescence in it, became increasingly apparent. In July 1970, a *New York Times* report based on a CIA briefing for the Senate Foreign Relations Committee stated that U.S. officials assumed that Israel already possessed atomic bombs or at least their easily assembled components. The report noted that the U.S. government was divided as to whether Israel had actually assembled nuclear weapons, but virtually all agreed that if Israel had not as yet attached the "last wire" to a nuclear bomb, it was in "very easy range" of doing so. The unnamed U.S. officials quoted by the *Times* denied that Israel had a reprocessing facility and implied that Israel's sole source of nuclear weapons material was the plutonium it had obtained from France in return for the plutonium-bearing spent fuel allegedly diverted from the Dimona reactor around 1968.[40] Despite these revelations, the United States significantly increased military aid to Israel several months later in response to growing Soviet aid to Egypt, indicating that Washington would tolerate Israel's clandestine acquisition of nuclear arms if necessary to advance other foreign policy objectives in the Middle East.[41]

In June 1974, President Nixon offered to sell nuclear power reactors to Israel and Egypt as a token of U.S. confidence in the durability of their rapprochement following the 1973 October War. The proposed sales—announced barely a month after India's nuclear test had dramatically underscored the risk of nuclear proliferation by less developed nations—were to be made without requiring either Israel or Egypt to ratify the Non-Proliferation Treaty (NPT), i.e., to renounce the development of nuclear weapons and accept IAEA safeguards on all of their nuclear installations. For Israel, ratification would have meant opening the Dimona site to international inspections. Since U.S. officials had believed since 1968 that Israel possessed a nuclear weapons capability, the willingness to expand U.S.-Israeli nuclear ties without placing any limitations on Israel's presumed military nuclear program was another indication of the Nixon administration's apparent willingness to tolerate that program.

Following Nixon's resignation in August 1974, the administration of Gerald Ford maintained this posture. Indeed, Ford administration witnesses were testifying in favor of the proposed sale even as the CIA was circulating within the U.S. government its summary of Israeli nuclear activities, which concluded:

We believe that Israel has already produced nuclear weapons. Our judgment is based on Israeli acquisition of large quantities of uranium, partly by clandestine means; the ambiguous nature of Israeli efforts in the field of uranium enrichment, and Israel's large investment in a costly missile system designed to accommodate nuclear warheads. We do not expect the Israelis to provide confirmation of widespread suspicions of their capability, either by nuclear testing or by threats of use, short of a grave threat to the nation's existence. Future emphasis is likely to be on improving weapon designs, manufacturing missiles more capable in terms of distance and accuracy than the existing 260-mile Jericho, and acquiring or perfecting weapons for aircraft delivery.[42]

In December 1974, as Congress continued to review the U.S.-Israeli reactor sale proposal, an Israeli official provided the first confirmation that his country had taken important steps toward developing nuclear arms. Israeli president Ephraim Katzir, during an interview with a group of science writers, stated, "It has always been our intention to develop the nuclear potential. We now have that potential." The newspaper account of the interview goes on to state, "The President said that if the need arose, Israel could convert capability into fact 'in a short time—even in a few days.' "[43]

In 1976, the United States and Israel negotiated and initialed a detailed agreement for nuclear cooperation (identical to a concurrently proposed U.S.-Egyptian accord), but the proposal was never submitted for congressional review because of growing congressional concerns over proliferation. Ultimately, the reactor sales were put off and eventually made conditional on Israeli and Egyptian adherence to the NPT or acceptance of comprehensive IAEA safeguards.[44] In 1981 Egypt ratified the NPT; in the same year, the United States signed an agreement for nuclear cooperation with Cairo permitting the sale of two nuclear power plants under particularly strong non-proliferation restrictions. Such sales to Israel remain prohibited, however, because of its refusal to place the Dimona facilities under safeguards—one of the few, if belated, steps the United States has taken to indicate its disapproval of Israel's reputed nuclear weapons program.

Apart from these political developments, Israel may also have made a major advance in its capabilities for manufacturing nuclear weapons material during 1974. Reportedly, two Israeli scientists successfully enriched uranium by using lasers, an experimental technique then also under development in the United States. Although the Israeli experiments produced only minuscule quantities, U.S. authorities considered the accomplishment important since it indicated that Israel might be able to use the technique in the future to produce highly enriched uranium for weapons.[45] However, subsequent CIA estimates of the size of Israel's presumed nuclear arsenal, discussed below, suggest that by 1981, at least, the laser enrichment technique was not contributing significantly to Israel's nuclear weapons capabilities.

Further Revelations and U.S. Response. In July 1975, the *Boston Globe* reported that "senior American analysts in the American security community" believed that Israel had produced more than ten nuclear weapons since the 1973 war, when Israeli officials became convinced that Arab oil wealth would permit Israel's enemies to acquire conventional arsenals that could eventually shift the Mideast balance of power against Israel.[46] The *Globe* report did not go into the details of how Israel had acquired the material for its weapons.

In early 1976, however, Carl Duckett, a senior CIA official, disclosed in a secret briefing to the Nuclear Regulatory Commission that Israel was making nuclear weapons from plutonium produced in Dimona. He went on to say that the amount of plutonium available from the reactor, presumably reprocessed in Israel, was so substantial that the CIA now regarded

the alleged earlier diversion of highly enriched uranium from NUMEC as academic.[47] At a second, sup-
posedly off-the-record briefing to members of the
American Institute of Aeronautics and Astronautics
(AIAA) in March 1976—the substance of which was
reported in the press shortly afterwards—Duckett estimated that the Israeli nuclear arsenal contained between ten and twenty Hiroshima-size bombs.[48]

Soon after the revelation of Duckett's briefing to the
AIAA, *Time* magazine ran a major story stating that
by late 1973 Israel's nuclear arsenal numbered thirteen
Hiroshima-size bombs. *Time* asserted that when
Israeli forces were faltering in the early stages of the
1973 Arab-Israeli War, Prime Minister Golda Meir
ordered that the nuclear weapons be assembled and
readied for use. Only when the war shifted in Israel's
favor were the weapons returned to their underground
bunkers. The *Time* report, which did not identify its
sources, stated that material for the weapons came
from the plutonium produced in the Dimona reactor
and reprocessed in an Israeli facility built between
1967 and 1969.[49] The *Time* account also stated that
former foreign minister Moshe Dayan

believes that a nuclear capability is essential to Israel. "Israel
has no choice. . . . With our manpower, we cannot physically, financially or economically go on acquiring more and
more tanks and more and more planes. Before long you will
have all of us maintaining and oiling the tanks."[50]

None of these revelations is known to have generated renewed attempts on the part of the United States
to curb Israel's apparent nuclear arms program. However, Congress did continue to hold up the proposed
nuclear power plant sale and blocked a 1975 proposal
to provide Pershing surface-to-surface missiles to Israel. Although the weapons were to be equipped with

conventional warheads, critics feared Israel might substitute nuclear explosives.[51]

In 1976, another official statement added to the confused picture of official Israeli views on nuclear weapons. During the visit of a U.S. Senate delegation, Prime Minister Meir responded to a question by Senator Howard Baker with one of the most categorical denials to date. While agreeing that Israeli scientists could produce nuclear weapons, she asserted that Israel had not done so and did not even possess the necessary nuclear materials for such an undertaking, a statement directly at odds with U.S. assessments since 1968.[52]

Independent Corroboration. Notwithstanding Meir's statement, by late 1977 the authoritative International Atomic Energy Agency, which monitors nuclear programs around the world, had concluded also that Israel could produce separated plutonium. The October 1977 *IAEA Bulletin,* an official publication of the Agency, listed the nuclear facilities not subject to its inspections. Included in this category was, "in Israel, a large research reactor and a pilot reprocessing facility."[53] The publication provided no further information on the Israeli facility, nor did it describe the basis for the Agency's conclusion.

Finally, in 1980, Francis Perrin, former head of the French Atomic Energy Commission, stated in an interview, "We are sure the Israelis have nuclear weapons. . . . They have sufficient facilities to produce one or two bombs a year."[54] Perrin also declared that France, by turning a blind eye to the activities of private French companies, "participated in the building of a plutonium extraction plant."[55] Given the long-standing ties between the French and Israeli nuclear programs, Perrin's statement represents an important piece of independent substantiation on these issues.

The South Atlantic "Flash." On September 22, 1979, a U.S. surveillance satellite detected a flash in the South Atlantic Ocean that displayed the characteristics of a nuclear explosion.[56] President Jimmy Carter's White House Office of Science and Technology Policy assembled a panel of scientific experts to investigate whether such an explosion had, in fact, taken place.

After analyzing extensive data from the satellite's sensors, the team found that certain aspects of the satellite's readings for this event varied significantly from those for known nuclear tests. This, along with other discrepancies such as the inability of U.S. search planes to detect any fallout near the supposed test site, led the panel to conclude that the event registered by the satellite was "probably not from a nuclear explosion" but, more likely, from a phenomenon occurring close to the satellite, such as the reflecting flash from a colliding meteorite.[57] Other government agencies, including the Defense Intelligence Agency and the Naval Research Laboratory, believed a test had taken place, however, and the matter has never been settled conclusively.[58]

According to a February 1980 article in the *Washington Post,* the CIA told a key congressional committee that if a test had taken place, "Israel is the leading candidate," with South Africa the second most likely possibility.[59]

The 1981 Bombing of Iraq's Reactor. The background to Israel's destruction of the Osirak reactor outside Baghdad appears in detail in the section on Iraq. Of importance here is that the event brought to light new information regarding nuclear developments in Israel. Two and a half weeks after the raid, for example, Moshe Dayan gave the most unequivocal acknowledgment to date of Israel's nuclear capabilities in a statement quoted by the *New York Times:*

We don't have any atomic bombs now, but we have the capacity, we can do that in a short time. We are not going to be the first ones to introduce nuclear weapons into the Middle East, but we do have the capacity to produce nuclear weapons, and if the Arabs are willing to introduce nuclear weapons into the Middle East, then Israel should not be too late in having nuclear weapons, too.[60]

Several days later, the CIA reportedly told the House Foreign Affairs Committee that "Israel was now believed to have between 10 and 20 nuclear weapons that could be delivered either by fighter-bombers or [by] Israel's domestically designed and built Jericho missile."[61] This report is noteworthy not only because it conforms with past CIA characterizations of Israel's nuclear capacity but because it also suggests that the CIA believed Israel's nuclear arsenal had not grown significantly since 1976, the date of Carl Duckett's briefing to the AIAA meeting.

Whether the 1981 CIA estimate implies that the Israeli nuclear arsenal was frozen at 1976 levels or that the arsenal increased slowly—say, from fourteen to nineteen weapons, which matches the reported one-bomb-per-year plutonium output for the Dimona reactor—the estimate makes it clear that Israel's presumed nuclear weapons production capability through 1981 was rather limited. According to one 1980 account, however, Israel had increased the Dimona reactor's capacity from twenty-five to seventy megawatts, allowing its plutonium output to be increased to twenty-five kilograms per year—enough for three to five atomic weapons.[62] If the reactor was modified in this way, Israel may now be able to build up its nuclear arsenal far more rapidly than in the past.

The CIA estimate also suggests that Israel's attempts to enrich uranium through the use of lasers—

under study since 1974—had not yet succeeded in producing significant quantities of highly enriched uranium, which could be used for nuclear weapons.[63]

Israeli Rocketry. In the mid-1960s, with French aid, Israel began to develop a 260-mile-range ballistic missile capable of carrying a nuclear warhead. Sources vary as to the status of the missile, known as Jericho, which is said to have a mobile launcher. The CIA's 1974 assessment of Israeli nuclear arms suggested that Jericho was already operational, and *Time* magazine's account of Israel's deployment of nuclear arms in the 1973 October War claimed that both Jerichos and aircraft were readied to deliver atomic warheads.[64] One more recent analysis has cautioned, however, against assuming that the Jericho (and the shorter-range Shavit) "are now capable of even rapid deployment as a nuclear system."[65]

Israel as a Nuclear Importer and Exporter. In addition to the nuclear assistance it has received over the years from the United States and France, Israel has also reportedly purchased heavy water for the Dimona reactor from Norway,[66] and uranium from a number of sources including Argentina, South Africa, France and from French-controlled uranium mines in Gabon, Niger, and the Central African Republic.[67] Israel is not known to be an exporter of nuclear commodities.

There have also been reports over the years of close Israeli-South African nuclear ties. Israel is said to have obtained uranium from South Africa during the 1960s. Some reports on South Africa's nuclear test site, discovered in 1977 and subsequently dismantled, state that an Israeli weapon was to be tested there. In addition, some accounts of the 1979 South Atlantic "flash" have also suggested that the event was a joint Israeli-South African test. One recent account, which describes extensive joint activities between the two countries in developing conventional arms, including guided missiles and jet aircraft, states that nuclear cooperation also extended to development of the Pelunduna research reactor.[68]

Given the secrecy with which both nations surround their nuclear programs, it is not possible to assess the validity of these accounts.

II. Developments of the Past Year

The past twelve months have been relatively uneventful in terms of developments that might significantly affect Israel's nuclear weapons capability in the near term. Apart from the previously discussed release of the 1961 Senate Foreign Relations Committee executive session minutes confirming other reports that Israel had kept the United States in the dark about the Dimona plant, no new information about the history or substance of Israel's nuclear capabilities has come to light, and the long-standing uncertainty concerning nuclear weapons in Israel remains.

Fusion Reactor

In mid-1983, a California-based group, the International Energy Systems Company, sought Israeli government support to set up an experimental fusion reactor in Israel. (The nuclear fusion process releases energy as the nuclei of hydrogen atoms are joined together.) Past investments in fusion research for energy purposes have been extremely costly and only marginally successful; thus far scientists have not been able to produce electricity from the process. Much of this research, some of which is classified, has a direct application to the development of fusion weapons, either hydrogen bombs, which can be many times more powerful than atomic weapons, or neutron bombs, which can be suitable for battlefield use.

Although the Israeli government has refused to allocate funds directly for the fusion project, it has offered to donate land for the reactor on the occupied West Bank. In addition, the Israeli treasury has provided guarantees worth $20-25 million to private Israeli firms investing in the project. It is too early to tell whether the project to build the reactor, known as a rigatron, has the potential for aiding an Israeli nuclear weapons program.[69]

Israel at the IAEA; Threat to Nuclear Programs

At the September 1982 IAEA General Conference, Arab states led a majority of IAEA members in a vote to deny Israel's credentials as a response to its destruction of Iraq's large research reactor in June of the previous year, and, it appeared, as an expression of disapproval of Israel's involvement in the recent massacres by Lebanese Christian militiamen at Palestinian refugee camps in Beirut. At the October 1983 session, however, after considerable behind-the-scenes maneuvering, Israel was permitted to participate fully.[70]

In the aftermath of the 1982 vote, the U.S. delegation to the IAEA walked out of the meeting to protest the Agency's politicization, stating that the United States would "reassess" its continued membership in the organization. Several months later, Congress suspended funding for the Agency pending the "certification" of Israel's status as a full participant in the IAEA.[71]

Withdrawal of the United States—the IAEA's most active member state and greatest financial supporter—confronted the Agency with a potentially grave crisis. U.S. representation and funding were restored, however, in mid-1983 after the Agency's Board of Governors accepted a finding by IAEA director general Blix in February that Israel was a member in good standing of the Agency.[72] Despite the Board's action, Israel's seating at the 1983 General Conference remained in doubt and appears to have been accomplished largely as the result of strong U.S. diplomatic efforts, including the open threat that the United States would withdraw from the Agency if Israel's credentials were again rejected.[73]

While permitting Israeli participation, the General Conference nevertheless adopted a resolution calling on Israel to "withdraw forthwith its threat to attack" nuclear installations in Iraq and other countries.[74] The resolution provided for the withholding of Agency research contracts, a boycott of Israeli products and materials, and a refusal to hold meetings in Israel, if that nation did not comply with the measure by the next General Conference in October 1984. Delegates from Israel and the United States both noted that Israel had declared to the U.N. secretary-general that it had no policy of attacking nuclear installations, and this declaration was repeated by the Israeli delegate at the General Conference.[75]

These statements were directly at odds, however, with one made several months earlier by Israeli defense minister Moshe Arens. At a June 1983 meeting with French defense officials in Paris, Arens declared that Israel would bomb any Arab nuclear reactor built "for military purposes."[76] Arens's June statement appeared to draw a distinction between nuclear reactors "for military purposes" and others, suggesting that Israel may not seek to interfere with construction by its rivals of safeguarded civilian nuclear power reactors, such as those planned by Libya, Egypt, and Syria. Nonetheless, the statement, which was apparently a

warning to France against rebuilding Iraq's large research reactor outside Baghdad, seemed to reaffirm
that Israel would act pre-emptively to protect its
nuclear superiority in the region.

Thus, Israel's announced policy as to how far it may
go to prevent the emergence of a nuclear-armed rival
remains ambiguous. As a practical matter, however,
Israel's destruction of the Iraqi research reactor in
1981 leaves few doubts that it will be prepared to
consider similar action in the future.

New Nuclear Power Plant

In January 1984, Israeli government officials announced the start of a $5-million study to select the site
for Israel's first nuclear power plant. The reactor under consideration, which is expected to cost between
$1 billion and $2 billion, is a relatively small, 250-
megawatt natural-uranium/heavy-water plant, nick-
named ISDU, an acronym for Israeli deuterium/-
uranium.[77]

As early as July 1981, Israel had expressed interest
in obtaining a natural-uranium/heavy-water power reactor. An advisory commission appointed by Israeli
energy minister Yitzhak Moda'i favored this alternative because of its potential for allowing Israel to
manufacture its own natural uranium fuel. That option
would be unavailable if the more widely used light
water reactor had been selected, since that type requires enriched uranium fuel and Israel lacks the necessary enrichment capacity. The commission believed
Israel would have little difficulty purchasing reactors
abroad and would be able to obtain easy credit terms
from Western manufacturers.[78] However, despite
reports stating that "international companies including British ones" hoped to work out a "new formula"

that might enable Israel to buy nuclear power plants without first signing the Non-Proliferation Treaty, the commission's final report, issued in December 1982, made clear that the negotiations had failed.[79]

According to Israeli press accounts, all the nuclear supplier nations that might have sold the reactor to Israel maintained a common front, insisting that Israel ratify the Non-Proliferation Treaty as a precondition.[80] This seemed to leave Israel with no alternative but to develop a nuclear power plant on its own. The commission found, however, that the difficulties involved in developing a nuclear power plant were formidable, and it recommended that the government of Israel "do everything within its powers" to reach an agreement with the nuclear suppliers.[81]

Notwithstanding this apparent impasse, advocates of an Israeli nuclear energy program persisted. Israeli science minister Yuval Ne'eman arranged for Dr. Edward Teller, the prominent American physicist, to visit Israel in December 1982 to advise the Israeli government on how it might proceed to develop an indigenous nuclear power industry. One press account suggested that Ne'eman and other Israeli nuclear power advocates believed that

the slump experienced at present by the companies who build the reactors may help Israel acquire the necessary components from those companies in "under and next to the table" deals. In such case, if indeed this is possible (and many doubt it), a domestic reactor will be a coverup for foreign components and knowhow purchased from various manufacturers without the knowledge of their governments under the claim that those parts are not exclusively for nuclear reactors.[82]

Indeed, in a December 17 interview, Ne'eman stated,

There is also the possibility of procuring information and spare parts abroad after we ourselves build the heart of the reactor. Then we will not be tied by international restrictions.[83]

The ISDU reactor proposal may have been developed with this approach in mind. If so, it could prove a serious challenge to the efforts of nuclear supplier countries to maintain an embargo on nuclear sales to Israel until it accepts broader international supervision of its nuclear program—to date the principal expression of Western disapproval of Israel's apparent development of nuclear weapons.

Moreover, if the ISDU reactor were not placed under IAEA safeguards, it could contribute directly and significantly to Israel's nuclear weapons capability. Such a reactor could produce more than fifty kilograms of high quality plutonium per year, depending in part on how it was operated, enough for six to ten atomic bombs—an output many times greater than that of the Dimona plant.[84] While Israel may not have sufficient reprocessing capacity at present to handle the much larger quantities of spent reactor fuel the ISDU reactor would produce, the assumed Dimona reprocessing unit could, in principle, be expanded or a new reprocessing plant built, as needed. If it accepts safeguards on the ISDU plant, however, Israel could not use the plant's output for nuclear explosives without incurring the severe political costs of violating the IAEA system.

Israel's decision on submitting the reactor to international oversight, which has not been announced, will thus be an important indication of whether it intends to retain the option of using the reactor to support the nation's presumed nuclear weapons program. Israel is said to have agreed to safeguards on the new reactor it was trying to buy abroad (though not on its activities at Dimona), and it may be ready to accept them on the ISDU reactor as well. Moreover, even if Israel is able to persuade some nuclear supplier governments to sell it important components for the plant, it may still have little choice but to accept such plant-specific safeguards, since all the nuclear supplier countries have made this a requirement for exports of major nuclear components.[85] Science Minister Ne'eman's statement, noted above, suggesting that Israel might be able to obtain information and spare parts abroad without being "tied to international restrictions" may indicate, however, that Israeli nuclear planners hope to bypass these requirements and keep the ISDU plant, like the Dimona reactor, free from IAEA oversight.

III. Prospects for Nuclear Weapons in Israel

Despite the secrecy surrounding the Israeli nuclear program and the studied ambiguity of Israeli official statements on nuclear matters over the years, there is broad consensus among experts in the field that Israel possesses a ready capability to deploy ten to twenty nuclear weapons. Indeed, few have harbored serious doubts on this score since the revelations of the mid- and late 1970s.

While important questions remain concerning parts of the historical record and the size and degree of sophistication of Israel's nuclear arsenal, attention has now shifted to the issue of how Israel can best use these capabilities to enhance its security.

One alternative would be for Israel to make its supposed nuclear deterrent overt, through an acknowledged nuclear test or a formal declaration. Some analysts believe that a declared nuclear weapons capability would be a more effective deterrent than an ambiguous one because it would reduce the risk of Arab aggression based on underestimation of Israel's strength.[86] And at least one strategist has argued that if the Arabs acquired nuclear capabilities to match Israel's, regional stability—and Israeli security—would be increased.[87]

On the other hand, there are strong incentives for Israel to keep its nuclear capabilities uncertain and undeclared. Disclosure would increase pressures on the Arab states to acquire similar capabilities—which current Israeli leaders strongly believe would be injurious to Israel—or to seek Soviet guarantees of nuclear retaliation against Israel should it use nuclear arms. An overt nuclear deterrent posture could also invite Arab countermeasures or pre-emptive actions against Israel's nuclear forces.

In addition, by declaring that it had nuclear arms, Israel would complicate its relations with the United States. Since Israeli use of nuclear weapons is usually thought of as a measure of last resort, Israel has had a continuing need for major American assistance in conventional weaponry for lesser military confrontations, such as that in Lebanon during 1982-83. Were Israel to disregard international non-proliferation norms and overtly declare that it possessed nuclear arms and intended to use them in certain circumstances, popular and congressional support for Israel might weaken, threatening cutbacks in U.S. assistance. Israel's currently ambiguous posture, on the other hand, has apparently permitted U.S. officials to overlook Israel's nuclear capabilities when making decisions on military aid.

From the standpoint of non-proliferation generally, Israel's crossing the threshold from a suspected to an overt nuclear weapons capability would be a serious setback. Even if stringent sanctions were imposed in response to Israel's action—and it is by no means clear that they would be—the "norm" of non-proliferation, already challenged by Israel's ambiguous nuclear activities, would be directly undercut. Nuclear arms would be further legitimized as an acceptable, increasingly common component of national defense programs, and other countries at the nuclear threshold would be encouraged to follow the Israeli example. If tough sanctions were not imposed, these effects would be greatly amplified.

Whatever the merits of an overt nuclear deterrent posture, there have been no indications in the past several years that Israel is moving toward adopting that stance. Most observers believe Israel will maintain its current posture of ambiguity as it refines its nuclear weapons designs and its delivery capabilities.

Finally, Israel may also seek to increase its nuclear-weapons production capability through enlargement of the Dimona plant—already reported by one source to have occurred—or by the construction of an unsafeguarded power reactor and, if needed, additional reprocessing capacity. Application of IAEA safeguards to the reactor would be an important signal that a major augmentation of Israel's nuclear weapons potential through this mechanism was not being planned.

ISRAEL

phosphate/uranium
mining area

0   50
MILES

Israel

Research Reactors

IRR I Nahal Soreq (light-water/highly enriched uranium, 5MWt)[a]
* supplier: United States
* start up: 1960
* fuel source: United States, through 1977 (expiration of U.S. agreement).
* safeguards: yes

IRR 2, Dimona (heavy-water/natural-uranium, 24-26 MWt)[b]
* supplier: France
* start up: 1963
* fuel source: Israel, South Africa(?), Argentina(?), Belgium(?), France(?), Niger(?), Central African Republic(?), Gabon(?)[c]
* heavy water: Norway[a], Israel(?)[a]
* safeguards: no

Uranium Resources/Active Mining Sites/Uranium Mills

* reasonably assured reserves: 30-60,000 tons is available from processing phosphate ores.[a]
* currently active site: phosphate deposits in the Negev near Beersheba.[d]
* mills in operation: phosphoric acid plants producing yellowcake as by-product, two in Haifa, one in southern Israel. Combined output, 100 tons.[a]

Uranium Purification (UO$_2$)

* capacity: sufficient to supply Dimona reactor (presumed)
* supplier: Israel(?)
* start up: ?
* safeguards: no

Heavy Water

Rehovot
* capacity: pilot scale[a]; sufficient to supply Dimona reactor (presumed).
* supplier: Israel
* start up: 1954(?)[a]
* safeguards: no

Fuel Fabrication

Dimona(?)[h]
* capacity: sufficient to supply Dimona reactor (presumed)
* supplier: Israel(?)
* start up: mid-1960s(?)
* safeguards: no

Reprocessing

Dimona(?)[k]
* capacity: unknown; only published estimate is 4-5 kilograms of plutonium from 3,400 kilograms spent fuel per year.[f] If matched to Dimona reactor's output, could produce 8-10 kilograms plutonium per year.[b]
* supplier: Israel and SGN (France)[g]
* start up: probably after 1969
* safeguards: no

Nahal Soreq
- capacity: laboratory-scale[i]
- supplier: Great Britain; some U.S. equipment(?).[i]
- start up: 1960(?)
- safeguards: no[j]

Enrichment
- type: laser(?)[e]
- capacity: 2-3 kilograms per year(?)[e]
- supplier: Israel
- start up: 1974(?)
- safeguards: no

UF$_6$ Conversion
- capacity: Small capacity to permit enrichment activities (presumed).
- supplier: Israel (?)
- start up: 1974(?)
- safeguards: no

Sources and Notes

a. *Israeli Nuclear Armament,* Report of the Secretary General, United Nations General Assembly A/36/431, September 18, 1981, pp. 8-11, 15-18.

b. At 24-26 megawatts, the reactor could produce 8-10 kilograms of plutonium per year. U.N., *Israeli Nuclear Armament,* p. 15. The capacity may have been raised to 70 MWt, "The Middle East's Nuclear Race," *Foreign Report,* August 13, 1980. The reactor could then produce about 25 kilograms of plutonium per year. U.N., *Israeli Nuclear Armament,* p. 16.

c. John R. Redick, *The Military Potential of Latin American Nuclear Energy Programs* (Beverly Hills, CA: Sage Publications, 1972) p. 13 (Argentina); personal communication with informed former U.S. official (Argentina); Bertrand Goldschmidt, *Le Défi Atomique* (Paris: Fayard, 1980) pp. 205-206 (initially, uranium bought on world market from a number of sources, mainly Western and African); Fuad Jabber, *Israel and Nuclear Weapons* (London: Chatto and Windus, 1971) p. 89 (first load of Dimona reportedly comprised of 10 tons from South Africa, 10 tons from Dead Sea phosphates, 4 tons from French sources); Christopher Raj, "Israel and Nuclear Weapons," in K. Subrahmanyam, ed. *Nuclear Myths and Realities* (ABC: New Delhi, 1981) p. 105. (South Africa, France, French-controlled uranium mines in Gabon, Central African Republic, and Niger); William Drozdiak "Uranium Loss is Admitted," *Washington Post,* May 3, 1977 (200 tons of yellowcake diverted on Mediterranean Sea from Belgium thought to wind up in Israel.)

d. "Yellowcake from Phosphates," *Business Review and Economic News from Israel* (Tel Aviv), reprinted in Foreign Broadcast Information Service/Nuclear Proliferation and Development, March 14, 1983, p. 28.

e. Robert Gillette, "Uranium Enrichment: Rumors of Israeli Progess with Lasers", *Science*, No. 183, March 22, 1974, p. 1172; U.N., *Israeli Nuclear Armament*, p. 15.

   CIA officials were convinced that Israel diverted approximately 100 kilograms of highly enriched uranium from the NUMEC plant in Apollo, Pennsylvania, between 1964 and 1966. Transcript of "Near Armageddon: The Spread of Nuclear Weapons in the Middle East," ABC News Close-Up, April 27, 1981, pp. 13-14 (Statement by former CIA official Carl Duckett). No concrete evidence that the material was diverted has come to light, however.

f. *International Military Review* (Moscow), No. 6, 1980, p. 20.

g. Weissmann and Krosney, *The Islamic Bomb*, (New York: Times Books, 1981) p. 113, citing Charles De Gaulle, *Memoirs of Hope: Renewal and Endeavor* (New York: Simon and Schuster, 1971), p. 266.

h. Fuad Jabber, *Israel and Nuclear Weapons* (London: Chatto and Windus, 1971), p. 45.

i. Ibid. p. 43.

j. Not listed in 1982 IAEA Annual Report among safeguarded installations.

k. IAEA Bulletin, Vol. 19, No. 5, p. 2; Weissman and Krosney, *The Islamic Bomb*, p. 110. See also discussion in text at footnotes 29, 47, and 49.

Libya

Libya's open support for international terrorism, its readiness to use military force overtly in Africa and to support insurgencies all over the world, and its bitter hostility toward Israel and the United States have raised fears that if it were to acquire nuclear arms, the result would be international blackmail and mayhem on a grand scale. Indeed, the image of a nuclear-armed Muammar el-Khadafi, contemptuous of world opinion and the value of innocent lives, has become the very symbol of the dangers posed by unrestrained proliferation.

Since its unsuccessful attempts during the 1970s to purchase nuclear weapons or the technology critical for their manufacture from China and a number of nations at the nuclear weapons threshold, Libya's nuclear program appears to have been limited to the training of large numbers of students abroad and the operation of a small Soviet-supplied research center at

Tajoura. These activities do not pose a near-term proliferation threat. Nonetheless, Khadafi's reported clandestine nuclear ties to Pakistan and continuing nuclear cooperation with Argentina, Belgium, and the Soviet Union may permit him eventually to accelerate Libya's nuclear program. Libya might be able to develop an unsophisticated reactor for producing plutonium and a simple reprocessing plant for extracting it within the next decade, although U.S. experts believe even this is beyond Libya's capabilities.

I. Background

Early Efforts. The story of Libya's initial attempt to acquire nuclear weapons is by now well known. According to Mohamed Heikal, confidant of then Egyptian president Gamal Abdel Nasser, in 1970 Libyan president Khadafi sent Abdul Jalloud, vice chairman of the Revolutionary Command Council, to Cairo to seek Nasser's assistance in obtaining atomic weapons from China. Although Nasser advised Jalloud that such arms were not sold internationally, Jalloud made a secret trip to China with Egyptian assistance to attempt to purchase them. Heikal states the Chinese were not willing to make the sale, but they apparently offered more general assistance in the field of nuclear research.[1]

Following this rebuff, Libya turned to a two-track program for bolstering its nuclear sector: clandestine activities directed at quickly obtaining nuclear weapons or the key materials and equipment for making them, and open activities aimed at building a nuclear research and energy program typical of developing countries. According to the most detailed investigation of the Libyan nuclear program published to date, following the first route, Libyan nuclear aides attempted in 1973 to purchase twenty large electromagnets from the French firm Thompson-CSF. Tripoli apparently intended to use the equipment to try to enrich uranium, employing a technique the United States had used for that purpose as part of the Manhattan Project but subsequently discarded as inefficient. The French government, however, refused to approve the sale.[2]

Also in 1973, Libya is said to have entered into an extraordinary secret agreement with then Pakistani President Zulfikar Ali Bhutto, under which Khadafi offered hundreds of millions of dollars to finance the Pakistani nuclear weapons program in return for "full access" to "the entire capability" Pakistan would develop. Among other elements of the arrangement, Libya specifically requested training in the operation of hot cells, the radiologically shielded units that can be used for extracting plutonium from spent reactor fuel.[3] Another report of the deal, citing Pakistani officials, states that Libya offered to finance a large reprocessing plant Pakistan was then negotiating to purchase from the French, in return for some of the plutonium it produced.[4] As discussed below, Libya also provided large amounts of uranium to Pakistan between 1978 and 1980, apparently in an attempt to persuade Pakistan not to renege on its part of the understanding.

In 1974, as part of a parallel effort to build an open nuclear program from the ground up, Libya sought assistance from the U.S. General Atomics Corporation, the manufacturer of research reactors widely used in developing countries. The State Department and the Congressional Joint Committee on Atomic Energy opposed extending nuclear cooperation to Libya, however, and no aid was provided.[5]

In the same year, again as part of what appeared to be a traditional nuclear development program, Libya concluded an agreement with Argentina under which the latter was to provide Tripoli with equipment and training in the area of uranium prospecting, extraction, and purification, as well as more general assistance.[6] By this time, Argentina, which had inaugurated its first nuclear power plant that year, had one of the more advanced nuclear programs in the developing world and had already mastered one of the key technologies necessary for the production of nuclear weapons—the extraction of plutonium from spent nuclear fuel in laboratory-scale hot cells.[7] It is not known whether the Libya-Argentina accord provided for training in this field, as Libya's secret accord with Pakistan reportedly did.

At the time, neither Argentina nor Libya was party to the Nuclear Non-Proliferation Treaty (NPT); thus Argentina could legally provide assistance to Libya without the application of International Atomic Energy Agency (IAEA) safeguards. Although Libya ratified the NPT in 1975, thereby agreeing to place all of its nuclear activities under the IAEA system, it did not conclude a safeguards agreement under the treaty until 1980. During the interim, Libya could have obtained nuclear aid from Argentina without notifying the Agency. In 1975, Libya also annexed a strip of land running across northern Chad that was said to contain major uranium deposits.[8] In principle, Libya would have been able to exploit these deposits with the aid obtained under its 1974 agreement with Argentina.

Soviet and French Reactor Agreements. Libya's adherence to the Non-Proliferation Treaty was probably a condition for receiving nuclear assistance from the Soviet Union. In 1975, Tripoli signed a nuclear cooperation agreement that provided for the USSR to build a small, ten megawatt research reactor in Libya and an associated atomic research center.[9] The reactor is believed to have begun operating in late 1981.[10]

In 1976, Libya pursued the apparently peaceful aspects of its nuclear development program by signing a nuclear cooperation agreement with France under which the latter was to sell Tripoli a six hundred-megawatt nuclear power plant.[11] The deal, however, was never consummated. Instead, in 1977, Libya signed another accord with the Soviet Union for the construction of a 440-megawatt nuclear power reactor.[12] It is not known whether Moscow attached any special non-proliferation conditions to the sale of the plant, such as the requirement imposed on Eastern European nations that plutonium-bearing spent fuel must be returned to the Soviet Union. Construction of the facility has been considerably delayed, however, and as late as March 1983, Libya and the Soviet Union were still negotiating the specifics of the reactor sale.[13]

Cooperation with Pakistan and India. During 1978, Colonel Khadafi apparently pursued his quest for nuclear weapons by seeking assistance from both Pakistan and India, a pair of countries engaged in a serious nuclear rivalry. In the case of the former, the Libyan leader reportedly sought to obtain leverage to enforce his secret 1973 understanding with Islamabad (for the transfer of Pakistani-developed nuclear-weapons-related technology) by supplying Pakistan with uranium concentrate (yellowcake) that was not subject to IAEA monitoring, for use in Pakistan's clandestine uranium enrichment program. As revealed in a detailed analysis of the episode published in 1981, Libya reportedly purchased several hundred tons of uranium concentrate from Niger between 1978 and 1980 and secretly transshipped substantial quantities of the material to Pakistan. As mentioned above, although Libya had ratified the Non-Proliferation Treaty, it had not yet formalized a safeguards agreement with the

IAEA. Such an agreement would have required Libya to place all yellowcake purchases on an inventory supervised by the IAEA and to export the material only to countries that had agreed to do likewise. Until Libya signed its safeguards agreement with the Agency in July 1980, however, it was able to import and export uranium concentrate without informing the Agency.[14]

While pursuing its secret dealings with Pakistan, Libya entered into an open nuclear cooperation agreement with India. During a visit to New Delhi in July 1978 for the signing of the accord, Libyan prime minister Jalloud was said to have pressed Indian nuclear officials for a commitment that India would assist Libya in obtaining an "independent nuclear capability."[15] When India, over the course of the following year, limited nuclear cooperation to strictly peaceful areas, Libya abruptly terminated its oil shipments to New Delhi—expected to amount to one million tons per year—in an attempt to compel India to share more sensitive nuclear technology. India refused and recalled its ambassador to Tripoli for consultations.[16]

Libyan Intentions. As the dealings with Pakistan and India unfolded, a high-ranking Libyan official openly confirmed his country's continuing interest in obtaining nuclear arms—despite its ratification of the Non-Proliferation Treaty. According to Jeremy Stone, director of the Federation of American Scientists, during a late 1978 Libyan-sponsored conference in Tripoli, Ahmed el-Shahati, head of the Foreign Liaison Office of the Libyan People's Congress, stated "unequivocally that Libya is seeking nuclear weapons."[17] As Stone later wrote:

That evening I dined privately with Shahati and his group of Western-trained people-to-people entrepreneurs. I opened the discussion by saying that our scientists were often

quite tolerant of anti-American statements and widely varying politics. But we did draw the line at the use of science for
killing innocent people. Were they going to persist in supporting terrorists, and were they seeking an atomic bomb?
They were. Shahati made no bones about it, saying they
would seek all weapons with which to defend themselves. To
be sure I understood, I asked again were they seeking to
maintain the right to get a bomb or actually trying to get the
bomb itself? It was the latter.[18]

The Federation subsequently wrote an open letter
to Soviet ambassador Anatoly Dobrynin, urging the
Soviet Union to reconsider its planned power reactor
sale to Libya on the ground that Tripoli could not be
relied upon to honor its renunciation of nuclear weapons under the Non-Proliferation Treaty. While it is
unlikely that this letter was an important factor in
Soviet decision-making, the Soviets have repeatedly
postponed transferring the facility to Tripoli, as noted
earlier, quite possibly out of concern over Khadafi's
nuclear intentions.

In early June 1981, the Jeckyl-and-Hyde nature of
Libya's nuclear activities was again highlighted. In an
interview with *Time* magazine just before Israel destroyed Iraq's large research reactor outside Baghdad,
Khadafi stated,

I have nothing but scorn for the notion of an Islamic bomb.
There is no such thing as an Islamic bomb or a "Christian
bomb." Any such weapon is a means of terrorizing human-
ity, and we are against the manufacture and acquisition of
nuclear weapons. This is in line with our definition of—and
opposition to—terrorism.[19]

Then, according to Arab intelligence sources quoted
in the *Economist* magazine's *Foreign Report* news-
letter, on June 10, three days after the Israeli raid, and

perhaps a week after the *Time* interview, Khadafi held a secret meeting with five trusted advisors at which he announced that he would use "all Libya's financial resources" to obtain a complete nuclear weapon from Pakistan or the technology to enrich uranium to weapons-grade, which Pakistan was using at its enrichment plant at Kahuta. According to the report, Khadafi sent a letter to Pakistani president Zia ul-Haq charging him with failing to live up to a 1980 agreement promising Libya that technology in return for $1.5 billion to support the Pakistani nuclear-weapons program. As a further inducement, Khadafi reportedly offered General Zia sophisticated anti-aircraft weapons to protect Pakistan's nuclear facilities against a possible raid by India.[20] No corroboration of these alleged new elements of the Libya-Pakistan connection have since come to light, however.

In addition to these alleged actions to advance Libya's nuclear-weapons program, three months later President Khadafi, in a speech commemorating the twelfth anniversary of his coming to power, declared his readiness to cause nuclear devastation to support Libya's foreign-policy interests. In a fiery response to the shooting down of two Libyan warplanes in the Gulf of Sidra by U.S. Navy jet fighters on August 19, he stated,

We are warning the peoples of Sicily, Crete, Turkey and all the states of the Mediterranean that if America again attacks the Gulf of Sidra, then we will intentionally attack the nuclear depots in their countries and cause an international catastrophe.[21]

Even if Khadafi's words are not taken literally, the very fact that he would make such threats once again demonstrates the intemperate hostility that has become his hallmark and that makes the image of a nuclear-armed Libya so menacing.

Cooperation with Belgium. Notwithstanding the continuing rumors of Libyan efforts to acquire atomic weapons and the Soviet Union's obvious reluctance to increase nuclear ties with Tripoli, two Belgian firms, Belgatom and Belgonucléaire significantly expanded their technical cooperation with Libya during 1981 and 1982. Under a long-standing, open-ended consulting contract with the Libyan Atomic Energy Commission, the firms provided technical assistance regarding the Soviet-supplied research center at Tajoura, and the pending Soviet-supplied nuclear power reactor, as well as feasibility studies concerning the development of a number of Libyan uranium deposits.[22]

By mid-1982 the United States had become sufficiently concerned about the level of cooperation between the two nations to urge Belgium to terminate the activities of these firms. Apparently the U.S. initiative met with little success: in December 1982, Libya was said to be negotiating the purchase of a major new facility from Belgonucléaire—a plant for producing uranium tetrafluoride (UF_4), discussed below.

Renewed Ties with Argentina. In 1982, Libyan ties with Argentina were also strengthened. During the Falklands War, Libya is said to have shipped more than $100 million worth of weapons to Argentina, including air-to-air missiles for use on Argentina's Mirage jets and 120 Soviet-made SA-7 anti-aircraft missiles.[23] It is possible that in return for this military aid, Libya sought nuclear technology from Argentina that might be used in a nuclear weapons program, since such a quid pro quo would be consistent with reported past transactions in which Khadafi sought to trade critically needed commodities—oil in the case of India and uranium not subject to IAEA monitoring in the case of

Pakistan—for sensitive nuclear technology. Moreover, according to a May 1983 report, Argentina and Libya did, in fact, increase their nuclear links after the Falklands War. The report states that Argentina had recently sent a forty-five member delegation to Tripoli to discuss increased Argentine nuclear and arms exports.[24]

At the time of this mission, Argentina was building both a reprocessing plant and an enrichment facility, although the latter was not disclosed publicly until November 1983. Libyan nuclear officials had expressed a keen interest in acquiring both types of facilities in past dealings with India and Pakistan. In a September 1983 congressional hearing, however, U.S. Ambassador-at-Large for Non-Proliferation Richard T. Kennedy stated that he had been assured by Argentine nuclear aides that no technology related to these sensitive areas was being transferred to Libya by Argentina.[25] Unfortunately, at the time, Argentina was misrepresenting its domestic nuclear activities to the United States by failing to disclose its secret enrichment plant—casting doubt on its assurances vis-à-vis its nuclear dealings with Tripoli. Whatever the substance of Libyan-Argentine nuclear trade, its future under Argentina's new president, Raul Alfonsín, remains to be seen.

Other Nuclear Aid for Libya. In addition to its approaches to the Soviet Union, Pakistan, India, the United States, Belgium, France, and Argentina, Libya has solicited aid from Finland to develop a safety system for Libya's planned Soviet-supplied power plant. Finland had built such a safety system for its own Soviet-supplied nuclear stations. With the delay in the construction of the Soviet plant in Libya, however, the relationship with Finland apparently petered out.[26]

Libya has also purchased significant quantities of

uranium from Niger—258 tons in 1978, 150 in 1979, 180 in 1980, and 1,212 in 1981—a portion of which is believed to have been shipped to Pakistan, as discussed above.[27]

Numerous Libyan scientists have also trained abroad, including some two hundred in the United States, between two and three hundred in Europe, and an even greater number in the Soviet Union.[28] In March 1983, however, the United States took steps to prohibit Libyan students from studying nuclear science at American institutions.[29]

Libyan Rocketry. Although Libya does not have an indigenous rocket or missile production capability, during the late 1970s it reportedly signed a $100-million contract with a German company called OTRAG to develop a ground-to-ground missile system with a range of 2,000 miles. The company reportedly set up a launching base at Jarmah, some 430 miles south of Tripoli. Although the company claimed that it was helping Libya to develop a satellite launching capability, U.S. intelligence officials believed that the activities were a cover for a military program. These officials noted that Libyan military officials, many of whom were connected with Libya's atomic energy program, directed the rocketry project and that a substantial part of the Libyan Atomic Energy Commission's budget reportedly was used to support OTRAG-related activities. The company ceased its activities in Libya in late 1981.[30]

II. Developments of the Past Year

Belgian Aid

In May 1984, Belgian nuclear officials announced that Belgium and Libya would shortly sign an agreement for nuclear cooperation.[31] The agreement was intended in part to provide the legal framework for the sale by Belgonucléaire of a uranium tetrafluoride plant to Tripoli, as mentioned above. Although the material produced in the plant would not itself be readily usable for nuclear weapons or other nuclear applications, production of uranium tetrafluoride is a key intermediate stage in creating a variety of materials that could contribute to a Libyan nuclear-weapons program. In particular, uranium metal can be easily made from tetrafluoride.

Some U.S. officials feared that Libya could use uranium metal as fuel in a crude natural-uranium/graphite reactor to produce plutonium. The technology for building such a reactor is not complex, and although the nuclear supplier countries strictly control exports of reactor-grade graphite, experts believe that Libya might nonetheless acquire this substance by circumventing these restrictions.[32]

The plutonium produced in the uranium metal fuel would then have to be separated in a reprocessing plant. Again, however, a crude reprocessing plant might be within the range of Libyan capabilities, especially if it were able to obtain technical assistance from Pakistan or, possibly, Argentina.[33]

Uranium tetrafluoride is also readily transformed into uranium hexafluoride, the gas used in the enrichment process. This might serve as feedstock if Libya were to build an enrichment plant under its supposed arrangement with Pakistan.

Unlike plants that produce uranium metal or uranium hexafluoride, the Belgonucléaire facility might not be subject to IAEA inspections despite Libya's adherence to the Non-Proliferation Treaty, since IAEA rules may exempt these plants whose output cannot be used directly in nuclear weapons, nuclear reactors, or the uranium-enrichment process. The issue has, apparently, never been decided by the Agency. If safeguards were not applied, and Libya took the plant's output and transformed it into metal without declaring the activity to the IAEA, the Agency would have no occasion to learn of the fact. Nor would the Agency have any way of discovering an undeclared reactor and reprocessing plant, since IAEA inspectors may visit only those facilities that are formally acknowledged by the country to be under safeguards.

If Libya were to produce uranium metal and build such clandestine facilities, it would face the continuing risk of detection by foreign intelligence operations. Since Libya would be violating its safeguards obligations under the Non-Proliferation Treaty if it did not declare these parts of its nuclear program to the IAEA and submit them to inspection, detection of such clandestine activities could lead to international censure and sanctions. However, Libya's continued support for international terrorism in the face of similar international denunciation suggests that it may not consider such costs unacceptable.

While recognizing that these scenarios were highly speculative, U.S. officials believed their concerns were justified because there appeared to be no logical use for the plant's output within Libya's nuclear energy and research program. Accordingly, Washington continued to press Belgium to block the sale. The outcome of these negotiations was still in doubt as of June 1984.

III. Prospects for Nuclear Weapons in Libya

As seen above, evidence from a wide range of sources suggests that acquiring nuclear weapons is one of President Khadafi's important goals. Libya has made little progress towards developing a nuclear capability, however, largely because its technological skills are limited and many nations are reluctant to provide it with nuclear aid.

Nonetheless, open nuclear assistance from Belgium, Argentina, and the Soviet Union is helping Libya create a nuclear infrastructure. Moreover, by its offers of critically needed economic assistance, unmonitored uranium, oil, and possibly arms, Libya has repeatedly tried to induce countries at the nuclear-weapons threshold to supply it with nuclear technology directly useful in the development of nuclear weapons. So far, Libya is not known to have succeeded in these efforts, but they may yet bear fruit.

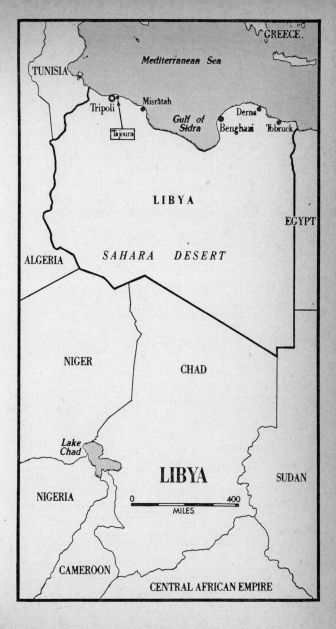

163

Libya

Research Reactor

Tajoura (light-water/highly-enriched uranium, 10 MWt)[a]
- supplier: USSR[a]
- fuel source: USSR[a]
- start up   1981[b]
- safeguards: yes[c]

Power Reactor Under Construction

Gulf of Sidra (light-water/low-enriched uranium, 440 MWe)[d]
- supplier: Atomenergoexport (USSR)[e]
- fuel source: USSR
- start up: planned 1986[d]
- safeguards: yes

Uranium Resources/Active Mining Sites/Uranium Mills

- reasonably assured
  reserves: none assessed, four active exploration projects.[f]
- currently active sites: none
- mills in operation: none

Uranium Tetrafluoride (UF₄)

Tripoli
- capacity: ?
- supplier: Belgonucléaire (Belgium)[g]
- start up: negotiations for purchase of plant still continuing
- safeguards: uncertain

Sources and Notes

a. Senate Foreign Relations committee, *Hearings on the Israeli Air Strike*, June 18, 19, and 25, 1981, 97th Congress, 1st Session (Washington, D.C.: U.S. General Printing Office, 1981) p. 40.

b. Claudia Wright, "Libya's Nuclear Program," *The Middle East*, February 1982, p. 47; *Hearings on the Israeli Air Strike*, p. 50.

c. International Atomic Energy Agency, *The Annual Report, 1982*, (Vienna, Austria: International Atomic Energy Agency, 1983), p. 81.

d. Claudia Wright, "Libya's Nuclear Program," p. 50.

e. Robin Miller, "Nuclear Power Plans Outlined," *Jamahiriyah Review*, Foreign Broadcast Information Service/Nuclear Development and Proliferation, March 22, 1982, p. 17.

f. OECD Nuclear Energy Agency and the International Atomic Energy Agency, *Uranium Resources, Production, and Demand* (Paris: OECD, 1983), p. 208. Libya reportedly purchased several hundred tons of uranium concentrate from Niger between 1978 and 1980. Steve Weissman and Herbert Krosney, *The Islamic Bomb*, (New York: Times Books, 1981), p. 210.

g. "Libya and Belgonucléaire of Belgium Are In Detailed Negotiation," *Nucleonics Week*, December 2, 1982, p. 4.

Iraq

Iraq's nuclear program, which may well have been aimed at developing nuclear arms by the mid-1990s, if not sooner, has been considered dormant since Israel's June 1981 bombing raid destroyed its centerpiece, the large French-supplied Osirak research reactor. The Iraqi government has declared that it intends to rebuild the facility, but preoccupied by the war with Iran, it has apparently not taken any steps in that direction. Iraq's 12.5 kilograms (1 kilogram = 2.2 pounds) of French-supplied highly enriched uranium fuel, possibly enough for a single, carefully designed nuclear weapon, could present a near-term proliferation threat that cannot be discounted in light of Iraq's readiness to use another unconventional weapon—lethal chemical agents—in its all-out war with Iran. Moreover, a recent report that Iraq has been seeking to obtain nuclear-weapons-usable plutonium from Italian black market sources, if true, would indicate that Baghdad's interest in obtaining nuclear weapons remains strong and that, despite the destruction of Osirak, its efforts to achieve this objective may be continuing.

I. Background

Early Developments. From the mid-1950s to the mid-1970s, Iraq's modest nuclear research program was typical of developing nations and had little significance for weapons. The program centered on the training abroad in nuclear science and technology[1] of a small number of Iraqi students and the operation of a two-megawatt, Soviet-supplied research reactor, the IRT-2000, which was completed in 1968 at the Tuwaitha Atomic Center.[2] Iraq ratified the Non-Proliferation Treaty in 1969.

Cooperation Agreement with France. In 1974, however, Iraq began a major expansion of its nuclear activities by concluding a nuclear cooperation agreement with France.[3] Under the agreement, France was to supply Baghdad with a large reactor and help build the Tuwaitha center into a "nuclear university" capable of training some six hundred scientists and technicians. In return, Iraq reportedly promised to buy French arms and to assure France a long-term supply of oil.[4]

Concern that Iraq had development of a nuclear weapons capability in mind when it entered into this accord first arose during the following year, when Iraq tried to purchase a five-hundred-megawatt natural-uranium/gas-graphite power reactor under the French agreement.[5] This reactor type was no longer considered an up-to-date model for generating electricity and had been supplanted in France by light-water reactors some years before. It was, however, particularly efficient in producing large quantities of plutonium; indeed, the natural-uranium/gas-graphite model still furnished plutonium for the French nuclear weapons program.[6] France rejected Iraq's proposal principally because it no longer possessed the manufacturing capability for natural-uranium/gas-graphite reactors.[7]

Instead, France offered Iraq a duplicate of a large, forty-megawatt materials-testing reactor and an associated eight-hundred-kilowatt mock-up of that reactor—both of which France operated at its Saclay Research Institute—an offer Iraq accepted.[8] (Iraq named the reactors Tammuz I and II, respectively, but they were known to the French as Osirak and Isis.)

This alternative posed its own proliferation dangers, and within months after the signing of the August 1976 sales contract for the plants, Israel, the United States, and several European governments protested to France.[9] They were alarmed that the reactors were to be fueled with highly enriched uranium that could be directly used for nuclear weapons. France had offered to provide Iraq with seventy-two kilograms initially, enough to fuel the reactor for a year—or to produce several nuclear bombs.[10] If Iraq elected to disregard the International Atomic Energy Agency (IAEA) safeguards covering the material and had prepared the necessary non-nuclear components of nuclear weapons in advance, the highly enriched material could give it a small nuclear arsenal in a matter of weeks.[11]

A second concern, which would become more important in subsequent years, was that Osirak, with a rating of forty megawatts, would give Iraq the ability to produce substantial quantities of plutonium. If natural (unenriched) uranium "targets" were placed in and around Osirak's highly enriched uranium core and irradiated, part of the natural uranium would be transmuted into plutonium. In theory, the Osirak reactor could produce approximately ten kilograms of plutonium per year in this manner, enough for possibly two nuclear weapons.[12] If Iraq were to acquire a reprocessing capability to extract the plutonium from the untransmuted uranium and other residues in the irradiated targets, it could obtain a stockpile of plutonium that, like its stockpile of new highly enriched uranium fuel, would give it the capability to assemble nuclear weapons quickly. Again, however, Iraq would have to violate IAEA safeguards openly to do this, unless it attempted to irradiate the targets and reprocess them clandestinely, a scenario that became increasingly implausible as discussed below.

Suspicions that Iraq had purchased Osirak for the purpose of obtaining nuclear weapons material were underscored by the fact that the forty-megawatt reactor was unusually large.[13] Typically, developing countries have acquired one-to-five-megawatt research reactors that use far smaller quantities of highly enriched uranium fuel and are incapable of producing plutonium in significant amounts.[14] Moreover, Iraq's decision to buy Osirak—a reactor that would not produce electricity—as a substitute for the natural-uranium/gas-graphite *power* reactor it had originally requested was hard to explain unless it was assumed that in both cases Iraq's underlying objective was to develop a nuclear explosives capability.

In 1978, after repeated protests by the United States, Israel, Saudi Arabia, Syria, and a number of other governments[15] against the proposed sale of the seventy-two kilograms of weapons-grade uranium, France attempted to persuade Iraq to accept an alternative fuel known as caramel.[16] With an enrichment level of only 7 percent, caramel would have been unusable for nuclear weapons. Although the new fuel had apparently been tested in the French reactor at Saclay on which Osirak was modeled, Iraq insisted on delivery of the weapons-grade fuel, claiming that the reliability of caramel had not been proven.[17] Iraq's insistence on obtaining weapons-grade material, when the caramel fuel would probably have sufficed for most of its legitimate research activities, has been taken as further evidence that the Osirak project veiled a nuclear weapons program.

France ultimately gave in to Iraqi demands, announcing its decision in March 1980. In the negotiations, however, Iraq accepted three important additional safeguards to prevent any misuse of Osirak and its fuel. First, France would not supply all seventy-two kilograms of fresh highly enriched uranium at once, but would transfer it in stages, as it was needed, so that no more than twenty-four kilograms (enough to load Osirak and reload it once) would be in Iraq at any time. Spent fuel would be returned promptly to France.[18] Although twenty-four kilograms would easily be enough for one nuclear device, half of the material would normally be in use in Osirak and highly radioactive, making it unsuitable for weapons without extensive processing.

Second, Iraq agreed to pre-irradiate all fresh highly enriched uranium fuel, when received, in the small Isis reactor.[19] While not precluding use of the material for nuclear arms, the pre-irradiation would make it difficult to move and work with the fuel without special precautions and radiological shielding to protect workers. Iraq received the first (and only) shipment, 12.5 kilograms of highly enriched uranium, in July 1980.

The third safeguard required French technicians to remain at Osirak and participate in research activities there through 1989. In principle, these technicians would help ensure both that the reactor's highly enriched uranium fuel was not diverted clandestinely and that significant amounts of unenriched uranium were

not secretly introduced into the core to produce plutonium.[20]

Although the efforts of the United States, Israel,
and other concerned nations failed to reverse France's
decision to provide highly enriched uranium to Iraq,
these safeguards did significantly reduce the proliferation threat posed by the transfer.

Assistance from Italy. Paralleling its dealings with
France in 1976, Iraq purchased from Italy five laboratories for the Tuwaitha center, including three hot
cells, lead-shielded rooms with remote-handling
equipment for examining and processing radioactive
materials.[21] U.S. officials believed that if Iraq produced plutonium by irradiating unenriched uranium
targets in Osirak, the hot cells could separate enough
plutonium for approximately one nuclear device per
year.[22] As in the case of the apparently oversized
Osirak reactor, the scale of the hot cells, officials believed, far exceeded the needs of a civilian nuclear
program, raising concerns that the hot cells, too, had
been acquired to aid an Iraqi nuclear weapons effort.

Apart from the hot cells, the Italian nuclear laboratories provided Iraq with the capability to purify processed uranium, or yellowcake, and fabricate it into
forms that could be inserted into the Osirak reactor.
Such facilities could legitimately be used to fabricate
nuclear fuel, but not for the type of reactors that Iraq
possessed, suggesting that the fuel fabrication laboratory had also been acquired to help Iraq produce plutonium.[23]

Between 1978 and 1980, the United States worked
intensively to persuade the Italian government to
block the sale, but without success.[24] Italy's rebuff to
the U.S. protest was based on factors similar to those
that led France to overrule foreign objections to its
export of highly enriched uranium. Italy depended

upon Iraq for nearly one third of its oil and had apparently agreed to provide nuclear assistance in return for assurances of a long-term oil supply. Moreover, it too was seeking to close an arms sale with Iraq (for eleven naval vessels worth $2.8 billion). Reneging on its promised nuclear transfer could have jeopardized both those arrangements.[25]

During 1980 and 1981, numerous Iraqi technicians reportedly studied reprocessing in Italy, and Iraq is said to have entered into negotiations with Italy for the purchase of a small-scale reprocessing plant.[26] Like Iraq's purchase of the hot cells, neither the training nor the acquisition of a larger reprocessing capability was in keeping with Iraq's limited civilian nuclear research needs.

Finally, it has also been reported that by the time of the June 7, 1981, Israeli raid, Iraq was trying to purchase a natural-uranium/heavy-water reactor from Italy that could generate in its spent fuel quantities of plutonium many times greater than Osirak could produce.[27] Used in conjunction with the small reprocessing facility then being pursued, the reactor would have enabled Iraq to produce plutonium for at least several weapons annually.

Iraq's Uranium Purchases. In concert with acquisition of the outsized Osirak reactor with its highly enriched uranium fuel and the unusually elaborate Italian nuclear laboratories, from 1979 through 1981 Iraq raised further suspicion by arranging a series of uranium purchases.

In January 1980, for example, after seven months of negotiations Brazil agreed to supply Iraq with a wide range of nuclear assistance, including large quantities of processed uranium ore (yellowcake).[28] Two months later, Iraq purchased 138 tons of yellowcake from Portugal, which was delivered in April of the following year. And in May 1981, it bought one hundred tons of the material from Niger.[29]

These purchases, which were duly reported to the IAEA pursuant to Iraq's Non-Proliferation Treaty obligations, alarmed IAEA and Western officials because the amounts of uranium involved greatly exceeded the possible needs of Iraq's research reactors, and even if it were assumed that Iraq intended to build a nuclear power reactor in the future, stockpiling uranium ten to fifteen years ahead of time was highly unusual.[30] On the other hand, if Iraq were seeking to produce plutonium in Osirak by irradiating uranium target specimens, the yellowcake was the missing link that made this alternative feasible.[31]

Two additional transactions during 1980 involving *depleted* uranium lent further credence to these concerns: Iraq's purchase from Italy of six tons of this material (along with four tons of yellowcake) and its attempted purchase of fabricated depleted uranium fuel pins from West Germany.[32] Depleted uranium is not useful as a nuclear fuel and could not have powered any Iraqi reactor, current or future. But depleted uranium, like natural uranium, can be irradiated to produce plutonium.

Moreover, the depleted uranium deals were at least partly clandestine and appear to have involved subterfuge, further suggesting that they were not part of Iraq's legitimate nuclear research program. In the first transaction, an Italian firm sold ten tons of depleted and natural uranium to Iraq, which it had purchased from a West German supplier, NUKEM. In buying the material, however, the Italian firm had reportedly indicated it was intended to be used in Italy, presumably because West Germany might not have permitted export of the material if it had known it was destined for Iraq.[33]

In the second transaction, Iraq attempted to obtain fabricated depleted uranium fuel pins directly from NUKEM. Iraq reportedly claimed the pins were being purchased for use in a yet-to-be-built training reactor. A more likely reason in the eyes of some experts, particularly since Iraq is not known to have had such a training reactor on order, was that the pins were intended to be inserted into Osirak and that Iraq was seeking to avoid the necessity of fabricating the pins itself.[34] NUKEM tried to subcontract portions of the job to Canadian and American firms reportedly without disclosing the ultimate destination of the finished product. When U.S. and Canadian regulatory officials looked into the matter, they discovered this, and the contract went no further.[35]

The unusual physical properties of depleted uranium and the clandestine aspects of Iraq's efforts to obtain this material are particularly strong indicators that Iraq was moving toward the undeclared acquisition of nuclear weapons material.

Statements of Intent. In addition to the mounting circumstantial evidence that Iraq was seeking to use its civilian nuclear program for military ends, Baghdad's belligerent foreign policy, support for radical and terrorist organizations, and intense hostility toward Israel contributed to fears that Iraq might be seeking to develop nuclear arms to advance its radical objectives and enhance its status in the Arab world. This view is supported by several official statements by Iraqi spokesmen indicating Baghdad's support for the development of nuclear arms by Arab nations in general or by Iraq itself.

Most telling is a 1975 statement by Saddam Hussein, then a member of the Revolutionary Command Council. In an interview with a Beirut magazine, he declared his nation's expanding nuclear program was "the first Arab attempt at nuclear arming."[36]

In 1977, after the conclusion of the nuclear contracts with France and Italy, Naim Haddad, also a member of Iraq's Revolutionary Command Council, reportedly stated at a meeting of the Arab League, "The Arabs must get an atom bomb. The Arab countries should possess whatever is necessary to defend themselves."[37] Haddad's unqualified enthusiasm for nuclear weapons at a time when Iraq was building a large nuclear program that would provide it with virtually all of the necessary components caused considerable concern in Israel and other countries.

Three years later, in July 1980, the *London Times* quoted Saddam Hussein, by now Iraq's president, as saying, "We have no program concerning the manufacture of the atomic bomb."[38] The article went on to state, however, that:

President Husain [sic] implied several times that Arab nations would be able to use atomic weapons, adding—after his denial of any intention to make a bomb—that "whoever wants to be our enemy can expect that enemy to be totally different in the very near future." Circumspect though this phrase may appear, it is no secret that Iraq's nuclear reactor is expected to be commissioned in five months.[39]

While not a direct contradiction of his disavowal of nuclear weapons, Hussein's statements raised serious doubts as to its credibility.

Finally, on October 4, 1980, shortly after an Iranian aircraft attacked the Osirak facility, an editorial in the Iraqi government-controlled newspaper *Al-Jumhuriyah* stated:

We ask Khomeini and his gang: Who will benefit from hitting the nuclear reactor in Iraq—Iran or the Zionist entity? The nuclear reactor cannot be a threat to Iran because Iraq looks upon the Iranian people as brothers. And if it were not for Khomeini's bloodthirsty bunch and its bitter arrogance and hatred, then there would not have been a war between Iraq and Iran. Instead, there would have been peace, friendship, and cooperation in the shadow of true Islam . . . .

The Zionist entity is the one that fears the Iraqi nuclear reactor. The entity has tried so hard to undermine Iraqi efforts to obtain nuclear technology. Further, that entity has warned that it will not stand with its hands tied behind its back in that regard, but rather it will try to destroy the Iraqi nuclear reactor by any means available to it, especially since the reactor constitutes a grave danger for "Israel."

That is what Begin and Zionist enemy circles have said. Those who tried to carry out the act are Khomeini, Bani-Sadr, and the suspicious defense minister Fakuri.[40]

Although the phrasing of the editorial is ambiguous—it may simply have been restating supposed Israeli views and fears—the likeliest interpretation is that the statement was asserting that Osirak in fact posed a danger to that country. Thus the statement appears to be an acknowledgment that Baghdad intended to use Osirak in the development of nuclear arms.

Against the foregoing, sometimes ambiguous statements, must be balanced Iraqi officials' repeated assurances to the International Atomic Energy Agency (IAEA), the United Nations, and similar bodies expressly denying this intent, as well as Iraq's early ratification of the Non-Proliferation Treaty.[41]

Efforts to Sabotage Iraq's Nuclear Program. Despite diplomatic interventions by the United States, Israel, and others, Iraq thus succeeded in acquiring nuclear technology, equipment, and materials that would give it access to highly enriched uranium and, potentially plutonium. Beginning in April 1979, however, its program became the target of a series of bombings and assassinations that dealt it several setbacks.

In April 1979, the core structures for Osirak and the smaller Isis reactor were destroyed by a bomb planted in a warehouse in Seine-sur-Mer, France, where the equipment was awaiting shipment to Iraq.[42] The previously unknown French Ecological Group claimed responsibility, although French officials speculated that Israeli agents had perpetrated the act. Others blamed the French government, charging that it was unhappy with the reactor sale but unwilling to renege openly on the contract. The issue was never resolved. In any event, France rebuilt the reactor cores and delivered them about six months later.[43]

This incident was followed in June 1980 by the murder of Dr. Yahya el-Meshad, an Egyptian nuclear scientist working for the Iraqi Atomic Energy Commission. At the time of the murder, France was preparing to ship the first 12.5 kilograms of highly enriched uranium fuel for Osirak.[44] Meshad, who was slain in his Paris hotel room, was in France to inspect the fuel prior to shipment. As in the case of the Seine-sur-Mer bombing, the perpetrator was not found, and suspicions focused on Israeli agents.

Two months later, a series of bombings occurred at the residences or offices of several officials of Iraq's key nuclear suppliers: SNIA-Techint, the Italian company supplying the hot cells to Iraq; its partner in the sale, Ansaldo Mercanico Nucleare; and Techniatome, the French government-owned subsidiary supplying the Osirak reactor. In addition, officials and workers in these and several other French and Italian companies received threatening letters from the Committee to Safeguard the Islamic Revolution, warning them to stop their work on Iraq's nuclear program.[45] Again, the parties actually responsible were never identified; this time speculation centered on Israel and Iran. The French and Italian firms involved went ahead with their nuclear exports despite the threats.

Iraq's nuclear program suffered a more serious setback on September 30, 1980—eight days after Iraq launched the war against Iran—when two Iranian Phantom jets attacked the Osirak reactor, then still under construction. Although the attack caused only modest damage to the reactor's dome and cooling system, the incident postponed the plant's planned start-up from December 1980 to mid-1981 or later.[46]

The Gulf War also impaired international monitoring of the Iraqi nuclear program. Of some four hundred French technicians working at the Osirak site, all but seventy returned to Europe after Iraq declared war on Iran; and the group shrank to seven or so after the Iranian raid.[47] Moreover, these workers were no longer on duty full time. Although they could still verify that the 12.5 kilograms of French highly enriched uranium were properly stored, they could not maintain constant surveillance over the center. Second, in November 1980, Iraq advised the IAEA to postpone a planned safeguards inspection of the facility and fuel in view of the wartime conditions.[48] IAEA inspections did not resume until January 18, 1981, some six and a half months after the previous inspection; however, all of the highly enriched uranium supplied by France was duly accounted for.[49]

Although these lapses in surveillance by the French technicians and the IAEA were temporary and did not result in any misuse of Iraq's nuclear material, they revealed the potential fragility of the measures intended to help ensure that Iraq's nuclear program would remain peaceful. In effect, the episode demonstrated that by declaring a national crisis, Iraq might be able to suspend international observation of its nuclear program for months at a time, if not longer.

Israel's plans for its June 1981 bombing reportedly began in earnest in January or February 1980 and accelerated during the summer after Israeli diplomatic efforts failed to persuade France and Italy to curtail their nuclear assistance to Baghdad.[50] Israel apparently scheduled its attack on Osirak for September— only to be forestalled by Iran's raid against the facility late that month. When it became clear that the damage from that raid was limited and that, with the return of the French workers in the early months of 1981, Osirak would be ready to start up later that year, Israel destroyed the reactor on June 7.[51]

Assessment of the Iraqi Program Prior to the Israeli Raid. Israel's surprise attack generated an inquiry into Iraq's nuclear capabilities.[52] As suggested above, considerable circumstantial evidence indicates that Iraq was seeking to develop a nuclear weapons capability through use of its expanded civilian nuclear program. To this must be added a statement by Iraqi president Saddam Hussein; in a speech to his cabinet on June 24, 1981, some two weeks after the Israeli raid, he called upon all peaceloving nations to, "assist the Arabs in one way or another to obtain the nuclear bomb in order to confront Israel's existing bombs."[53] While not necessarily reflecting his thinking before the raid, Hussein's June 24 statement is consistent with several previous official Iraqi pronouncements and suggests that Iraq had long harbored the goal of bending its nuclear program to develop nuclear arms.

Two routes were theoretically available to Iraq for acquiring the necessary nuclear material for weapons. It could either use Osirak's highly enriched uranium fuel, or it could produce plutonium in the reactor and subsequently extract the material in the Italian hot cells.

With respect to the highly enriched uranium route, there is little dispute that the IAEA safeguards covering the reactor were technically capable of detecting efforts to remove small quantities of Osirak's fuel surreptitiously. In addition, Iraq would have had to deceive the French technicians working with the reactor. This strategy, moreover, would have taken considerable time, and if Iraq were found out before it had obtained the quantity necessary for a single weapon, France would certainly have terminated further supplies, making it impossible for Iraq to accumulate the quantity of highly enriched uranium it needed.[54]

On the other hand, once France had supplied the fresh highly enriched uranium fuel, Iraq might have considered abrogating IAEA safeguards and seizing all of the material abruptly, perhaps after restricting French and IAEA access to the reactor (as it did during the early stages of the Iran-Iraq war) to delay detection for a number of months. Detection would be certain ultimately, however, and in response, France would have cut off further fuel shipments. At best, Iraq would by then have one or conceivably two untested nuclear weapons—an uncertain long-term deterrent and an inviting target for pre-emptive attack by its adversaries.

Secretly acquiring enough plutonium for nuclear weapons would have been even more difficult. To use Osirak to produce the maximum eight to sixteen kilograms of plutonium per year while avoiding French or IAEA detection appears to have been virtually impossible, since among other steps, it would have necessitated either major structural modifications of the reactor's easily observed interior or the insertion of hundreds of uranium targets and rearrangement of scores of fuel elements—all of which would be most difficult to conceal.[55] Moreover, using the reactor in this fashion would have led to unusually high fuel consumption, which would undoubtedly have prompted French and IAEA inquiries and led to restrictions on further fuel shipments.

Iraq might have succeeded in irradiating smaller quantities of uranium in the reactor without detection or might have used the reactor's neutron-beam chamber for this purpose. The neutron beam chamber is a channel beneath the reactor intended for irradiation of target specimens—which the IAEA might not have routinely inspected.

These strategies, however, like the larger-scale secret plutonium production option, would have necessitated secret fabrication of the uranium targets and their subsequent reprocessing. Once the Italian laboratories were placed under IAEA inspection, detection of these activities would have been highly likely.[56]

It is also possible that Iraq might have openly produced small amounts of plutonium over a number of years as part of its safeguarded nuclear research program. The Non-Proliferation Treaty does not prohibit this activity, provided it is subject to Agency inspections. Though France might have objected initially, it might eventually have gone along, as it did in supplying Osirak's highly enriched uranium fuel, provided the plutonium production did not have obvious earmarks of an attempt to develop nuclear arms. Apart from the weapons material this would have given Iraq, it also would have provided valuable training and experience that Iraq could have later used if its negotiations with Italy for a pilot-scale reprocessing plant had been successful.

Taken together, the French controls and IAEA safeguards would have made it very difficult for Iraq to obtain nuclear weapons material from Osirak in any quantity. Nonetheless, there is considerable evidence that such an illicit goal was a central objective of the Iraqi nuclear program.

These two conclusions are not as incompatible as they may at first appear. In the mid-1970s Iraq may have anticipated that by using Osirak and the Italian hot cells, it could obtain substantial quantities of weapons-usable material, only to find that its plans were unexpectedly thwarted by new French non-proliferation controls. Under its original game plan, it would have had at least three bombs' worth of highly enriched uranium on hand at all times and, given France's permissive attitude in the mid-1970s, it might have expected that as long as IAEA safeguards were applied it could openly produce and separate one bomb's worth of plutonium annually. If the non-nuclear components for atomic weapons were assembled in advance, this would have provided Baghdad with a ready nuclear weapons option that it could have exercised quickly by abrogating IAEA safeguards or withdrawing from the Non-Proliferation Treaty (NPT).

As France imposed new restrictions on Osirak and its fuel, Iraq appears to have revised its plans and integrated the facility into a longer-term strategy for accumulating nuclear weapons material. Indeed, in the immediate aftermath of the Israeli raid, the United States appears to have seen Osirak as part of such a longer-range plan. On June 9, 1981, for example, State Department spokesman Dean Fischer stated, "We have no evidence that Iraq has violated its commitments under the [Non-Proliferation] Treaty." He went on to say, however, that the United States was concerned that the Iraqi nuclear program could "pose a threat at some point in the future."[57] A senior Senate staff expert has outlined the following scenario suggesting how Iraq might have used its civilian nuclear program (assuming Osirak had remained available) to aid its quest for nuclear weapons:

While fully complying with its NPT and bilateral obligations, Iraq gains essential hands-on experience in reactor operation and reprocessing through use of Osirak and the Italian-supplied hot cells, while training numerous specialists at home and abroad. Gradually, over the next two to four years enough plutonium is separated openly for one or more nuclear weapons. Enough highly enriched uranium, in the form of Osirak fuel, for another weapon is also available from time to time. Secretly, Iraq also begins testing and manufacturing the non-nuclear components for atomic weapons. From this point on, Iraq could quickly assemble actual weapons in a matter of weeks without violating the NPT until the moment of assembly. The size of Iraq's potential nuclear arsenal would now be of the same order of magnitude as that of the United States at the time of the Hiroshima bombing.

Simultaneously, and still fully adhering to its non-proliferation commitments, Iraq uses its oil supply leverage, as it has apparently done in the past, to conclude the purchase from Italy of the natural uranium reactor and small reprocessing plant mentioned earlier. Once these are in place, perhaps five to eight years later, Iraq could begin separating larger quantities of plutonium from the new reactor's spent fuel; this could be done openly, under IAEA safeguards. Larger numbers of weapons could now be assembled in a national crisis. At this point, Iraq would have achieved rough parity with Israel.

If Iraq moved to actual weapons manufacture it would violate the NPT and its other non-proliferation commitments. However, in the event of a regional crisis—or even on the pretext of some act of Israeli belligerence—Iraq could legally withdraw from the Treaty on ninety days' notice. While a violation of Iraq's bilateral commitments might trigger a nuclear supply cut-off, Iraq could continue to manufacture plutonium by irradiating uranium from its stockpile in either the Osirak reactor (until its supply of highly enriched uranium fuel was exhausted) or in the larger reactor purchased from Italy.[58]

II. Developments of the Past Year

Rebuilding Osirak

Immediately after the Israeli raid, France announced that it had terminated nuclear assistance to Iraq.[59] Baghdad, however, stated that it planned to press ahead with its nuclear program, and in mid-July Saudi Arabia announced that it would finance Osirak's reconstruction.[60] By late summer, after negotiations with the Mitterand government, Iraq announced that France had agreed in principle to rebuild the reactor—but under more stringent controls.[61]

France revealed the specific terms of its plan early in 1982. Iraq would have to accept low-enriched caramel fuel for the plant; French technicians would remain at the site permanently; and, in addition, Iraq would have to include other states in the operation of the installation, making it a regional research center.[62] Iraq did not indicate whether it would agree to any of these new measures.[63] Although France and Iraq had settled outstanding issues concerning payments for the demolished facility by September 1983, they had not as yet reached any substantive agreement to rebuild it.[64] As of mid-1984, no significant reconstruction work was known to have begun on Osirak.[65]

In late 1982, Italy advised U.S. officials that it did not plan to offer additional nuclear equipment to Iraq.[66]

Iraq's Use of Chemical Weapons

On March 26, 1984, a United Nations-sponsored team of military and medical experts concluded that "chemical weapons in the form of aerial bombs have been used" in Iran.[67] The report, in effect, confirmed a March 5 statement by the U.S. State Department declaring that Iraq had used such weapons against Iran in their nearly four-year-old conflict. According to the U.N. report, the lethal chemical agents used against Iran were mustard gas and a nerve agent known as Tabun.[68]

Iraq's use of chemical weapons directly violated its obligations under the 1925 Geneva Protocol, which it ratified in 1931, prohibiting the "use in war of asphyxiating, poisonous or other gases." Baghdad's action also defied the long-standing moral taboo against the use of these inhuman weapons that has, with only a handful of exceptions, prevailed since World War I. The development thus casts serious doubt on Iraq's intention to uphold its commitment to another treaty it has ratified that seeks to control unconventional weapons: the Nuclear Non-Proliferation Treaty, prohibiting the manufacture of nuclear explosives. It also raises questions whether, if Iraq had obtained nuclear arms, it would have hesitated to use them during the Gulf War. Indeed, Iraqi officials, while denying that their nation had used poison gas, insisted on its right to use any weapon to defend itself against invasion.[69] At least one Israeli politician has cited these events as justifying, in retrospect, Israel's destruction of the Osirak reactor.[70]

As indicated above, Iraq has not yet rebuilt its nuclear program. Nevertheless, Iraq's apparent desperation to end the war with Iran, coupled with its flagrant disregard of its arms control commitments, raises a more immediate proliferation concern. The Israeli raid did not destroy the 12.5 kilograms of French-supplied highly enriched uranium fuel for Osirak. This material may be sufficient to manufacture a single nuclear weapon, especially if it is combined with a smaller amount of highly enriched fuel previously supplied by the Soviet Union for Iraq's IRT-2000 research reactor. If confronted by an overwhelming Iranian invasion force, Iraqi leaders might seriously consider using this material to threaten Teheran with even a single untested nuclear weapon. An additional risk is that even if Iraq's current leadership does not use the French fuel in this manner, the material might fall into less responsible hands if an Iranian victory led to a period of political turmoil and internal strife within Iraq.

The measures taken to prevent misuse of the Osirak fuel may not be sufficient in this setting. Although the IAEA periodically inspects the French-supplied fuel, inspections were suspended at the Osirak site for a total of six months during 1980-81 because of the on-going hostilities with Iran. In any event, Iraq's blatant violation of the Geneva Protocol suggests Baghdad would have few qualms about openly abrogating its IAEA safeguards commitments. As for France's precaution of lightly irradiating the Osirak fuel, a number of U.S. experts believe this would no longer interfere with building a nuclear device, since the radiation level of the material would have diminished. Similarly, Iraq's building such a device would not be precluded by the fact that it now possesses substantially less than the twenty-five kilograms of highly enriched uranium the IAEA considers to be the minimum needed to make a crude bomb. According to several U.S. experts, the amount on hand might be sufficient if Iraq used a number of widely published weapons design improvements.[71]

Soviet Offer of Nuclear Power Reactor to Iraq

On March 22, 1984, Baghdad announced that the Soviet Union had agreed to build Iraq's first nuclear power plant.[72] The facility is likely to be a light-water reactor using low-enriched uranium fuel that cannot be directly used for nuclear weapons. However, plutonium produced in that fuel could be extracted, either in the Italian hot cells or in other facilities that Iraq might acquire by the time the Soviet plant is completed, probably not before the middle 1990s. One important non-proliferation measure that Moscow may require is that spent fuel from the reactor be returned to the Soviet Union without reprocessing. Soviet reactors exported to Eastern Europe are subject to this restriction.

Whether the Soviet Union will require tough non-proliferation controls of this kind, however, is uncertain. The very fact that Moscow decided to make a major new nuclear transfer to Iraq when it appeared that Iraq had initiated a nuclear-weapons development program and when it had only recently violated a major arms limitation treaty, suggests that the Soviet Union's interest in strengthening its ties to Iraq may outweigh its concerns over the possibility of proliferation there. On the other hand, the Soviet-Iraqi nuclear-sales agreement may amount to little more than a symbolic gesture. The Soviets made a similar commitment to Libya in 1977 but have yet to supply the nuclear power plant as promised.

Attempt to Purchase Plutonium

According to Italian news reports published as this book went to press, sometime over the past four years Iraq appears to have adopted a clandestine strategy to obtain nuclear arms unrelated to Osirak, by purchasing plutonium on the black market. In June 1984, after a four-year investigation, Italian authorities arraigned Colonel Massimo Pugliese, a former member of the Italian secret service, and twenty-nine other individuals, charging them with conspiring to export weapons illegally to Iraq and Somalia. Among the items Iraq was to have bought were thirty-four kilograms of plutonium (enough for four to six weapons), a metric ton of uranium (probably yellowcake), two metric tons of plastic explosives, and other equipment.[73]

When Iraq may have placed the order for the plutonium was not disclosed. If this occurred at about the time the Italian investigation began, apparently in early 1980, it would roughly coincide with France's imposition of new restrictions on the use of Osirak, which limited its potential for aiding Iraq in developing nuclear arms in the near term. The attempted plutonium purchase may thus have been an alternative strategy for obtaining nuclear arms relatively quickly, while Osirak was integrated into a longer-term nuclear weapons development program, as hypothesized above. It is also possible that the plutonium purchase order was placed after Osirak was destroyed, when indigenous production of nuclear weapons material no longer appeared feasible.

It seems unlikely that the Pugliese ring could have delivered the material to Iraq, however, since plutonium is subject to strict export controls and security measures. The episode is significant, nonetheless, because, if the facts as they have been alleged by Italian authorities are correct, there would no longer seem to be any question of Iraq's intent to obtain nuclear weapons as rapidly as possible or of its readiness to break its Non-Proliferation Treaty pledges not to manufacture such arms and to maintain IAEA safeguards on all of its nuclear activities.

III. Prospects for Nuclear Weapons in Iraq

Since the destruction of the Osirak reactor in 1981, Iraq's indigenous nuclear program has been dormant. The 12.5 kilograms of French-supplied highly enriched uranium fuel at the Osirak site, however, may pose an immediate, if limited, proliferation danger. In the longer term, French and Soviet nuclear assistance may revitalize Iraq's nuclear program, although any reconstruction of the Osirak plant with French aid would be subject to much more stringent non-proliferation measures than were applied to the facility originally.

In addition, Iraq's ongoing war with Iran has cut Iraqi oil exports to a trickle, and this is likely to restrict for some time Baghdad's ability to build a serious nuclear program. Without the leverage it once enjoyed as a major oil supplier, Iraq will have difficulty obtaining any but the most innocent nuclear commodities from the nuclear supplier countries. Moreover, the costs of the war, coupled with the loss of oil revenues, have taken a severe economic toll on Iraq, which is likely to preclude expenditures necessary for a substantial nuclear program.

On the other hand, the recent revelations in the Italian press of Iraq's attempt to purchase plutonium from black market sources would appear to indicate that its efforts to acquire nuclear arms have not ceased and to raise added doubts as to Iraq's commitment to the Non-Proliferation Treaty.

SOVIET UNION

TURKEY

SYRIA

Mosul

Arbela

Kirkuk

Sulaymaniyah

IRAN

Tigris River

Euphrates

I R A Q

Baghdad
(Tuwaitha)

Karbala

Hillah

Najaf

River

JORDAN

Basra

SAUDI ARABIA

Persian
Gulf

IRAQ

0   300

MILES

Iraq

Research Reactors

Osirak, Tammuz I (light-water/highly enriched uranium, 40 MWt)
- supplier: France
- start up: Destroyed by Israel June 1981, prior to start up; future status uncertain.
- fuel source: France
- safeguards: yes

Isis, Tammuz II (light-water/highly enriched uranium, 800 KWt[a])
- supplier: France
- start up: 1980 (?)
- fuel source: France
- safeguards: yes

IRT-2000 (light-water/highly enriched uranium, 5 MWt)[c]
- supplier: Soviet Union
- start up: 1968
- fuel source: Soviet Union[c]
- safeguards: yes

Uranium Resources/Active Mining Sites/Uranium Mills
- reasonably assured reserves: none
- currently active site: none
- mills in operation: none[d]

Uranium Purification (UO$_6$)

Tuwaitha (laboratory scale)
- capacity: ?
- supplier: Italy
- start up: not operating (?)
- safeguards: yes

Fuel Fabrication

Tuwaitha
- capacity: ?
- supplier: Italy
- start up: not operating (?)
- safeguards: yes

Reprocessing
- capacity: 8 kg plutonium per year[e]
- supplier: Italy
- start up: not operating (?)
- safeguards: yes

Sources and Notes

a. Steve Weissman and Herbert Krosney, *The Islamic Bomb* (New York: Times Books, 1981), pp. 94, 100, 266.

b. Congressional Research Service, *Analysis of Six Issues About Nuclear Capabilities of India, Iraq, Libya, and Pakistan,* prepared for the Subcommittee of Arms Control, Oceans, and International Operations and Environment of the Senate Foreign Relations Committee (1982).

c. Jed C. Snyder, "The Road to Osiraq: Baghdad's Quest for the Bomb," *The Middle East Journal,* (Autumn 1983), p. 1.

d. Yellowcake supplied from Portugal, Brazil, and Niger, *Congressional Research Service, Six Issues,* p. 46.

e. Richard Burt, "U.S. Says Italy Sells Iraq Atomic Bomb Technology," *New York Times,* March 18, 1980, p. 1. Five to ten kg of plutonium per year, Weissman and Krosney, *The Islamic Bomb,* p. 268.

Chapter IV:
Latin America

Introduction

Argentina and Brazil pose the only serious risks of proliferation in Latin America for the remainder of this century. Chile and Cuba are sometimes mentioned as potential proliferators—largely because they have refused to implement non-proliferation treaties barring the development of nuclear arms—but their nuclear development programs are so rudimentary as to rule out any danger for the foreseeable future.

Both Argentina and Brazil have declared repeatedly that their programs are dedicated exclusively to peaceful ends. Although there is no publicly available information to indicate that either nation is actively seeking to develop nuclear arms, both are constructing enrichment and reprocessing plants capable of producing readily usable nuclear weapons material, both have rejected placing all their nuclear activities under International Atomic Energy Agency (IAEA) safeguards, and both have refused to renounce nuclear explosives through binding treaty pledges under the Nuclear Non-Proliferation Treaty or the Treaty of Tlatelolco. These actions raise fears that Argentina and Brazil may be working quietly towards nuclear weapons capabilities that could be exercised without violating international undertakings.

Why these nations might pursue this course is less clear. Neither faces a serious external security threat or a nuclear-armed regional rival, the usual spurs to proliferation. While Argentina, in the wake of the Falklands War, might reason that a small nuclear deterrent could in the future avert interventions similar to Britain's, all the elements of its nuclear program that might contribute to such a deterrent were initiated well before the Falklands crisis.

The best explanation is that both nations view nuclear development as a potentially critical factor in their long-standing competition for regional pre-eminence and, at a minimum, an area in which neither can afford to fall far behind. Over the years, nationalistic desires for nuclear mastery, combined with concerns about their neighbor's nuclear program, have propelled Buenos Aires and Brasilia ever closer to attaining de facto nuclear weapons capabilities.

The process seems to have been one of action and reaction. By the early 1970s, responding to Argentina's nuclear accomplishments, some Brazilian analysts feared that Buenos Aires might be tempted to build nuclear weapons in order to close the widening military and economic gap between the two states resulting from Brazil's extraordinary growth. These concerns reportedly influenced Brazil's decision in 1975 to purchase enrichment and reprocessing technology subject to international inspection. Argentina, in turn, stimulated by these developments and its desire to attain nuclear independence from the advanced supplier countries, soon initiated its own enrichment and large-scale reprocessing projects, the former in secret, rapidly matching the Brazilian effort in these sensitive areas, while accepting far more limited international oversight of its nuclear program. Recently, Brazil's Figueiredo government, apparently responding to these developments, has intensified its own efforts to develop capabilities for producing nuclear weapons material. Today, Argentina is possibly five years ahead of its northern rival and can probably achieve a nuclear weapons capability in the next several years if it diligently pursues its present course. Brazil is unlikely to complete the requirements for building nuclear arms before the early 1990s.

While neither nation may be planning now to develop or test nuclear explosives, efforts to maintain rough parity in the race to acquire the capacity to accumulate nuclear weapons material—and thus the capacity to produce a bomb quickly once a decision to do so has been taken—have been manifest for over a decade. Once nuclear weapons material is in hand, the temptation to proceed further (for example, through the test of a "peaceful nuclear explosive") may prove far stronger than it appears today.

Nevertheless, external political pressures, fears of triggering an active nuclear arms race, and increasing cooperation between Argentina and Brazil in the nuclear field are important countervailing factors; so, too, are financial constraints. Furthermore, most—but not all—of the pathways to development of a nuclear device would require violation of clear-cut international obligations, including IAEA safeguards, that would carry considerable diplomatic costs.

Argentina's new civilian government is currently reappraising the Argentine nuclear program. Should it significantly alter the program's direction, either by accepting increased international supervision over it or by suspending development of its more provocative facilities, Brazil might well be prepared to follow suit, and the incipient race in Latin America to develop nuclear weapons capabilities might be halted or at least deferred.

Argentina

I. Background

Argentina's nuclear program, which dates from 1950, is the most advanced in Latin America. Over the years Argentina has worked consistently to minimize International Atomic Energy Agency (IAEA) safeguards and treaty constraints on its nuclear affairs, while striving to attain nuclear self-sufficiency. Through these efforts, it has both preserved its right to develop nuclear explosives and made steady progress toward achieving the capability for doing so.

Early Capabilities. The early phase of Argentina's nuclear development began on a false note in 1951 when former Third Reich scientist, Ronald Richter, director of a team of Argentine nuclear researchers, fraudulently claimed to have conducted the first controlled nuclear fusion experiments. Even so, under the auspices of its National Atomic Energy Commission

(CNEA), established the previous year, Argentina's nuclear specialists were soon conducting serious research on a range of subjects.[1] CNEA began to produce uranium in 1953 and annual output reached 58,000 tons of ore by 1965, by which time two small uranium mills were also in operation. In 1955 Argentina signed an agreement for nuclear cooperation with the United States. Under that accord, Argentina built its first research reactor (the RA-1) in 1958 using U.S plans. That early assistance in developing domestic capabilities enabled Argentina to build three additional research reactors on its own by 1967. Despite this unusually high degree of self-sufficiency, Argentina was obliged to accept IAEA safeguards on these facilities (and on a German-supplied research reactor that began operating in 1972) because they used enriched uranium fuel imported from the United States, imported equipment, or both.

First Nuclear Power Plant and Avoidance of Safeguards. In the mid-1960s, Argentina began negotiations to purchase its first nuclear power plant, and according to the former head of the Argentine nuclear power program, selected not a German natural-uranium/heavy-water reactor, as widely reported, but a French natural-uranium/gas-graphite reactor. At the last minute, however, France backed out of the deal without explanation.[2] One factor that triggered Argentine interest in the French reactor was that it used natural uranium fuel, thus avoiding ongoing dependence on the United States, then the sole supplier of the enriched-uranium fuel that the more widely used U.S.-style light-water reactors would have required.[3] Another factor that may have influenced Argentina was that the reactor was particularly well suited to producing plutonium for nuclear explosives and is a model similar to the one France uses to produce plutonium for its own nuclear weapons program. What arrangements might have covered the sale had it gone through are not known, nor is the extent to which French proliferation concerns influenced its decision to cancel the deal.

After a careful study of alternatives, CNEA solicited bids from other vendors and in 1968 ordered a 320-megawatt natural-uranium/heavy-water reactor, known as Atucha I, from the West German firm Siemens AG. Argentine officials attributed this choice to the favorable commercial terms of the German bid and, again, a desire to avoid reliance on the United States for fuel.[4] Argentina remained dependent on the United States to supply the 340 metric tons of heavy water (a metric ton = 2200 pounds) for the plant and, until the early 1980s, had to rely on another external supplier, West Germany, to fabricate Argentine uranium concentrate into fuel rods for the reactor. The choice of the West German reactor thus provided no greater independence than would have been offered by a U.S. light-water reactor, which has led to speculation that there was a secret military purpose behind its selection. Some observers have noted, for example, that the natural-uranium reactor would produce more plutonium in its spent fuel than a U.S.-style reactor and could be refueled without shutting down, making it more difficult to safeguard. These points appear to be at least technically accurate, and Brazil is reported to have taken them seriously.[5] Others have claimed the selection was based on a secret offer from West German nuclear aides to assist Argentina in building a laboratory-scale reprocessing plant to permit extraction of the plutonium from spent fuel. Such a facility was built in 1969, in fact, but the project was initiated prior to conclusion of the West German reactor sale. German officials have denied assisting the effort.[6]

Argentina also sought to maintain autonomy over

its use of its first nuclear power plant by limiting IAEA oversight of the facility. Although Buenos Aires acceded to West Germany's requirement that the plant be subject to an IAEA safeguards agreement, Argentina insisted when it negotiated the accord with the Agency several years later that safeguards would be applied to the plant only for an initial term of five years, to be extended, "as both parties deem convenient," i.e., only if Argentina subsequently agreed to extensions.[7] This effort to exploit the loophole in the Atucha I agreement with Bonn might have succeeded but for the fact that to obtain heavy water for the reactor from the United States (and, subsequently, fuel fabrication technology from West Germany), Argentina was obliged to accept long-term safeguards on the plant. The Atucha I plant began generating electricity in 1974.

Argentina's 1968 attempt to lay the groundwork for limiting application of IAEA safeguards to its nuclear program coincided roughly with a series of parallel actions in other settings to avoid restrictions on its nuclear affairs. In the negotiations on the text of the 1967 Treaty of Tlatelolco, Argentina supported Brazil's proposed wording that sought to preserve the right of treaty parties to conduct "peaceful nuclear explosions." Although this wording was approved, Argentina nonetheless refused to ratify the accord after signing it in 1967. Argentina also refused to join the Nuclear Non-Proliferation Treaty (NPT) when it was opened for signature in 1968 and, indeed, was one of only a handful of nations to abstain from the June 1968 U.N. General Assembly vote commending the treaty.[8] Both treaties would have required Argentina to accept IAEA safeguards on all of its nuclear activities indefinitely. Argentina has continually objected to the Non-Proliferation Treaty on grounds that its prohibition of nuclear arms and requirement of full-scope safeguards apply only to states that had not tested a nuclear weapon by 1967, while those that had conducted such a test, the "nuclear weapon states," remain free to pursue the arms race.[9] Its objections to the Tlatelolco Treaty have varied over the years, as discussed below.

Initial Reprocessing Activities. In concert with rejection of these accords and its efforts to limit the duration of safeguards on Atucha I, the CNEA began to construct a laboratory-scale reprocessing facility for extracting nuclear-weapons-usable plutonium from spent reactor fuel.[10] According to the U.S. Department of State, the plant consisted "essentially of a number of laboratory hot cells for handling radioactive materials" that "became operational in 1969 and operated intermittently until it was dismantled in 1973."[11] Despite Argentina's rejection of the Tlatelolco and Non-Proliferation Treaties, the United States granted approval to Argentina to reprocess approximately thirteen kilograms (1 kilogram = 2.2 pounds) of U.S.-supplied spent medium-enriched uranium fuel from the RA-1 research reactor.[12] The plant produced only inconsequential amounts of plutonium, "less, and probably a great deal less than one kilogram," according to the State Department, although other sources have alleged that larger amounts were obtained.[13] Even if its output was trivial, however, the plant provided Argentine nuclear scientists with invaluable experience in this portion of the nuclear fuel cycle and laid the basis for development, a decade later, of a larger reprocessing facility.

Second Nuclear Power Plant. In 1972 Argentina solicited bids for a second six hundred-megawatt nuclear power plant to be located at Embalse. In the hopes of achieving greater autonomy, Argentina again selected a natural-uranium/heavy-water plant, this time to be purchased from the consortium of Atomic Energy of Canada Limited and Italimpianti, the Italian engineering firm.

The precise reason for the selection of the Canadian plant is unclear. Reportedly a Canadian offer of an ancillary technology-transfer agreement was a key factor, but bribery and the plant's superior plutonium production capabilities in comparison to light-water reactors have also been identified as playing a role.[14]

Once again, Argentine negotiators sought to minimize restrictions on use of the plant and reportedly gained Canada's agreement that IAEA safeguards coverage would be limited to fifteen years. In the aftermath of Argentina's negotiations on Atucha I, however, the IAEA Board of Governors had upgraded the requirements for safeguards agreements. Moreover, following India's 1974 nuclear test, Canada sought to enhance the non-proliferation controls over the Embalse plant. Argentina ultimately accepted an agreement that extended IAEA safeguards coverage for as long as the Embalse reactor or any plutonium produced in it remained in Argentina and potentially useful for nuclear weapons.[15] The Embalse reactor began generating electricity in 1983.

Gaining Nuclear Autonomy and Access to Nuclear Weapons Material. Argentina's military government, which took power in March 1976, accelerated its predecessor's efforts to achieve nuclear self-sufficiency, motivated in large part by Brazil's 1975 deal with West Germany to obtain a complete "nuclear fuel cycle," including reprocessing and enrichment capabilities, with their obvious military potential.[16] Indeed, in 1977 the CNEA began to construct a small reprocessing facility at the Ezeiza Atomic Center. The facility, first announced in 1978, was to produce ten to twenty kilograms of plutonium per year, enough nuclear material for several weapons.[17]

CNEA spokesmen at the time stated that since the facility was based on indigenous technology, it would not be subject to IAEA safeguards except when reprocessing fuel from reactors under IAEA safeguards.[18] Nonetheless, the Italian company Techint, which had sold Iraq a hot-cell reprocessing unit in 1976, apparently participated in the construction of the facility through an Argentine entity of the same name, raising the possibility that important technology was transferred from Italy under the arrangement.[19] If substantial foreign assistance was provided, Argentina's grounds for limiting the application of safeguards may be open to challenge.

Concern that the plant might ultimately be aimed at assisting Argentina to obtain a nuclear weapons capability has been heightened by the fact that given Argentina's small nuclear power program and ample uranium resources, there appears to be no obvious non-military need for the plant's plutonium output. CNEA's then-president, Carlos Castro Madero, repeatedly defended the plant, however, by arguing that using mixed plutonium-uranium fuel in Argentina's nuclear power reactors would allow uranium savings of 50 percent. In addition, he argued that Argentina needed to demonstrate its mastery of this technology in order to be taken as a serious nuclear supplier in Latin America[20] and that excess output could be sold for breeder reactor programs abroad, presumably in Western Europe and Japan.[21] (While work on the facility apparently has continued steadily since this period, the plant has been substantially delayed and is not expected to start up until at least 1986.[22])

Despite these public justifications for the installation, privately Castro Madero acknowledged that it was being built as a response to Brazil's purchase of reprocessing and enrichment plants from West Germany in 1975. The revelation was made during Argentine-U.S. negotiations in 1977-78 on the possible sale of heavy-water production technology to Argentina, discussed below. According to a former U.S. government official familiar with these negotiations, the United States hinted it might be prepared to sell the technology on the condition that Argentina halt construction of the Ezeiza reprocessing plant. Castro Madero responded that the deal would have been acceptable several years earlier, but now that Brazil had suddenly pushed ahead of Argentina, abandonment of the Ezeiza project could not be considered.[23]

The CNEA began work on another secret project at roughly the same time: construction of a small uranium enrichment facility. This facility, whose existence was not announced until late 1983, could eventually supply highly enriched uranium suitable for nuclear weapons, although, like the Ezeiza reprocessing plant, Argentina has justified it as a necessary part of its civilian nuclear energy program. Quite possibly, however, it, too, was motivated by a desire to match the enrichment capability West Germany was providing Brazil as part of their 1975 deal.

In the mid- to late 1970s Argentina's military government also took steps to develop indigenous means for producing nuclear fuel and heavy water. In order to achieve autonomy as rapidly as possible, while also minimizing the application of IAEA safeguards to its nuclear program, the CNEA imported key technology and equipment for one of each of the plants it would need, accepting IAEA coverage on these facilities while simultaneously developing a parallel, unsafeguarded facility based on indigenous technology.

At the Ezeiza Atomic Center, for example, a commercial-scale fuel fabrication line to produce fuel for the Atucha I reactor, based on West German technology, was well advanced by 1979. Efforts to build fuel fabrication lines for Argentina's other nuclear reactors, based on indigenous technology, also were proceeding. Elsewhere, an experimental plant was operating for converting uranium concentrate, or "yellowcake," into purified uranium dioxide (UO_2) to serve as feed stock for the fabrication process. One unit of this plant also relied on equipment from West Germany; a second was indigenous.[24]

Heavy-Water Technology and the Tlatelolco Treaty. Obtaining the capability to produce heavy water, however, proved particularly difficult because of the strong restrictions enforced by the nuclear supplier countries. The United States, for one, feared that with its own heavy-water manufacturing capability, Argentina would have the full range of facilities needed to develop atomic weapons as well as added opportunities to avoid international safeguards. Moreover, Buenos Aires would be far less vulnerable to the threat of a nuclear supply cutoff in the event that it someday moved in the direction of developing such arms overtly. These restrictions led the CNEA as early as 1975 to begin research for development of a purely domestic heavy-water-manufacturing capability.[25]

Possibly in the hopes that nuclear supplier restrictions might be eased, Argentine president Jorge Rafael Videla agreed in a September 1977 meeting with U.S. president Jimmy Carter to ratify the Treaty of Tlatelolco.[26] It became clear, however, that unless Argentina were prepared to abandon the Ezeiza reprocessing plant, the United States was willing to sell only heavy water to Argentina, not equipment for its manufacture. Shortly afterwards Argentina reverted to its traditional opposition to the accord. Its principal stated objection raised in the course of negotiating the full-scope safeguards agreement called for by the treaty was that the IAEA, the United States, Britain, and the USSR had interpreted the treaty in a manner that would preclude parties from developing peaceful nuclear explosives, an option Argentina was not prepared to give up.[27] Argentina's change of heart on ratification of the treaty also coincided with protracted delays in U.S. enriched-uranium exports (needed for Argentina's research reactors), caused by human rights and proliferation concerns in the United States.[28]

With the possibility of U.S. heavy-water-manufacturing assistance apparently foreclosed, the CNEA began in February 1979 to construct an experimental two to four metric-tons-per-year heavy-water production plant at Atucha using its domestically developed technology. For comparison, Argentina's planned research reactor, the RA-7, will need 50 metric tons for its initial charge; the Atucha I plant required 320 metric tons of the material. Argentina has refused safeguards on the plant, claiming it is being built without foreign assistance. According to an Argentine nuclear spokesman quoted in the press, however, Argentina has purchased important components for the plant abroad—including some from the United States—by employing "subterfuges and intermediaries." If so, Argentina's basis for refusing safeguards may be invalid and some exports may have occurred in conflict with the export standards adopted by the major nuclear supplier countries in the mid-1970s, known as the Nuclear Suppliers' Guidelines.[29]

Concurrent with initiation of the Atucha heavy-water plant, the CNEA solicited construction bids from foreign vendors for a 250-metric-ton-per-year heavy-water facility in conjunction with bids for Argentina's third nuclear power plant, to be situated at the Atucha I site.[30]

Atucha II and Avoidance of Full-Scope Safeguards. The United States continued to press Argentina to ratify the Tlatelolco accord, spurred by reports that the CNEA was also developing a large, unsafeguarded natural-uranium/heavy-water research reactor—the RA-7. The United States feared that plutonium-bearing spent fuel from the reactor could be reprocessed in the then recently announced Ezeiza plant without international supervision to produce plutonium for perhaps several nuclear weapons per year. U.S. non-proliferation officials also began parallel attempts to persuade Canada and West Germany—the two leading contenders for the Atucha II reactor and commercial heavy-water plant contracts—to make Argentina's ratification of the treaty, or separate acceptance of full-scope safeguards (i.e., IAEA inspection of all Argentina's nuclear activities present and future), a condition for the sale.

Although Canada had previously adopted this stance, West Germany had rejected it when it had been proposed as a uniform nuclear export condition during the 1974-77 meetings of the Nuclear Suppliers Group.[31] Washington feared that unless West Germany joined Canada in conditioning the sale on Argentina's acceptance of full-scope safeguards Canada's tough non-proliferation stand would be undercut and Argentina would feel little pressure to accept wider safeguards.

By arguing that inclusion of the sensitive heavy-water plant merited non-proliferation controls beyond those West Germany had been willing to impose in the past—and by playing on the possibility that Bonn might need to buy substantial quantities of U.S. heavy water for the first charge of the Atucha II reactor—the

United States persuaded West Germany to require full-scope safeguards as a condition for the sale, consistent with Canada's policy.[32]

In October, 1979, the CNEA decided to split the project, however, accepting a bid of the West German Kraftwerk Union (KWU) to build a natural-uranium/heavy-water nuclear power plant at Atucha (Atucha II) and a bid submitted by the Swiss Sulzer Brothers firm to construct the 250-metric-ton-per-year heavy-water production facility at Arroyito. Since the Swiss were not insisting that Argentina accept full-scope safeguards as a condition for purchasing the heavy-water plant, Germany argued that it was not obliged to demand full safeguards for the purchase of the less sensitive Atucha II reactor.[33] Although Castro Madero denied that Argentina had accepted the far more costly West German-Swiss bid[34] in order to avoid stringent safeguards, off-the-record comments by other Argentine officials involved and the details of the deal itself support the view that the safeguards question was a factor.[35]

In the following months as the West German and Swiss governments reviewed export authorizations for the two plants, the United States urged them to reconsider the decision not to require full safeguards coverage as a condition for the sales.[36] In the end, amid rumors that U.S. pressure was easing, the West Europeans prevailed, insisting that their sales fully complied with the Nuclear Suppliers' Guidelines.[37] Nevertheless, U.S. criticism prompted Bonn and Berne to insist upon unusually strong safeguards, including the requirement that any facilities based on technology transferred in conjunction with the two plants would also be under safeguards. However, the agreement did not preclude Argentina's pursuit of its expanding parallel unsafeguarded nuclear activities.

U.S. Support for Heavy-Water Plant. Upon taking office in January 1981, the Reagan administration took a conciliatory approach in its efforts to reduce the risks of Argentine proliferation and, among other efforts to improve nuclear relations, in mid-1981 approved the export of a sophisticated Foxboro Corporation process control computer to Argentina for use in the Sulzer Brothers heavy-water plant.[38]

Despite these overtures, little changed in Argentina's public declarations concerning its stance on the NPT, the Treaty of Tlatelolco, or its reservation of the right to develop peaceful nuclear explosives (PNEs).[39] Nevertheless, then CNEA president Castro Madero underscored that Argentina had no intention of developing PNEs and that he believed that the development of nuclear weapons by any Latin American nation would serve no purpose and would trigger a wasteful nuclear arms race.[40]

The Falklands Crisis. The 1982 Falklands War appeared to have little visible impact on the Argentine nuclear program. Buenos Aires condemned British use of nuclear submarines as contrary to the principles of non-proliferation and accused the British of bringing tactical nuclear weapons into the area.[41] In response, Argentina declared, it would consider itself free to pursue development of nuclear submarines, and a CNEA feasibility study was launched. Argentina continued to pledge, however, not to build nuclear arms.[42]

Nuclear Imports and Exports. Despite its considerable degree of autonomy, Argentina has depended on outside sources for a variety of key nuclear materials and equipment. Between 1980 and 1982, for example, it imported 6 metric tons of heavy water from the USSR to make up for losses at Atucha I (1.5 metric tons per year) and reportedly obtained an additional quantity of the material from the People's Republic of China.[43] Similarly, the Soviet Union provided one hundred kilograms of 20 percent enriched fuel for Argentine research reactors, and Buenos Aires made arrangements to purchase twelve kilograms of the material from China, although the deal may have been postponed in 1982 because of Argentina's growing economic problems.[44] In addition, Argentina had imported three zirconium-rolling mills from the USSR (after being turned down by France)[45] and has been importing fabricated fuel from Canada for the Embalse reactor.[46] The CNEA had also arranged with KWU to have the lower portion of the Atucha II power plant vessel manufactured in Brazil by a joint KWU-Brazilian Nuclear Corporation subsidiary. A U.S. firm, Combustion Engineering, had originally won the order for the vessel, but the export was prohibited under the 1978 U.S. Nuclear Non-Proliferation Act.[47] Finally, Argentina was apparently relying on French assistance in the construction of its uranium-concentrating plants.[48] These transactions indicate that Argentina continues to require substantial imports from the nuclear supplier nations to support its nuclear power program, although its level of self-sufficiency is steadily increasing.

At the same time, Argentina has also become a nuclear exporter in its own right. By mid-1983 it had supplied Peru with two research reactors, some fourteen kilograms of U.S.-supplied enriched uranium, and associated laboratories;[49] had agreed to construct an experimental reactor, associated research facilities, and pilot uranium treatment plant in Colombia;[50] and was holding discussions with Uruguay on building a nuclear research center there.[51] In addition, it was said to have exported uranium concentrate to Israel and to be planning further uranium exports.[52] Castro Madero has also repeatedly indicated that Argentina might export nuclear-weapons-usable plutonium once its Ezeiza reprocessing plant starts up.[53]

Argentina also has signed numerous nuclear cooperation agreements under which a range of exports may be offered, including those with Peru, India, Yugoslavia, Colombia, Uruguay, Romania, Chile, Paraguay, Ecuador, Bolivia, Venezuela and Libya.[54] Argentina's nuclear ties to Libya, including the possibility that Argentina might have offered Libya technology on nuclear-weapons-material production facilities in return for $100 million in arms shipments during the Falklands War, are discussed in the chapter on Libya.

Given Argentina's reluctance to adopt strict non-proliferation controls over its domestic nuclear program, these exports have raised fears that Argentina might not insist on tough limitations on the use of material and equipment it supplies to others. Argentina's declared policy, however, is to require that its nuclear export recipients place Argentine equipment and material under IAEA safeguards.[55]

Nuclear Cooperation with Brazil. CNEA has signed contracts with the government-owned Brazilian Nuclear Corporation (NUCLEBRAS) for the lease to Brazil of 240 metric tons of uranium concentrate, which Brazil subsequently "returned" when its uranium-mining activities were expanded, and for the supply of 160,000 meters of zircaloy tubing to manufacture fuel elements for future Brazilian nuclear power plants.[56] In addition, the CNEA made two agreements with Brazil's National Atomic Energy Commission for the exchange of technical information and for reciprocal use of training centers.[57]

Taken together with the CNEA-NUCLEBRAS agreement for the manufacture of a major portion of the Atucha II pressure vessel,[58] the nuclear ties between the two nations have been quite substantial and demonstrate that their nuclear relationship has not been exclusively competitive. Indeed, Castro Madero has called the relationship one of "mutual respect and sincere cooperation,"[59] and has stressed that Brazil supported Argentina's endeavors to complete its far-reaching nuclear program in the face of advanced supplier nation attempts to restrict it.[60] Nevertheless, Argentina's effort to maintain a clear lead over Brazil in the highly symbolic nuclear field leaves little doubt that the dominant theme in their nuclear relations is rivalry.

II. Developments of the Past Year

From mid-1983 to mid-1984, the past trends of Argentina's nuclear development were largely reaffirmed, although the apparent openness of the nation's new government to added non-proliferation measures has raised hopes that major changes in the program may ultimately be implemented. In November 1983, CNEA president Castro Madero dramatically announced that Argentina had been clandestinely developing an additional part of the nuclear fuel cycle that could provide direct access to nuclear-weapons-usable highly enriched uranium. In subsequent months, Argentina's newly elected civilian leaders reiterated their nation's unwillingness to join the Non-Proliferation Treaty or, at least in the near term, to ratify the Treaty of Tlatelolco. Nevertheless, the government's prompt actions to bring Argentina's nuclear program under civilian control and to introduce legislation prohibiting development of nuclear weapons gave evidence of its intent to restrict the nation's nuclear program to peaceful ends. Coupled with budget cuts that may slow development of the more provocative elements of the Argentine nuclear program, these changes may portend a major reduction in the danger of Argentine proliferation.

During this period, finally, efforts of interested foreign nations, especially the United States, to influence Argentina's nuclear policies remained tentative and appeared to have little impact on their direction.

U.S. Approval of West German Heavy-Water Sale to Argentina. On August 2, 1983, the U.S. Department of Energy approved West Germany's request to transfer 143 metric tons of U.S.-origin heavy water to Argentina.[61] A portion of the material was intended to make up losses at the the Atucha I and Embalse reactors, but the bulk of it was to be added to Argentina's stockpile of heavy water, apparently for later use in the Atucha II reactor.[62] The U.S. right to approve the transfer arose from its having originally supplied the material to West Germany for use in demonstration reactors.[63]

The U.S. approval was immediately criticized in Congress as an attempt by the Reagan administration to undercut the provisions of the 1978 Nuclear Non-Proliferation Act forbidding U.S. export of nuclear reactors and fuel to nations refusing to accept full-scope safeguards.[64] Although the 1978 act did not bar exports or retransfers of nuclear "components" (including heavy water) to such countries, the congressional critics charged that approval of the heavy-water sale ran counter to the basic purpose of the act's embargo, namely, putting pressure on hold-out nations to adopt full-scope safeguards by denying aid to their nuclear programs.[65] They also contended that the approval was part of a pattern of Reagan administration actions extending nuclear trade to nations with unsafeguarded facilities by exploiting loopholes in and otherwise circumventing the 1978 act.[66]

The Reagan administration defended its decision to approve the heavy-water transfer on the grounds that all the requirements of U.S. law were met and that the heavy water and any plutonium produced through its use in Argentina would be under IAEA safeguards. Furthermore, they pointed out that the Carter administration had permitted exports of certain nuclear components to Argentina.[67] In addition, the approval was justified as part of the administration's broader policy of seeking to gain tightened non-proliferation controls by using lesser nuclear transactions as goodwill gestures to establish a dialogue with nuclear officials in countries of proliferation concern.[68]

Additionally, administration officials apparently feared the possibility that another supplier might be willing to provide the heavy water without safeguards. The principal alternative commercial suppliers appear to have been Canada, the Soviet Union, and China.[69] However, with Canada apparently unwilling to enter into new nuclear trade with Argentina unless it accepted full-scope safeguards, and with Argentina already having difficulty negotiating with the USSR and China for small quantities of heavy water,[70] it appears that the risk of another supplier's stepping in was not a serious one. In fact, U.S. control over large quantities of needed heavy water appeared to offer it a certain amount of leverage for negotiating with Argentina for stricter non-proliferation measures.[71]

For its part, West Germany defended the transfer on the grounds that Argentina's nuclear program was already fully under safeguards, a view the IAEA itself appears to accept.[72] Thus, in Bonn's view, U.S. critics had no right to complain that Germany was making imprudent nuclear exports.

This view of the safeguards status of the Argentine nuclear program was not, however, accepted by the

U.S. State Department, which, as noted, supported the heavy-water transfer on other grounds. U.S. experts believed Argentina had been operating an unsafeguarded uranium purification plant at Córdoba and had reserved the right to fabricate material from it into fuel elements in the pilot fuel fabrication line at Ezeiza without safeguards. Since Argentina had not, apparently, formally declared these aspects of its program to the IAEA (it is currently using safeguarded material in the pilot fuel fabrication line), the IAEA— and West Germany—were able to claim that in Argentina "all substantial nuclear activities known to the Agency" are under safeguards.[73]

Finally, Great Britain, only recently victorious in the Falklands War, had also acquiesced in the transfer. In the 1970s, Britain's Central Electricity Generating Board, expecting to embark on a heavy-water reactor construction program, had taken an option on one hundred metric tons of the West German material. After the Board decided to develop light-water reactors instead, the option went unexercised until, in 1981, West Germany pressed for the British to take the material or relinquish it so that it could be sold to Argentina. Before the matter was resolved, the Falklands conflict erupted. Afterwards, Britain chose not to take the material, which would have deprived Argentina of its use, reportedly because Britain would have been forced to construct storage facilities.[74]

Thus three of the principal nuclear suppliers had together agreed to a major new sale to Argentina of needed material, probably not otherwise available, despite Argentina's continued rejection of full-scope safeguards, its reservation of the right to conduct peaceful nuclear explosives, and its active development of a reprocessing plant that would shortly be able to provide it with nuclear weapons material.[75]

Revelation of Secret Uranium
Enrichment Plant.

On November 18, 1983, just weeks before the installation of Raul Alfonsín, Argentina's first democratically
elected leader since 1973, CNEA president Castro
Madero made the startling announcement that after a
series of successful pilot experiments, Argentina had
completed construction of a "medium size" uranium
enrichment plant using the gaseous diffusion method.
The project to build the facility and develop its complex technology had been initiated in 1978, he revealed, and conducted in total secrecy.[76]

The facility, in the city of Pilcaniyeu, appeared to
represent a major technological and political accomplishment for Argentina, since only a handful of nations, generally the world's most advanced, had previously mastered the enrichment process.[77] The new
enrichment plant also posed a major new proliferation
danger, because in principle it could shortly provide
Argentina with the capability to enrich uranium to
weapons grade levels. Although so far the plant had
apparently produced only a few kilograms of slightly
enriched uranium,[78] the CNEA hoped it would be able
to turn out five hundred kilograms of 20 percent enriched uranium a year by 1985, a capability which U.S.
experts feared could easily be transformed into an
annual production of 100 kilograms of 90 percent enriched material, enough for four to six nuclear weapons.[79] Asserting that the $62.5 million plant was essen-
tially indigenous, since only 15 percent of it had been
imported,[80] CNEA spokesmen declared that Argentina did not intend to place it under IAEA safeguards,[81] a decision further heightening concerns that
the plant might someday be used for nuclear weapons.

Castro Madero and Argentine president-elect Raul Alfonsín strongly insisted, however, that the plant would be used strictly for peaceful purposes, and the former cited the public disclosure of the theretofore secret facility as proof that it was not part of a covert nuclear weapons development program.[82] Castro Madero also reiterated earlier declarations that it would be "absolutely useless and non-productive" for Argentina to develop nuclear weapons and would be "inviting or provoking other countries to do the same."[83]

The CNEA president offered a number of justifications for the construction of the plant and for the secrecy surrounding the project. The decision to undertake development of an enrichment capability, he said, was made in view of the 1978 U.S. cutoff of enriched uranium for Argentina's research reactors, which were needed to produce radioisotopes for medicine and agriculture;[84] to enable Argentina to provide fuel for the enriched-uranium research reactors it was hoping to export to other Latin American countries, thereby putting Argentina on an equal footing with other suppliers of such reactors (principally the United States);[85] and to permit the use of slightly (one percent) enriched uranium in Argentina's own heavy-water power reactors, an option Castro Madero claimed could cut the reactors' uranium consumption by 50 percent.[86]

These rationales left a number of questions unresolved. First, the plant's announced capacity in 1985 of 500 kilograms per year of 20 percent enriched uranium would be over sixteen times greater than the yearly 20-to-30 kilogram demand of Argentina's research reactors and expected exports for this material. Replacement of terminated U.S. enriched-uranium exports thus hardly seems to have been the principal justification for construction of the plant, and, indeed, Castro Madero claimed that after "sufficient stocks" of 20 percent material were in hand, the plant would be shifted over to producing fifteen metric tons of 1 percent enriched material for Argentina's power reactors.[87] The use of slightly enriched material in heavy-water reactors, however, though theoretically feasible, is not practiced by any other nation operating such plants. Critics have also argued that the full costs of producing this 1 percent material would far outweigh any savings.[88]

This suggests that undeclared rationales for the project may have been important. First, Argentine nuclear planners may have sought to keep pace with Brazil, which under its 1975 deal with West Germany, proposed to construct both reprocessing and enrichment plants. The 1978 decision to build the Pilcaniyeu enrichment facility took place at approximately the same time as the decision to build the Ezeiza reprocessing plant, so the two may have been considered together as a way of responding to the Brazilian program.

Secondly, CNEA planners may have believed that an enrichment plant had the potential for providing the quickest route to obtaining nuclear weapons material not subject to IAEA safeguards for use in a possible future nuclear explosives program. To obtain unsafeguarded plutonium using the Ezeiza reprocessing facility, a large unsafeguarded research reactor (the RA-7) would also have to be built, along with unsafeguarded uranium purification and fuel fabrication facilities and heavy-water plants. Even after all these installations were in place, moreover, perhaps only enough unsafeguarded plutonium for one or two explosive devices per year could be produced, depending in part on the size of the RA-7. The enrichment

route, in contrast, held out the possibility of both bypassing safeguards through construction of a single,
albeit technically complex, facility and of creating far
greater quantities of nuclear weapons material.[89]

Plainly, the secrecy surrounding the Argentine enrichment project suggests its objectives went beyond
contributing to Argentina's highly publicized nuclear
energy and research program. Nonetheless, CNEA
president Castro Madero defended keeping the program under wraps on the ground that the United States
and other nuclear suppliers would have brought strong
pressures to bear to thwart the effort.[90] Moreover, he
claimed he did not want to create false expectations
regarding the project which, had it failed, might have
looked like an embarrassing replay of the 1951 Richter
affair.[91]

The Reagan administration's measured reaction to
the announcement of the Pilcaniyeu plant was limited
to calling upon Argentina to place the facility under
IAEA safeguards. Privately, U.S. officials were dis-
mayed at the apparent failure of American intelligence
efforts to discover a plant that had been under development for five years.[92] Far more disturbing, U.S. officials saw development of the facility as a major setback
for American non-proliferation efforts, some compar-
ing its significance to India's 1974 nuclear test. Not
only did the facility offer the potential for a major
Argentine nuclear weapons program, but the nation's
ability to master the gaseous diffusion process (if in
fact it has done so) established a dangerous precedent
that others might follow. Equally troubling was that
the elaborate network of export controls established
by the Nuclear Suppliers Group in 1976 to curb the
spread of sensitive nuclear technology had apparently
been impotent against Argentina's ability to manufacture many components for the Pilcaniyeu plant on its

own. Nor had the export-monitoring efforts of nuclear supplier countries spotted, much less prevented, Argentina's importation of some 15 percent of the equipment needed for the facility.

Presumably, the equipment imported was the most sophisticated required in the installation, since this would have been the most difficult for Argentina to fabricate on its own. This suggests that—as in the case of the Ezeiza reprocessing plant, for which Argentina may have obtained important technical assistance from the Italian Techint firm, and the Atucha heavy-water plant—Argentina's assertions that it need not place the Pilcaniyeu facility under safeguards may be subject to challenge. Also of importance is the identity of the firms and exporting nations that provided material to Argentina, since the 1977 U.S. Foreign Assistance Act and the 1978 U.S. Non-Proliferation Act require the imposition of foreign assistance and nuclear trade sanctions against nations exporting nuclear enrichment and reprocessing equipment to non-nuclear-weapon states.[93]

As U.S. government experts developed a better picture of the facility, some became increasingly skeptical of Castro Madero's claims, concluding that construction of even a far smaller plant than he envisioned before the end of the decade would be a major accomplishment. Among other obstacles, they noted, would be the cost of a facility of the size announced and the substantial quantities of electricity it would use. The Argentines would also have to rely far more heavily on outside assistance for many key components. For example, even if Argentina were able to custom-make compressors for its experimental enrichment unit that could handle the highly corrosive uranium hexafluoride gas used in the process, the compressors would be needed in such great numbers for the pilot plant that they would probably have to be purchased abroad. These compressors are on the Nuclear Suppliers' trigger list and could not be exported without the application of IAEA safeguards. If these assessments are correct, the Pilcaniyeu plant may pose a less serious proliferation threat than originally thought. Moreover, there may be important opportunities to use supplier country export controls over key equipment to bring the facility under the IAEA system or, possibly, halt it altogether. Other analysts, however, believe that the equipment used in the facility is relatively unsophisticated and that supplier country export restrictions may have only a limited impact.

Despite its concerns, the United States apparently held back from taking any major diplomatic initiatives with respect to the new Argentine enrichment capability, preferring to await the inauguration of the Alfonsín government.

Brazil's reaction to Castro Madero's announcement was also cautious. Publicly, Brazil offered its congratulations on the important scientific and technological achievement of its southern neighbor.[94] Press accounts suggested, however, that beneath the surface, the Figueiredo government was considerably more ambivalent. One Brazilian press analysis of the new developments stated they "substantially altered the technological situation and the atomic diplomacy and geopolitics of Argentina." The same article noted that "the relationship between the capacity to enrich uranium and to produce an atomic bomb is direct and close" and observed that Argentina had conducted studies of the feasibility of developing nuclear engines for submarines.[95] While not an expression of Brazilian government views, the analysis undoubtedly mirrored the thinking of many officials, and, indeed, within a month of the Argentine announcement, Brazilian military leaders had declared that their nation would shortly have an unsafeguarded uranium enrichment capability of its own.

The announcement of the Pilcaniyeu facility also helps explain the intense efforts on the part of Argentina to avoid the application of full-scope safeguards in 1979-80 at the time the bids for the Atucha II reactor and the Arroyito heavy-water production plant were accepted. Acceptance of comprehensive IAEA oversight would have necessitated disclosure of the enrichment facility and closed off what might have then appeared a promising route for obtaining nuclear weapons material without international restrictions. The existence of the secret enrichment plant also means that Argentina was not acting in good faith with West Germany, Britain, and the United States when they agreed to aid the Argentine nuclear program in August 1983 through the sale of 143 metric tons of heavy water. Whether the sale would have been approved had the enrichment plant's existence been known is a matter of speculation, but plainly, new considerations would have entered into the approving nations' decision-making on the sale. Although much, if not all, of the heavy water involved was still in West Germany after revelation of the enrichment plant in November, no steps are known to have been taken to rescind the prior approval of the sale, possibly because none of the supplier countries involved wanted to embarrass the new government of Raul Alfonsín.

Argentina's Nuclear Policies Under the Alfonsín Government

The inauguration of Raul Alfonsín as Argentina's president in early December 1983 appeared to signal a major shift in Argentine nuclear policy. Following the announcement of the Pilcaniyeu enrichment plant, for example, President-elect Alfonsín immediately issued a statement declaring that the facility would be used exclusively for peaceful purposes. Even before taking office, he announced that one of his first acts would be to establish an advisory commission to review Argentina's nuclear program and to draft legislation formalizing the country's nuclear policies and placing their implementation under civilian control.[96] In other pre-inauguration statements, top policy makers of the incoming government declared that Argentina might be willing to accept international safeguards on all its nuclear facilities and possibly ratify the Treaty of Tlatelolco if the United States aided it in obtaining a satisfactory settlement of the Falklands crisis.[97]

In December, CNEA president Castro Madero resigned and was replaced the following month by a civilian engineer, Alberto Constantini, seemingly a signal that major changes in the direction of Argentina's nuclear program were under way. By February, however, this trend appeared far less certain. Constantini, for example, retained the agency's board of directors and endorsed its goal of using domestic technology to master the nuclear fuel cycle (a term usually taken to include reprocessing and enrichment). Moreover, press reports indicated that the commission appointed by President Alfonsín to study the CNEA nuclear program also intended to recommend continuation of the agency's previous policies, including completion of the indigenous, unsafeguarded pilot heavy-water production plant at Atucha and continued work on the Ezeiza reprocessing plant; nor, according to CNEA chairman Constantini, would research on the production of enriched uranium at Pilcaniyeu be slowed.[98] Similarly, in a series of interviews and statements, Argentine foreign minister

Dante Caputo stated that the Alfonsín government would maintain Argentina's long-standing objections to the Non-Proliferation Treaty as a discriminatory accord that condemned non-nuclear-weapon states to permanent inferiority. On the other hand, Caputo stressed that the new government was actively considering ratification of the Treaty of Tlatelolco and that it believed it would be advisable for Argentina to "agree to an inspection system which will vouch for our peaceful nuclear development."[99]

Argentine leaders appeared to move away from early ratification of the Tlatelolco Treaty in subsequent weeks by imposing major new preconditions on such an action. In a letter to Senator Charles Percy, chairman of the Foreign Relations Committee, Foreign Minister Caputo stated that prior to ratification there was a "need to clarify Argentina's safeguards agreements with the International Atomic Energy Agency" to reflect the "particularities" of the Tlatelolco Treaty in contrast to the Non-Proliferation Treaty. Caputo's statement apparently refers to the long-standing Argentina-IAEA dispute over whether safeguards agreements under the Tlatelolco accord must permit parties to detonate peaceful nuclear explosives—thus, in effect, declaring that Argentina continued to reserve its right to pursue this course. Since this had been a non-negotiable issue with the IAEA, interposing it as a precondition plainly indicated that the Alfonsín government was far from ready to ratify the Tlatelolco accord. In addition, Argentina wanted to establish a means for verifying whether nuclear weapon states had violated Protocol II of the Tlatelolco Treaty by introducing nuclear weapons into the Latin American nuclear-weapons-free zone, as some sources indicated Britain had done during the Falklands War.[100] Alfonsín's reluctance to ratify the treaty was confirmed in early April when, despite urgings from Mexican president Miguel de la Madrid, Argentine government spokesmen stated that their nation was not then prepared to adhere to the accord.[101]

Domestic political opposition from Perónist and right-wing parties appears to be the principal factor restraining the Alfonsín government from ratifying the treaty, which the president himself is said to favor.[102] With Argentina's new government seeking to prosecute the nation's former military leaders for human rights violations, to resolve the longstanding Beagle Islands dispute with Chile, to impose austerity measures and bring down inflation, and to work out a settlement with Great Britain over the Falklands, it appears that a conscious decision has been made to postpone a possible confrontation over the basic direction of the Argentine nuclear program.

Indeed, in June President Alfonsín announced that an accord had been signed with the Perónists and other smaller parties, establishing agreed upon principles for addressing the major issues facing the country. According to press accounts, the need to achieve consensus in this document eliminated the possibility that Argentina would ratify the Tlatelolco or Non-Proliferation Treaties.[103]

Important decisions on the CNEA's budget, however, remain to be made. From the standpoint of proliferation, the critical decisions here will be whether funds will be available for the early completion of the Pilcaniyeu enrichment plant, scheduled to start up in 1985, and the Ezeiza reprocessing facility, scheduled to start up in 1986, both of which could provide access to nuclear weapons material, although, at the latter plant, only under IAEA safeguards, since Argentina currently lacks a source of unsafeguarded spent fuel. Deferral of these facilities, like a decision to ratify the

Treaty of Tlatelolco, could substantially reduce the threat of Argentine proliferation.

Expanding Export Opportunities

In September 1983, as noted earlier, Argentina and Chile ratified the nuclear cooperation agreement that had been signed in 1976. In addition, Argentina agreed to expand nuclear aid to Algeria in the areas of radiology and preparation of preliminary studies for the construction of a nuclear power plant.[104] Argentine nuclear organizations were also asked by an American firm to participate in a portion of the Egyptian El Dabaa nuclear power plant project bid.[105]

These developments highlight the increasingly important role Argentina is likely to play as a nuclear supplier in future years.

III. Prospects for Nuclear Weapons in Argentina

With operating uranium mines, mills, purification plants, fuel fabrication facilities, and nuclear reactors, with successful demonstrations of reprocessing and enrichment, and with proven nuclear engineering, construction, and component-manufacturing capabilities, there is little question that Argentina today has the general scientific and industrial infrastructure necessary for the development of nuclear weapons. Indeed, Argentine officials have said as much since the mid-1970s, when the nation's nuclear specialists first separated small amounts of plutonium.[106] At present, however, the nation lacks facilities—enrichment and reprocessing plants—for the production of nuclear weapons materials in significant quantities, although both types of plant are under development.

If Argentina chooses to move closer to the possession of nuclear arms, it has several options. First, it could complete the Ezeiza reprocessing plant and begin openly to reprocess spent fuel from the safeguarded Atucha I or Embalse reactors, producing significant quantities of plutonium that would also be under safeguards. Once a stockpile of plutonium was available, Argentina would have a de facto nuclear weapons capability, although the political costs of using the material for weapons would be high, since Argentina would have to violate its safeguards agreements to do so.

Second, if the Ezeiza plant were completed, Argentina might attempt to obtain unsafeguarded plutonium openly. The material would then be available for weapons without the necessity of violating international pledges. This time-consuming option would require completing the unsafeguarded natural-uranium/heavy-water RA-7 research reactor and building up an unsafeguarded capability to produce heavy water using technology from its indigenous pilot heavy-water plant at Atucha. A capability to produce unsafeguarded fuel for such a reactor is already largely in place. Plutonium-bearing spent fuel from the reactor could then be reprocessed at Ezeiza on an unsafeguarded basis, under the arrangements currently covering the plant.

Another, quicker approach would be to obtain unsafeguarded plutonium partly through clandestine efforts, by bypassing safeguards and placing "extra" fuel in the Embalse reactor (which many believe is difficult to safeguard because it does not need to be shut down for refueling). Press accounts in September 1983 stated that the CIA believed the Argentine military had, in fact, developed a secret plan along these lines, but other U.S. officials reportedly discounted this because they found the alleged plan highly unrealistic.[107]

Completion of the unsafeguarded Pilcaniyeu enrichment plant could provide another route to quantities of nuclear weapons material that Argentina would be legally free to use for any purpose, including nuclear weapons. Estimates of the time required for this plan vary from one to two years—the announced timetable for completing the plant—to five years or more, the view of some U.S. government officials.

The acquisition of nuclear weapons material by any of these routes would undoubtedly be seen as a significant step towards developing a nuclear weapons capability, however, and would inevitably trigger responsive action by Brazil, much as Argentina's previous steps in this direction appear to have done. Moreover, despite its lagging nuclear program, in the long term, Brazil's considerably greater resources could permit it to outstrip any nuclear weapons capability Argentina might develop, eliminating any short-term advantage Buenos Aires might enjoy.[108]

Given these strong disincentives, it seems unlikely that the Alfonsín government will accelerate the more provocative elements of the nation's nuclear program or otherwise signal an interest in developing a nuclear weapons capability. If, in the end, Argentina's new leaders are not prepared to reverse the direction of their program by accepting added non-proliferation commitments or suspending development of enrichment and reprocessing capabilities, their most likely course will be continuation of the disquieting yet still ambiguous path of their predecessors of moving toward a nuclear capability, but at a very cautious pace.

BOLIVIA

PARAGUAY

Salta

Tucuman

Resistencia
Corrientes

Parana River

BRAZIL

Pacific
Ocean

Los Gigantes   Córdoba

Santa Fe

URUGUAY

Mendoza

Rio Tercero
(Embalse)

Rosario

La Estela

Atucha

San Rafael

Buenos Aires
(Constituyentes)
(Ezeiza)

Rio de
la Plata

Malargüe

ARGENTINA

Mar del Plata

CHILE

Arroyito

Bahia Blanca

Neuquen

Atlantic
Ocean

Pilcaniyeu

San Carlos
de Bariloche

Rawson

Comodoro
Rivadavia

ARGENTINA

uranium mining area

0   400

MILES

Rio Gallegos

231

Argentina

Power Reactors/Operating or Under Construction

Atucha I (heavy-water/natural-uranium, 320 MWe)
- supplier: Siemens AG (West Germany)
- start up: 1974
- fuel source: Argentina and West Germany (for some process steps); Argentina, only, after 1984 (est.).[a]
- heavy water: initial charge, U.S., West Germany.[b]
- safeguards: yes

Embalse (heavy-water/natural-uranium, 600 MWe)
- supplier: Atomic Energy of Canada Ltd. (Canada) and Italimpianti (Italy)
- start up: 1983
- fuel source: Canada and Argentina through 1985; Argentina, only, after 1985 (est.).[a]
- heavy water: initial charge, Canada[e]
- safeguards: yes

Atucha II (heavy-water/natural-uranium, 745 MWe)
- supplier: Kraftwerk Union (West Germany)
- start up: 1989 (est.)[c]
- fuel source: Argentina
- heavy water: Argentina and West Germany[r]
- safeguards: yes

Uranium Resources/Active Mining Sites/Uranium Mills

- reasonably assured reserves: 23,000 metric tons[f]
- currently active sites: San Rafael[f], Los Gigantes[g]
- mills in operation: San Rafael, Los Gigantes, Marlagüe, La Estela[f]

Uranium Purification (UO₂)

Córdoba
- capacity: 150 metric tons per year, planned 330 metric tons per year[h]
- supplier: Kraftwerk Union (West Germany) and Argentina
- start up: 1982 (West German line), 1983 (?) (Argentinian line)[c]
- safeguards: One of two production lines is safeguarded because of West German equipment.

Córdoba[s]
- capacity: unknown; 180 tons UO_2 produced to date
- supplier: Argentina
- start up: ?
- safeguards: no

UF₆ Conversion

- Capacity presumed (to serve pilot enrichment plant)

Heavy Water

Arroyito (industrial scale)
- capacity: 250 metric tons per year
- supplier: Sulzer Brothers (Switzerland)
- start up: 1985 (est.)[i]
- safeguards: yes

Atucha (pilot scale)
- capacity: 2-4 metric tons per year[t]
- supplier: Argentina (with possible foreign aid)[d]
- start up: 1984 (est.)[i]
- safeguards: no

232

Enrichment

Pilcaniyeu

- type: gaseous diffusion
- capacity: experimental; 500 kg per year of 20% enriched uranium by 1985 (est.)[j]
- supplier: Argentina
- start up: 1983 (experimental unit)
- safeguards: no

Fuel Fabrication

Ezeiza

- capacity: all requirements for Atucha I, 1984 (est.); all requirements for Embalse, 1985 (est.); all requirements for Atucha II, 1987 (est.).[a]
- supplier: Atucha I line, West Germany; Embalse line (CANDU) Argentina.[j]
- start up: 1982[a]
- safeguards: Atucha line safeguarded, Embalse line safeguarded only when fabricating safeguarded UO_2.[k]

Constituyentes (pilot plant for highly enriched uranium)[l]

Reprocessing

Ezeiza

- capacity: 15 kg plutonium, 5 metric tons spent fuel per year [e]
- supplier: Argentina (possible Italian aid)[m]
- start up: 1986 (est.)[m]
- safeguards: only when safeguarded fuel is processed.[n]

Ezeiza

- capacity: laboratory scale
- supplier: Argentina
- start up: 1969; operated intermittantly until dismantled in 1973.[e]
- safeguards: no

Research Reactors [l,o]

RA-0, Córdoba (tank/medium-enriched uranium, 1 Wt)

- supplier: Argentina
- start up: 1965
- safeguards: no

RA-1, Constituyentes (tank/medium-enriched uranium, less than 1 MWt)

- supplier: Argentina
- start up: 1958
- safeguards: yes

RA-2, Constituyentes (tank/highly enriched uranium, less than 1 MWt)

- supplier: Argentina
- start up: 1966
- safeguards: yes

RA-3, Ezeiza (pool/highly enriched uranium, 5 MWt)[u]

- supplier: Argentina
- start up: 1967
- safeguards: yes

RA-4, Rosario (homogenous, medium-enriched uranium, less that 1 MWt)

- supplier: West Germany
- start up: 1972
- safeguards: yes

RA-6, San Carlos de Bariloche (MTR, highly enriched uranium, 500 KWt[p, u]

- supplier: Argentina
- start up: 1982
- safeguards: only when safeguarded fuel is present.

RA-7, planned (heavy-water/natural-uranium 40-100 MWt)[q]

- supplier: Argentina
- start up: (?)
- safeguards: no

Sources and Notes

a. "Fuel Fabrication Factory Opened," *Nuclear Engineering International*, May 1982, p. 8; "Nuclear Firms Advance Level of Technology to Meet Objectives," *Energia Nuclear*, translated in Foreign Broadcast Information Service/Nuclear Proliferation and Development, hereafter FBIS/NDP, pp. 15-17.

b. John Redick, "The Military Potential of Latin American Nuclear Programs," International Studies Series, Sage Publications, 1972, p. 13; personal communication.

   Between 1980 and 1982, Argentina imported 6 metric tons of heavy water each from the USSR and the People's Republic of China to make up for losses at Atucha I. Richard Kessler, "U.S. Approval for West Germany to Sell 143 Tonnes of Heavy Water to Argentina," *Nucleonics Week*, August 25, 1983, p. 7; Judith Miller, "U.S. Is Holding Up Peking Atom Talks," *New York Times*, September 19, 1982. Additional heavy water was obtained from West Germany (with U.S. permission) in 1983. Kessler, "U.S. Approval."

c. Carlos Castro Madero, "Argentina's Nuclear Energy Program," *Nuclear Europe*, July-August 1983, pp. 31-33.

d. Burt Solomon, "Argentina Bent on Home-Grown Nuclear Program," *Energy Daily*, November 9, 1982, p. 3.

e. Powell A. Moore, Assistant Secretary of State for Congressional Relations, to Senator Gary Hart, August 19, 1982.

f. Reasonably Assured Reserves at less than $130 per kilogram. OECD Nuclear Energy Agency and the International Atomic Energy Agency, *Uranium, Resources Production and Demand* (Paris: OECD, 1983), pp. 61-62, 89.

g. "Uranium Concentrate Plant," *TELAM, Noticias Argentinas* (Buenos Aires), November 16, 1982, translated in Foreign Broadcast Information Service/Latin America, December 9, 1982, p. B4.

h. "Argentina to Start Producing U0$_2$ This Year," *Nuclear Fuel*, September 13, 1982, p. 15.

i. Richard Kessler, "U.S. Approval for West Germany to Sell 143 Tonnes of Heavy Water to Argentina," *Nucleonics Week*, August 25, 1983, p. 7.

j. "CNEA Chairman Makes Announcement," *TELAM* (Buenos Aires) 2102 GMT, November 18, 1983, translated in FBIS/NDP, December 12, 1983, p. 7; Milton R. Benjamin, "Argentina Seen Capable of 4 A-Bombs a Year," *Washington Post*, December 9, 1983.

k. Personal communication with informed U.S. official.

l. International Atomic Energy Agency, *Annual Report for 1982*, p. 84.

m. Robert Laufer, "Argentina Looks to Reprocessing to Fill Its Own Needs Plus Plutonium Sales," *Nuclear Fuel*, November 8, 1982, p. 3.

n. Safeguarded when processing safeguarded spent fuel only. Currently only safeguarded spent fuel is available.

o. Pilat and Donnelly, "An Analysis of Argentina's Nuclear Power Program and Its Closeness to Nuclear Weapons," December 2, 1982.

p. "Research Reactor Inaugurated," *Nuclear Engineering International*, June 1983, p. 10.

q. Sometimes referred to as *RA-5*.

r. Some of the 143 metric tons of heavy water sold to Argentina by West Germany in 1983 (with U.S. permission) was to be available for Atucha II. Personal communication with U.S. and West German officials.

s. Reportedly a second facility in Cordoba; scheduled to be closed after domestic line at larger Cordoba plant is opened; personal communication with knowledgeable U.S. official.

t. May not be capable of producing reactor-grade heavy water.

u. Currently being converted to 20 percent enriched uranium.

Brazil

I. Background

Like Argentina, Brazil currently lacks the enrichment or reprocessing capabilities necessary to produce nuclear weapons material. Brazil's nuclear development has closely followed its southern neighbor's in its measured progress toward acquiring those facilities while avoiding treaty obligations that would foreclose Brasilia's right to manufacture nuclear weapons at a later time. Although important differences exist between the Brazilian and Argentine approaches to nuclear development, and while Argentina appears perhaps five years closer to having a capability to produce nuclear weapons material in significant quantity, Brazil has consistently taken the steps necessary to avoid falling substantially behind, and this appears to be the key factor determining the direction of its nuclear program today. If existing trends continue, Brazil could have the nuclear materials required for a de facto nuclear weapons capability in the early 1990s.

Early capabilities. Brazil's nuclear program was initiated under the National Research Council in 1951, the year Argentina claimed its researchers, headed by former Third Reich scientist Ronald Richter, had mastered the nuclear fusion process. Although this claim was soon discredited, Brazilian leaders may have been responding to Argentina's interest in obtaining the key to the H-bomb when, in 1953, they sent the president of the National Research Council, Admiral Alvaro Alberto, to West Germany to purchase three experimental ultracentrifuges from a team led by another former Third Reich scientist, Wilhelm Groth. The clandestine export of this equipment, which held the potential for allowing Brazil to enrich uranium to weapons-grade, was blocked at the last minute when it was uncovered by U.S. occupation authorities. Alvaro soon resigned under U.S. pressure, but the impounded centrifuges were exported to Brazil several years later, after the end of the Allied occupation.[1] As discussed below, Brazil's pursuit of ultracentrifuge uranium enrichment technology continued in subsequent years.

Like Argentina, Brazil signed an agreement for nuclear cooperation in 1955 with the United States. The following year, Brazilian nuclear research and policy functions were transferred to the Comissao Nacional de Energia Nuclear (CNEN), and in 1957 the CNEN inaugurated Brazil's first research reactor, supplied under the U.S. agreement, and thereby virtually tied with Argentina for the honor of operating Latin America's first such facility.[2] Like the two additional research reactors Brazil would have in operation by 1965, this one used U.S.-supplied medium-enriched (20 percent) fuel and was subject to IAEA safeguards.

First Nuclear Power Plant and Continuing Uranium Enrichment Research. In the early 1960s Brazil selected a French natural-uranium reactor to launch its nuclear power program, the course Argentina would also pursue.[3] These negotiations were abandoned in 1964, however, when the military took power, and Brazil did not order its first nuclear power plant—a 626-megawatt U.S. (Westinghouse) enriched-uranium/light-water reactor, known as Angra I—until 1971, three years after Argentina initiated construction of its first nuclear power reactor, Atucha I. Although choosing the Westinghouse plant meant Brazil would be entirely dependent on the United States for enriched-uranium fuel, attractive financing and wide international acceptance of the Westinghouse technology clinched the sale for the United States. In any event, Brazil's nuclear planners believed the nation lacked sufficient uranium reserves to fuel its own reactors, so that selecting a natural-uranium/heavy-water reactor would not have promised independence from foreign suppliers comparable to that Argentina was striving to achieve.[4] The Angra I plant began generating electricity in 1982.

During the mid-to-late 1960s, while Argentina was pressing ahead with the Atucha plant and its laboratory-scale reprocessing activities, Brazil pursued a parallel track aimed at mastering a different part of the nuclear fuel cycle that could ultimately provide access to nuclear weapons material: uranium enrichment using centrifuges. A 1967 nuclear agreement with France and a similar 1969 agreement with West Germany, for example, both provided for joint research in this area.[5] It does not appear that these activities, whose results have not been publicized, were subject to IAEA safeguards.

Rejection of Non-Proliferation Accords. During this period, Brazil also avoided making treaty commitments that would preclude its future development of nuclear arms. Like Argentina, it refused to adhere to the 1968 Nuclear Non-Proliferation Treaty, and it joined Argentina and a handful of other nations in abstaining from the U.N. resolution endorsing the treaty. Brazil has argued that the accord improperly freezes non-nuclear-weapon states in an inferior status and places unequal demands on them.[6]

Similarly, although Brazil offered the first resolution calling for a Latin American nuclear-weapons-free zone in 1962 and actively supported early efforts to negotiate the Treaty of Tlatelolco, its posture changed dramatically to one of obstruction following the military takeover of 1964. Brazil was responsible for the inclusion of the treaty's provisions preserving the right of parties to conduct peaceful nuclear explosions (which Brazil claimed could be important to the economic development of its vast interior) and for the treaty's entry-into-force provisions requiring ratification by all eligible states (unless waived) for the treaty to become fully effective.[7] Brazil has both signed and ratified the accord, but because it has not waived this provision, the treaty is not binding upon it. Nevertheless, Brazil has committed itself "not to perform any act which defeats the objectives of the treaty."[8] While apparently a firm declaration against developing nuclear weapons, the pledge has not impeded Brazil from undertaking nuclear activities without the application of International Atomic Energy Agency (IAEA) safeguards that the treaty would require.[9] Nor does it appear to rule out Brazil's manufacturing peaceful nuclear explosives, since Brazil interprets the treaty as permitting this.

Another indication of Brazil's interest in retaining the option to build nuclear weapons was a 1967 CNEN feasibility study examining the time that would be needed and the cost of such an undertaking. The study concluded the project would take fifteen years and cost about $550 million.[10]

The 1975 Deal with West Germany. Although Brazil's extraordinary economic boom during the late 1960s and early 1970s far surpassed the growth rates achieved by its southern rival, by 1975 the Brazilian nuclear program had fallen decidedly behind. By this time Buenos Aires had extracted plutonium from spent reactor fuel, and in 1974 it began to operate the Atucha I nuclear power plant, the first in Latin America. In June 1975, however, Brazil signed a massive multibillion-dollar nuclear sales agreement with West Germany that held the promise of rapidly making Brasilia the continent's nuclear leader.

Under the deal, Brazil was to build two German-supplied 1300-megawatt low-enriched-uranium/light-water nuclear power reactors by 1985, with the option to purchase six more for completion by 1990. West Germany would assist Brazilian uranium exploration efforts in two areas of the country in return for 20 percent of the ore produced, and the Germans would provide a pilot fuel fabrication plant to supply the reactors, to be followed by a commercial plant. In addition, West Germany agreed to provide Brazil with a pilot reprocessing plant and to assist it in building a large-scale enrichment plant using the jet-nozzle technique—technologies that could provide Brazil with significant quantities of plutonium and highly enriched uranium. Although all of the equipment and technology transferred were to be subject to unusually strong IAEA safeguards, described below, West Germany did not require Brazil to agree to accept full-scope safeguards (i.e., to place all of its nuclear activities, present and future, under international inspection).

Anticipated Benefits. From the Brazilian standpoint, the deal promised many benefits. First, it provided a response to growing concerns that Argentina might be developing nuclear weapons to compensate for Brazil's growing lead in economic and conventional military power.[11] Second, Brazilian officials hoped to enhance the nation's energy security. As the largest oil importer in the developing world, Brazil had been badly shaken by the 1973 oil embargo. Its plans to use nuclear energy as a partial alternative had been unexpectedly set back in 1974, however, when because of an apparent shortage of enrichment capacity the United States changed its enriched uranium sales policy and refused to make a firm commitment to supply enriched uranium for Brazil's second and third nuclear power plants (then in the planning stage).[12] West German aid in uranium exploration and the construction in Brazil of fuel fabrication and enrichment plants offered the hope that Brazil might achieve nuclear fuel self-sufficiency. Finally, obtaining closely held nuclear technology from an advanced supplier nation was an important diplomatic achievement, underscoring Brazil's leadership in the developing world and enhancing the prestige of President Ernesto Geisel at home.

For Germany, the agreement meant a vital boost for its nuclear reactor industry at a time when domestic orders were falling, as well as an opportunity to break the U.S. near-monopoly on nuclear power plant sales to the developing world. West Germany also hoped to enhance its own energy security by gaining access to an important new source of uranium.[13]

When it was announced, barely a year after India's May 1974 nuclear test, this first-time-ever sale of both reprocessing and enrichment capabilities raised grave proliferation concerns in Washington and Buenos Aires, especially in view of Brazil's rejection of the

Non-Proliferation and Tlatelolco Treaties and its repeated expressions of interest in developing nuclear explosives.[14]

U.S. Response. To reduce the effectiveness of any U.S. opposition that might emerge to the sale, West German negotiators apparently tried to present the United States with a *fait accompli*, officially informing them only after the fact that an agreement in principle had been reached with the Brazilians in mid-February of 1975.[15] In fact, the U.S. reaction to the sale was somewhat mixed. While Congress and the press condemned West Germany's offer to sell enrichment and reprocessing technology as "sweeteners" to clinch the multibillion-dollar reactor sales, the Ford administration was more muted in its response, voicing its disapproval only through middle-ranking officials and ultimately accepting that the Germans, having made a commitment, would not be moved.[16]

Special Safeguards. West German nuclear spokesmen tried to deflect U.S. criticism in part by stressing that the safeguards covering the deal were stronger than those required by the Non-Proliferation Treaty for nuclear exports. IAEA safeguards would extend not only to exported items and nuclear material (i.e., plutonium) produced through their use, but also to any facilities that Brazil might build based on West German technology and to nuclear material produced in them.[17]

Under the Brazil-West Germany-IAEA agreement covering the deal, Germany was to describe to the Agency any technical information it provided Brazil in the principal areas of the deal; thereafter any plants built using that information would be subject to safeguards. Recognizing that ambiguities might arise (if, for example, Brazil argued that it was building a particular facility using information in the public literature rather than German-supplied data), the agreement specified that for a period of twenty years any plant built in Brazil would automatically be treated as though it were a replicated facility if it incorporated the same physical or chemical processes as those specified by West Germany and communicated to the IAEA.[18]

As broad as these restrictions were, however, they did not amount to full-scope safeguards because, as Brazilian officials stressed at the time, they did not oblige Brazil to place all indigenously developed nuclear technology and materials under the IAEA system and thus did not prevent Brazil from developing nuclear explosives by this route.[19] The agreement, for example, left Brazil free to pursue uranium enrichment without safeguards as long as a technology such as centrifuge or laser enrichment, rather than the jet-nozzle process being supplied by West Germany, was used. Moreover, any reprocessing plant Brazil might build before receiving relevant German technical information that had to be reported to the IAEA was also apparently exempt from mandatory IAEA safeguards under the deal. Brazil would later exploit one, and by some accounts both, of these loopholes.

Secret West German Controls. Another facet of the 1975 deal that would help reduce the risk of Brazil's exploiting for military purposes technology it received from West Germany emerged only in 1979 in the course of a Brazilian congressional investigation. This inquiry brought to light a 1975 stockholders agreement under which West Germany's Kraftwerk Union (KWU), the key German supplier under the deal, was given actual control of NUCLEN, the joint KWU-Brazilian entity formed to transfer technology to Brazil, as well as to construct the reactors and the reprocessing and enrichment plants. Although KWU owned only 25 percent of NUCLEN's stock, while 75 percent was owned by the Brazilian Nuclear Corporation (NUCLEBRAS), the stockholders' agreement gave KWU the right to appoint four voting members to a "technical committee" with the power to review all important NUCLEN decisions; the fifth member of the committee, representing Brazilian interests, had no vote. Thus, through KWU, West Germany maintained total control over the timing and extent of the nuclear technology that would be transferred to Brazil, a valuable non-proliferation tool, since West Germany would be in a position to hold back potentially sensitive reprocessing and enrichment information if it appeared Brazil was moving towards developing nuclear arms.[20]

Added Dutch Restrictions on Reprocessing. High-level U.S. interventions with Bonn and Brasilia early in the Carter administration to try to undo the most sensitive parts of the deal proved unsuccessful. However, in June 1977, West Germany announced that, until further notice, it would not approve additional reprocessing and enrichment plant exports. In light of this pledge and the slowing pace of the Brazilian nuclear program, the United States muted its criticism of the deal, Assistant Secretary of State Terence Todman stating during a visit to Brazil in mid-1977 that "The United States considers Brazil and Germany to be sovereign nations that can sign any agreement they see fit."[21]

While West Germany refused further restrictions of its exports to Brazil, an important additional restriction was imposed by the Netherlands on Brazil's use of the pilot reprocessing plant it intended to build with West German help. The first two reactors built under the 1975 deal, Angra II and III, were to be fueled initially with enriched uranium from the West German-British-Dutch uranium enrichment consortium, URENCO. In 1978, however, concerned over Brazil's continuing refusal to accept full-scope safeguards and over the prospect that the weapons-usable plutonium produced in URENCO-supplied fuel might subsequently be extracted in the German-supplied pilot reprocessing plant, the Dutch made the export of the URENCO material conditional on Brazil's agreeing that any plutonium extracted from the fuel would be stored under multilateral control. If an international plutonium storage regime within the framework of the IAEA were not in place two years before the scheduled reprocessing of the URENCO-supplied fuel, then the three URENCO countries and Brazil would together establish a separate ad hoc storage regime. By this approach Brazil would not gain complete control of substantial quantities of plutonium, at least until its own enrichment plant was operating and supplying fuel for Angra II and III.[22]

The U.S. Fuel Embargo. Imposition of these restrictions roughly coincided with passage of the U.S. Nuclear Non-Proliferation Act of 1978 that prohibited (after 1980) exports of enriched-uranium fuel to countries refusing to accept full-scope safeguards. The United States had contracted in 1973 to supply enriched fuel for Brazil's first nuclear power plant, the U.S.-supplied Angra I reactor. The 1978 law meant that the United States would not honor this contract. Brazil was able to circumvent this embargo in 1981, however, with the tacit approval of the Reagan administration, by taking URENCO fuel earmarked for Angra II and using it as reload material for Angra I.[23] Nonetheless, the Dutch-imposed restrictions on the URENCO fuel meant that part of the plutonium produced in the Angra I reactor could not be extracted unless subsequently placed under an international storage regime.[24]

Progress Despite Major Delays. Brazil's implementation of its deal with West Germany, and of its nuclear power program generally, have been beset by major delays and cost overruns. The U.S.-supplied Angra I plant, for example, did not begin generating electricity until March 1982, some five years after its originally planned start-up date, and by then its cost had increased from $350 million to $1.5 billion. The first two power plants to be built under the Bonn-Brasilia accord, Angra II and III, have also suffered at least a five-year delay because of foundation problems discovered in 1979. The combined cost of the two facilities had increased from $565 million to $2 billion as of 1982.[25] With the solicitation of bids for Brazil's next two power plants, Iguape I and II, now postponed because of budget cuts necessitated by Brazil's financial crisis, it is entirely possible that Brazil will have only three operating nuclear power plants by the end of the century.[26]

Although Brazil's German-supplied jet-nozzle enrichment plant has been beset by comparable delays and cost overruns, Brazil appears to have made slow but steady progress in developing this facility and mastering its technology. In 1980 an experimental jet-nozzle plant was moved from West Germany to Belo Horizonte, and construction of the first "cascade" of a commercial-scale facility at Resende has been under way for several years. Plans call for expansion of this initial module of the plant to permit the production of sixty-four metric tons of low-enriched uranium fuel in 1988, sufficient for fueling the three Angra power plants.[27] In 1983, funds that were to have gone to nuclear power plant construction were shifted to this project to avoid further delays, even as the overall budget for implementing the West German deal was cut some 40 percent.[28]

This facility will be dedicated to the production of low-enriched material and subject to IAEA safeguards that have a strong likelihood of detecting any misuse of the plant for the production of weapons-grade material. Nevertheless, the facility will provide valuable experience for Brazilian technicians in dealing with the uranium enrichment process, experience that may be transferable to Brazil's parallel research and development activities aimed at mastering alternative enrichment techniques.

The West German-supplied pilot reprocessing plant included in the 1975 deal is also moving forward, if slowly. From 1980 to 1982, Brazilian technicians were training in Germany, where engineering work on the design of the plant was also under way. However, not until 1983 was a site selected for the facility—it is to be part of the atomic complex at Resende—and it is now expected to begin operation in 1986.[29] As noted below, however, other reprocessing activities not directly related to the 1975 deal may already have taken place in Brazil.

Brazil's joint efforts with West Germany to identify additional uranium reserves have proved successful and by late 1983 Brazil had located 160,000 metric tons of measured and indicated reserves, the seventh largest uranium resource base in the world.[30] Brazil has also successfully completed with West German assistance the construction of a fuel fabrication facility that will manufacture the fuel rods and assemblies needed for the three Angra reactors, using enriched uranium from URENCO until domestic supplies are available from Resende.[31]

The Parallel Program. Whatever the long-term proliferation risks inherent in the transfers of sensitive technology to Brazil under the 1975 deal, the German and Dutch restrictions on Brazil's nuclear activities and

Brazil's slow progress in implementing the arrangement have considerably reduced these dangers in the near term. Not only is all activity under the West German agreement subject to IAEA safeguards, but in addition, Brazil will have only limited access to materials that can be directly used for nuclear weapons, since at least through 1990, on the one hand, highly enriched uranium is not expected to be produced at the Resende enrichment plant, while on the other, any plutonium extracted in the Resende reprocessing plant would have to be transferred promptly to storage under multilateral auspices. Moreover, any facilities built using the same nuclear technology as these installations will be subject to safeguards.

During the early 1980s, however, Brazil began to accelerate a series of unsafeguarded nuclear research, development, and demonstration efforts outside the ambit of the West German accord, which were apparently aimed at building capabilities necessary for the development of nuclear explosives. These activities have been carried out in a series of research institutes around the country, principally the Instituto des Pesquisas Energeticas e Nucleares (IPEN) in São Paulo and the Brazilian air force's Centro Téchnico Aerospacial (CTA) in São José dos Campos.

In 1983 Brazilian president Joao Figueiredo placed all nuclear research facilities, including IPEN, under the control of the national government, apparently in order to strengthen military control of these institutions.[32] In addition, Colonel Durvaldo Gonçalves, reportedly the leading advocate of Brazilian nuclear weapons acquisition, was appointed head of IPEN in 1983.[33]

Activities at IPEN. The precise nature of the activities at IPEN, which is located at the University of São Paulo, is apparently known to the U.S. government but has not been disclosed publicly. In a November 1981 letter to Senator Charles Percy explaining why the United States believes Brazil has not placed all of its relevant nuclear activities under IAEA safeguards and is therefore ineligible to receive U.S. nuclear fuel and reactor exports under the 1978 Non-Proliferation Act, the State Department noted:

The dialogue [with the Brazilian government] included discussion of safeguards at certain specific nuclear research facilities at the University of São Paulo which, in Brazil's view, were indigenous and so small as to not require safeguards under IAEA definitions. The U.S. advised Brazil that in our view, the nature and level of safeguards at these facilities could be determined by the IAEA, but that based on what we knew of them we believed the facilities would have to be declared to the IAEA and appropriate safeguards be maintained for the applicable U.S. legal criterion [i.e. the full-scope safeguards requirement] to be met.[34]

One facility at IPEN is apparently a plant for the purification of uranium to reactor grade, that is, to a level that would permit it to be irradiated in a reactor to produce plutonium. U.S. officials believe more than ten metric tons of purified unenriched material has been produced.[35] In addition, IPEN apparently contains a small reprocessing unit that would be capable of extracting plutonium from such irradiated material or from spent reactor fuel. Some sources set the output of the unit at five kilograms (1 kilogram = 2.2 pounds) of plutonium per year (possibly enough for a single bomb), while others state it can produce only several grams.[36] West Germany is said to have provided the radiation protection equipment for the facility, possibly as a gift.[37] A second, larger reprocessing unit is said by one source to be under development. The center also appears to have a plant for transforming yellowcake into gaseous uranium hexafluoride, the material used in the enrichment process.[38]

Alleged Reprocessing. In February 1983 the *Washington Post* reported that researchers at IPEN had, in fact, produced plutonium by irradiating natural uranium in the five-megawatt U.S.-supplied research reactor at the center and then reprocessing it to obtain a few grams of plutonium using the laboratory-scale facility. The small scale of this activity, which reportedly was not intended to produce the five to eight kilograms of plutonium necessary for a nuclear weapon but rather to give Brazil needed experience in reprocessing, would closely parallel efforts by Argentina in the 1969-1972 period to perform such experiments.

Brazil's ambassador to the United States issued a denial of the charges in the story, stating that "IPEN's reprocessing facility is actually an analysis laboratory to handle material safely. Its purpose is to train experts on nuclear safety." He went on to say that "the laboratory has not handled any irradiated material."[39] Nevertheless, in a follow-up story the *Post* quoted the Brazilian mines and energy minister César Cals as acknowledging that some plutonium had been "produced" using a U.S.-made test reactor as part of Brazil's peaceful nuclear program.[40] Whether this meant only that uranium specimens had been irradiated in the reactor to produce the material in the specimens or that contrary to the assertion of the Brazilian ambassador such specimens had also been reprocessed to extract the plutonium was not clear.

U.S. Reaction. Although the U.S. agreement for cooperation with Brazil prohibits the reprocessing of U.S. fuel supplied for the reactor without U.S. permission, such permission arguably would not be required if Brazil placed extra material in the reactor and reprocessed it, as the *Washington Post* suggested. Similarly, the trilateral agreement between the IAEA, the United States, and Brazil covering the reactor exempts minor quantities of plutonium from safeguards coverage, although exemptions must be declared to the Agency. None had been declared by Brazil.

Although Brazil appeared to have taken advantage of the loopholes in its agreement with Washington covering the IPEN reactor to "produce" plutonium, the United States, rather than publicly challenging Brazil's skirting of U.S. controls, chose to exculpate its behavior, declaring:

1. It is the opinion of the United States that Brazil is not developing nuclear weapons. Anyone who claims having obtained any information to the contrary from the U.S. intelligence service is absolutely wrong;
2. The U.S. government is convinced that Brazil has strictly abided by all multilateral and bilateral nuclear safeguards agreements of which it is a signatory.[41]

The U.S. statement did not, however, deny that the reprocessing had taken place, although U.S. officials have given such denials privately.

Why the United States sought to exonerate Brazil so completely is unclear. However, since 1981, the Reagan administration has been attempting to take a more conciliatory approach in dealing with Brazil on proliferation matters and, indeed, at the time the *Post* story broke, it was considering the specific goodwill gesture of releasing Brazil from its 1973 uranium enrichment contract for the Angra I fuel, a step that would have facilitated Brazil's obtaining fuel for that reactor from URENCO.[42]

If Brazil did engage in small-scale reprocessing at IPEN, one reason may have been to lay the groundwork for a later claim that its scientists had mastered reprocessing on their own and that therefore the subsequently transferred West German data on various aspects of reprocessing did not have to be "declared" to the IAEA under the West Germany-Brazil-IAEA agreement. This might allow Brazil to argue that a subsequently built reprocessing plant, using the same processes as those in the IPEN unit and the yet-to-be-built West German-supplied reprocessing plant, was not covered by safeguards under the "replication" clause of the West Germany-Brazil-IAEA safeguards agreement, since it did not use technology that had been declared to the Agency.

Enrichment Research. In addition to these activities at IPEN, in early 1983 the secretary-general of Brazil's National Security Council, Danilo Venturini, announced that IPEN would continue a major program—secretly initiated in 1978—to develop ultracentrifuge enrichment technology as part of an alternative line of research to the Brazilian-German agreement. The IPEN program called for construction of a laboratory-scale enrichment plant by 1987 and a semi-industrial unit three years later.[43] Presumably, such a plant would be unsafeguarded and, in principle, could produce highly enriched uranium in sufficient quantities to permit the manufacture of nuclear weapons. IPEN technicians have already completed an unsafeguarded laboratory-scale plant for producing the uranium hexafluoride gas used in enrichment experiments, and an unsafeguarded pilot-scale plant was scheduled to operate at IPEN in 1984.[44]

The decision to pursue this research effort was made in 1978 at a federal summit that included representatives of the National Intelligence Service, the CNEN, and NUCLEBRAS. Reportedly, the participants sought to establish a two-track program, one dealing with the production of nuclear electricity and the other, with uranium enrichment as part of a national security effort.[45] Investigation of laser enrichment would also be included in the $100-million project.[46]

Research on laser enrichment was apparently also being undertaken at the CTA in São José dos Campos, although government sources gave this effort little publicity until late 1983, following Argentina's announcement that it had mastered the enrichment process using the gaseous diffusion method.[47]

Brazilian Rocketry. Brazil has by far the most advanced rocketry program in Latin America, which dates back to 1961. Since the inauguration of the Barreira do Inferno rocket base in 1965, Brazil, in conjunction with West Germany, has conducted hundreds of test launchings of battlefield and sounding (weather) rockets.[48] Recently, the Brazilian space program has concentrated on increasing the altitude range of its launch vehicles, and in late 1984 Brasilia plans to test-launch a Sonda IV rocket capable of reaching over six hundred miles.[49] These developments, along with the advanced state of Brazil's aircraft and basic industries, suggest that Brazil has the resources to develop a nuclear missile program, although Brazil's progress in developing guidance systems and payload designs, and therefore its proximity to an operational missile capability, is uncertain.

Nuclear Imports and Exports. In addition to its nuclear trade relations with the United States and West Germany, Brazil has entered into nuclear cooperation agreements with a number of additional countries, including Algeria, Argentina, Bolivia, Britain, Chile, Colombia, Ecuador, France, Iraq, Israel (a convention), Italy, Paraguay, the People's Republic of China, Peru, Portugal, Spain, Switzerland, Uruguay, Venezuela, and the European Atomic Community (Euratom).[50] Under its agreement with France, it has imported a safeguarded plant for converting uranium concentrate into uranium hexafluoride gas to be used in the enrichment process at Resende and is also receiving assistance in the construction of a major uranium-ore processing mill at Itataia. Its accord with Rome provides for Italy to build an experimental breeder reactor at a new Brazilian research center, Campo di Roma, in Itaguaí, but the project has been postponed.[51] Brazil "borrowed," and then returned, natural uranium from Argentina and has imported zircaloy tubing for the fabrication of fuel elements from that country.[52] Brazil has also purchased natural uranium from South Africa to be enriched by URENCO in order to fuel the Angra I reactor.[53]

Brazil also intends to become a major nuclear exporter. With its large uranium reserves and its planned uranium enrichment capability, Brazilian nuclear officials hope to make Brazil a significant exporter of enriched uranium by the end of the century and to finance part of Brazil's nuclear development through advance sales of this material.[54] In addition, with West German assistance, Brazil has developed a capability for manufacturing heavy nuclear equipment, including pressure vessels, steam generators, and pressurizers, which it also hopes to sell abroad in the years ahead.[55] Given the slowdown in the Brazilian enrichment program and the drastically reduced projections for nuclear power growth around the world, however, the commercial potential for Brazil's nuclear exports remains uncertain. Brazil has not stated whether it will require its export recipients to place Brazilian-origin nuclear commodities under IAEA safeguards.

In January 1980 Brazil signed a nuclear cooperation agreement with Iraq under which Brazil was to supply Baghdad with natural and low-enriched uranium, finished fuel elements, and technology and engineering services for reactor construction. According to press accounts, in order to obtain the nuclear accord, Iraq threatened Brazil—which was then receiving 80 percent of the oil it needed from the Middle East, half of it from Iraq—with major oil price increases. Apparently, Brazil refused to transfer any of the nuclear technology relating to enrichment or reprocessing that it was obtaining from West Germany, since such retransfers were prohibited without the latter's consent.[56] It is not known, however, whether Brazil may have considered sharing technology in these fields that it had developed on its own at IPEN and CTA. Brazil reportedly agreed to supply Iraq with 70 metric tons of uranium oxide, some eight tons of which were shipped prior to the time that Israel destroyed Iraq's nuclear reactor.[57] Iraq and Brazil agreed to inform the IAEA of their negotiations so that appropriate safeguards could be applied to the transactions.

II. Developments of the Past Year

During the past twelve months, Brazil accelerated certain parts of its nuclear program that could contribute directly to the development of nuclear weapons. At the same time, Brazilian military officials and the Brazilian press began to speak with increasing openness about the desirability of acquiring such a capability. Much of this was a response to Argentina's announcement in late 1983 of its indigenous enrichment plant at Pilcaniyeu. France responded to these developments in the Brazilian program by holding back equipment needed for the Resende enrichment plant, while the United States reacted more ambivalently by expanding military links to Brasilia and easing nuclear restrictions.

Announcement of Major New Research Reactor

In late October 1983, CNEN chairman Rex Nazare announced that Brazil was designing its first entirely indigenous research reactor for the purpose of radio-isotope production. Construction would begin in mid-1984, with the plant expected to begin operation between 1988 and 1989. The CNEN announcement did not specify the size of the reactor and stated that details as to the type of uranium fuel it would use and where that fuel would be procured—whether from an outside supplier or from Brazil's own enrichment facilities—would be announced sometime in 1984.

Nazare explained the rationale for developing an indigenous research reactor with the somewhat cryptic comment that "in view of the ever greater difficulties in the nuclear area at the international level, the continuous operation of the atomic reactors that exist in the country is impracticable, not permitting self-sufficiency in radioisotopes, although the percentage of national participation is growing."[58] This was an apparent reference to the fact that U.S. supplies of enriched uranium for Brazil's existing isotope-producing research reactors had been suspended under the 1978 Non-Proliferation Act because of Brazil's unwillingness to place all of its nuclear installations under IAEA safeguards.

The 20 percent enriched uranium required for Brazil's research reactors, however, can be obtained on the international market, from the Soviet Union or China, for example, nations from whom Argentina has made such purchases in recent years. Moreover, any new research reactor developed by Brazil would require comparable fuel—unless a natural-uranium/heavy-water reactor were built, in which case heavy water would have to be purchased abroad. Thus, unless Brazil were planning to supply its new reactor with indigenously produced enriched uranium, from the Resende enrichment plant, for example, it is not evident how a new research reactor would ease "difficulties in the nuclear area at the international level." On the other hand, if Brazil were intending to produce research reactor fuel indigenously, such fuel could be used in its existing isotope-producing reactors to circumvent the U.S. supply cutoff. Again, development of a new research reactor would not appear to be necessary for the production of radioisotopes.

This suggests another possible purpose behind the project: construction of a large research reactor capable of producing significant quantities of plutonium that might contribute to a future nuclear weapons capability. Indeed, Brazil itself appears to have experimented with this approach at the IPEN facility, as discussed earlier, irradiating natural uranium in the U.S.-supplied research reactor there and, according to some reports, then reprocessing the material to extract small quantities of plutonium.[59] An indigenously built reactor, if fueled with unsafeguarded enriched uranium from the planned IPEN centrifuge enrichment unit, could operate without IAEA supervision. Argentina also has a large unsafeguarded research reactor on the drawing boards. Possibly Brazil's planned facility is a response to this Argentine installation.

U.S. government experts give little credence to this scenario. They believe the planned reactor will be too small to pose a proliferation threat and point out that if Brazil succeeds in producing enriched uranium at IPEN, upgrading it to weapons-grade would be a more direct and efficient route to the bomb than using the material as fuel in a new research reactor to produce plutonium.[60] Until further details of the planned facility are known, it will be impossible to make a clear judgment as to its potential contribution to a Brazilian nuclear weapons capability.

Response to Announcement of Argentine Enrichment Capability

Initially, Brazil reacted with studied indifference to the November 18, 1983, announcement that Argentina had succeeded in producing enriched uranium. One press account immediately after the Argentine disclosure stated that Brazil's military ministers had "revealed that the Brazilian Army is not concerned over the Argentine announcement," and Brazilian president Figueiredo addressed a letter to his Argentine counterpart expressing his "deep satisfaction" over Argentina's mastering of the uranium enrichment process.[61]

Public comment quickly turned to the strategic implications of the Argentine achievement and the need for a Brazilian response. On November 22, the respected *O Estado de São Paulo,* after pointing out that both Argentina and Brazil had reserved the right to produce nuclear explosives by refusing to ratify the Non-Proliferation Treaty or to become formally bound by the Tlatelolco Treaty, stated:

Since the purpose of the use [peaceful or military] will not be known until the moment of the use of the explosive, it is valid to suppose that the two governments are conscientiously pursuing the objective of mastering the technology that will permit them access to the bomb.

From that perspective one cannot let the announcement made by [Argentine] Rear Admiral Madero last Friday pass without comment; although on a laboratory scale, Argentina today has the technical conditions to produce the Atomic Bomb.[62]

Only a few days later, physicist José Goldemberg, long-time critic of the Brazilian nuclear program, predicted that Brazilian nuclear officials would use the Argentine success as a pretext for accelerating the Resende jet-nozzle enrichment plant.[63] Indeed, on the heels of this comment the Brazilian government was reported to have begun a debate with an eye to "catching up with Argentina on the mastery of nuclear technology."[64] Under discussion were increased funding for the first uranium enrichment unit at the Resende site and completion of the German-supplied Resende spent fuel reprocessing plant. At the end of November, barely two weeks after the Argentine announcement, a senior member of the Brazilian army, General Pires Gonçalves, in an unusually open declaration of the military potential of Brazil's nuclear program, stated that "Brazil will soon conclude the uranium technology cycle that will allow manufacture of the atomic bomb."[65]

In the following weeks, the Brazilian press continued to play up the military potential of Brazil's nuclear program, apparently encouraged by the nation's military leaders, who seemed eager to show that Argentina's new capabilities did not leave Brazil at a strategic disadvantage. On December 9, *O Estado de São Paulo* revealed that Brasília had prepared a contingency plan for future development of atomic weapons:

The Brazilian nuclear bomb is theoretically defined, and the date has already been established for adopting a decision about its construction: 1990. It is at that time that the military scientific research bodies and the civilian research institutions in the atomic sector will have completed a long process of acquiring knowledge and training personnel to provide the country with total technological independence in this sector. Everything will then depend on the determination of the government to establish the terms of a possible program designed to create a nuclear-equipped tactical and strategic security force in Brazil.

Under the plan, the article continued, Brazil's "main strategic nuclear weapon" would be a twenty to thirty kiloton bomb using plutonium that would be carried by a medium-range missile based on a satellite-launch vehicle that Brazil is currently developing. The necessary nuclear research activities are being conducted principally at the CTA in São José dos Campos and include development of laser uranium enrichment technology (presumably suited to manufacturing highly enriched uranium) and breeder reactors for the purpose, the article stated, of producing large quantities of plutonium.[66]

In an interview published the following day, Waldyr Vasconcellos, chief of the Armed Forces General Staff, stated that Brazil "is preparing to master nuclear technology completely" and "will be able to produce armaments, including the atomic bomb." He went on to state that studies were currently "advanced and could lead to the manufacture of an atomic bomb," but asserted that the goal of the effort "is for peaceful purposes." The same article quoted military sources in Brasilia as stating that research at São José dos Campos was advanced and that scientists there "certainly know the techniques for the manufacture of the bomb." These sources claimed, however, that Brazil had no interest in producing nuclear weapons because that would encourage nuclear competition in Latin America and would be very costly. The article also stated that the new commander of the São José dos Campos research center, Brigadier General Hugo de Oliveira Piva, confirmed that Brazil would be in a position to build an atomic weapon by 1990. The article continued:

He gave assurance that there is no Brazilian plan to produce an atomic bomb but he acknowledged that the development of the latest nuclear technology is also guaranteeing the country's progress in connection with uses of atomic technology for weaponry.

U.S. embassy officials were apparently unperturbed by these startling new characterizations of Brazil's nuclear program. The article quoted one U.S. official as stating: "Nothing leads the American government to believe that Brazil is really producing its bomb. We are persuaded that the Brazilian government has meticulously honored [its] international safeguard agreements."[67]

On December 13, Energy Minister César Cals, responsible for implementing the Brazilian-West German nuclear deal, also stressed the importance of the unsafeguarded parallel nuclear research program being conducted at São José dos Campos. Cals stated that the government's current priority was the "conquest of the atom," meaning the development of enrichment and reprocessing using "native" technology. A day later Cals issued a clarifying note, apparently fearful that his remarks might be misinterpreted to suggest Brazil was launched on a nuclear weapons development program: "Any reading, deductions or inferences leading to the conclusion that Brazil is attempting to evade the peaceful uses of nuclear technology do not have the slightest grounds and are devoid of any substance."[68]

Others in the Figueiredo government were obviously seeking to create a different impression, however. On December 15, the *Correio Braziliense* carried a further elaboration by certain unnamed scientists involved in unsafeguarded nuclear research at São José dos Campos and other sites to the effect that Cals' remarks "should be only understood to apply in the jurisdiction of the ministries and in the context of the Brazilian-West German FRG nuclear agreement." In the words of these experts,

There is no intention of building military nuclear devices at this time, and probably that decision will not be made, but it would be naive to believe that a decision made by the current government could be binding on Brazilian governments in the 1990s when the geo-political picture will certainly be different, and the national sovereignty will have to be discussed in the light of the situation in the next decade. . . . In the medium-term Brazil might decide to use nuclear technology in any of the alternatives inherent in the possession of the complete nuclear fuel cycle.[69]

By the end of January, Brazil's navy minister, Admiral Eduardo da Silva Fonseca Maximiano, echoed his army colleagues in an interview:

[Reporter] We are going to have the byproduct of nuclear research, and we will be in a position to manufacture the bomb in the 1990's. Whenever we reach that point, what will be necessary to build the bomb?

[Maximiano] The decision of a future government. But today I want to make something clear: we, the military are not going after the bomb. With the development of nuclear research, however, one day the country will inevitably have the material necessary to build the bomb. *It is a good thing to have that capacity.* But just because we possess that capacity, manufacturing the bomb will make no sense because we do not intend to go to war against anyone. Where would we drop the bomb? On our heads? So we will not build any nuclear device.[70] [Emphases added.]

Admiral Fonseca Maximiano also acknowledged that Brazil was studying the feasibility of developing nuclear submarines that would require the production of highly enriched uranium. Asked whether such uranium might be produced at Resende—which Brazilian nuclear officials have long stated would be dedicated to the production of low-enriched uranium only—he replied, "Why not?"[71] This was a strong hint that at least some elements of the Brazilian elite saw the safeguarded German-supplied plant as a potential source of weapons-grade material.

Despite the confusion created by these exchanges, the implications they raise are sobering. Important elements of the Brazilian scientific and technical community are engaged in research that they believe is laying the foundation for a possible Brazilian nuclear weapons program and that is enjoying increased prominence and legitimacy in Brazilian government circles.

Budget Priority. What appeared to be the first concrete response to the Argentine enrichment plant was made by NUCLEBRAS chief Darió Gomes. In early January, he announced that although budget cuts would require NUCLEBRAS to postpone all orders for supplies that were to be placed during 1984 and to slow construction of the Angra II nuclear plant, the Resende uranium enrichment facility would not be affected because "it has priority status within the nuclear program."[72] In March, plans to produce enriched uranium at Resende by 1985 were disclosed.[73]

French Restrictions. During December 1983, as the Brazilian response to the Argentine enrichment program evolved, Brazil was also negotiating with Alsthom-Atlantíque, the French state-controlled engineering group, to purchase compressors needed for the expansion of the Resende enrichment plant from its demonstration phase to industrial-scale production. Reportedly, Brazil considered the French compressors superior to those available in West Germany and needed them to improve the efficiency of the jet-nozzle process at the enrichment plant.[74]

French Foreign Ministry officials, apparently concerned over Brazil's failure to accept full-scope safeguards and over the proliferation risks of aiding it in mastering the enrichment process, refused to issue export licenses for the compressors, stating that time would be needed to "reflect" about whether approval would be given.[75] Contributing to French concerns were doubts about the commercial justification for building the enrichment plant, whose development was predicated originally on Brazil's previous plan to construct eight nuclear power reactors supplied by West Germany. Brazil now plans to construct only two of these power reactors, and enriched-uranium supply contracts with URENCO already cover most of their requirements. French government officials believed that "Brazil's intentions were not as pure as they might be."[76] In response to the French rebuff, Brazil announced that the order for the pumps would be placed with West Germany.

Strengthening of U.S.-Brazilian Ties

Despite the increasingly explicit signs of Brazil's interest in the military aspects of nuclear energy, Washington's public posture was one of growing leniency towards Brasilia. In February, the United States signed a major new memorandum of understanding for military-industrial cooperation with Brazil and simultaneously released it from the onerous 1973 uranium enrichment contract.[77]

The signing of the military agreement, which provided for the co-production in Brazil of U.S.-designed military equipment, was the centerpiece of Secretary of State George Shultz's visit to Brasilia in early February 1984 and appeared to symbolize the improvement in relations between the countries. U.S. criticism of Brazil's human rights policies and of its efforts to acquire enrichment and reprocessing technology had led to difficult relations during the Carter administration. Indeed, Brazil had severed military ties in 1977 in the face of an imminent cutoff of U.S. military assistance on human rights grounds, and under the 1977 Symington amendment to the U.S. Foreign Assistance Act, Brazil remains ineligible for direct U.S. economic or military assistance because of its importation of nuclear enrichment and reprocessing equipment.[78]

The Reagan administration has not attempted to suspend the Symington amendment to permit military assistance to Brazil, as it has to allow such aid to Pakistan. Nevertheless, its efforts to rekindle military relations through the memorandum of understanding may have been taken as a sign that U.S. concerns over the risks of Brazilian proliferation had diminished.

Export of enriched uranium to Brazil has been prohibited since 1980 under the U.S. Non-Proliferation Act because of Brasilia's unwillingness to accept international safeguards on all of its nuclear installations. The 1973 enrichment contract provided for the imposition of termination charges against Brazil if it did not take delivery of the enriched uranium on schedule. In 1981, the United States temporarily suspended application of the penalty provision, thus allowing Brazil to turn to URENCO for the first reload of the Angra I plant without suffering economic hardship. The decision to suspend the 1973 contract indefinitely, also formalized during the Shultz visit, meant that Brazil would not face penalties if it sought additional fuel supplies for Angra I from other sources.[79] With Brazil's senior military leaders openly declaring that the nation was seeking the technology for a near-term nuclear weapons capability, this gesture, like the signing of the U.S.-Brazilian military accord, may also have given the appearance of reduced U.S. concern over the direction of Brazil's nuclear program.

Expanding Export Opportunities

In late 1983 and during the first half of early 1984, Brazil continued its active pursuit of export markets for its nuclear materials and equipment. In December, Brazil's heavy equipment manufacturing corporation (NUCLEP) presented a bid to the West German firm KWU to serve as subcontractor for part of the latter's bid to supply nuclear power reactors to Egypt and Turkey.[80]

In May 1984 Brazil signed an agreement for nuclear cooperation with the People's Republic of China. The accord covered basic research, planning, construction, and operation of nuclear research and power reactors and the production of radioisotopes. It was not disclosed whether, under the accord, Brazil will sell China equipment for its growing nuclear power program.[81] Finally, Brazil and Venezuela signed a nuclear cooperation agreement in January 1984. Although Venezuela does not have a nuclear power program, the two nations will carry out preliminary research in this area.[82]

All of these initiatives testify to Brazil's expanding pretensions as a nuclear supplier, and, depending on the conditions Brazil places on its nuclear exports, could raise the possibility of new proliferation dangers.

III. Prospects for Nuclear Weapons in Brazil

Although Brazil is plainly behind Argentina in nuclear development, its considerable nuclear infrastructure and underlying technological and industrial base leave little doubt that it, too, possesses the raw scientific and technical capabilities necessary to design and fabricate nuclear weapons. For the time being, however, Brazil lacks a source of plutonium or highly enriched uranium and is not likely to have one until 1990 at the earliest.

Several options would be available to Brazil if it chose to move closer to the possession of nuclear arms. First, and most directly, it could build an unsafeguarded ultracentrifuge or laser uranium enrichment facility based on its ongoing research in these fields. Under currently announced plans, a semi-industrial-scale centrifuge unit is to be built at IPEN by 1990. Details of other unsafeguarded enrichment research have not been disclosed.

A second route, development of an unsafeguarded plutonium production capability, may be considerably more difficult. Although Brazil has a source of unsafeguarded reactor-grade uranium at IPEN, all of its nuclear power and research reactors are under safeguards; a new reactor would have to be built indigenously if Brazil wanted to acquire plutonium not subject to international supervision. A large research reactor could do the job, but fueling it would be a major problem. Such reactors either use natural uranium surrounded by heavy water—a commodity Brazil has no capacity for producing and which is difficult to purchase on the international market without safeguards—or highly enriched uranium surrounded by normal, or light, water. As noted earlier, however, Brazil currently has no source of highly enriched uranium. If it did have a source of such uranium, it would not need to develop a plutonium production capability, since the highly enriched uranium itself could be used to build nuclear weapons.

Brazil's third option would be to acquire significant quantities of highly enriched uranium under safeguards. This would provide Brazil with a de facto nuclear weapons capability, but one that could be exercised only at great political cost. By 1988, Brazil is hoping to produce sixty metric tons of low-enriched uranium per year at the Resende enrichment facility. Since this plant will be dedicated to producing low-enriched uranium, IAEA inspectors would be likely to detect any attempt to switch the plant to the production of highly enriched material. Still, one Brazilian official has hinted that the Resende plant might be used for producing highly enriched uranium, ostensibly for nuclear submarine fuel.[83]

Finally, Brazil could obtain a stockpile of plutonium under safeguards. By completing the Resende reprocessing plant, now scheduled to begin operation in 1986, Brazil could in principle reprocess fuel from the Angra I reactor to obtain plutonium. However, the enriched uranium originally used to fuel Angra I was supplied by the United States and under the U.S.-Brazil agreement, U.S. approval for reprocessing that material would have to be obtained. It is unlikely such approval would be granted. In recent years, the United States has limited such authorizations to reprocessing in the nuclear weapon states and in Japan. The fuel used in Angra I after its initial loading will be supplied by URENCO for several years, at least, and will be subject to the Dutch-imposed requirement that any plutonium extracted from the fuel be stored under multinational auspices. This would prevent Brazil from maintaining substantial stocks of plutonium under its direct control, although Brazil would probably obtain access to some quantities of this material before consigning it to the international storage regime.[84] Not until about 1990 will Brazil be able to load the Angra I plant with domestically enriched fuel. Brazil could subsequently reprocess this material at will and store the resulting plutonium under Brazilian control—all under IAEA safeguards, however.

In sum, while Brazil now lacks the capacity to produce nuclear weapons material in quantity, it is pressing to complete in the next five years facilities that could provide such a capability, and one option being actively pursued—the centrifuge enrichment unit at IPEN—would provide unsafeguarded material that could be freely used for nuclear explosives.

From the available evidence, Brazil appears to be developing its enrichment and reprocessing capabilities in large part to avoid falling behind Argentina's comparable efforts. Given Argentina's lead—its partially unsafeguarded reprocessing plant has been under construction since 1977 and its unsafeguarded enrichment capability has already been demonstrated—Brazil is not inclined to slow its own efforts in these fields. The priority given IPEN's centrifuge research and the Resende enrichment and reprocessing plants demonstrates this commitment. Should the Alfonsín government decide to slow the more provocative elements of Argentina's nuclear activities or agree to added non-proliferation pledges, however, Brazilian officials might reconsider this posture so as to avoid the risk of Brazilian activities in the reprocessing and enrichment fields rekindling the Argentine program. Moreover, like Argentina, Brazil would have to weigh the costs of developing a de facto nuclear weapons capability on its relations with the United States and other advanced Western nations on whom it, too, depends for nuclear aid, export markets, and financing.

One additional factor of importance for assessing near-term prospects for proliferation in Brazil is that the elections now scheduled for 1985 will restore civilian government. The nation's new leadership could change the direction of Brazil's nuclear program, by accepting new non-proliferation commitments, slowing development of reprocessing and enrichment capabilities, or both. Even for a new civilian government, however, Argentina's nuclear posture will likely be the decisive factor in determining Brazil's nuclear policy.

BRAZIL

⬡ uranium mining area

0 — 800
MILES

Brazil

Power Reactors/Operating or Under Construction

Angra I (light-water/low-enriched uranium, 626 MWe)
- supplier: Westinghouse (U.S.)
- start up: 1982
- fuel source: Initial load, U.S.; current reloads URENCO (W. German, British, Dutch)[a]; Brazil enriched uranium, only, after 1986. (est.).[b]
- safeguards: yes

Angra II (light-water/low-enriched uranium, 1300 MWe)
- supplier: Kraftwerk Union (West Germany)
- start up: 1989 (est.)[c]
- fuel source: Initial load, URENCO (W. German, British, Dutch); subsequent loads, Brazil enriched uranium.[b]
- safeguards: yes

Angra III (light-water/low-enriched uranium, 1300 MWe)
- supplier: Kraftwerk Union (West Germany)
- start up: 1990 (est.)[c]
- fuel source: Initial load, URENCO (W. German, British, Dutch), subsequent loads, Brazil enriched uranium.[b]
- safeguards: yes

Uranium Resources/Active Mining Sites/Uranium Mills

- reasonably assured reserves: 163,000 metric tons[d]
- currently active site: Poços de Caldas
- mills in operation: Poços de Caldas

Uranium Purification (UO$_2$)

IPEN, São Paulo
- capacity: excess of 10 metric tons per year[e]
- supplier: Brazil, with some W. German equipment.[f]
- start up: 1981 (?)[e]
- safeguards: no

UF$_6$ Conversion

Resende
- capacity: planned 500 metric tons per year (eventually 2000 metric tons per year)[g]
- supplier: P.U.K. (France)[h]
- start up: after 1984[g]
- safeguards: yes

IPEN, São Paulo (pilot scale)
- capacity: 25 kg of UF$_6$ per hour by 1984 (est.)[i]
- supplier: Brazil[i, j]
- start up: after 1984[g]
- safeguards: no

IPEN, São Paulo (laboratory scale)
- capacity: (?) (50 kg. UF$_6$ produced by 1982).[i]
- supplier: Brazil (with some foreign assistance)[i]
- start up: 1981-1982[i]
- safeguards: no

Enrichment

Resende
- type: jet-nozzle
- capacity: 64 metric tons low-enriched uranium in 1988.[k]
- supplier: Kraftwerk Union (West Germany)[l]
- start up: first cascade 1985 (est.)[m]
- safeguards: yes

Belo Horizonte
- type: jet-nozzle
- capacity: laboratory scale
- supplier: Kraftwerk Union (West Germany)
- start up: 1980[n]
- safeguards: yes

IPEN, São Paulo
- type: ultracentrifuge
- capacity: lab scale until 1990, semi-industrial capacity thereafter
- supplier: Brazil
- start up: 1987, lab scale; 1990 semi-industrial unit[o]
- safeguards: no

Fuel Fabrication

Resende
- capacity: Planned 100 tons per year for Angra I, II, III[p]
- supplier: West Germany
- start up: 1982[q]
- safeguards: yes

IPEN, São Paulo (pilot plant)

Reprocessing

Resende
- capacity: pilot scale, 10 kg spent fuel per day[r]
- supplier: West Germany
- start up: 1986 (est.)[s]
- safeguards: yes[t]

IPEN, São Paulo (laboratory scale)
- capacity: varying estimates[u]
- supplier: Brazil with some West German equipment[f]
- start up: 1981 (?)[f] 1983 (?)[u]
- safeguards: only when safeguarded fuel is processed[w]

Principal Research Reactors[x,y]

IEAR-1, São Paulo (Pool/highly-enriched uranium[v] , 5 MWt)
- supplier: United States
- start up: 1957
- safeguards: yes

RIEN-1, Rio de Janeiro (Argonaut/medium-enriched uranium, 10 KWt)
- supplier: Brazil
- start up: 1965
- safeguards: yes

Triga-UMG, Belo Horizonte (Triga I/medium-enriched uranium 100 KWt)
- supplier: United States
- start up: 1960
- safeguards: yes

Sources and Notes

a. "German Uranium for Angra." *Jornal do Brasil*, translated in Foreign Broadcast Information Service/Nuclear Proliferation and Development, hereafter FBIS/NDP, January 18, 1982, p. 28.

b. Assis Mendonca, "Germany Denies Having Negotiated Another Process." *O Estado de São Paulo*, translated in FBIS/NDP, May 13, 1982, p. 21.

c. "Gomes Comments on Program Changes, Equipment, Uranium Exports," *O Estado de São Paulo*, translated in FBIS/NDP, December 20, 1983, p. 58.

d. Reasonably Assured Reserves at less than $130 kilogram, OECD Nuclear Energy Agency and the International Atomic Energy Agency, *Uranium: Resources, Production, and Demand*, (Paris: OECD, 1983), p. 98.

e. personal communication with informed U.S. official.

f. Bernardo Kucinski, "Argentine Boast Spurs Brazil into Race for Bomb," *The Guardian*, reprinted in FBIS/NDP, February 19, 1982, pp. 6-8.

g. "Researchers Developing Brazil's Know-how on UF-6 Beyond the Plant Now Being Built," *Nuclear Fuel*, September 27, 1982, p. 13, (Planned start-up, 1984); *Nuclear Engineering International*, March 1984, p. 8, (construction will resume in 1984).

h. "Uranium Enrichment Plant in Itataia Confirmed," *O Estado de São Paulo*, translated in FBIS/NDP, January 25, 1982, p. 22.

i. "IPEN Produces Uranium Hexafluoride on Laboratory Scale," *Jornal do Brasil*, translated in FBIS/NDP, July 28, 1982, p. 18.

j. personal communication with informed U.S. official.

k. "Unfavorable Aspects of Nuclear Accord Coming to Light," *Estado de São Paulo*, April 1, 1982 translated in FBIS/NDP, May 3, 1982, p. 11.

l. "KWU Recommends Development of Jet-Nozzle Enrichment Process Here," *O Estado de Sao Paulo*, translated in FBIS/NDP, June 3, 1982, p. 22.

m. "Uranium Enrichment Production," *Jornal de Comercio, AFP*, (Paris) March 11, 1984, translated in FBIS/NDP, March 29, 1984, p. 12; "Uranium Enrichment Test," *O Globo*, February 18, 1984, translated in FBIS/NDP March 29, 1984, p. 12 (first cascade to be tested in late 1984.)

n. Charles Thurston, "Critics See Brazil as Taken For a Ride on Its 'Last Train' to SWU Technology," *Nuclear Fuel*, April 26, 1982, p. 3.

o. Eneas Filho, "Ten Billion Cruzeiros to be Allocated for Nuclear Research," *Jornal do Brasil*, translated in FBIS/NDP, March 21, 1983, p. 28.

p. "Operation of Fuel Elements Factory in Resende Discussed," *Manchete*, (Rio de Janeiro), translated in FBIS/NDP, December 6, 1982, pp. 18-21.

q. Juan de Onis, "Brazil's Crash Program Slows to Realistic Pace," *International Herald Tribune*, October 1982.

r. William W. Lowrance, "Nuclear Futures For Sale: To Brazil From West Germany, 1975," *International Security*, Fall 1976, p. 152.

s. "Resende Site of Uranium Reprocessing Plant Confirmed," *O Estado de São Paulo*, translated in FBIS/NDP, May 10, 1983, p. 21. Later start-up date probable; reportedly little construction to date, (personal communication with informed U.S. official.)

t. International storage also required for any plutonium reprocessed from URENCO fuel.

u. Milton R. Benjamin "Brazil Takes Steps Toward Nuclear Weapons Potential," *Washington Post*, February 3, 1983. But see, "The laboratory has not handled any radioactive material," February 13, 1983, *Washington Post* letter to the editor from Antonio Azeredo da Silveira. U.S. officials concur. (Personal communication). Minute quantities, (scientist Roberto Hukay in "Report on IPEN Reactor," *Jornal do Brasil*, translated in FBIS/NDP, February 18, 1983, p. 5.) Five kg plutonium per year (Kucinski, "Argentine Boast Spurs Brazil into Race for the Bomb.")

v. Currently 90 percent enriched uranium, soon to be converted to 20 percent enriched uranium.

w. Currently, only safeguarded fuel is available.

x. James Katz and Onkar Marwah, *Nuclear Power in Developing Countries* (Lexington, MA: Lexington Books, 1982), p. 100.

y. International Atomic Energy Agency, *The Annual Report for 1981*, p. 70.

Chapter V:
Africa

Introduction

The only African nation posing a significant proliferation risk today is South Africa; indeed, no other
state in the region has more than the most rudimentary
nuclear program. South Africa has the capability to
produce highly enriched uranium for nuclear weapons
and may have accumulated enough material for between fifteen and twenty-five nuclear explosives of the
size used on Hiroshima.[1] If reports that it imported
substantial quantities of low-enriched uranium from
China in 1981 are true, it could rapidly enrich this
material further to weapons-grade, substantially increasing its stockpile of nuclear explosive material.
Although South Africa is not known to have manufactured nuclear weapons or to have tested them, it is
generally believed to have been preparing a test in
1977. It may also have detonated a nuclear device in
September 1979, when a U.S. surveillance satellite
observed signals that some experts have interpreted as

coming from a nuclear explosion in the Indian or South Atlantic ocean.

Although South Africa is the only nation in the region with a nuclear capability, other nations have recently begun to discuss the desirability of obtaining nuclear arms. In 1980, for example, Chuba Okadigbo, a senior advisor to then Nigerian president Shehu Shagari, stated in an address to the Foreign Policy Association in New York that Nigeria could obtain the technology and materials needed for a nuclear bomb and intended to build one "if it is necessary to bring South Africa to the negotiating table." Okadigbo, who stated that he was speaking for the Nigerian government on the matter, continued, "We won't allow Africa to be subjected to nuclear blackmail," and added that it would be "unreasonable to expect" that other African nations will not seek a nuclear weapon to meet South Africa's presumed capability.[2]

Similarly, in June 1983, the secretary-general of the Organization of African Unity, Edem Kodjo of Togo, said at the nineteenth summit meeting of black African states, "Let us not be told especially about denuclearizing Africa when South Africa already has a nuclear arsenal. Against whom is it manufacturing its atomic bomb? Against us, of course, and the duty of the African states that can is to resolutely embark on the nuclear path. Such will be easily done within the framework of a community."[3]

Notwithstanding these statements of intent, no steps appear to have been taken toward achieving this objective. While the long-term potential for further proliferation on the African continent remains, it is hard to imagine a second nation obtaining a nuclear weapons capability for the remainder of this century.

South Africa

I. Background

The earliest phase of the South African involvement in the nuclear field was devoted exclusively to a military objective: supplying uranium for the nuclear weapons programs of the United States and Great Britain. At the end of the Second World War, South African prime minister Jan Smuts ordered a secret survey of his country's uranium resources at the request of Great Britain, which had collaborated with the United States on developing the atomic bomb.[1] In 1949 the South African Atomic Energy Institute was established, and in 1950 it entered into an agreement with the British-U.S. Combined Development Agency to promote South African uranium production.[2]

The Combined Development Agency purchased the entire output of South Africa's mining operations through much of the 1950s, financed the development of South Africa's uranium resources, and assisted South Africa in perfecting the technology for extracting and processing uranium.[3] By 1955 South Africa was operating nineteen mines and twelve extraction plants.[4]

In May 1954, the United States built upon the activities of the Combined Development Agency to organize an international consultative group of uranium supplier countries, known as the Western Suppliers Group (a precursor of the 1975 Nuclear Suppliers Group). The purpose of the organization was to help prevent the spread of nuclear capabilities by requiring bilateral, and later, International Atomic Energy Agency (IAEA) safeguards on uranium sales. South Africa was a charter member of the group, which also included Britain, Canada, France, Belgium, and Australia, along with the United States.[5] South Africa also participated in the development of a second multilateral institution dedicated to curbing the spread of nuclear weapons, the International Atomic Energy Agency, which was founded in 1957. South Africa was given a permanent seat on the IAEA board as the nation with the "most advanced" nuclear program in its region.

U.S. Assistance. The United States and South Africa signed a nuclear cooperation agreement in 1957. Under the agreement, nearly one hundred South African nationals were trained at American institutions through 1970, including Drs. A.J.A. Roux and W. L. Grant, who later played key roles in developing South Africa's uranium enrichment capability.[6] Under the accord, the United States sold Pretoria a five-megawatt, high-enriched-uranium/light-water research reactor called SAFARI I. Located at the National Nuclear Research Centre at Pelindaba, the reactor was completed in March 1965.[7] The reactor has been under IAEA safeguards since 1967 and was upgraded to twenty megawatts in 1969. Built by the Allis Chalmers Corporation, it was fueled with U.S.-supplied 90 percent enriched uranium, some one hundred kilograms of which was supplied to South Africa between 1965 and 1976.[8]

In 1967 South Africa commissioned a second, smaller reactor, Pelunduna-Zero, which used low-enriched uranium and heavy water. The United States supplied 606 kilograms of 2 percent enriched uranium and 5.45 kilograms of heavy water for the plant under the U.S.-South Africa nuclear agreement which required the application of IAEA safeguards to all such exports. As a result, this reactor, like SAFARI I, was apparently placed under the IAEA system. It has since been decommissioned.[9]

While neither of these reactors is known to have played a direct role in South Africa's nuclear weapons development program, they were undoubtedly important in training South African nuclear specialists and permitting experiments that helped in the design of nuclear explosives.[10] Indeed, by 1977, only months before it was accused of developing a nuclear bomb, the president of South Africa's Atomic Energy Board, A.J.A. Roux, stated: "We can ascribe our degree of advancement today in large measure to training and assistance so willingly provided by the United States of America during the early years of our nuclear program when several of the Western nations cooperated in initiating our scientists and engineers into nuclear science."[11]

As important as U.S. assistance may have been to South Africa, from the U.S. standpoint the nuclear relationship was increasingly troubled because South Africa's policy of racial separation (apartheid) made U.S.-South African nuclear cooperation potentially embarrassing for U.S. leaders. In the fall of 1964, for example, the Johnson administration delayed shipment of the highly enriched uranium fuel needed to permit the start-up of the SAFARI I reactor, apparently fearing that news of the shipment, with the close ties to South Africa it implied, might interfere with the conduct of U.S. African policy, then in a sensitive stage because of the Congo crisis. To make the export more acceptable to potential critics, Washington insisted that Pretoria agree to enter into an accord with the IAEA to permit the agency to inspect the SAFARI I reactor in lieu of the United States, as was then planned. (At the time, the United States, in order to promote wider acceptance of the IAEA safeguards system, was requiring all of its nuclear export recipients to accept this change-over when their agreements expired. However, in the case of South Africa, whose agreement was not due for renewal until 1969, Washington accelerated the imposition of this condition.) South Africa reportedly agreed to the new terms, and the fuel was shipped in February 1965 without publicity.[12]

Development of Nuclear Weapons Capability. The first hint that Pretoria might be considering the development of its own nuclear explosives came in 1965, when one of the members of South Africa's Atomic Energy Board, Dr. Andries Visser, advocated building a nuclear arsenal for "prestige purposes" and reportedly stated, "We should have the bomb to prevent aggression from loud-mouthed Afro-Asiatic states . . . money is no problem. The capital for such a bomb is available."[13] Visser apparently was responding to a finding by the South African Atomic Energy Board that production of a single nuclear weapon would cost the equivalent of $70 million, nearly a quarter of the country's defense budget at the time.[14] Later that year,

Prime Minister H. F. Verwoerd offered a second veiled hint of South Africa's interest in nuclear arms during the inauguration ceremony for the SAFARI I reactor, urging that "it is the duty of South Africa to consider not only the military uses of the material but also to do all in its power to direct its uses to peaceful purposes."[15]

In December 1968, General H. J. Martin, then army chief of staff, reportedly stated that South Africa was ready to make its own nuclear weapons and that this readiness was linked with work he was doing on the development of missiles. His statement was quickly repudiated by then minister of defense (now prime minister) P. W. Botha.[16] Earlier in 1968, South Africa had refused to sign the just-completed Non-Proliferation Treaty. In addition to voicing the common argument that the Non-Proliferation Treaty did not obligate the nuclear-weapon states to reduce their arsenals, Pretoria expressed concern over the treaty's impact on the commercial aspects of nuclear energy in South Africa. Among other fears mentioned by South Africa's delegate in the U.N. debate on the Non-Proliferation Treaty were that South Africa might ultimately have to submit its gold mines—where uranium is obtained as a by-product—to international inspection and that hard-earned technological advances important to South Africa's competitiveness in the uranium field might be compromised by the inspection regime.[17] (In fact, the IAEA safeguards system developed to implement the Non-Proliferation Treaty's full-scope safeguards requirement does not call for IAEA oversight of mining activities, partly as a concession to South Africa aimed at gaining its adherence to the pact.)

Notwithstanding this declared position, South Africa may well have rejected the treaty in order to retain its legal option to develop nuclear weapons at a later point. The 1960s were a period of rapid decolonialization in Africa, and South African leaders became increasingly concerned about the nation's long-term security, as evidenced by the sixfold increase in South African defense expenditures between 1961 and 1968.[18] Moreover, as noted above, some in the South African government favored the acquisition of nuclear arms, and it is known that during the 1960s South Africa was working actively to develop a technique for enriching uranium that could provide the technological capability for manufacturing nuclear arms.[19] Against this background, there may have been wide consensus within the South African government against giving up the option to build nuclear arms.

While refusing to sign the pact in 1968, the South African delegate to the United Nations expressed his support for the treaty and stated that South Africa was resolved "to do absolutely nothing in the context of uranium sales to foreign buyers which might conceivably contribute to an addition to the ranks of nuclear weapon states," an apparent pledge to make uranium exports only when they would be subject to IAEA monitoring.[20] Reportedly, in the late 1950s and early 1960s South Africa had supplied Israel with uranium for use in the Dimona reactor without requiring application of IAEA safeguards.[21]

Uranium Enrichment Capability. In July 1970, Prime Minister John Vorster announced to parliament that the South African Atomic Energy Board had successfully developed a new process, "unique in its concept," of uranium enrichment.[22] Although the process has remained secret, details revealed at professional meetings in the 1970s indicate that its distinguishing feature is a "high-performance stationary-walled centrifuge."[23] The process is believed to be somewhat similar to the Becker jet-nozzle method developed in West Germany. South Africa hoped to commercialize the process and, by enriching uranium prior to export, greatly increase the value of a commodity then expected to be in demand as nuclear energy programs around the world expanded.

Although the technology also appeared to have military potential, since it would permit the manufacture of highly enriched uranium, in announcing the new technology Vorster stated that South Africa was "prepared to collaborate in the exploitation of this process with any non-communist country desiring to do so." And indeed at least one contact with the West German firm STEAG (Steinkohlen-Elektrizitats AG), which had the rights to develop the West German Becker jet-nozzle process, was reported openly in the press.[24] Since, presumably, any such foreign participation would have made it very difficult for South Africa to use its uranium enrichment capability for nuclear weapons, the fact that external aid was sought may mean that Pretoria had no intention at that time of exploiting the new technology's military potential.

Although the original attempt to obtain overt assistance from STEAG was blocked by the West German government, cooperation between the firm and South Africa's uranium enrichment corporation appears to have proceeded on a clandestine basis. STEAG is believed to have assisted South Africa in the engineering of a pilot enrichment plant that was completed in 1975 at Valindaba. Based on documents stolen from the South African embassy in West Germany by the African National Congress, a black political organization banned in South Africa, some West German government officials may also have helped to provide this assistance, including West Germany's senior air officer and representative to NATO's military committee,

Lieutenant General Guenter Rall. Rall is said to have made a secret trip to South Africa traveling under an assumed name to visit its nuclear research center. The documents indicate, moreover, that between 1969 and 1975, numerous South African nationals visited the West German research center at Karlsruhe, where research on uranium enrichment was also being conducted.[25]

This has led to the charge that the "unique" South African enrichment process is really the Becker process with slight modifications. Other authorities believe that the South African process is distinctive, although this does not rule out the possibility that STEAG used its knowledge of the Becker process to aid South Africa in developing the Valindaba plant.[26] In either case, by working through back channels, South Africa was able to avoid the application of IAEA safeguards to the pilot enrichment installation.[27]

Whether or not South Africa had substantial assistance in the basic engineering and design of the plant from STEAG, other outside assistance appears to have been critically needed. In 1965, or shortly thereafter, for example, Great Britain is said to have agreed to license technology to South Africa for transforming uranium yellowcake into uranium hexafluoride gas, the feedstock necessary for the enrichment process.[28] In addition, key component parts for the Valindaba facility were purchased from German, French, and U.S. firms—for example, separating elements from Siemens AG and Messerschmidt-Boelkow-Blohm GmbH (West Germany); compressors from GHH-Sterkrade (West Germany), Hispano-Suiza (France), and Sulzer Brothers (Switzerland); process control computers from Foxboro Corporation (United States); and slide valves from Leybold-Hereaus (West

Germany).[29] Today, as a result of guidelines adopted by the Nuclear Suppliers Group, many of these components could not be purchased by South Africa unless the facilities in which they were being used were subject to IAEA safeguards. This requirement is also mandated by the Non-Proliferation Treaty in the case of all suppliers that have ratified that document. At the time of some of the transfers to South Africa, however, the Suppliers' Guidelines had not yet been agreed to and, indeed, some of the arrangements, such as the licensing of the British hexafluoride technology, may have predated the Non-Proliferation Treaty itself.

U.S. Response in the 1970s. Through the early 1970s, the United States appears not to have attempted to dissuade South Africa from developing the pilot enrichment plant at Valindaba. Indeed, in 1973, the U.S. Commerce Department authorized the export of the Foxboro Corporation computers, noted earlier, for use in the facility. These were the most powerful industrial-process control computers available and were modified to South African specifications for use in the plant.[30] Although the export is said to have been authorized without the knowledge of U.S. officials responsible for non-proliferation policy, the apparent lack of attention to Pretoria's enrichment plant contrasts sharply with the strong U.S. efforts to discourage Taiwan from obtaining an unsafeguarded reprocessing unit during this same period and with the initiative, however shortlived, to discourage India from manufacturing explosives using plutonium from the CIRUS research reactor, which contained U.S. heavy water.[31]

Moreover, in mid-1974, as the Valindaba plant with its obvious military potential was nearing completion, the United States signed a major amendment of its existing nuclear agreement with South Africa to permit greatly expanded cooperation. The United States agreed to enrich all the fuel that would be needed for two large nuclear power plants South Africa was then planning to build at Koeberg.[32] No hearings were held on the agreement, which, after laying before Congress for thirty days of Congressional session, became effective on June 22, 1974, less than one month after India's nuclear test. On July 12, obviously responding to the test, the vice-president of South Africa's Atomic Energy Board, Dr. Louw Alberts, declared that South Africa had the technology and resources to produce an atomic bomb.[33] A month later, the U.S. Department of Energy signed the enrichment-services contract with South Africa contemplated by the agreement for cooperation.[34] At the time, judging by a CIA assessment of South African nuclear weapons capabilities dated September 4, 1974, the U.S. government was well aware of the military potential of South Africa's nuclear program:

. . . it [South Africa] apparently has developed a technology for enriching uranium that could be used for producing weapons-grade material. South Africa probably would go forward with a nuclear weapons program if it saw a serious threat from African neighbors beginning to emerge. So serious a threat is highly unlikely in the 1970s.[35]

Why the Nixon administration took such a laissez-faire stance towards the South African nuclear program in the early 1970s is not clear. One element may have been that the overall Nixon strategy for dealing with South Africa was to avoid confrontation so that a dialogue, particularly on Pretoria's racial policies, could be established.[36] As noted earlier, Congress, too, seemed uninterested in South Africa's growing nuclear weapons capability.[37] More active U.S. scrutiny of South Africa's nuclear program might possibly have resulted in exposure of the apparently unauthorized West German aid for the Valindaba pilot enrichment plant.

Moreover, it is also possible that South Africa acquired the nuclear weapons capability inherent in the Valindaba facility without a specific decision having been taken by top leaders to build the plant for this purpose. Ample commercial justification existed at the time for the development of a South African enrichment capability, while the utility to Pretoria of nuclear arms then and now remains uncertain. On the other hand, Pretoria's refusal to sign the Non-Proliferation Treaty suggests that it was deliberately seeking to maintain the option to develop unsafeguarded nuclear installations that might eventually provide a nuclear weapons capability without violating any international agreements. In either case, if top South African leaders had faced an international outcry in the early 1970s objecting to the plant as a grave proliferation threat, it is possible that South Africa might have accepted some limitations on its use (possibly IAEA safeguards or an agreement that its output be restricted exclusively to low-enrichment uranium to be verified more informally).[38]

The start-up of the Valindaba pilot uranium enrichment plant took place in April 1975, although full operation was not achieved until 1977.[39] The maximum production of the plant, assuming that it used natural uranium feed, could be fifty kilograms per year of highly enriched uranium, enough for two to three weapons annually, depending on their design. In a 1976 interview with *Newsweek* magazine, South African prime minister John Vorster acknowledged the military potential of the plant. Asked if South Africa's defenses included a nuclear capability, he replied, "We are only interested in the peaceful applications of nuclear power. But we can enrich uranium, and we have the capability. We did not sign the Nuclear Non-Proliferation Treaty."[40]

In 1975, South African Atomic Energy Board president Roux announced that his country would build a commercial-scale enrichment plant capable of producing five thousand tons of low-enriched uranium per year, most of it intended for export.[41] By 1978, however, the decision was made to build a smaller facility, said to be capable of producing fifty tons of low enriched material per year, enough for the two 1,000 megawatt Koeberg nuclear power plants that Pretoria purchased from France in 1976.

Although the United States had been slow to react to South Africa's acquisition of the Valindaba pilot enrichment plant, in 1975 and 1976 congressional pressure began to mount for taking a harder stand against the South African nuclear program. The first target was the export of highly enriched uranium for the SAFARI I reactor. As a result of a law suit by the Congressional Black Caucus and broad congressional objections to the shipment of material directly usable for nuclear weapons to South Africa, the Ford administration suspended SAFARI fuel exports in early 1975.[42]

Similarly, in 1976, congressional opposition led to the cancellation of a proposed sale of two nuclear power plants by the General Electric Corporation to South Africa. The Ford administration had been prepared to approve the sale on the grounds that the plants would be safeguarded and that maintaining ties to the South African government would encourage their constructive participation in current negotiations on the transition to majority rule in Rhodesia.[43] Opposition to the GE sale was based only partly on nonproliferation concerns; more important was the fear that the highly visible sale would give the appearance that U.S. objections to South Africa's racial policies were easing.[44]

In May, South Africa, which had previously signed a letter of intent with General Electric for the facilities, accepted a French bid to build the plants. Under the French-South African agreement for the reactors, both plants were to be subject to IAEA safeguards. In addition, France insisted that any spent fuel from the facility be returned to France for reprocessing, ruling out use of plutonium in the material for a possible South African nuclear weapons program.[45] Congressional opposition to the reactor sale notwithstanding, the U.S. contract to supply fuel for the Koeberg plants remained intact.

Discovery of Test Site. South African concern over its long-term security intensified in the mid-1970s. In 1974, Angola and Mozambique gained their independence from Portugal and established black, Marxist governments. Rhodesia, too, was moving toward black rule, while at home the Soweto riots in 1976 underscored the danger of internal violence against the Afrikaner regime. South Africa's response to these mounting challenges had been the continuing buildup of its military power, with defense expenditures doubling between 1975 and 1977.[46] Inauguration of the Carter administration in January 1977 with its outspoken opposition to apartheid and support for majority rule in Namibia, moreover, meant that Pretoria would find little support in Washington.

In 1977, new evidence emerged of South Africa's interest in developing nuclear arms. Early in the year, Information and Interior Minister Connie Mulder broadly hinted that this was the aim of Pretoria's nuclear program. Describing his country's defense posture, he stated: "We will use all means at our disposal, whatever they may be. It is true that we have just completed our own pilot plant that uses very advanced technology, and we have major uranium resources."[47]

On August 6, the Soviet Union notified the United States that one of its surveillance satellites had observed what appeared to be a nuclear test site in the Kalahari Desert. A U.S. observation satellite shortly confirmed the Soviet finding, and over the next two weeks the United States worked with France, Great Britain, and West Germany to develop a concerted response to the impending test. As a result of the joint efforts of these and possibly other governments, reportedly including a threat to break diplomatic relations and a warning by France that a test might jeopardize the completion of the Koeberg reactors, South Africa agreed not to go forward with it. On August 23, President Carter announced that: "South Africa has informed us that they do not intend to develop nuclear explosive devices for any purpose, either peaceful or as a weapon, that the Kalahari test site which has been in question is not designed for the use of nuclear explosives, and that no nuclear explosive test will be taken in South Africa now or in the future."[48]

In October, however, South African prime minister John Vorster stated on the U.S. television program "Issues and Answers": "I am not aware of any promise that I gave to President Carter. I repeated a statement which I have made very often, that as far as South Africa is concerned, we are only interested in peaceful development of nuclear facilities."[49]

In response, the State Department declared that all the assurances announced by President Carter as having been received from South Africa were in fact contained in an October 13 letter from Prime Minister Vorster to President Carter and that similar assurances had been given in September to the U.S. ambassador in Pretoria. Several days later, however, the dispute was revived when South African finance minister Owen Horwood stated at a political gathering in Durban that his government reserved the right to depart from its assurances that its nuclear program was for peaceful purposes only. These remarks, however, were corrected within hours by South African foreign minister Roeloff Botha: "Assurances given to the United States, French, British, and German governments regarding South Africa's intentions in the fuel and nuclear technology area reflect firm government policy."[50]

The upshot of the episode remains somewhat ambiguous. Pretoria has apparently stood by its pledge not to conduct a test "in South Africa," but construction at the supposed test site reportedly continued until December 1977.[51] Moreover, as discussed below, it appeared in 1979 that Pretoria might have conducted a test in the South Atlantic. In addition, South Africa's continued unwillingness to permit international inspection of the Valindaba pilot enrichment plant meant that Pretoria remained free to accumulate highly enriched uranium there and to prepare nuclear explosives without fear of detection, notwithstanding its contrary assurances to the United States. Why the United States and other Western governments did not insist that Pretoria accept IAEA safeguards on the plant, at a time when they were reportedly prepared to break diplomatic relations if South Africa conducted a *test,* is not clear. Apparently, the Western response was tailored to addressing the immediate crisis of an impending nuclear detonation, and the option of demanding an additional major concession from Pretoria was not actively considered.[52]

South Africa's motives for readying a nuclear test at that time are unclear, but an obvious factor was the siege mentality brought on by the developments in the early and mid-1970s noted earlier. Given South Africa's overwhelming conventional military superiority in comparison to its neighbors, the test was probably intended as a political gesture to symbolize the implacable resolve of the nation's Afrikaner leadership to preserve white rule against all odds.[53]

Later in 1977, the United Nations Security Council adopted a mandatory arms embargo against South Africa. The embargo had been under consideration when the Kalahari test site was first exposed, and some observers believe that the crisis over the Kalahari incident contributed to passage of that resolution.[54] This setback at the United Nations followed Pretoria's ouster from its permanent position on the IAEA Board of Governors in June. Both episodes undoubtedly intensified Pretoria's sense of isolation and may have provided additional support for those within the South African leadership favoring development of nuclear arms.

Opposition to Safeguards. Through the late 1970s, the Carter administration continued to withhold fuel for the SAFARI I reactor and to press South Africa to ratify the Non-Proliferation Treaty—although not with the forcefulness that had been brought to bear in 1977 to head off the Kalahari test. In 1978, the U.S. Nuclear Non-Proliferation Act effectively codified that standard by prohibiting (after March 1980) U.S. nuclear fuel exports to countries refusing to place all of their nuclear installations under IAEA safeguards.[55]

In 1979, it appeared that South Africa might be considering acceptance of the treaty. In December of that year, the IAEA General Conference voted to reject Pretoria's credentials, effectively ousting it from meaningful participation in key Agency activities. In arguing against the rejection of South Africa's credentials, IAEA director general Sigvard Eklund stated that South Africa appeared ready to sign the treaty, implicitly warning that Pretoria's expulsion from the Agency would undermine efforts to achieve this result.

By 1980, South Africa apparently had agreed that if a specific set of conditions was satisfied, it would join the accord. These conditions included resumption of American supplies of highly enriched uranium for the SAFARI I reactor, U.S. willingness to export low-enriched uranium for the Koeberg power stations, U.S. agreement to permit exports of nonsensitive items for the Valindaba enrichment plant, and support for South Africa's reinstatement on the IAEA Board of Governors.[56] One of these requirements, the supply of low-enriched fuel for the Koeberg power plants, was looming as an increasingly important concern for South Africa, since the twin facilities were expected to be completed in 1982 and 1983; South African officials were beginning to fear that the plants might not be able to start up because of the U.S. fuel embargo.[57]

The urgency of bringing South Africa's pilot-scale enrichment plant at Valindaba under IAEA safeguards was underscored in early 1981 when South Africa announced that it had successfully enriched uranium to 41 percent, sufficient to fuel the SAFARI I plant. Having reached this level of enrichment, producing weapons-grade material in the 90 percent range would not be a serious technological challenge.[58]

When the Reagan administration took office in January 1981, U.S. nuclear fuel exports to South Africa were barred by the full-scope safeguards requirement in the Non-Proliferation Act. In November 1981, however, South Africa announced that it had obtained low-enriched uranium fuel for the two French-supplied Koeberg reactors expected to begin operations in 1982 and 1983.[59] France had agreed to fabricate the uranium into fuel elements pursuant to a pre-existing contract. Although the Koeberg reactors were themselves under international safeguards and thus would not contribute directly to a South African nuclear weapons program, the effect of France's honoring its fuel fabrication contract was to undercut the U.S. embargo on nuclear fuel sales to South Africa, an embargo intended to pressure Pretoria to accept full-scope safeguards—or at least to penalize it for refusal to do so.

Where South Africa had obtained the low-enriched uranium fuel remained a mystery for a number of weeks until it was learned that the material had been purchased from a consortium of Swiss utilities building the Kaiseraugst nuclear unit near Basel.[60] That plant had been severely delayed and was not expected to be completed for another ten years. Additional material was purchased from Synatom, a Belgian nuclear fuel supply company. Material from both sources had been enriched at France's Eurodif facility at Tricastin and was awaiting export to Switzerland and Belgium. South Africa purchased the material while it was still in France and arranged for its delivery to the French fuel fabrication plant.

In December it was learned that two American uranium brokers, Edlow International and SWUCO, Inc., had arranged the transaction for the various parties.[61] Moreover, it was subsequently revealed that the U.S. State Department had been advised of the transaction before it was consummated by Edlow and SWUCO and had taken no steps to discourage them from proceeding with the deal, nor to dissuade France from fabricating the fuel into fuel elements for the Koeberg plants.[62]

State Department aides defended their action on the

ground that the Edlow and SWUCO activities were not in violation of U.S. law, since no U.S. material was involved. More important, they argued that allowing the transaction was consistent with the Reagan administration's conciliatory non-proliferation policy of permitting limited nuclear commerce in nonsensitive areas as a goodwill gesture while negotiations on tougher controls continued.[63]

In May 1982, the Reagan administration pursued this initiative by announcing that it would permit the export to South Africa of certain nuclear component parts and "dual-use" items, i.e., commodities with a wide range of industrial uses sometimes employed for a nuclear-related purpose.[64] Although the Non-Proliferation Act prohibited U.S. exports of nuclear fuel and reactors to nations not accepting full-scope safeguards, it did not similarly preclude sales of these lesser nuclear items.

Congressional critics charged that while its actions were legal, the administration, by providing such cooperation, was once again undercutting the policy embodied in the Non-Proliferation Act of bringing pressure on South Africa through nuclear trade restrictions. Other congressional activists emphasized that making the highly visible nuclear sales would be perceived as a gesture of support for South Africa's racial policies. (Indeed, in December 1982, the African National Congress, the outlawed black guerrilla group, set off four bombs at the Koeberg reactor construction site, damaging key components and graphically demonstrating that South Africa's nuclear program had become symbolically linked to the issue of continued white minority rule.)[65] Eventually this combined congressional criticism led the Reagan administration to delay the exports indefinitely. South Africa's rejection of additional safeguards, however, continued.

Possible Chinese Aid. In late 1981, as South Africa was announcing that it had circumvented the U.S. embargo on nuclear fuel for the Koeberg plant, reports surfaced that Pretoria had obtained low-enriched uranium not only from Europe, but also from the People's Republic of China.[66] Although China denied that it had sold material to South Africa, by late 1982 it was widely believed within the U.S. government that such a transfer of low-enriched uranium had taken place, possibly through intermediaries, without the requirement that South Africa place the material under IAEA safeguards. Depending on the quantity of low-enriched uranium provided and the peculiarities of the Valindaba pilot enrichment plant, the receipt of this material may have significantly increased South Africa's nuclear weapons capability.[67]

Most of the effort required to enrich uranium to weapons grade is expended in enriching uranium from its natural state (0.7 percent U^{235}) to the low enriched level (3 percent U^{235}). By substituting low-enriched uranium for natural uranium as the feed for the Valindaba plant, South Africa may thereby be able to increase considerably the plant's capacity to produce highly enriched material usable for weapons. Since fuel purchases for a power plant would normally involve tens of tons of low-enriched uranium (thirty tons are needed for a typical commercial power plant reload), it is possible that South Africa now has sufficient low-enriched uranium feedstock to double or perhaps triple the high-enriched uranium output of the Valindaba pilot plant, greatly increasing the size of Pretoria's potential nuclear arsenal. Inasmuch as any Chinese-supplied material would not be under IAEA safeguards, South Africa could use it for nuclear arms without apparently violating any international undertakings.

The VELA Incident. On September 22, 1979, a U.S. VELA satellite recorded a signal resembling the flash from a nuclear test.[68] Since the satellite at that time was observing the southern Atlantic and Indian oceans, speculation immediately arose that South Africa had conducted a nuclear test at sea. Such a test would not have been ruled out by the assurances given to President Carter in 1977 that Pretoria would not conduct a test *in* South Africa. The size of the apparent test was small, two to four kilotons, suggesting that either a battlefield nuclear weapon or, possibly, the trigger for a thermonuclear device (hydrogen bomb) had been detonated—or that a larger device had fizzled. In each of the forty-one previous cases in which a VELA satellite had observed the distinctive double-humped curve of a nuclear test, corroborative evidence had also been available to verify that a nuclear test had taken place. In the case of the South Atlantic "flash," however, no such evidence was obtained.

The Carter White House convened a panel of scientific experts to review the signal obtained by the satellite to try to determine whether any test had in fact taken place. After analyzing extensive data from the satellite's sensors, the team found that certain aspects of its readings of the event varied significantly from those of other known nuclear tests. This, along with other discrepancies, led the panel to conclude that the event registered by the satellite was "probably not from a nuclear explosion" but, more likely, from a phenomenon occurring close to the satellite, such as the reflecting flash from a colliding meteorite.[69] Other government agencies, however, including the Defense Intelligence Agency and the Naval Research Laboratory, concluded that a test had taken place, and the matter has never been settled conclusively. (A 1981 U.N. study group summarized the evidence brought to light by various U.S. government agencies; the summary is reprinted as Appendix G.)

If, notwithstanding the conclusion of the White House experts panel, a nuclear test in fact took place, it is by no means clear which nation or nations may have been responsible. Reportedly, the CIA told a key congressional committee that "Israel is the leading candidate," with South Africa the second most likely possibility.[70] Others have suggested that South Africa and Israel might have conducted a joint test or that India, or possibly France, was responsible.[71]

From the standpoint of South Africa's nuclear capabilities, the episode may have been less important than is generally believed. There is little question that since the 1977 Kalahari incident, virtually all observers believe that South Africa has been capable of developing nuclear arms using highly enriched uranium from the Valindaba plant and that it has given serious consideration to this option, which it could implement quickly if the need arose. Even if the 1979 event ultimately proves to have been a test, and even if Pretoria could be connected to it, this would say little more about its nuclear capabilities. While the event may have been the test of a sophisticated low-yield nuclear device, which would attest to South Africa's nuclear weapons design and fabrication capabilities, it could as easily have been a fizzle of a device intended to produce a larger yield, which would lead to the opposite conclusion about South Africa's skills.

South Africa as a Nuclear Exporter. With its substantial uranium reserves and extensive mining and milling industry, South Africa has annually produced between 11 and 15 percent of the uranium used in the free world for more than a decade.[72] Through the late 1970s and early 1980s, South Africa had significant uranium supply contracts with the United States, Great Britain,

France, West Germany, and Taiwan, among other nations.[73] Although during the late 1970s, as noted earlier, South Africa had hoped to develop a substantial uranium enrichment industry, these plans have been abandoned and the semi-commercial enrichment plant at Valindaba will be devoted to producing material for domestic use. South Africa's uranium exports are in the form of unenriched uranium concentrate (yellowcake).

Given the current glut of uranium on world markets and the availability of alternative suppliers, South Africa's uranium production capabilities are not likely to offer it significant leverage with the advanced Western nations in its negotiations over its nuclear program or other issues.[74]

Cooperation with Israel. Over the years there have been repeated reports of Israeli-South African nuclear cooperation. It has been alleged, for example, that South Africa provided Israel with uranium not subject to IAEA monitoring for use in the Dimona reactor, that the device to be tested in the Kalahari Desert in 1977 was Israeli, and that the two nations conducted a joint nuclear test in the South Atlantic in 1979.[75] One recent account, which describes extensive joint activities between the two countries in developing conventional arms, including guided missiles and jet aircraft, states that nuclear cooperation also extended to development of the Pelunduna research reactor.[76] It has not been possible to assess the validity of these accounts.

Given the secrecy with which both nations surround their nuclear programs, it has not been possible to assess the validity of these accounts.

II. Developments of the Past Year

Continuing Safeguards Negotiations

Since taking office in January 1981, the Reagan administration has attempted to gain South Africa's acceptance of wider safeguards by adopting a more conciliatory posture than that of the Ford and Carter administrations, offering small inducements to Pretoria in the nuclear field rather than applying nuclear export sanctions broadly. This trend continued during 1983 as the Reagan administration authorized the Westinghouse Corporation to offer South Africa technical services for managing the Koeberg reactor.[77] Once again, congressional reaction was sharp, and the incident contributed to growing support for legislation to prohibit all trade in nuclear commodities and services to nations not accepting full-scope safeguards. Indeed, by early 1984, legislation had passed in both the House and the Senate that would prohibit sales of nuclear components and the transfer of technology such as the Westinghouse management services deal in such cases.[78]

Reportedly, the administration's strategy has been to persuade Pretoria that it can permit safeguards on the semi-commercial-scale uranium enrichment plant it is now constructing without risking disclosure of its technological secrets. The key to the U.S. initiative is an agreement known as the Hexapartite Safeguards Project, which went into effect in March 1983 among six nations and organizations operating or planning commercial uranium enrichment plants—Australia, West Germany, Japan, the Netherlands, the United States, and the French-led nuclear uranium enrichment group, Eurodif. The agreement, signed after two years of negotiations, provides for a safeguards plan intended to be applicable to all enrichment facilities under the IAEA system and designed to ensure the protection of industrial secrets embodied in the plants.

Armed with this arrangement, which U.S. officials apparently told Pretoria was developed with South Africa's concerns in mind, the United States has argued that Pretoria no longer has grounds for objecting to safeguarding its soon-to-be-completed enrichment plant. At the same time, the United States reportedly was hoping to avoid the need for safeguards on the existing pilot-scale facility by persuading South Africa to dismantle it. The United States would then provide the more highly enriched uranium fuel needed for the SAFARI I reactor which, with slight modifications, could be operated on 20 percent enriched material not readily usable for nuclear weapons.[79] As part of the overall deal, the United States would agree to support South Africa's reintegration into the IAEA and to waive multimillion-dollar penalties contained in the U.S.-South African fuel agreement for the Koeberg plant, which the United States could seek to enforce if South Africa refused to make payments under the contract.

Although this strategy has yet to bear fruit—South Africa has maintained its objections to safeguards on its enrichment plant—in February 1984 Pretoria pledged that its conduct in nuclear affairs would be in accordance with "the spirit, principles and goals," of the Nuclear Non-Proliferation Treaty.[80] In effect, this was a reaffirmation of South Africa's declaration in 1968, noted earlier, that exports of nuclear materials (in particular, uranium) would not be made to non-nuclear-weapon countries without IAEA monitoring. South Africa also agreed to reopen negotiations on safeguarding its semi-commercial-scale enrichment facility at Valindaba, although not with respect to its pilot facility.[81] In return, the United States is said to have agreed to waive the penalty provisions in the 1974 Koeberg fuel contract.

While South Africa's pledge was far short of the hoped-for modification of its safeguards policy, it nevertheless revealed a willingness to negotiate seriously with the Reagan administration. Moreover, as discussed elsewhere, transactions in yellowcake have been an important element of clandestine nuclear commerce, assisting Pakistan's nuclear weapons program and possibly Israel's as well. Hence, South Africa's reaffirmation of its export practices is a useful contribution to international controls and may be valuable as a model that can be used to encourage the adoption of responsible export policies by other emerging nuclear supplier states not party to the Non-Proliferation Treaty.

III. Prospects for Nuclear Weapons in South Africa

South Africa now possesses the capability to produce at least fifty kilograms per year of highly enriched uranium, enough for two or possibly three nuclear weapons, and its capabilities may be considerably larger if it has received substantial quantities of unsafeguarded low-enriched uranium that can be used as feedstock in the enrichment process. South Africa has been able to accumulate highly-enriched material since early 1977 or possibly since 1975, when completion of the Valindaba pilot enrichment plant was announced Assuming that early production rates were lower than the plant's designed capacity, South Africa might have accumulated 375 kilograms of nuclear weapons material by mid-1984, enough for between fifteen and twenty-five nuclear devices[82] before taking into account possible additions based on the upgrading of unsafeguarded low-enriched uranium South Africa may have obtained from China. If South Africa were able to triple the output of the enrichment plant by using low-enriched uranium feed and operated the plant in this fashion throughout 1982, 1983, and the first half of 1984, a total of 650 kilograms of highly enriched uranium could be available, enough for a stockpile of more than forty weapons, roughly the size of the U.S. nuclear weapons arsenal in 1948.[83] Since the Valindaba pilot-scale facility is not under safeguards, South Africa remains legally free to use highly enriched material it produces for nuclear explosives.

In the next several years, South Africa is expected to complete construction of its semi-commercial scale uranium enrichment facility twenty to thirty times larger than the Valindaba pilot plant. Although Pretoria has stated that the facility is intended to produce low-enriched uranium (not usable for nuclear weapons) to fuel the Koeberg power reactors, there would probably be little difficulty modifying this installation to produce highly enriched material. In principle, this could allow South Africa to produce between 40 and 100 nuclear devices per year depending on their design and the plant's capacity.

South Africa has indicated, however, that it may be prepared to put this newer installation under IAEA safeguards. If it takes this step and pledges that the facility is dedicated to producing nonweapons-grade, low-enriched material, South Africa would not be able to turn the plant to military use without accepting grave diplomatic costs. Thus, a decision on safeguards at the plant could significantly reduce Pretoria's long-term nuclear weapons material production capability.

South Africa's refusal to place its small pilot plant under international inspections, its test preparations in 1977, and the continuing hints by some of its leaders that the nation may some day turn to the development of nuclear arms have given South Africa a de facto nuclear deterrent. Even if nuclear weapons have not been assembled and integrated with Pretoria's military forces, few informed observers doubt that Pretoria possesses the capability to assemble such weapons rapidly.

Why South Africa has sought to achieve this capability and when its leaders might consider using nuclear weapons are more difficult questions. Observers appear to be unanimous that the key to understanding the South African nuclear explosives program is the Afrikaner mentality. Fixated on survival in the face of what the Botha government characterizes as a "total onslaught" by Communist inspired and supported black African forces, South African leaders have built up the nation's military might to the point of unquestioned superiority against any potential adversary.[84] South Africa has recently demonstrated its conventional military capabilities, forcing Mozambique and apparently Angola to come to terms and reduce support for insurgent guerrilla activities in South Africa proper and in Namibia. In such a context, the added intimidating effect of nuclear weapons is hardly necessary. Indeed, it is difficult to imagine the situation in which South Africa might resort to the use of nuclear weapons to deal with an external enemy. As for internal enemies, nuclear arms are even less relevant.

Nevertheless, South Africa's leaders may value a nuclear weapons capability for the aura of invincibility and permanence such arms would give the white minority government in Pretoria. Pretoria may thus see nuclear weapons as offsetting the continuing international challenge to its legitimacy.

Whatever South Africa's reasons for developing its nuclear capability, Pretoria seems to have little to gain by giving it up at this juncture. As long as it remains committed to apartheid, there is little likelihood that its ties to the Western democracies, particularly the United States, could be strengthened sufficiently to compensate for the loss of its nuclear option, however limited its practical utility.

Settlement of the Namibian question, together with an extended period of peaceful co-existence with the Marxist regimes in Mozambique, Zimbabwe, and Angola, may eventually lessen the extreme defensiveness that pervades South Africa's current leadership and open the way for international oversight of all of South Africa's nuclear program. The likelihood of such a change of position in the near term, however, appears to be small.

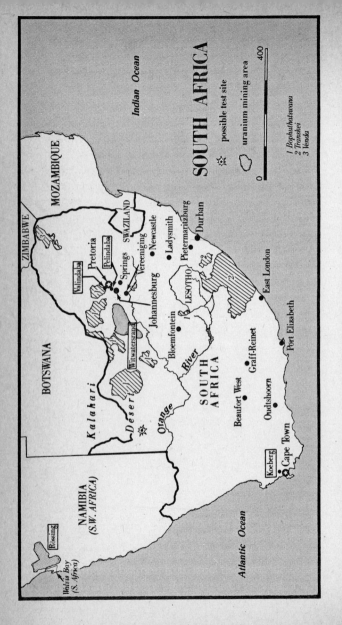

SOUTH AFRICA

☆ possible test site

⬭ uranium mining area

1 Bophuthatswana
2 Transkei
3 Venda

0 |————| 400

Indian Ocean

MOZAMBIQUE

ZIMBABWE

SWAZILAND

Pretoria
Pelindaba
Valindaba
Springs
Vereeniging
Johannesburg
Witwatersrand
Newcastle
Ladysmith
Pietermaritzburg
Durban

BOTSWANA

Kalahari

Desert

LESOTHO

Orange

River

Bloemfontein

SOUTH
AFRICA

East London

Beaufort West

Graff-Reinet

Oudtshoorn

Port Elizabeth

NAMIBIA
(S.W. AFRICA)

Rössing

Walvis Bay
(S. Africa)

Atlantic Ocean

Koeberg

Cape Town

South Africa

Power Reactors/Operating or Under Construction

Koeberg I (light-water/low-enriched uranium, 922 MWe)
- supplier: Framatome (France)
- start up: 1984[a]
- fuel source: Switzerland; Belgium; China (?) for initial loads; S. Africa after 1987.[b]
- safeguards: yes

Koeberg II (light-water/low-enriched uranium, 922 MWe)
- supplier: Framatome (France)
- start up: 1985 (est.)
- fuel source: ?
- safeguards: yes

Uranium Resources/Active Mining Sites/Uranium Mills

- reasonably assured reserves:
  South Africa: 313,000 metric tons[c]
  Namibia: 135,000 metric tons[d]
- currently active sites: South Africa: Witwatersrand Basin, Palabora
  Namibia: Rössing
- mills in operation: South Africa: Witwatersrand Group
           Blyvooruitzicht
           Chemwes
           East Rand Gold and Uranium
           Harmony (3 mills)
           Hartebeestfontein
           Joint Metallurgical Scheme
           Randfontein
           Vaal Reefs (3 mills)
           Western Deep Levels
        Driefontein
        Palabora
  Namibia: Rössing

UF$_6$ Conversion

Valindaba
- capacity: Sufficient for Valindaba pilot-scale enrichment plant (presumed).
- supplier: Great Britain (?)[e]
- start up: prior to 1975
- safeguards: no

Enrichment

Valindaba (pilot plant)
- type: stationary-wall centrifuge/jet-nozzle[f]
- capacity: 50 kg high-enriched uranium per year[g]
- supplier: Siemens AG (West Germany), Messerschmidt-Boelkow-Bloem GmbH (West Germany), GHH-Sterkrade (West Germany), Hispano-Suiza (France), and Sulzer Brothers (Switzerland), Foxboro Corporation (U.S.), and Leybold-Heraus (West Germany).[h]
- start up: 1975; full operation in 1977.[i]
- safeguards: no

Valindaba (semi-commercial plant)
- type: stationary-wall centrifuge/jet-nozzle[f]
- capacity: 50 metric tons of low-enriched uranium per year[g]
- supplier: South Africa
- start up: 1987 (est.)[j]
- safeguards: no

Research Reactors

SAFARI I, Pelindaba (light-water/high-enriched uranium, 20 MWt)
- supplier: Allis Chalmers Corporation (U.S.)
- start up: 1965
- fuel source: United States;[k] after 1981, South Africa.
- safeguards: yes

Pelunduna Zero (SAFARI II) (heavy-water/low-enriched uranium, 0 MWt)
- supplier: South Africa
- start up: 1967[l] (now decommissioned)
- fuel source: United States
- heavy water: United States
- safeguards: yes

Sources and Notes

a. "Koeberg Ups Power," *Rand Daily Mail*, Foreign Broadcast Information Service/Nuclear Proliferation and Development, April 17, 1984, p. 36.

b. Ann MacLachlan, "U.S. Firm Plays Role in South Africa Purchase of Uranium," *Energy Daily*, December 10, 1981. George Lardner.Jr., and Don Oberdorfer, "China Was Source of Atomic Fuel for South Africa, U.S. Believes," *Washington Post*, November 18, 1981. The fuel obtained from Switzerland and Belgium was enriched and fabricated in France; U.S. uranium brokers helped arrange the sale with the knowledge of the U.S. State Department. The United States was to supply fuel for the plant, but U.S. fuel exports to South Africa have been prohibited by law since 1980.

c. Reserves at less than $130 per kg; *Uranium Resources, Production, and Demand*, A Joint Report of the OECD Nuclear Energy Agency and the International Atomic Energy Agency (Paris: OECD, 1983), p. 251, 258.

d. Reserves at less than $130 per kg; *Uranium Resources, Production, and Demand*, A Joint Report of the OECD Nuclear Energy Agency and the International Atomic Energy Agency (OECD: Paris, 1982), p. 139.

e. J. E. Spence, "The Republic of South Africa: Proliferation and the Politics of 'Outward Movement,' " in Lawrence and Larus, eds., *Nuclear Proliferation Phase II*. (Lawrence, KA: University Press of Kansas), p. 217.

f. Possibly based on German jet-nozzle process, degree of similarity uncertain.

g. Department of Political and Security Council Affairs, United Nations Centre for Disarmament, Report of the Secretary General, *South Africa's Plan and Capability in the Nuclear Field*, Report A/35/402 (New York: United Nations, 1981), p. 22.

h. C. Raja Mohan, "Atomic Teeth to Apartheid: South Africa and Nuclear Weapons," in K. Subrahmanyam, *Nuclear Myths and Realities* (ABC, New Delhi, 1981), p. 123.

i. David Fishlock, "The South African Nuclear Weapons Scare," prepared for Congressional Research Service, December 1977, p. CRS-5.

j. Rob Laufer, "Inside Valindaba: South African Enrichment Plant Steadily Taking Shape," *Nucleonics Week*, April 8, 1982, p. 1.

k. U.S. exports ceased in 1975.

l. J. E. Spence, "South Africa: the Nuclear Option," *African Affairs*, October 1981, p. 441. The reactor is presently decommissioned; (Robert Jaster, "Politics and the Afrikaner Bomb," *Orbis*, Winter 1984, p. 827.)

Important
Related Developments
of the Year

Introduction

As seen in the preceding chapters, the international non-proliferation regime, consisting of treaties, international institutions, multilateral export control arrangements, country-to-country agreements, and individual nuclear-supplier country practices, has had a significant impact in restraining the spread of nuclear weapons. Several important developments affecting the regime took place from mid-1983 to mid-1984.

Two involve China. In recent years, China, alone among the nuclear supplier countries, is known to have sharply deviated from accepted norms for nuclear transfers by making unsafeguarded sales of nuclear materials and, reportedly, assisting Pakistan to design nuclear weapons and to build its unsafeguarded uranium enrichment plant at Kahuta. As an inducement to encourage China to tighten its nuclear export practices, the United States has proposed to sell it nuclear power reactors and related technology. But in mid-1984, the United States halted efforts to conclude a nuclear trade agreement with Peking because of the latter's continuing laxity in offering nuclear aid. On a separate front, during 1984, China offered to accept spent nuclear power reactor fuel from Western Europe for long-term storage. The storage of such material in nuclear weapon states has long been considered a potentially valuable non-proliferation tool, since it eliminates the risk that non-nuclear-weapon nations where spent fuel is accumulating might reprocess this material to extract its weapons-usable plutonium. The details of negotiations on the U.S.-China nuclear trade pact and the Chinese spent fuel storage offer are discussed in the first part of this chapter.

Also during the past year, the nuclear supplier countries expanded the list of items they would place under strict export controls and for the first time since the late 1970s, the Western suppliers convened as a group to discuss additional joint efforts to strengthen the non-proliferation regime. These developments, proposed new U.S. non-proliferation legislation, and the International Atomic Energy Agency's safeguards activities during the past year are reviewed in the second half of this chapter.

China

I. U.S.-China Nuclear Negotiations

During a visit by President Ronald Reagan to Peking in April 1984, the United States and the People's Republic of China initialed an agreement for nuclear cooperation that had been under negotiation for more than two years. Talks on the accord had been stalled because of U.S. concerns over China's unsafeguarded nuclear exports to Pakistan and other emerging nuclear powers and because of disputes over the controls covering nuclear equipment to be supplied by the United States under the pact. With these issues apparently resolved, both nations anticipated a profitable nuclear trade relationship. In June 1984, however, the Reagan administration suspended the process of executive branch and congressional review necessary for the formal approval of the accord subsequent to its initialing, apparently because of concern that China was continuing to assist Pakistan's nuclear weapons program.

China is a nuclear weapon state, having tested its first atomic bomb in 1964, and is now believed to possess a stockpile of several hundred nuclear weapons.[1] Peking also has medium-range missiles (700-mile range) and intermediate-range missiles (up to 3,500-mile range) and is developing intercontinental ballistic missiles capable of reaching the United States, as well as nuclear-missile-carrying submarines. Unlike the other nuclear weapon countries and many emerging ones, China has no nuclear power plants. Recently, it has turned to the West to develop this energy resource.

The Chinese nuclear power program calls for the completion of ten thousand megawatts of generating capacity (the equivalent of ten large, U.S.-style power reactors) by the year 2000.[2] Negotiations with Western suppliers have been under way for several years on two specific projects: a pair of nine-hundred-megawatt nuclear power plants in Guangdong province, near Hong Kong, intended in large part to supply electricity to that city, and two smaller, three-hundred-megawatt power plants to be built near Shanghai, sometimes referred to as the 728 Project.[3] France is expected to supply the nuclear portion of the Guangdong units and Great Britain the non-nuclear turbines, while the reactors for the Shanghai plants will be built by China itself with major components purchased abroad.[4] The U.S. Westinghouse Electric Corporation has hoped to become a major supplier for the latter project and has applied for licenses to export a number of major components for the installation.[5] Japan, West Germany, and Italy have also been seeking to make nuclear sales to China.[6]

The United States appears to have taken an early

step towards opening nuclear trade with China in 1979, when the Carter administration authorized Framatome, France's government-controlled reactor manufacturing corporation, to offer Peking a nuclear power reactor for the Guangdong project. Framatome had originally obtained the design for the plant under license from Westinghouse with the proviso that Washington's approval would have to be obtained before French reactors based on this design could be exported to third countries.[7] The proposed French sale, which is still being negotiated with Peking, was controversial because China had stated it would not accept IAEA safeguards on the facility. At the time, the Carter administration was not prepared to authorize U.S. sales of nuclear equipment to Peking without such safeguards. Nonetheless, it consented to the proposed French sale, apparently because it was seeking France's cooperation on more pressing non-proliferation issues and believed that, with a pre-existing nuclear arsenal, Peking was unlikely to use the French plant for military ends. It was also understood that France would have the right to monitor China's use of French-supplied nuclear equipment and that China had agreed to restrictions on retransferring the equipment to other nations.[8]

China's Nuclear Exports

Serious negotiations between the United States and China on direct nuclear cooperation began sometime in 1981 after the Reagan administration took office.[9] Talks were suspended the same year, however, apparently because China had been exporting nuclear commodities to countries of high proliferation concern without imposing any restrictions on how those commodities could be used. According to press accounts,

China had recently shipped 3 percent enriched uranium to South Africa, 20 percent enriched uranium to Argentina for use in its research reactors, and heavy water to Argentina and possibly to India and South Africa, as well.[10] China has strongly denied exporting low-enriched uranium to South Africa, but has not expressly disclaimed making the other transfers.[11] (Argentina confirmed the purchase of 20 percent enriched uranium from Peking for a research reactor.)[12]

China was said not to have required recipients to place any of these transfers under IAEA safeguards. No other nuclear supplier has made such unsafeguarded transfers for more than a decade; they are prohibited by the Nuclear Non-Proliferation Treaty and would also violate the Nuclear Suppliers' Guidelines. (Indeed, some nuclear suppliers, such as the United States, Sweden, Canada, and Australia, have embargoed virtually all nuclear sales to South Africa, India, and Argentina because of their refusal to accept safeguards on *all* of their nuclear installations.) China is not a party to the Non-Proliferation Treaty, nor has it adhered to the export standards of the Nuclear Suppliers Group.

Significantly, because of the particular commodities and recipient countries said to be involved, China's unsafeguarded exports may have contributed directly to the spread of nuclear weapons around the world. The reported sale of unsafeguarded low-enriched uranium to South Africa, for example, may have allowed Pretoria to triple the production of weapons-grade uranium at its Valindaba enrichment plant by using low-enriched uranium as feed instead of natural uranium.[13] Similarly, if China supplied heavy water to India, as has been reported, it may have subsequently allowed New Delhi to start up the Madras I nuclear power plant. The Madras plant is India's first unsafeguarded nuclear power station and is capable of producing approximately forty kilograms (1 kilogram = 2.2 pounds) of plutonium in its spent fuel annually, enough material for up to eight nuclear weapons. Because Madras I is unsafeguarded, India could extract this material in its Tarapur reprocessing plant without the IAEA monitoring that would cover the reprocessing of spent fuel from all of India's other nuclear power plants, which are under safeguards. In essence, New Delhi's ability to run the Madras plant means it can substantially increase the amount of plutonium available for nuclear arms.

More troubling than these transactions were reports that China had given Pakistan detailed nuclear weapons design information and also aided it in building a centrifuge uranium enrichment plant to produce highly enriched uranium for atomic bombs.[14] If these reports are accurate, China's assistance would have been the most direct act of proliferation by a nuclear weapon state in more than two decades.

Against this background, the Reagan administration suspended talks with Peking on nuclear cooperation in mid-1981. It also imposed a nuclear embargo against China, refusing to authorize the transfer of either nuclear power reactor technology or nuclear components to Peking. Such transfers are not explicitly prohibited by the U.S. Non-Proliferation Act, even in the absence of an agreement for cooperation, but they do require special authorizations or export licenses, which the administration declined to grant.[15]

China's nuclear assistance to Pakistan and other nations, however, did not apparently lead the Reagan administration to impose sanctions beyond the nuclear area. In early 1984, for example, the United States and China signed agreements to encourage the exchange of scientific and technological information and to promote the transfer of U.S. technology to China in the fields of offshore oil and coal development.[16] U.S. regulations limiting the transfer of non-nuclear technologies to China were also eased during this period.[17] Nor, apparently, did the administration attempt to gain the support of other potential nuclear suppliers to establish a multilateral nuclear embargo against Peking or to take other steps against China until it agreed to tighten its nuclear export practices.[18]

Areas of Dispute

In mid-1983, however, China seemed ready to adopt a more restrictive nuclear transfer policy. Consequently, the United States reopened negotiations with Peking on a nuclear trade agreement.[19] As the negotiations continued, however, three principal areas of dispute emerged.

Verification. The first concerned the application of safeguards to facilities in China using U.S. nuclear exports. As noted previously, China objected to IAEA inspections as an undue intrusion on its sovereignty. Washington and Peking were, however, able to reach agreement on a bilateral verification arrangement that, according to a Reagan administration spokesman, consisted of "consultations, exchanges of information and visits to facilities subject to the [Sino-U.S. nuclear] agreement in order to assure that the provisions of the agreement are effectively carried out."[20]

Although the United States has relied on the IAEA since the late 1960s to perform inspections under its nuclear cooperation agreements, Washington has employed the bilateral-inspection alternative on occasion, and all U.S. agreements specify that if IAEA safeguards prove to be unsatisfactory, the United

States shall have the right to implement such bilateral inspections in their place. In practice, the U.S. experience with bilateral inspections appears to have been poor in at least two controversial instances. During the 1960s, for example, Israel informally agreed to permit U.S. visits to the Dimona reactor but reportedly limited their scope to the point where the inspectors were unable to determine whether or not the facility was being used for military purposes.[21] It has also been rumored that during the late 1960s the United States encountered difficulties in conducting bilateral inspections of the Tarapur nuclear power plants in India.

Based on available information, the United States will probably have to negotiate most of the important details of the verification arrangements with Peking on an ad hoc basis after the broad agreement for cooperation is concluded, and it will be difficult to assess in advance whether the total package of inspection rights will ultimately prove satisfactory. In contrast, when the IAEA applies safeguards, it uses a standardized approach for implementing its monitoring and record-keeping requirements. While negotiations often are required to work out fine points of the implementation arrangements, the overall contours of the final IAEA safeguards arrangements are predictable.

Prior Consent. Whatever the remaining uncertainties, U.S. and Chinese negotiators apparently found a mutually satisfactory formula for addressing the safeguards question. Nonetheless, differences persisted through early 1984 on the question of whether China would have to obtain prior U.S. consent before it could reprocess spent fuel from a reactor using U.S. exports in order to extract weapons-usable plutonium. Such prior-consent rights are a standard part of U.S. nuclear accords and are specifically required by the 1978 Nuclear Non-Proliferation Act.[22] From the U.S.

standpoint, the issue had importance because nuclear power plants, the facilities for which the U.S. was expected to supply components, produce large quantities of plutonium in their spent fuel. If China were free to reprocess the fuel at will, this plutonium could be readily used to manufacture nuclear weapons should China ever decide to violate its pledge (presumed to be part of the U.S.-China accord) not to do so. With the possibility that tons of plutonium might eventually be available—enough for possibly hundreds of weapons—the potential contribution to China's nuclear arsenal could be substantial. If it possessed a right of prior consent, however, the United States could prevent reprocessing and ensure that the plutonium produced in China's power reactors using U.S. components did not become readily available for nuclear weapons.

Although China had initially objected to granting the United States prior-consent rights over the reprocessing of spent fuel produced in reactors containing equipment of U.S. origin, by early 1984 it had apparently acquiesced. But the language embodying this understanding was said by U.S. negotiators to be "unorthodox," raising concerns in Congress that the U.S. approval right might not be ironclad.[23] Until the text of the Sino-U.S. cooperation agreement is made public, therefore, it will be impossible to assess the strength of U.S. reprocessing controls.

Although the two issues are not known to have been linked in the U.S.-China negotiations, the effectiveness of U.S. prior-approval rights over reprocessing as a means of preventing China from using U.S. nuclear aid to produce nuclear arms is critically dependent on the adequacy of the safeguards that are applied to reactors using U.S. equipment. In essence, only by making thorough, ongoing inspections of such reactors can the United States be sure that no spent fuel has been improperly removed for reprocessing without the required U.S. authorization. Thus, a U.S. reprocessing veto, even if totally unambiguous, might not accomplish its objective if safeguards proved to be deficient.

Nuclear Export Practices. The third issue impeding conclusion of the Sino-U.S. nuclear accord was Washington's insistence that Peking tighten its nuclear export practices. Washington's stance was not based solely on the desire to reduce the risks of proliferation; it was also apparently required by law: the Atomic Energy Act prohibits nuclear cooperation with any nation that has assisted a non-nuclear-weapon country to acquire a nuclear weapons capability and that has "failed to take steps which, in the President's judgement, represent sufficient progress toward terminating such assistance."[24] (Although the law allows the President to waive this prohibition, exercising the waiver would not have been feasible politically, given the controversy surrounding the U.S.-China accord. It would have amounted to President Reagan's declaring that he was prepared to sign the agreement even though he knew China was assisting other nations to obtain nuclear arms.)

Apparently as a result of continuing negotiations with the United States, however, China for the first time applied for membership in the International Atomic Energy Agency, a seeming indication of its readiness to adopt stricter non-proliferation policies more harmonious with those of the United States. China formally became a member of the 112-nation organization on January 6, 1984.[25] In addition, Peking apparently informed Washington privately that in the future it would require the application of IAEA safeguards to all of its nuclear exports, a major strengthening of its nuclear export practices.[26] China continued to refuse to ratify the Non-Proliferation Treaty, however, which would have made the application of safeguards to its exports a legal requirement, and it refused to adopt publicly the guidelines of the Nuclear Suppliers Group, which would have also constituted a formal pledge to require such safeguards and to exercise restraint in making exports of enrichment and reprocessing technology.

In addition, during a visit to Washington in January 1984, Chinese premier Zhao Ziyang stated in a toast at a White House dinner that "we do not engage in nuclear proliferation ourselves, nor do we help other countries develop nuclear weapons."[27] Zhao's statement, repeated in a January 11 meeting with a group of congressional leaders, represented a major shift from China's previous stance under Chairman Mao that any country had the right to acquire nuclear weapons.[28] Because the statement was not phrased in the future tense, however—i.e., China did not explicitly state that it would not assist nations in developing nuclear weapons in the future—U.S. officials sought further clarification and were apparently assured in private discussions that the statement was intended to cover the future as well.[29] Neither the pledge itself nor the subsequent private assurances were included in the text of the Sino-U.S. nuclear agreement or otherwise reduced to writing, however.

Congressional Review

Based on these various understandings, U.S. ambassador-at-large Richard T. Kennedy and China's commissioner of science and technology Gia Weiwen initialed the U.S.-China agreement for nuclear cooperation on April 30, during President Reagan's visit to Peking.[30]

Presumably, U.S. officials believed China's pledges constituted "sufficient progress" towards ending any aid it may have been providing other nations in developing nuclear weapons so as to remove the possible legal prohibition on U.S. cooperation. Nevertheless, under the Atomic Energy Act, a number of steps, including an interagency review and the preparation of a detailed Non-Proliferation Assessment Statement, had to be completed before the agreement could be formally signed by Secretary of State George Shultz. In addition, before becoming effective, the agreement had to be presented to Congress for a sixty-day review. Under the statute, only days when both houses of Congress were in session counted towards this review period; since long congressional recesses were anticipated for the presidential nominating conventions and the elections, it soon became clear that unless the agreements were submitted to Congress by early June, the review period might not expire until the end of the congressional session, in which case it would have to be started anew when the ninety-ninth Congress convened in January 1985.

Under the Atomic Energy Act, Congress may veto any agreement for cooperation during the review period by a majority vote of both the House and Senate. In June 1983, however, a series of Supreme Court decisions had invalidated such "legislative vetoes."[31] This meant that while the Sino-U.S. accord could not go into effect until the expiration of the sixty-day review period, outright rejection of the agreement by Congress could be accomplished only by the enactment of a statute—for example, an act precluding the Nuclear Regulatory Commission from expending funds to license nuclear exports to China—which could easily be stalled in the legislative process by those supporting the agreement. And since the President would belikely to veto any legislation to block the agreement, a two-thirds majority of both houses of Congress—to override the veto—would be needed as a practical matter to stop the accord. (In contrast, the invalidated congressional veto mechanism in the Non-Proliferation Act had provided for expedited procedures precluding legislative delaying tactics, and no presidential action was needed.)

In early 1984, an amendment to the Atomic Energy Act to require passage of a law or joint resolution *before* a new agreement for nuclear cooperation could become effective was adopted by the Senate as a rider to another bill (the Export Administration Act Amendments of 1983) by a vote of 70 to 16. Whether this new requirement would apply to the China agreement depended on whether it was enacted prior to the formal signing of that accord by Secretary of State Shultz. As of July 1984, it remained uncertain which might be completed first, since the bill containing the rider was awaiting action by a House-Senate conference committee.

Implementation Delayed

Congressional opposition to the accord began to build slowly soon after it was initialed, as conservatives concerned about expanding U.S. ties with China joined liberals concerned about the ambiguities thought to exist in the agreement and Peking's reluctance to give the United States explicit assurances concerning its nuclear export practices.[32] By early June, it became clear that the Reagan administration was delaying submitting the agreement to Congress. The reason, according to administration sources, was that China was continuing to aid Pakistan's nuclear weapons program by providing assistance for its ultracentrifuge enrichment plant at Kahuta. Administration spokesmen declared that some evidence of this was available before President Reagan's visit to Peking, but that the information had become firmer after the visit.[33] Administration sources also indicated that as late as 1983 China had assisted Pakistan by providing nuclear weapons design information, specifically data pertaining to a low-yield uranium-based nuclear device tested in China's fourth nuclear detonation, which took place in 1966.[34]

During early June, U.S. ambassador to Peking Arthur W. Hummel, Jr., was said to have sought a clarification from the Chinese Foreign Ministry on whether aid to Pakistan was in fact continuing, but China reportedly refused to provide any new assurances. However, Premier Zhao's statement that "we do not engage in nuclear proliferation ourselves, nor do we help other nations to develop nuclear weapons" was reaffirmed in a document adopted by the National People's Congress, China's parliament, in May; and on June 20, a Chinese Foreign Ministry spokesman called Zhao's statement a "solemn principled position" and reiterated a second statement also adopted by the National People's Congress that "we by no means favor the Nuclear Non-Proliferation Treaty, nor do we engage in such proliferation by helping other countries to develop nuclear weapons."[35] If aid to Pakistan was continuing notwithstanding these various pledges, serious questions as to the credibility of China's nuclear assurances would be raised.

As of late July 1984, the status of the U.S.-China accords remained uncertain. Given the new revelations about China's nuclear transfers, the requirement that the agreement lie before Congress for sixty days while both houses are in session, and the approach of the presidential election in which President Reagan could be criticized by both Republican conservatives and Democratic opponents for allowing the agreement to go forward before China's non-proliferation posture had been clarified, it seemed unlikely that the agreement could go into effect before the end of 1984.

Attitudes of Other Suppliers. An important related issue is the attitude of other nuclear supplier countries, specifically France, Great Britain, West Germany, and Japan, all of which have increased nuclear ties to China in the past year.[36] If China has, in fact, engaged in activities directly contributing to proliferation as has been reported in the American press, it is possible the United States will urge the other nuclear suppliers to place an embargo on nuclear exports to Peking and perhaps to impose additional sanctions. Since all the nuclear suppliers have been in competition to obtain nuclear orders from China, however, it is uncertain whether the suppliers will stand together and place the issue of nuclear proliferation ahead of possible commercial gain. Indeed, in January 1984, while the United States was maintaining a nuclear embargo against China pending clarification of its nuclear export policies, a West German firm, Klein, Schanzlin, and Becker AG, won the contract previously promised Westinghouse to supply the reactor coolant pumps for the Shanghai reactors.[37]

On the other hand, it appeared in July that at least one other supplier, Japan had reservations about nuclear trade with Peking. Reportedly Tokyo was refusing to conclude a nuclear cooperation agreement until China agreed to more stringent safeguards measures on Japanese nuclear imports.[38]

II. Chinese Offer to Accept Nuclear Waste from the West

In February 1984, several West German companies announced that they had signed a letter of intent with China to receive and store radioactive waste from European nuclear reactors in remote areas of China. The West German companies involved in the deal, which might be worth as much as $4.5 billion, were NUKEM, a nuclear fuel company; one of its subsidiaries specializing in the transportation of nuclear material, Transnuclear; and Alfred Hempel, a privately owned company specializing in trade with Eastern bloc nations.[39] Reportedly, under the terms being arranged, China would sign fifteen-to-twenty-year contracts with Western European utilities to accept spent reactor fuel. The fuel would be stored for approximately fifty years in an above-ground, monitored, storage facility, with a permanent repository for the fuel to be built subsequently. All the facilities were expected to be built in the Gobi Desert.[40]

The offer presented a number of non-proliferation issues, since China's obtaining large quantities of plutonium-bearing spent fuel from the West raised the possibility that Peking might subsequently extract the nuclear weapons material from it.[41] Apparently, China had agreed in the course of its discussion with its West German partners to allow IAEA monitoring of all spent fuel received in China, a significant departure from its prior opposition to allowing IAEA inspectors to supervise nuclear activities within the country.[42]

According to press accounts, the West German companies involved had not consulted either their government or the IAEA during the course of the negotiations, and the West German government seemed hostile to the idea of German utilities sending their spent fuel to China. Similarly, France, Britain, and Belgium, which, like Germany, are each developing reprocessing as part of an overall nuclear waste disposal program, were not expected to be interested in having their electric utilities participate in the arrangement. The West German sponsors of the proposal, however, expected to find customers in Switzerland, Italy, Spain, the Netherlands, Yugoslavia, Finland, and especially Austria, where a completed nuclear power plant had been sitting idle since 1978, in large part because Austria had no mechanism for disposing of its spent fuel.[43]

Any proposals to transfer spent fuel produced from material that had originally come from Australia, Canada, or the United States would require approval of those countries, however. U.S. State Department officials, reacting to the Chinese spent fuel storage offer, were largely noncommittal, although they stressed the desirability of having the IAEA monitor any storage installation.[44]

During the late 1970s, the Carter administration had proposed taking back U.S.-supplied spent fuel and storing it in the United States as a non-proliferation measure aimed at providing an alternative to reprocessing. At the time, reprocessing to extract plutonium and unused uranium from spent fuel and separating the highly radioactive waste products was the recognized approach for dealing with nuclear waste, notwithstanding the proliferation potential involved in creating separated plutonium. The Carter administration promoted the alternative concept of long-term storage of spent fuel, and the U.S. take-back offer was part of this initiative. Carter officials hoped to interest nations such as India, Taiwan, South Korea, and other potential nuclear weapon states in this option. But because of domestic political opposition to storing foreign nuclear waste in the United States, the proposal was not implemented.[45] The Chinese spent fuel storage proposal, however, would not likely advance non-proliferation goals to the same extent as the earlier U.S. proposals, since China would be taking spent fuel from Western Europe where there is little danger of proliferation.

Whether China and its West German partners will succeed in finding customers for their spent fuel storage program, in overcoming the technological challenges of transporting and storing the material, and in arranging appropriate non-proliferation measures remains to be seen. Given these difficulties, it is likely to be many years before the program could become operational.

Controls and
Safeguards

I. Nuclear Suppliers Strengthen Controls, Renew Meetings

Zangger Committee.

On January 24, 1984, the State Department announced that new international controls restricting the export of components for ultracentrifuge enrichment plants had been adopted by the twenty-one-member-Non-Proliferation Treaty Exporters Committee, also known as the Zangger Committee after its Swiss chairman. Under the new controls, all supplier nations that are parties to the treaty have agreed not to make exports of key components for such facilities unless safeguards will be applied to the installation using them.[1]

The Non-Proliferation Treaty requires safeguards for exports of items "especially designed or prepared" for the processing, use, or production of enriched uranium or plutonium. In the mid-1970s, nuclear exporter countries that were parties to the Non-Proliferation Treaty had adopted a "trigger list" of specific items deemed to fall within this category. (It was called a trigger list because the export of items on it was to trigger the application of IAEA safeguards to the transfer). At the time, however, international concern was focused on the spread of reprocessing capabilities, and until 1984, the Zangger list included only a handful of specific items used in ultracentrifuge enrichment plants, such as centrifuge assemblies themselves and special compressors and seals. In the late 1970s, when Pakistan's efforts to purchase the component parts for its ultracentrifuge enrichment plant at Kahuta became known, serious negotiations were begun to refine the trigger list in this area.

At that time, Pakistan was seeking to purchase dual-use items, i.e., equipment that could be used in either a nuclear or non-nuclear industrial setting, which raised a new problem. Switzerland is reported to have taken the position that items such as vacuum valves and uranium-hexafluoride-gas-feed equipment custom-made for Pakistan's enrichment facility could be exported without the application of safeguards, since they were not specifically mentioned on the Zangger list—even though the Non-Proliferation Treaty itself stated that safeguards were to be applied with respect to equipment "especially designed or prepared" for such plants. In 1984, the Zangger list was upgraded to specify, in detail, the particular types of equipment for ultracentrifuge plants whose export would trigger safeguards.

The Nuclear Suppliers Group—an entity distinct from the Non-Proliferation Treaty Exporters Committee because it includes France which is not a party to the treaty—has also established a trigger list. Historically this list has been roughly the same as the Zangger

Committee's, and a revision of this list to make it more specific concerning exports of components for ultra-centrifuge enrichment plants is now under consideration.

Suppliers Group Meets

In July 1984, at the request of the United States, the Western members of the Nuclear Suppliers Group met formally for the first time in seven years to consider new measures for further strengthening nuclear export controls.[2] Four East Bloc members of the Suppliers Group did not attend by mutual agreement.

Formal meetings of the group had been discontinued in 1977 to avoid intensifying the concerns of nuclear importer countries that the group's efforts to coordinate export controls and safeguards policy were a veiled attempt to restrict the flow of nuclear technology needed for peaceful nuclear energy and research programs. Since 1977, Suppliers Group activities had been coordinated through bilateral negotiations or meetings of small groups of supplier countries.

The Reagan administration, reversing its prior opposition to a formal suppliers' meeting, reportedly believed a meeting was called for in order to address several new developments. One was the emergence of new "second tier" suppliers such as Brazil and China. Discussions at the meeting, held in Luxembourg, addressed how to approach these nations to encourage their adoption of export policies consistent with those of the Nuclear Suppliers' Guidelines.

A second issue under discussion were the efforts of countries, such as Pakistan, to circumvent existing controls by purchasing components, subcomponents, and dual-use items for facilities whose direct export had been effectively embargoed. In addition, the meeting addressed plans by Belgium to aid Libya with nuclear training and equipment. (Belgium is also said to be considering new assistance to Pakistan to help it complete its New Labs reprocessing plant; this, too, may have been discussed.)[3]

Finally, the United States also pursued its initiative to gain Suppliers Group agreement to ban future nuclear sales to nations refusing to accept IAEA safeguards on all of their nuclear installations. Exports to Argentina, Brazil, India, Israel, Pakistan, and South Africa could be affected. France and West Germany have long opposed this added restriction on new nuclear sales, and once again, no agreement was reached on its adoption. However, the group agreed to give further study to this export standard.[4]

Australia, Belgium, Canada, France, West Germany, Italy, Japan, the Netherlands, Sweden, Switzerland, Britain, and the United States attended the meeting. Australia, formerly an observer at Nuclear Suppliers Group sessions, became a full participant. According to State Department spokesmen, Eastern Bloc members of the group did not attend because Western members wanted to conduct an initial round of talks before moving to broader discussions.[5]

It is still too early to judge whether this revival of the Suppliers Group will make a significant contribution to international efforts to curb proliferation.

II. Revision in U.S. Non-Proliferation Laws

No significant changes in the statutes governing U.S. non-proliferation and nuclear export policy were enacted during the past year.

In July 1983, an amendment to the International Monetary Fund (IMF) authorization bill passed the House of Representatives, empowering the U.S.

executive director of the IMF to take into account, when making loan decisions, whether the recipient state had detonated a nuclear device or was a party to the Non-Proliferation Treaty. U.S. law already required this of U.S. directors at other multilateral financial institutions.[6] The amendment was dropped from the bill, however, prior to enactment.[7]

As of July 1, 1984, legislation had passed both the House and the Senate to prohibit U.S. exports of nuclear components and transfers of nuclear technology to nations refusing to accept IAEA safeguards on all their nuclear facilities—in effect, applying the same export standards now governing U.S. exports of nuclear fuel and reactors to these lesser transfers. As described in the sections on Argentina, Brazil, South Africa, and India, this legislation was largely a response to a series of actions by the Reagan administration permitting such lesser exports and technology transfers to these nations in the hope of improving the atmosphere for negotiations on their adoption of stronger non-proliferation measures. The amendments, which would revise the U.S. Atomic Energy Act (previously amended by the 1978 Non-Proliferation Act), were attached as riders to the Export Administration Act Amendments of 1983, H.R. 7781 and S. 979.

The legislation was opposed by the Reagan administration, not only because it wanted to retain the authority to use lesser exports as bargaining chips in certain cases, but also because it believed that a further tightening of U.S. export rules would complicate ongoing negotiations with other nuclear suppliers. These were aimed at gaining the agreement of all suppliers that new reactor and fuel exports would be made only to countries accepting full-scope safeguards; this would harmonize supplier group policy with that of the

United States under the 1978 Non-Proliferation Act. In the negotiations, Washington has not sought to make full-scope safeguards a condition for the sale of nuclear components and for nuclear technology transfers, however, as the pending legislation would require. The Reagan administration argued that a shift in U.S. law might make some suppliers afraid that even if they agreed to strengthened restrictions on reactor and fuel sales, Washington would soon seek additional limitations covering these other areas.

A separate rider to the Senate version of the Export Administration Act Amendments would require passage of a law or joint resolution before new agreements for nuclear cooperation (such as the nearly completed U.S.-China accord) could become effective.[8] As of July 1984, these bills were awaiting action by a House-Senate conference committee.

III. International Atomic Energy Agency Safeguards Activities

Important developments of the past year at the IAEA pertaining to the controversy concerning the rejection of Israel's credentials to the 1982 IAEA General Conference, the issue of Israel's policy towards military attacks on peaceful nuclear installations, and China's decision to become a member of the Agency have been covered in previous sections.

Safeguards. According to the IAEA's annual Safeguards Implementation Report, the Agency detected "no anomaly during 1983 which would indicate the diversion of a significant amount of safeguarded material or the misuse of facilities or equipment subject to safeguards."[9] The Agency carried out 1,840 inspections during 1983 at 520 nuclear installations around the world. More than 230 automatic photo and television surveillance systems operated in the field, and 6,600 seals applied to nuclear material were detached and subsequently verified at the IAEA headquarters in Vienna. More than 1,150 plutonium and uranium samples were analyzed, and nearly 3,000 analytical results were reported. Accounting and other safeguards data comprising 800,000 data entries were processed and stored in the Agency's computer.

About 420, mostly minor, discrepancies or irregularities were found. All but one, which is still being investigated, were eventually explained to the Agency's satisfaction. No details concerning these events were disclosed to the public, however, because of the Agency's long-standing policy of maintaining the confidentiality of its safeguards activities.

By the end of 1983, safeguards had actually been applied in forty-three non-nuclear-weapon countries which had signed the Non-Proliferation Treaty, the Tlatelolco Treaty, or both. Safeguards were applied in ten non-nuclear-weapon states not party to either of these treaties. In six of these states, the Agency reported, significant facilities not safeguarded by the IAEA were known to be in operation or under construction. (The Agency did not specify which countries these were, but its 1982 annual report lists India, Israel, Pakistan, and South Africa in this category; possibly Brazil and Argentina, where the United States believes unsafeguarded activities are taking place, have been added.)

The Safeguards Implementation Report also describes problem areas and instances in which the Agency's safeguards goals have not been met. This portion of the document does not name individual countries or facilities but characterizes the safeguards activities category by category (reviewing, for example, whether the Agency was able to meet its safeguards objectives for light-water reactors, or natural-uranium/heavy-water reactors, reprocessing plants, and the like). Problems, such as the frequency of video camera failures or generic inadequacies in accounting for certain kinds of materials, are also described in general terms. The document, although it is made available to every member government, is not released to the public. In past years, the United States has sought to change this practice, but objections from other members have kept the document confidential.

The Agency's budget for safeguards activities was $30.9 million in 1983 and $32.5 million in 1984. This is supplemented by about $3 million in "extra budgetary" resources, principally voluntary contributions from certain member states, including the United States. By way of comparison, the budget for the Washington, D.C., Metropolitan Police Department for 1984 is $134 million and the cost of a single F-16 fighter is $17 million.

* * *

International efforts to slow nuclear proliferation have not been without success. It is ten years since a new nation detonated a nuclear device and twenty years since an additional nation declared unambiguously that it had attained nuclear weapons status. Nations once thought to be very likely proliferators in the short term—Iraq, South Korea, Taiwan, Libya—have apparently made little progress toward achieving nuclear capabilities and some have seen their programs set back dramatically. Many fewer nations are likely to possess nuclear weapons at the end of the century than was widely expected in the 1960s.

Still, the dangers of nuclear proliferation persist and will be with us always. As the events of the past year make clear, at least eight nations are moving to acquire nuclear weapons capabilities, or to expand already existing, if incipient, capabilities. Additional nations no doubt wait in the wings—and will seek such capabilities if circumstances permit.

Only the continued cooperation of the nuclear supplier countries and responsible behavior on the part of all the great powers will contain the danger of nuclear proliferation. The record of international cooperation in this area is impressive, particularly in view of the tensions and hostilities that characterize other aspects of great power relations. But much more could be done. It is to be hoped that the United States will continue to exercise leadership to strengthen the international non-proliferation regime, and to take specific steps to contain the most pressing cases of potential proliferation. All the world will benefit from this diligence.

Notes

Chapter II:
Asia Introduction

1. According to the report of the House International Relations Committee on its 1978 investigation into Korean-American relations ("Koreagate"),

There are indications in the early 1970's, some steps were taken which appeared designed to pave the way for an ROK [Republic of Korea] nuclear weapons program. Specifics on this matter came from a subcommittee staff interview (on February 28, 1978) with a former high-ranking Korean Government official who was a member of the WEC [the secret Weapons Exploitation Committee of senior Korean officials]. He told the subcommittee that the WEC voted unanimously to proceed with the development of nuclear weapons. Subsequently, the Korean Government discussed purchase of a nuclear fuel reprocessing facility from France and a mixed-oxide fuel reprocessing lab from Belgium. The explosion of an Indian nuclear device in April 1974 using fissionable material produced with the assistance of a Canadian NRX research reactor led to greater caution by nuclear technology suppliers, however, and the Belgians and the Canadians withdrew offers for certain technology. Negotiations between the ROK and France continued for some time over a reprocessing facility. Ultimately, it appears that by some time in 1975, any ROK nuclear weapons program had been canceled and the negotiations for purchase of a fuel reprocessing facility also ended. (House Committee on International Relations, Subcommittee on International Organizations, *Investigation of Korean-American Relations,* 95th Congress, 2nd Session, 1978, p. 80).

According to a former U.S. official directly involved in U.S.-Korean nuclear affairs at the time, the contract for the French plant was in fact concluded and subsequently canceled by Korea.

A lengthy news report following up the House investigation of these matters suggested that Korea, in addition to negotiating the purchase of the reprocessing plant, had acquired numerous other components needed for nuclear weapons. The report quotes a "government arms-control analyst" as saying that the reprocessing plant was "practically the last thing on the list of things they needed, from special machine tools to the non-nuclear components of weapons . . . They were running all over the world picking up material and equipment." According to the report:

> Shortly after the Indian test, a small group of intelligence and technical experts, including one from the U.S. Atomic Energy Commission, is said to have begun canvassing U.S. embassies for signs of similar activities on the part of governments considered likely to seek nuclear weapons. The basic approach was to search embassy files for requests by foreign governments to import materials and equipment on a "critical list" of items considered indicative of an interest in atomic weapons. Among these items, sources said, were such things as equipment for machining plutonium metal, bulk orders of beryllium and boron, and exotic, explosive chemicals and shaped-charge technology needed to detonate fission weapons.

> "When they got to Korea, everything snapped into place," the analyst said. Simply by rummaging through embassy files for references to material and equipment that the Korean government had sought to import from U.S. industry and through military channels, a "substantial number" of items on the critical list came to light (Robert Gillette, "U.S. Squelched Apparent S. Korea A-Bomb Drive," *Los Angeles Times*, November 4, 1978).

2. Michael Weisskopf, "Taiwan, Nearing Limits of U.S. Arms Supply, To Build Own Jets," *Washington Post*, March 3, 1984. In the late 1960s and particularly during the mid-1970s, when the United States was opening friendly relations with mainland China, Taiwan made repeated attempts, some apparently secret, to develop a reprocessing capability. Because of Taiwan's precarious security situation and the lack of any clear need for this capability as part of Taiwan's nuclear energy program, U.S. officials came to believe that these efforts were aimed at eventually producing plutonium for nuclear weapons.

In 1969, for example, Taiwan sought to buy a reprocessing plant from the United States, but the Nixon administration denied this request and barred U.S. firms from selling key components for such plants (Edward Schumacher, "Taiwan Seen Reprocessing Nuclear Fuel," *Washington Post*, August 29, 1976). Taiwan then turned to other possible suppliers—in particular, France, from whom it sought to purchase a large reprocessing facility. When the United States intervened, discussions on the sales were broken off. France, however, apparently supplied a number of component parts useful for a reprocessing facility [Steve Weissman and Herbert Krosney, *The Islamic Bomb*, (New York: Times Books, 1981), pp. 152-153].

From 1974 to 1976, Taiwan tried to negotiate an agreement with the British for the reprocessing of Taiwanese spent fuel in England and the return of the plutonium to Taiwan. Once again, the United States stepped in, this time to insist that any plutonium produced under this arrangement be shipped to the United States, instead (Melinda Liu, "Accounting for the N-Factor," *Far Eastern Economic Review*, December 17, 1976, p. 33).

By 1974, the U.S. CIA had concluded:

Taipei conducts its small nuclear program with a weapon option in mind, and it will be in a position to fabricate a nuclear device after five years or so. Taipei's role in the world is changing radically, and concern over the possibility of complete isolation is mounting. Its decisions will be much influenced by U.S. policies in two key areas—support for the island's security and attitudes about the possibility of a nuclear-armed Taiwan. Taipei's present course probably is leading it toward development of nuclear weapons (CIA, "Prospects for Further Proliferation of Nuclear Weapons," DCI NIO 1945/74, "Sanitized Copy," September 4, 1974).

Despite U.S. interventions, by 1975 Taiwan was constructing a hot cell (a laboratory-scale reprocessing unit) on its own. The facility was apparently constructed with components purchased from around the world, including some from France (Schumacher, "Taiwan Seen Reprocessing"). Although the facility was capable of producing only tiny amounts of plutonium it would have provided Taiwan with valuable experience in this field (Ibid.). In that year, Taiwan asked the United States for permission to reprocess a small amount of spent fuel from a U.S.-supplied research reactor in Taiwan, but the United States did not reply to the inquiry (Don Oberdorfer, "Taiwan to Curb A-Role," *Washington Post*, September 23, 1976).

In 1976 reports surfaced that Taiwan may have been secretly extracting plutonium from spent fuel at a clandestine reprocessing facility of some kind (Schumacher, "Taiwan Seen Reprocessing;" Oberdorfer, "Taiwan to Curb A-Role"). Although in congressional hearings, U.S. officials stated that no reprocessing had actually taken place and that such a facility had not, in fact, been built, U.S. suspicions over Taiwan's activities in this area became so intense that the Ford administration insisted Taiwan cease all activities in the reprocessing field, dismantle the hot cell laboratory, and pledge not to engage in any activities related to reprocessing [Senate Subcommittee on Arms Control, International Organizations, and Security Agreements, *Hearings on Nonproliferation Issues,* September 22, 1976 (Washington, D.C.: U.S. Government Printing Office, 1976), pp. 346-371].

3. "Taiwan Makes Nuclear Arms Claim," *Washington Post,* May 15, 1983.

4. "Cabinet Rules Out Developing Nuclear Weapons," *Chung Yang Jih Pao* (Taipei), November 19, 1983, translated in Foreign Broadcast Information Service/Nuclear Development and Proliferation, December 20, 1983, p. 25.

India

1. David Hart, *Nuclear Power in India* (London: Allen and Unwin, 1983), pp. 32, 49.

2. Shyam Bhatia, *India's Nuclear Bomb* (New Delhi: Vikas, 1979), p. 100.

3. Roberta Wohlstetter, *"The Buddha Smiles": Absent-minded Peaceful Aid and the Indian Bomb,* Energy Research and Development Administration, Monograph 3, Contract No. (49-1)-3747, April 30, 1977, pp. 30-31.

4. Ibid., pp. 73-75.

5. Hart, *Nuclear Power in India,* pp. 37, 50-51.

6. Wohlstetter, *The Buddha Smiles,* p. 73.

7. Ibid., p. 74.

8. Ibid., p. 35.

9. IAEA/CS/OR.7, pp. 49-50, as cited in Wohlstetter, *The Buddha Smiles,* pp. 49-50.

10. Wohlstetter, *The Buddha Smiles,* pp. 55, 63; Bhatia, *India's Nuclear Bomb,* p. 150; N. Seshagiri, *The Bomb!* (New Delhi: Vikas, 1975), p. 119; Hart, *Nuclear Power in India,* p. 54. Estimates of the plant's capacity vary. See table at end of India section. It was originally rated at 100 tons per year (Wohlstetter, p. 55) but Hart's more conservative figure of thirty tons per year probably reflects more accurately actual operating experience.

11. Remarks of Bertrand Goldschmidt at Conference on the Atoms for Peace Program (Center for Strategic and International Studies, Georgetown University, Washington, D.C., December 1983); Wohlstetter, *The Buddha Smiles,* p. 63.

12. *Difficulties in Determining If Nuclear Training of Foreigners Contributes to Weapons Proliferation,* U.S. General Accounting Office, Report ID-79-2, April 23, 1979, pp. 18, 21; Wohlstetter, *The Buddha Smiles,* pp. 61-69. By 1974, the United States had trained 1,100 Indians in nuclear sciences, more trainees than for any other nation except Britain (Wohlstetter, p. 28, citing U.S. Atomic Energy Commission data).

13. Bhatia, *India's Nuclear Bomb,* pp. 54-69.

14. Ibid., p. 150. See also K. Subrahmanyam, "India: Keeping the Option Open," in Robert M. Lawrence and Joel Larus, eds., *Nuclear Proliferation Phase II* (Lawrence, Kansas: University Press of Kansas, 1974), p. 115. (Nehru "kept our nuclear option open"). Under this analysis, 1958—the year Nehru gave the Indian Atomic Energy Commission its broad mandate and the

year the decision was made to build the Trombay reprocessing plant—may mark the beginning of the Indian nuclear explosives program. (Brought to author's attention by Thomas W. Graham, Center for International Affairs, Massachusetts Institute of Technology).

15. Bhatia, *India's Nuclear Bomb*, pp. 106, 109.

16. T. T. Poulose, *Perspectives of India's Nuclear Policy* (New Delhi: Young Asia, 1978), pp. 56-58; Bhatia, *India's Nuclear Bomb*, pp. 109 ff.

17. Bhatia, *India's Nuclear Bomb*, p. 114.

18. Poulose, *India's Nuclear Policy*, p. 57.

19. Bhatia, *India's Nuclear Bomb*, p. 120. At the time, the idea that nuclear explosives might have peaceful applications was widely accepted, and both the United States and the Soviet Union were openly conducting experimental peaceful nuclear explosive programs. This lent a patina of legitimacy to Shastri's proposals and allowed him to stop short of an outright endorsement of nuclear arms.

20. Wohlstetter, *The Buddha Smiles,* p. 109. At this time, significantly, the Trombay reprocessing plant was nearing completion. Whatever the motivation may have been for initiating this project in 1958, the plant had plainly become the key to developing an Indian nuclear explosives capability, as Bhabha must have appreciated when he declared on October 16 that India could quickly produce nuclear weapons.

21. Richard K. Betts, "Incentives for Nuclear Weapons," in Joseph A. Yager, ed., *Nonproliferation and U.S. Foreign Policy* (Washington, D.C.: Brookings Institution, 1980), p. 121, n. 10.

22. Wohlstetter, *The Buddha Smiles*, p. 106.

23. Poulose, *India's Nuclear Policy*, p. 173.

24. The Trombay reprocessing plant apparently performed some plutonium extraction prior to its formal inauguration in 1966, however, and as of 1965 the U.S. CIA believed India had sufficient plutonium available to build a nuclear explosive [Bhatia, *India's Nuclear Bomb*, p. 142; Betts, "Incentives for Nuclear Weapons," p. 108, n. 76, citing Donald F. Chamberlain, Director of Scientific Intelligence, Central Intelligence Agency Memorandum for NSC, "The Indian Nuclear Weapon Capability," October 18, 1965 (Box 16, National Security Files, Vietnam Country File, Southwest Asia Special Intelligence Material File, Lyndon Baines Johnson Library, Austin, Texas, Vol. VII)].

25. Bhatia, *India's Nuclear Bomb*, p. 140.

26. Ibid., p. 143; see also Seshagiri, *The Bomb!*, p. 121.

27. Betts, "Incentives for Nuclear Weapons," p. 111.

28. Poulose, *India's Nuclear Policy*, pp. 118-123; Statement of Trivedi, October 31, 1966, First Committee Meeting, United Nations General Assembly, 21st session, New York, United Nations (1967), as cited in Wohlstetter, *The Buddha Smiles*, p. 113.

29. Poulose, *India's Nuclear Policy*, p. 62.

30. Wohlstetter, *The Buddha Smiles*, pp. 114-115.

31. Ernest W. Lefever, *Nuclear Arms in the Third World: U.S. Policy Dilemma* (Washington, D.C.: Brookings Institution, 1979), p. 33; Wohlstetter, *The Buddha Smiles*, p. 117.

32. Aide-Memoire from the U.S. Atomic Energy Commission to the Indian Atomic Energy Commission in Bombay, November 16, 1970, declassified September 19, 1980 (author's files).

33. Wohlstetter, *The Buddha Smiles*, pp. 118-119.

34. *Toronto Star*, July 11, 1974, as cited in Wohlstetter, *The Buddha Smiles*, p. 117.

35. *Toronto Star*, July 11, 1974, as cited in Wohlstetter, *The Buddha Smiles*, p. 118.

36. Sources disagree on the date when the decision to proceed with a test was made. See Stephen M. Meyer, *The Dynamic of Nuclear Proliferation* (Chicago, University of Chicago Press, 1984), p. 123 (decision in 1972); Bhatia, *India's Nuclear Bomb*, p. 143 (decision in 1970); Hart, *Nuclear Power in India*, p. 57 (decision in 1971, citing statement by Indian defense minister Jogjivan Ram, May 19, 1974).

37. In 1975, after several years of civil unrest, Mrs. Gandhi declared a "state of emergency," suspending many civil and political rights.

38. This is the interpretation of Bhatia, *India's Nuclear Bomb*, p. 146.

39. Seshagari, *The Bomb!*, pp. 5-6.

40. Some analysts disagree with this view, however. See Onkar Marwah, "India's Nuclear and Space Programs: Intent and Policy," *International Security*, Fall 1977, pp. 104-105; Poulose, *India's Nuclear Policy*, p. 116 ("What was demonstrated through the nuclear implosion technique in 1974 was a very small and sophisticated nuclear device which could also be carried in an aircraft. It was the product of ten years' labor."); personal communication with Pakistani military analyst, May 1984.

41. Dr. Homi Sethna, Chairman of the Indian Atomic Energy Commission, at a press conference on May 18, 1974, as cited in Wohlstetter, *The Buddha Smiles*, p. 120.

42. *Times of India*, May 23, 1974, and *Karachi Overseas Service*,

May 19, 1974, as cited in Wohlstetter, *The Buddha Smiles*, p. 122.

43 *Kahyan International*, March 7, 1975, as cited in Wohlstetter, *The Buddha Smiles*, p. 122.

44. Lefever, *Nuclear Arms*, p. 36.

45. Wohlstetter, *The Buddha Smiles*, p. 123.

46. Ibid., p. 134.

47. Ibid., p. 132.

48. *U.S.-India Agreement for Cooperation Concerning the Civil Uses of Atomic Energy*, August 8, 1963, 14 U.S.T. 1484, Article VII (A).

49. Homi N. Sethna to Dixy Lee Ray, September 17, 1974, reprinted in Wohlstetter, *The Buddha Smiles*, p. 212.

50. Steve Weissman and Herbert Krosney, *The Islamic Bomb* (New York: Times Books, 1981), p. 134. This more than offset the $25 million cut in U.S. bilateral aid to India in 1974 and possibly the contemporaneous aid cuts by Britain and Japan (Betts, "Incentives for Nuclear Weapons," p. 352).

51. Lefever, *Nuclear Arms*, p. 36; Lars Schoultz, "Politics, Economics, and U.S. Participation in Multilateral Development Banks," *International Organization*, Summer 1982, p. 558; personal communication with knowledgeable U.S. officials. In June, on the heels of the Indian test, President Nixon, during a trip to the Middle East, promised nuclear power plants to Israel and Egypt without the requirement that they sign the Non-Proliferation Treaty or place all their nuclear installations under IAEA safeguards. Reacting to this lenient attitude toward new nuclear sales and the administration's mild response to the Pokharan test, Congress passed an amendment to the Atomic Energy Act to permit it to reject new nuclear agreements by a majority vote of both houses [Atomic Energy Act, section 123, 42 U.S.C. 2153 (1974)].

52. Wohlstetter, *The Buddha Smiles*, pp. 140-156. In a letter to Senator Abraham Ribicoff of August 2, 1976, Secretary of State Henry Kissinger ultimately acknowledged that there was "a high probability" that U.S. heavy water was used in CIRUS at that time. Kissinger noted that the U.S. heavy water was probably commingled with Indian-produced heavy water and argued that in any event, India had by 1974 produced enough of its own heavy water to replace the U.S. supplies several times over so that U.S. material was not "essential" to the Indian test (author's files). In effect, this position declared that restrictions on the use of the U.S. material were a nullity.

53. Thomas O'Toole, "Earlier Try of Indian Bomb Told," *Washington Post,* July 13, 1974; personal communication with knowledgeable former U.S. official. The *Post* story has never been confirmed.

54. Assuming the CIRUS reactor began full operation in 1964 and could produce nine kilograms of plutonium in its spent fuel annually, by 1974 ninety kilograms would have been available. Part of this (fifteen kilograms) was used for the Pokharan test and twenty-one kilograms reportedly had been used to fuel the Purnima plant (Seshagiri, *The Bomb!,* p. 121). The Trombay reprocessing plant was closed in 1974. Thus, the stockpile of separated plutonium stayed constant until 1978, or possibly 1982, when the Tarapur reprocessing plant is believed to have begun operating [Thomas O'Toole, "India Reported Operating Its Second Reprocessing Plant," *Washington Post,* May 25, 1978; "India to Start Producing Plutonium," *New York Times,* April 17, 1982 (test runs during 1981)].

55. Hart, *Nuclear Power in India,* p. 47. As a result of a series of technical problems, labor disputes, and mishaps, India's heavy-water production program has been seriously delayed. Total production in 1981, for example, was only forty-five metric tons, less than a quarter of the design capacity of the four heavy-water plants that India had completed by this date ("Indian Nuclear Reactors: Heavy Going," *Economist,* August 7, 1982). The RAPP II reactor requires 230 metric tons of heavy water.

56. The new IAEA measures specified that safeguards would apply to the reactors (once the Soviet heavy water was introduced) and to any plutonium produced in them, as well as to any additional plutonium that this material might produce if it were subsequently used as reactor fuel in the breeder reactors India planned as part of its long-term nuclear energy strategy. In addition, safeguards would endure until safeguarded materials were no longer potentially useful for the production of nuclear explosives, i.e., indefinitely, rather than for a fixed number of years. These concepts are referred to as "pursuit" and "perpetuity," respectively, and would become the focus of a subsequent controversy regarding the Tarapur reactors discussed below.

It may be noted, however, that by providing India with substantial quantities of heavy water while not requiring it to accept comprehensive safeguards, the Soviet Union in effect allowed India to continue to use its small supplies of unsafeguarded heavy water for unsafeguarded activities—for example, filling the CIRUS, R-5, and later the Madras I reactors—that might contribute to a nuclear weapons program. Had the Soviets offered smaller quantities of the material, India might have been obliged to devote all of its unsafeguarded heavy water output, and possibly quantities of that material already in use in the CIRUS reactor, to charging the Rajasthan I and II reactors (Wohlstetter, *The Buddha Smiles*, p. 146).

57. The 1978 Nuclear Non-Proliferation Act prohibited U.S. exports of nuclear fuel (and reactors) after March 1980 to nations refusing to accept full-scope IAEA safeguards unless the president issued a special waiver, which could, in turn, be overridden by a majority vote of both houses of Congress. India steadfastly refused to accept this requirement and accused the United States of unilaterally amending the 1963 agreement for cooperation covering the Tarapur plants by imposing new conditions for India's receipt of fresh fuel. Citing veiled threats from New Delhi, Carter administration officials feared that if the U.S. fuel shipments were not made, India would declare the United States to be in breach of the 1963 accord and consider itself free to disregard important non-proliferation controls in the agreement, specifically the requirement that the Tarapur reactors and their plutonium-bearing spent fuel remain under IAEA safeguards and that U.S. permission be obtained before the spent fuel could be reprocessed to extract plutonium. (The administration also argued that because the United States had been responsible for delays in processing the pending export licenses, they should be treated like licenses approved before March 1980, to which the full-scope safeguards export criterion did not apply.)

Congressional opponents of the transfer argued that the exports represented the first test of the Non-Proliferation Act's cutoff provisions and that waiving the act in the case of India—which of all the countries not accepting full-scope safeguards was the only one to have detonated a nuclear device and to have violated an agreement with the United States in order to do so—would be taken as a sign by other would-be proliferators that the United States was not serious about stopping the spread of nuclear weapons. President Carter exercised the special waiver provisions of the act to permit the fuel export; although the House voted decisively to override the waiver, President Carter won a narrow victory in the Senate, allowing him to authorize two fuel shipments to India. Under the terms of an arrangement to gain the support of key members of the Senate, however, Carter authorized the first of the two pending fuel shipments in late 1980 but declared that the second would be authorized only when needed by India, perhaps a year later, and on condition that New Delhi took no further steps towards developing nuclear arms. In April 1981, shortly after the Reagan administration took office, intelligence reports quoted in the press stated that India appeared to be readying a site for a second nuclear test (Roger Gale, "Is That Another Bomb You're Building, Mrs. Gandhi?," *The Energy Daily,* April 27, 1981, p. 1). These reports effectively eliminated the possibility of further U.S. fuel shipments to India.

58. "India Reported Ready to Renege on Nuclear Pact," *Wall Street Journal,* April 20, 1981; Don Oberdorfer, "U.S., India Falter in Attempts to End Atomic Pact," *Washington Post,* November 14, 1981.

59. Bernard Weinraub, "Reagan and Mrs. Gandhi Resolve Dispute on Nuclear Fuel for India," *New York Times,* July 30, 1982; Robert F. Goheen, "Problems of Proliferation: U.S. Policy and the Third World," *World Politics,* January 1983, p. 200. Critics charged that this arrangement undermined the cutoff provisions of the 1978 act, which were intended to pressure India into accepting comprehensive IAEA inspections by denying it needed nuclear commodities if it refused (Senator John H. Glenn, "Is the Tarapur Agreement Any Good?" *Washington Post,* August 1, 1982).

60. "Gandhi Talks to House on Nuclear Developments," *New Delhi Patriot,* December 4, 1980, reprinted in *Foreign Broadcast Information Service/Nuclear Development and Proliferation* (hereafter FBIS/NDP), January 26, 1981, p. 4 (delays in Indian nuclear power program "mainly due to embargo").

61. Pakistan's original agreement with France would have required such inspections on the larger reprocessing facility at Chashma and on any subsequently built reprocessing plant that used the same basic technology. This provision has not been enforced since France's withdrawal from the deal, however.

62. Betts, "Incentives for Nuclear Weapons," p. 112; Lefever, *Nuclear Arms,* p. 38.

63. Betts, "Incentives for Nuclear Weapons," p. 113; Michael T. Kaufman, "India Gives Warning of Atom-Arms Race," *New York Times,* August 16, 1979.

64. "India to Keep Nuclear Options,'" *New York Times,* July 28, 1979.

65. Michael T. Kaufman, "India Gives Warning."

66. K. K. Sharma, "India Hints It May Scrap Nuclear Arms Abstinence," *Washington Star,* November 3, 1979.

67. Ibid.

68. "Gandhi Says National Interest May Require Nuclear Blast," *Washington Post*, March 14, 1980.

69. "Indian Enrichment Experiments Ostensibly for Weapons Purposes Continue," *Nucleonics Week*, April 10, 1980, p. 12. India has continued laboratory-scale activities in this field ("India Is Pursuing Uranium Enrichment Technology," *Nuclear Fuel*, February 28, 1983, p. 3).

70. Judith Miller, "Cranston Says India and Pakistan Are Preparing for Nuclear Testing," *New York Times*, April 28, 1981; Roger Gale, "India To Press 'Start Button' on Nuclear Fuel Reprocessing Plant," *Energy Daily*, February 5, 1981; Yogi Aggarwal, "India Makes Another Bomb," *Sunday Observer* (Bombay), August 30, 1981 (government had one atomic bomb ready in April, could prepare another one in weeks); K. Subrahmanyam, "Bomb—The Only Answer," *Times of India*, "Sunday Review," April 26, 1981, p. 1.

71. Stuart Auerbach, "Arms for Pakistan Spur Gandhi's Fears, Hawks' Calls for A-Weapons," *Washington Post*, May 3, 1981; Subrahmanyam, "The Only Answer."

72. Ravi Desai, "The Pressure in India for Nuclear Weapons," *Wall Street Journal*, July 13, 1981. It is again possible, however, that some of this activity, especially preparation of a test site, was intended as a warning to Pakistan not to proceed too far toward developing nuclear arms rather than as part of a genuine recommencement of India's nuclear explosives program.

73. Gale, "India to Press 'Start Button.' "

74. Don Oberdorfer, "U.S., Pakistan Progressing on New Aid Plan," *Washington Post*, April 22, 1981.

75. Foreign Assistance Act of 1961, section 669, 22 U.S.C. 2429a (1977).

76. Subrahmanyam, "The Only Answer."

77. A. G. Noorani, "The Sudden Volte-Face II," *Indian Express*, August 31, 1982, reprinted in FBIS/Asia, September 9, 1982; "CPI-M Leader Comments on Tarapur Fuel Arrangements," *The Patriot*, September 3, 1982, reprinted in FBIS/NDP, October 8, 1982, p. 25. See Export-Import Bank Act, 12 U.S.C. 635(b)(4).

78. International Financial Institutions Act, 22 U.S.C. 262g(b)(3), 1977. This formula replaced the 1974 provision requiring the United States to oppose all IDA loans to India. The provision does not apply to the U.S. representatives to the International Monetary Fund.

79. Other factors that may be restraining influences on India's nucle-

ar weapons policy are discussed in Section III, below.

80. "Venkataraman on Pakistan's Nuclear Plans," *Delhi Domestic Service,* 0730 GMT, March 2, 1982, translated in FBIS/Asia, March 4, 1982, p. E3.

81. Milton R. Benjamin, "India Said To Eye Raid on Pakistani A-Plants," *Washington Post,* December 20, 1982.

82. William Claiborne, "India Denies Plan To Hit Pakistani Nuclear Plants," *Washington Post,* December 23, 1982. Recent improvements in Indo-Pakistani relations are discussed below.

83. "Questions Raised About Agreement on Tarapur Fuel," *Times of India,* August 27, 1982, reprinted in FBIS/NDP, October 8, 1982, p. 32.

84. A portion of the Tarapur spent fuel was irradiated for only short periods, because some fuel elements were defective and were removed from the reactor earlier than would be normal. Thus, at least some of the Tarapur spent fuel may contain "low burn-up" plutonium ideally suited for nuclear weapons. India's 1974 assurances that it would use the Tarapur plutonium "exclusively for the needs of the Station," however, had no expiration date and, in principle, would continue to apply to the material. Nonetheless, without safeguards it would be difficult to verify India's compliance with this pledge. Moreover, it remains in doubt whether India considers itself bound by this commitment in perpetuity.

85. "Reportage on Indo-French Negotiations on Fuel," *The Statesman* (Calcutta), November 6, 1982, reprinted in FBIS/NDP, December 6, 1982, p. 11.

86. "Spokesman States Right to Reprocess Spent Fuel," *Delhi Domestic Service,* 0240 GMT, August 1, 1982, reprinted in FBIS/NDP, August 23, 1982, p. 9.

87. Pearl Marshall, "India Claims Unilateral Right To Reprocess U.S.-Origin Fuel," *Nucleonics Week,* December 18, 1980, p.1.

88. Wohlstetter, *The Buddha Smiles,* p. 114.

89. Stuart Auerbach, "India Becomes 6th Country to Put Satellite in Orbit," *Washington Post,* July 19, 1980.

90. But see "India's Rocket Could Meet Military Ambitions," *New Scientist,* August 26, 1982, p. 555 (solid propellant in satellite rocket "ideally suited for missiles;" rocket could be converted to military uses "in six *months*").

91. Rodney Jones, *Small Nuclear Forces,* Washington Papers 103 (Washington, D.C.: Center for Strategic and International Studies, Georgetown University, 1984), p. 27 (possible IRBM between 1990-2000).

92. Hart, *Nuclear Power in India*, p. 87.
93. "Attractive Terms of Soviet Nuclear Offer Told," *The Hindu*, December 13, 1982, reprinted in FBIS/NDP, February 4, 1983, p. 36.
94. Hart, *Nuclear Power in India*, pp. 52-53.
95. See chapters on Argentina and Libya; "India's Offer of Nuclear Cooperation," *Delhi Domestic Service*, 0830 GMT August 27, 1982, translated in FBIS/NDP, September 1982; "Nuclear Fuel Complex Gets Order From West Germany," *The Patriot*, April 8, 1982, reprinted in FBIS/NDP, May 18, 1982, p.12.
96. Agreements with the following nations were known to be in effect as of 1980: Afghanistan, Algeria, Argentina, Belgium, Czechoslovakia, West Germany, France, Hungary, Iraq, Italy, Libya, Poland, Romania, Syria, the United States, the USSR, and Yugoslavia. Agreements had previously been signed with Bangladesh, Brazil, Canada, Denmark, Egypt, East Germany, Iran, the Philippines, Spain, and the United Kingdom (Thomas W. Graham, "South Asian Nuclear Proliferation and National Security Chronology," Center for International Affairs, Massachusetts Institute of Technology, 1984).
97. Bhatia, *India's Nuclear Bomb*, p. 144; "New AEC Chief," *Times of India*, August 6, 1983, FBIS/NDP September 27, 1984, p. 26.
98. "Bhabha Atomic Center Director," *Times of India*, March 8, 1984, FBIS/NDP, April 9, 1984, p. 22.
99. Shyam Bhatia, "Zia Forced To Put Off Nuclear Test," *Sunday Observer* (London), January 2, 1983, p. 5.
100. Milton R. Benjamin, "U.S. Is Delaying Nuclear Exports to India," *Washington Post*, June 23, 1983.
101. *The Hindu* (Madras), March 20, 1983, as cited in *Nuclear Exports to India: Parts for the Tarapur Atomic Power Station*, Issue Brief IB-83-118 (Washington, D.C.: Congressional Research Service, 1983).
102. Atomic Energy Act, Sec. 129(1)(D) (added to the Atomic Energy Act by the 1978 Non-Proliferation Act) 42 U.S.C. Sec. 2158. The provision prohibits all U.S. nuclear exports to any non-nuclear-weapon nation found to be "engaging in activities involving source [i.e., natural uranium] or special nuclear [i.e., enriched uranium or plutonium] materials and having direct significance for the manufacture or acquisition of nuclear explosive devices," except under circumstances explained in the text.
103. Benjamin, "U.S. Delaying Nuclear Exports." Also, Richard Ottinger, Chairman of the House Subcommittee on Energy,

Conservation, and Power, to Ronald Reagan, December 1, 1982 (opposition to French fuel supply). Under the 1978 Nuclear Non-Proliferation Act, U.S.-origin components, unlike fuel or reactors, could be exported to nations not accepting full-scope safeguards. Thus, but for section 129 of the Act, the exports would have been permissible.

It is also possible that India's position that safeguards on the Tarapur reactors would cease in 1993 might have been interpreted by the Nuclear Regulatory Commission—which issues U.S. nuclear export licenses—as not satisfying one of the export criteria that do apply to nuclear component exports, the requirement that IAEA safeguards "apply" to them. In this case, too, the president would have had to issue a waiver in order to allow the exports to be made, resulting in equal political embarrassment since congressional opponents would surely have raised the reports of India's 1981 test preparations in arguing against the transfers.

104. William Claiborne, "Shultz Promises Parts for India's Reactor," *Washington Post,* July 1, 1983.

105. Immediately after Shultz's announcement, House and Senate members sent a letter to the White House condemning the sale [Claiborne, "Schultz Promises Parts;" also John H. Glenn to Ronald Reagan July 7, 1983 (serious radiation hazards at Tarapur would not be remedied by spare parts even if supplied)].

106. See Boschwitz-Glenn Resolution, S. Res. 1981, 98th Congress, 1st Session (1983); The Export Administration Act Amendments, H.R. 7781 and S. 979, 98th Congress, 2nd Session (1984). This legislation was still awaiting action by a House-Senate conference committee as of July 1984. Reactor and fuel exports to such countries were already banned under the 1978 act.

107. Victor Gilinsky, "Why Help India Make the Bomb?" *Wall Street Journal,* July 5, 1983.

108. Other factors influencing Indian nuclear explosives policy are discussed in Section III.

109. Milton R. Benjamin, "India Storing Weapon Grade Plutonium," *Washington Post,* February 20, 1983; Pearl Marshall, "India Reprocesses RAPP Fuel Under IAEA Eyes," *Nuclear Fuel,* February 14, 1983, p. 12.

110. H. N. Sethna, "Nuclear Power—Fast Breeder Reactors," Dr. H. L. Ray Memorial Lecture (Indian Institute of Chemical Engineers, Calcutta, May 31, 1977).

111. Congressional Research Service, *Analysis of Six Issues about the Nuclear Capabilities of India, Iraq, Libya and Pakistan,*

(Washington, D.C.: U.S. Government Printing Office, 1982), report prepared for the Subcommittee on Arms Control, Oceans, International Operations, and Environment of the Senate Foreign Relations Committee, January 1982, p. 2; Mohan Ram, "Nuclear Mirage," *Far Eastern Economic Review,* December 4, 1981, p. 24. A third reprocessing plant is planned near Kalpakkam to handle fuel from India's fifth and sixth power reactors, Madras I and II, from the Fast Breeder Test Reactor, also at Kalpakkam.

112. These low and high estimates are based on the alternative assumptions that India continues to use the fifteen-kilograms-of-plutonium-per-device design apparently used for the 1974 test, as the more conservative estimate, or uses five kilograms per weapon, a more generous estimate based on the requirements of moderately complex designs drawn from the open literature.

113. This point is thoughtfully analyzed by Wohlstetter, *The Buddha Smiles,* pp. 67-70.

114. H. N. Sethna, "Nuclear Power Development in India with Special Reference to Reprocessing" (paper presented at the Atomic Industrial Forum Conference, Tokyo, March 1983). An additional parallel with past events is the civil unrest now plaguing the Punjab; civil strife was also widespread in 1974. Some analysts have suggested that a desire to create a distraction from this turmoil was a factor leading to the 1974 test.

115. "Reportage on Opening, Problems of Kalpakkam N-Plant," *Times of India,* July 24, 1983, reprinted in FBIS/NDP, September 19, 1983, p. 15.

116. In fact, at least a quarter of the plant, mostly special steel alloys, was imported [S. Parthasarthy, "Point of Departure Noted," *The Hindu* (Madras) July 23, 1983, reprinted in FBIS/NDP, September 19, 1983, p. 15.]

117. Pearl Marshall, "India, Wanting No Constraints, Loathe to Seek Heavy Water from Soviet," *Nucleonics Week,* February 18, 1982, p. 4.

118. Praful Bidwai, "Causes of Early Shutdown," *Times of India,* July 27, 1983, reprinted in FBIS/NDP, September 19, 1983, p. 22. This report, it may be noted, indicated that one hundred tons of virgin heavy water had been shipped to Madras from Bombay (near Trombay); possibly this material had been intended for the R-5, India's second unsafeguarded plutonium-producing reactor, shortly expected to begin operating. Removal of the heavy water to Madras could result in a postponement of the R-5's start-up date.

119. It is also possible that India took very dilute (for example, 3 percent pure) but easily upgraded heavy water and substituted it for more highly concentrated material (for example, 30 percent pure), arguing that they were "equivalent" since neither was reactor-grade (99 percent pure). The 30 percent material could then have been diluted to produce ten times the quantity of the easily upgraded 3 percent material, which then could be improved to reactor-grade in India's heavy-water plants. Although India's agreement with the Soviet Union seems to rule out this strategy, its earlier agreement with Canada covering a portion of the heavy water in Rajastan I is more ambiguous on what constitutes "equivalent" heavy water.

120. Bidwai, "Causes of Early Shutdown."

121. Judith Miller, "U.S. Is Holding Up Peking Atom Talks," *New York Times,* September 19, 1982. China's aiding a potential nuclear adversary obtain unsafeguarded plutonium seems an unlikely turn of events, but at least one additional source, an Indian academic, has alleged the transaction took place. (Personal communication)

122. Some analysts discount the possibility that Madras might be used for this purpose, believing that the unsafeguarded R-5 reactor and the refurbished Trombay reprocessing plant, which produce enough plutonium for from three to possibly ten nuclear weapons per year, would be more likely sources for the material if India wanted to expand its nuclear explosives program. Nevertheless, the Madras reactor and the Tarapur reprocessing plant could produce about triple this amount of plutonium, and this capacity could well be needed if India decided on a serious nuclear weapons strategy. Moreover, in view of the considerable funds and effort India has expended to keep the Madras plant free from safeguards, this option appears a valid cause for concern.

123. Richard P. Cronin, "Prospects for Nuclear Proliferation in South Asia," *Middle East Journal,* Autumn 1983, p. 610.

124. Onkar Marwah, "India's Nuclear and Space Programs: Intent and Policy," *International Security,* Fall 1977, pp. 110-111 (cites study for U.S. Arms Control and Disarmament Agency that concluded India would suffer financial insolvency if it added cost of nuclear force to current defense expenditures).

125. Betts, "Incentives for Nuclear Weapons," p. 123. In addition, India's show of restraint has permitted it to remain a vocal advocate of nuclear disarmament.

126. Indeed, just the opposite may be true: once India acquires sub-

stantial quantities of plutonium from its peaceful nuclear energy program, building a nuclear deterrent will be so close at hand as to become a tempting option. Rather than constraining the decision to build a nuclear force, India's resource base would then invite it.

127. Richard P. Cronin, "Prospects for Nuclear Proliferation," pp. 608-609; Graham, "South Asia Nuclear Proliferation."

Pakistan

1. U.S. General Accounting Office, *Difficulties in Determining If Nuclear Training of Foreigners Contributes to Weapons Proliferation*, Report ID-79-2, April 23, 1979, pp. 20-23. Among this group was the head of Pakistan's atomic energy program. By 1974, 120 Pakistani nuclear experts had been trained (Roberta Wohlstetter, *"The Buddha Smiles": Absent-minded Peaceful Aid and the Indian Bomb*, Monograph 3, Energy Research and Development Administration, Contract No. (49-1)-3747, April 30, 1977, p. 28, citing U.S. Atomic Energy Commission data).

2. On Bhutto's role, see Zulfikar Ali Bhutto, *"If I Am Assassinated . . ."* (New Delhi: Vikas, 1979), pp. 135-138. On small reprocessing lab, see Steve Weissman and Herbert Krosney, *The Islamic Bomb*, (New York: Times Books, 1981), p. 81.

3. Bhutto, *"If I Am Assassinated . . .,"* pp. 137-138.

4. Zulfikar Ali Bhutto, *The Myth of Independence* (London: Oxford University Press, 1969), p. 153. Bhutto may have been even more emphatic in 1965, when he reportedly made the remark, "If India builds the bomb, we will eat leaves or grass, even go hungry, but we will have to get one of our own." (Weissman and Krosney, *The Islamic Bomb*, p. 162).

5. Weissman and Krosney, *Islamic Bomb*, pp. 43-46. The authors' information comes from two participants in the meeting. The date of this meeting, some two years before India's nuclear test, is significant because it shows that Pakistan's quest for nuclear arms was not stimulated by a direct nuclear threat from India. Rather, more generalized concerns over the disparity in conventional military strength and nuclear potential between the two nations seem to have been decisive.

6. Weissman and Krosney, *Islamic Bomb*, p. 75.

7. Zalmay Khallizad, "Pakistan: The Making of a Nuclear Power," *Asian Survey*, June 1976, p. 589; D. K. Palit and P. K. S. Namboodiri, *Pakistan's Islamic Bomb* (New Delhi: Vikas, 1979), p. 20.

8. Weissman and Krosney, *Islamic Bomb*, p. 75. Although Weissman and Krosney offer the rough estimate that the plant could produce 800 kilograms of plutonium per year, India's similarly-sized Tarapur reprocessing plant is said to have an output of 135 to 150 kilograms. The more conservative estimate is used here. See India section, note 109 and accompanying text.

9. Palit and Namboodiri, *Pakistan's Islamic Bomb*, p. 16. Weissman and Krosney also state, based on interviews with Pakistani

officials, that in 1973 and 1974 Islamabad asked France for certain types of analyses that were specifically relevant for the production of a nuclear weapon. Although the aid was not given, the request plainly put France on notice as to Pakistan's apparent interest in developing nuclear arms (Weissman and Krosney, *Islamic Bomb*, p. 76).

10. Weissman and Krosney, *Islamic Bomb*, p. 83.

11. Milton R. Benjamin, "Pakistan Building Secret Nuclear Plant," *Washington Post*, September 23, 1980. The New Labs is a separate facility from the small reprocessing laboratory noted earlier (Weissman and Krosney, *The Islamic Bomb*, p. 81; Thomas W. Graham, "South Asian Nuclear Proliferation and National Security Chronology," Center for International Affairs, Massachusetts Institute of Technology, 1984).

12. Weissman and Krosney, *Islamic Bomb*, p. 175

13. A report on the investigation is reprinted in K. Subrahmanyam, ed., *Nuclear Myths and Realities: India's Dilemma* (New Delhi: ABC, 1981), App. I to Ch. 8.

14. Shirin Tahir-Kheli, *The United States and Pakistan: The Evolution of an Influence Relationship* (New York: Praeger, 1982), pp. 63-64.

15. Palit and Namboodiri, *Pakistan's Islamic Bomb*, p. 36; Khallizad, "Pakistan," p. 583.

16. Sheikh R. Ali, "Pakistan's Islamic Bomb," *Asia Pacific Community*, Spring 1982, p. 77.

17. Tahir-Kheli, *The U.S. and Pakistan*, p. 89, citing figures from the International Institute for Strategic Studies, *The Military Balance: 1979-1980* (London, 1980), p. 106. According to another acccount of Pakistani-Arab relations, in addition to these ties there are about 5,000 troops in Saudi Arabia alone, including a large training group for the Royal Guards, most of whose officers are Pakistanis. Pakistani forces were reported to have been deployed in Jordan after the Camp David agreement and on the Yemen border at the time of border clashes in February 1979. Palit and Namboodiri, *Pakistan's Islamic Bomb*, pp. 42-43.

18. Weissman and Krosney, *Islamic Bomb*, pp. 62-65.

19. See chapter on Libya.

20. The original London Suppliers Club included the United States, the Soviet Union, Great Britain, France, West Germany, Japan, and Canada. As time went on, the following states joined: Belgium, Czechoslovakia, East Germany, Italy, the Netherlands, Poland, Sweden, and Switzerland. Australia and Finland indicated their compliance with the guidelines in later communi-

cations to the International Atomic Energy Agency.

21. Weissman and Krosney, *Islamic Bomb*, p. 164.
22. Tahir-Kheli, *The U.S. and Pakistan*, p. 88.
23. Foreign Assistance Act of 1961, Sec. 669 (1976) 22 U.S.C. 2429.
24. Tahir-Kheli, *The U.S. and Pakistan*, p. 124.
25. Ibid., pp. 127-129; Communique of the French Council for External Nuclear Policy, December 16, 1976, as cited in Charles N. Van Doren, *Nuclear Supply and Non-Proliferation: The IAEA Committee on Assurances of Supply*, Congressional Research Service Report 83-202 S (Library of Congress: Washington, D.C., 1983, p. CRS-192);
26. Tahir-Kheli, *The U.S. and Pakistan*, p. 129; personal communication with knowledgeable former U.S. officials.
27. The Symington amendment the amendment was not formally invoked against Pakistan, however.
28. Personal communication with a knowledgeable French official.
29. Weissman and Krosney, *Islamic Bomb*, p. 167; "Pakistan for the First Time Has Officially Acknowledged It Is Building Its Own Reprocessing Plant," *Nuclear Fuel*, September 17, 1979, p. 10; "The Last Two French Engineers Overseeing the Civil Work at Pakistan's . . .," *Nucleonics Week*, July 12, 1979, p. 6. According to a knowledgeable former U.S. official, the actual aid provided by French personnel during this period was nominal, and Washington saw the French presence as beneficial since it allowed monitoring of Pakistan activities at the site.
30. The Canadian policy was triggered by India's 1974 test and resulted in the termination of nuclear assistance to both India and Pakistan in 1976.
31. Based on Weissman and Krosney, *Islamic Bomb*, pp. 182-192.
32. At the time, military aid to Pakistan was marginal, and economic assistance was limited to $40 million (Tahir-Kheli, *The U.S. and Pakistan*, p. 134). Between October 1978, when the U.S. aid pipeline had been reopened following France's termination of its agreement with Pakistan for the sale of the Chashma reprocessing plant, and the subsequent termination of aid in early 1979, the Carter administration had offered to supply F-5 fighters to Pakistan. No specific nuclear strings were attached, but undoubtedly it was hoped that by increasing Pakistan's conventional military strength, its incentives for developing nuclear weapons would be reduced. Pakistan rejected the limited-range F-5s as not powerful enough in comparison to India's capabilities. In fact, the Carter administration had previously offered the F-5 to Pakistan in June 1977 in lieu of the more powerful A-7 which Pakistan was seek-

ing. At that point, too, Pakistan had rejected the F-5 offer. Ultimately, Pakistan turned to France for its military aircraft, purchasing the Mirage V. (Don Oberdorfer, "Arms Sale to Pakistan Urged to Stave Off A-Bomb There," *Washington Post,* August 6, 1979; Tahir-Kheli, *The U.S. and Pakistan,* pp. 90-91.

33. Senate Subcommittee on Energy, Nuclear Proliferation, and Federal Services of the Committee on Governmental Affairs, *Hearing on Nuclear Proliferation: The Situation in India and Pakistan,* May 1, 1979 (Washington, D.C.: U.S. Government Printing Office, 1979), p. 10. Pakistan's one nuclear power plant, it may be noted, does not require enriched uranium, and as mentioned earlier, although a considerable long-term nuclear energy plan had been drawn up involving numerous low-enriched-uranium/light-water power plants, none of these had gone beyond the planning stage as late as mid-1984.

34. "Address to the Nation," *The Moslem,* July 28, 1979, as cited in Tahir-Kheli, *The U.S. and Pakistan,* p. 135.

35. Richard Burt, "U.S. Aides Say Pakistan Is Reported to Be Building an A-Bomb Site," *New York Times,* August 17, 1979.

36. Richard Burt, "U.S. Will Press Pakistan to Halt A-Arms Project," *New York Times,* August 12, 1979. India may well have been the intelligence source cited by administration officials in the August 17 story (see note 35) on the supposed Pakistani nuclear weapons test site. On August 15, India's new prime minister, Charan Singh, had warned the Indian parliament that his government would review its earlier stand of not building nuclear weapons if Pakistan pursued its nuclear bomb program. In an August 15 address on the thirty-second anniversary of India's independence from Britain, he stated: "We know they are making the bomb. Why are they making the bomb? Against whom is it aimed? The bomb is aimed at us. It poses a danger to India's peace and security. But if Pakistan persists in its efforts to complete the bomb and continues to collect the materials for it we shall have to reconsider our earlier view" (Peter Niesewand, "India To Revise Nuclear Plans if Pakistan Acts, Leader Says," *Washington Post,* August 15, 1979).

37. Burt, "Pakistan Reported Building A-Bomb Site."

38. Burt, "U.S. Will Press Pakistan."

39. Michael T. Kaufman, "Pakistan Perplexed by U.S. Stand on Nuclear Arms," *New York Times,* August 9, 1979. Section 701 of the International Financial Institutions Act of 1977 (22 U.S.C. 262g), as noted elsewhere, requires American executive directors at multilateral lending institutions to take into account in the

course of making loan decisions whether a nation is a party to the Nuclear Non-Proliferation Treaty.

40. "Pakistan for the First Time Has Officially Acknowledged It Is Building Its Own Reprocessing Plant," *Nuclear Fuel*, September 17, 1979, p. 10. Pakistan justified the facility as necessary to allow it to extract plutonium from spent reactor fuel to be reused in breeder reactors. Pakistani Atomic Energy Commission chairman Munir Khan stated that the reprocessing plant would be part of an enlarged Pakistani nuclear power program entailing the construction of the sixteen or more nuclear power plants by the year 2000.

41. Don Oberdorfer, "Uranium Parley with Pakistanis Inconclusive," *Washington Post*, October 18, 1979.

42. Shahi reportedly assured Washington that Pakistan would not manufacture nuclear weapons or aid other countries to do so (Don Oberdorfer, "Effort to Block Pakistan from A-Bomb Faltering," *Washington Post*, October 20, 1979; personal communication with former U.S. Official). As noted below, however, even as these assurances were being given, Pakistani purchasing agents were obtaining key technology from Western Europe for the Kahuta plant and uranium from Libya to be upgraded in the facility.

43. Bernard Gwertzman, "White House Seeks Long-Term Aid to Bolster the Defense of Pakistan," *New York Times*, February 1, 1980.

44. Gwertzman, "White House Seeks Long-Term Aid," Tahir-Kheli, *The U.S. and Pakistan*, pp. 102-103.

45. John J. Fialka, "West Concerned by Signs of Libyan-Pakistan A-Effort," *Washington Star*, November 25, 1979.

46. IAEA document INFCIRC/248.

47. Fialka, "West Concerned;" "Niger Says It Sold Uranium to Libya, Use for Nuclear Weaponry Feared," *Washington Star*, April 14, 1981; Weissman and Krosney, *Islamic Bomb*, pp. 212-213.

48. "Niger Says Adherence to IAEA Safeguards Will Be Required for Export of Uranium," *Nuclear Fuel*, March 31, 1980, p. 2.

49. Fialka, "Niger Sold Uranium to Libya."

50. "Niger Says Adherence Required," *Nuclear Fuel*.

51. "Swiss To Allow Firms To Sell Nuclear Technology to Pakistan," *Washington Star*, September 23, 1980; Richard Burt, "Nuclear Issue Mars U.S. Ties with Swiss," *New York Times*, September 23, 1980; Leonard Downie, Jr., "Swiss Send Aid to Pakistan," *Washington Post*, September 21, 1980.

52. Leonard Downie, Jr. "Swiss, U.S. Prepare to Resume Nuclear Cooperation," *Washington Post,* December 31, 1980.

53. Leonard Downie, Jr., "US, Swiss at Impasse on A-Policy," *Washington Post,* September 22, 1980; "Swiss Investigate Exports to Pakistan While U.S. Withholds Okay on Pu Sale," *Nuclear Fuel,* September 29, 1980, p. 17.

54. "Swiss Firms May Avoid Further Deals, But Honor Existing Pacts With Pakistan," *Nuclear Fuel,* November 10, 1980, p. 1; Downie, "Swiss, U.S. to Resume Cooperation." In March 1981, one Swiss firm, CORA Engineering AG, which had been continuing exports to Pakistan, stated that all further transfers would be halted as a result of a bomb attack and threats against company executives by opponents of the nuclear facility ("Firm Halts Supplies to Pakistani A-Unit," *Washington Post,* March 20, 1981; "Swiss Firm Discontinues Sale of Nuclear Components to Pakistan," *Le Figaro,* March 17, 1981, translated in Foreign Broadcast Information Service/Nuclear Development and Proliferation (hereafter FBIS/NDP), April 21, 1981, p. 1.

55. "Pakistan Makes Its Own Nuclear Fuel," *Washington Star,* September 1, 1980; "Pakistan's KANUPP Reactor Is Now Operating on Domestically Fabricated Fuel," *Nucleonics Week,* September 4, 1980, p. 11. Canadian plans for the plant had apparently been provided before Ottowa terminated nuclear aid to Pakistan.

56. Milton R. Benjamin, "Pakistan Building Secret Nuclear Plant," *Washington Post,* September 23, 1980. U.S. experts apparently identified the facility well before the *Post* story and may have had some success in retarding its completion. (Personal communication with knowledgeable former U.S. official).

57. In June 1984, Senator Alan Cranston declared that the facility had conducted tests with nonradioactive materials in 1982 and had subsequently processed radioactive material—by implication, spent fuel. (*Congressional Record,* 90th Congress, 2nd Session, June 21, 1984, p. S 7901). U.S. officials denied the allegation, however. (Personal communication with knowledgeable U.S. officials; see also Ann MacLachlan, "Belgians Awaiting Government Approval to Complete Pakistani Reprocessing Lab," *Nuclear Fuel,* March 26, 1984, p. 9.)

58. Benjamin, "Pakistan Building Secret Plant."

59. Weissman and Krosney, *Islamic Bomb,* pp. 214-215.

60. Richard M. Weintraub, "Pakistan Said To Receive Nuclear Arms Parts Illegally Via Canada," *Washington Post,* December 7, 1980.

61. Barry Schweid, "Turks Ship U.S. A-Tools to Pakistan," *Washington Post,* June 28, 1981. Turkey apparently adopted the same attitude Switzerland had, claiming that the Non-Proliferation Treaty "trigger list" (items whose export would require safeguards) did not explicitly identify the items re-exported from Turkey as being subject to controls. After considerable U.S. urging, however, Turkey agreed to reconsider its position.

62. John M. Geddes, "Bonn Says Firm Illegally Sent Pakistan Gear That Can Be Used for Atomic Bombs," *Wall Street Journal,* July 16, 1981.

63. Ibid.

64. Don Oberdorfer, "US, Pakistan Progressing on New Aid Package," *Washington Post,* April 22, 1981.

65. Senate Subcommittee on Energy, Nuclear Proliferation, and Government Processes of the Committee on Governmental Affairs, *Hearing on Nuclear Non-Proliferation Policy,* 97th Congress, 1st Session, June 24, 1981 (Washington, D.C.: U.S. Government Printing Office, 1981), pp. 16-17.

66. Ibid., p. 16. President Zia reiterated these assurances during a visit to Washington in December 1982.

67. Ibid., pp. 16, 18-19.

68. Ibid., p. 18; Bernard Gwertzman, "Pakistan Blast Could End Aid," *New York Times,* September 17, 1981; Foreign Assistance Act of 1961, Sec. 670(b)(2), 22 U.S.C. 2429a(b)(2) (1981).

69. Alan Cranston, "Nuclear Arms Race in South Asia Endangers U.S. Security Interests," *Congressional Record,* 97th Congress, 1st Session, April 27, 1981, p. S 3929.

70. Schweid, "Turks Ship U.S. A-Tools."

71. Judith Miller, "U.S. Aides Studying Pakistani Reactor," *New York Times,* September 30, 1981.

72. Leslie Maitland, "U.S. Studying Foiled Bid to Export a Key Reactor Metal to Pakistan," *New York Times,* November 20, 1981.

73. Foreign Assistance Act of 1961, Sec. 670(b)(2), 22 U.S.C. 2429a(b)(2) (1981). Under the amendment, U.S. aid would be cut off automatically, although the president could continue assistance for sixty days if he determined that termination of assistance would be detrimental to the national security of the United States. After that time, however, aid would cease unless restored by vote of both houses of Congress.

74. "IAEA Is Facing Major Problems in Safeguarding Pakistan's KANUPP Power Station," *Nucleonics Week,* October 8, 1981, p. 6; "The Delicate Negotiations Between IAEA and Pakistan

Aimed at Upgrading . . .," *Nucleonics Week*, November 12, 1981, p. 4. The two primary areas of concern with respect to IAEA monitoring of the facility were the absence of surveillance equipment at an emergency hatch through which spent fuel might be surreptitiously removed and the lack of backup cameras for several key areas of the station. IAEA concerns had first arisen in late 1980.

75. Milton R. Benjamin, "Pakistan Backs Atomic Safeguards," *Washington Post*, November 17, 1982.

76. Ibid.; Ann MacLachlan, "IAEA Completes Its Desired Ungrading of Safeguards at KANUPP," *Nucleonics Week*, March 3, 1983, p. 1.

77. "Two Primary Deficiencies in IAEA Safeguards at Pakistan's KANUPP . . .," *Nucleonics Week*, September 23, 1982, p. 2.

78. Albert Wohlstetter et al., *Swords from Plowshares: The Military Potential of Civilian Nuclear Energy* (Chicago: University of Chicago Press, 1977), p. 195.

79. Small exemptions are sometimes permitted to this rule, but these must be formally requested and approved by the IAEA. Pakistan, according to knowledgeable U.S. officials, has not sought such an exemption.

80. Ambassador Ronald I. Spiers, "Speech to the Karachi Institute of Foreign Relations," on April 20, 1982, (International Communication Agency news release on same day), p. 13. Although neither of Pakistan's reprocessing plants is inspected by the IAEA, U.S. intelligence monitoring could presumably detect any reprocessing activity, since this would require processing of highly radioactive material.

81. "Pakistan Could Be Ready To Accept Bids for a 600-900-Mw Nuclear Unit," *Nucleonics Week*, October 8, 1981, p. 2. Pakistan has been assisted by a Spanish engineering firm, Sener, in developing the studies necessary for the procurement of such an installation.

82. "Statement on United States Nuclear Nonproliferation Policy," July 16, 1981, *Public Papers of the Presidents of the United States, Ronald Reagan* (Government Printing Office: Washington, D.C., 1981) p. 630.

83. "Cheysson Discusses Nuclear Plant," *Washington Post*, March 30, 1983.

84. "Deadline for Chashma Tenders Ends," *Dawn* (Karachi), August 3, 1983, reprinted in FBIS/NDP, September 2, 1983, p. 42.

85. "While the Pakistan Atomic Energy Commission Has Post-

poned the Deadline . . .," *Nucleonics Week*, November 10, 1983, p. 80; "Pakistan Has Indefinitely Postponed . . .," *Nucleonics Week*, April 5, 1984, p. 6.

86. Personal communication with knowledgeable French official; "Financing Prospects for Pakistan's Proposed Chashma Station Look So Dim," *Nucleonics Week*, March 24, 1983, p. 5.

87. As discussed in Chapter 6, the administration was also success-ful in tightening the Nuclear Suppliers' Guidelines to prohibit export of key enrichment plant components unless IAEA safe-guards were applied to the installation in which they were to be used.

88. Russell Warren Howe, "Pakistani's Are Closer to Producing Nuclear Weapon," *Washington Times*, July 26, 1984.

89. "Scientist Affirms Pakistan Capable of Uranium Enrichment, Weapons Production," *Nawa-I-Waqt*, February 10, 1984, trans-lated in FBIS/NDP, March 5, 1984, p. 32; "Pakistan's Nuclear Chief Says It Could Build Bomb," *Washington Post*, February 10, 1984.

90. "Scientist Affirms Pakistan Capable," *Nawa-I-Waqt*, FBIS/-NDP, pp. 43-44.

91. "Zia Chastises Western Media for Accounts of Khan's Remarks on Weapons Capability," *Nuclear Fuel*, February 27, 1984, p. 11.

92. "Zia Chastises Western Media," *Nuclear Fuel*, p. 11.

93. "Pakistan Names Kahuta Facility for Khan," *Nuclear Fuel*, January 16, 1984, p. 5.

94. Alan Cranston, "Nuclear Proliferation and U.S. National Secu-rity Interests."

95. Personal communication with knowledgeable U.S. officials; see also note 70 and accompanying text.

96. "3 Pakistanis Indicted on A-Arms Charges," *Washington Post*, July 17, 1984; Rick Atkinson, "Nuclear Parts Sought by Paki-stanis," *Washington Post*, July 21, 1984. The Pakistanis attempt-ed to export fifty high-speed electronic switches known as "kry-tons." It is not known how many are needed in a single weapon. (The switches are also used in the strobe lights placed atop large buildings to warn away aircraft). (Atkinson, "Parts Sought").

97. Rob Laufer, "Interview with Malone: Defense of Policy and Assessment of 'Hot Spots,'" *Nucleonics Week*, August 19, 1982, p. 2.

98. Judith Miller, "U.S. Is Holding Up Peking Atom Talks," *New York Times*, September 19, 1982.

99. Milton R. Benjamin, "China Aids Pakistan on A-Weapons,"

Washington Post, February 28, 1983.

100. Leslie H. Gelb, "Peking Said To Balk at Nuclear Pledges," *New York Times,* June 23, 1984. A report in the Indian press three months earlier quoted Indian foreign secretary Rasgottra as stating that China had actually tested a Pakistani nuclear device, but India's foreign minister subsequently disclaimed this. *(Times of India,* March 27, 1984, as cited in Thomas W. Graham, "South Asian Nuclear Proliferation and National Security Chronology." Center for International Affairs, Massachusetts Institute of Technology, (1984)).

101. "PRC Denies Nuclear Cooperation with Pakistan," *AFP,* 1220 GMT, February 26, 1983, reprinted in FBIS/NDP, March 21, 1983, p. 9.

102. Mike Knapik, "U.S.-China Nuclear Accord Now Faces Congressional Scrutiny," *Nucleonics Week,* May 3, 1984, p. 9.

103. Don Oberdorfer, "Arms Issue Snags Pact with China," *Washington Post,* June 15, 1984. U.S.-China nuclear discussions are analyzed in Chapter VI.

104. Senate Foreign Relations Committee, *United States Interests in South Asia; A Staff Report,* April 1984 (Washington, D.C.: U.S. Government Printing Office, 1984) pp. 30-31. See also, Senate Report 98-400; International Security and Development Act of 1984 (S-2582) (Washington, D.C.: U.S. Government Printing Office, 1984).

105. Russell Warren Howe, "Study Confirms Pakistan's Nuclear Bomb Know-How," *Washington Times,* July 25, 1984.

106. "3 Pakistani's Indicted," *Washington Post.* Pakistan should have little trouble finding or improvising substitutes for these items.

107. P. K. S. Namboodiri, "Pakistan's Nuclear Posture," in *Nuclear Myths,* p. 161.

108. Cranston, "Nuclear Proliferation and U.S. National Security," personal communication with knowledgeable U.S. official. See also, Ann MacLachlan, "Belgians Awaiting Government Approval to Complete Pakistani Reprocessing Lab," *Nuclear Fuel,* March 26, 1984, p. 9.

Chapter III:
Middle East Introduction

1. "Iraq's Bid for Plutonium Foiled," *The Energy Daily*, June 15, 1984, p. 2.
2. *Jane's Defence Weekly*, April 28, 1984, p. 635; Bernard Gwertzman, "U.S. Urges Ban in Atom Sales to Iran," *New York Times*, April 26, 1984.
3. Gwertzman, "U.S. Urges Ban."
4. *Jane's Defence Weekly*, May 5, 1984, p. 675.
5. Mohammed El-Sayed Selim, "Egypt," in James E. Katz and Onkar S. Marwah, eds., *Nuclear Power in Developing Countries* (Lexington, MA: Lexington Books, 1982), pp. 138-139.
6. "The Trail to Crazy Island," *Wall Street Journal*, March 16, 1984.
7. "Soviet A-Arms in Egypt in 1973, General Says," *Washington Post*, May 21, 1983.

Israel

1. Fuad Jabber, *Israel and Nuclear Weapons* (London: Chatto and Windus, 1971), ch. 1.
2. U.S. General Accounting Office, *Difficulties in Determining If Nuclear Training of Foreigners Contributes to Weapons Proliferation*, ID-79-2 (Washington, D.C., 1979), pp. 18-21. Between 1955 and 1965, nineteen Israeli scientists studied various subjects at U.S. government installations, including reprocessing and plutonium fabrication; Jabber, *Israel and Nuclear Weapons*, p.43 (hot cell).
3. Jabber, *Israel and Nuclear Weapons*, p. 33.
4. Secretary General of the United Nations, *Israeli Nuclear Armament*, U.N. General Assembly document A/36/431, 36th Session, September 18, 1981, p. 15. Norway is said to have provided the original charge of heavy water for the plant, while Israel reportedly obtained the uranium fuel from a number of sources including domestic phosphate deposits, Argentina, South Africa, France, and French-controlled mines in Gabon, Central African Republic, and Niger. Additional uranium was reportedly obtained clandestinely from Belgium. [John R. Redick, *Military Potential of Latin American Nuclear Energy Programs* (Beverly Hills, CA: Sage Publications, 1972), p. 13 (Argentina); personal communication

with informed former U.S. official (Argentina); Bertrand Goldschmidt, *Le Défi Atomique* (Paris: Fayard. 1980) pp. 205-206 (initially, uranium bought on world market from a number of sources, mainly Western and African); Jabber, *Israel and Nuclear Weapons,*) p.89 (first load of Dimona reportedly comprised of 10 tons from South Africa, 10 tons from Dead Sea phosphates, 4 tons from French sources); Christopher Raj, "Israel and Nuclear Weapons," in K. Subrahmanyam. ed. *Nuclear Myths and Realities* (ABC: New Delhi, 1981) p. 105 (South Africa, France, French-controlled uranium mines in Gabon, Central African Republic, and Niger); William Drozdiak "Uranium Loss is Admitted." *Washington Post*, May 3, 1977 (200 tons of yellowcake diverted on Mediterranean Sea from Belgium thought to wind up in Israel).

5. Jabber, *Israel and Nuclear Weapons*, p. 33.

6. Peter Pringle and James Spigelman, *The Nuclear Barons* (New York: Holt, Rinehart, and Winston, 1981), p. 296. President Charles De Gaulle's memoirs imply that some form of cooperation on reprocessing took place. Referring to the reduction of French nuclear aid to Israel in 1960, he states, "So ended, in particular the cooperation offered by us for the beginning, near Beersheba, of a plant for the transformation of uranium into plutonium from which one fine day there could emerge some atomic bombs." Charles De Gaulle, *Memoirs of Hope: Renewal and Endeavor* (New York: Simon and Schuster, 1971), p. 266.

7. Robert E. Harkavy, *The Spectre of a Middle Eastern Holocaust: The Strategic and Diplomatic Implications of the Israeli Nuclear Weapons Program*, Graduate School of International Studies, University of Denver (1977), p. 7. See section on Israeli rocketry, below.

8. Steve Weissman and Herbert Krosney, *The Islamic Bomb* (New York: Times Books, 1981), p. 113; Roger F. Pajak, *Nuclear Proliferation in the Middle East: Implications for the Superpowers*, National Defense University Monograph 82-1 (Washington, D.C., 1982), p. 31.

9. Weissman and Krosney, *Islamic Bomb*, p. 114.

10. Whether a nation today would need to test an atomic weapon to validate its design is an open question. The United States, for example, did not test the type of weapon (with a core of highly enriched uranium) it used to destroy Hiroshima, although the bomb used on Nagasaki (with a plutonium core) was tested in advance. Information on atomic weapons design has been widely published, and today's more powerful computers can run "tests"

of alternative design approaches. If Israel was attempting to develop nuclear weapons in the late 1950s, however, not all of this technology would have been available, and the data obtained from France would have been especially useful. In any event, the fact that Israel is not known to have conducted a nuclear test is not incompatible with the existence of an active Israeli nuclear weapons development program.

11. Executive Sessions of the Senate Foreign Relations Committee (Historical Series), Vol. XIII, Pt. 1, 87th Congress, 1st Session, 1961 (1984), pp. 7-8. The transcript of this session was released in April 1984.

12. Jabber, *Israel and Nuclear Weapons,* p. 35.

13. Ibid., p. 36.

14. Efraim Inbar, "The Israeli Basement—With Bombs or Without?" *Crossroads,* Winter-Spring 1982, p. 89.

15. Simha Flapan, "Nuclear Power in the Middle East (Part 1)," *New Outlook,* July 1974, p. 51.

16. Inbar, "Israeli Basement," p. 88. Eshkol's opposition may have been based on budgetary considerations, however, rather than qualms about developing weapons of mass destruction, as such.

17. Flapan, "Nuclear Power," p. 51. In conjunction with Israel's acceptance of inspections, the United States for the first time agreed to sell conventional arms—Hawk surface-to-air missiles—to Israel, strengthening Israel's conventional deterrent.

18. Ibid. Eshkol reorganized the commission to place it directly under the control of the prime minister, appointed members expert in the civilian uses of nuclear energy, and named himself as chairman.

19. Yair Evron, "Israel and the Atom: The Uses and Misuses of Ambiguity," *Orbis,* Winter 1974, p. 133, n. 25.

20. Flapan, "Nuclear Power," p. 51.

21. Weissman and Krosney, *Islamic Bomb,* p. 117; Hedrick Smith, "U.S. Assumes the Israelis Have A-bomb or Its Parts," *New York Times,* July 18, 1970, p. 1; Jabber, *Israel and Nuclear Weapons,* p. 70.

22. Weissman and Krosney, *Islamic Bomb,* pp. 117-118. Israel's source of spent fuel for such a transaction is also unclear, although one account states that U.S. inspectors believed "fissile material" was diverted from the Dimona reactor in 1968. Smith, "Israelis Have A-bomb."

23. Smith, "Israelis Have A-bomb."

24. John W. Finney, "Uranium Losses Spur Drive for Tighter U.S.

Controls of Fissionable Materials," *New York Times,* September 18, 1966.

25. Transcript of "Near Armageddon: The Spread of Nuclear Weapons in the Middle East," on ABC News Close-up, April 27, 1981, pp. 13-14.

26. Weissman and Krosney, *Islamic Bomb,* pp. 108-109; Smith, "Israelis Have A-bomb;" U.S. Nuclear Regulatory Commission, *Inquiry into the Testimony of the Executive Director for Operations,* Vol. III (Interviews), February 1978, p. 178.

27. U.S. Nuclear Regulatory Commission, *Safeguards Summary Event List,* NUREG-0525, rev. 3, December 1980.

28. Pringle and Spigelman, *Nuclear Barons,* p. 296; "How Israel Got the Bomb," *Time,* April 12, 1976, p. 39. There has been considerable speculation over why Israeli defense leaders would decide to build up Israel's nuclear weapons soon after winning its major military victory. Among the hypotheses regarding the motivations for such a decision are: fears that Egypt was developing chemical/radiological weapons (Harkavy); concerns over increased Soviet assistance to Egypt and wavering U.S. support for Israel (Inbar); and the realization that victory gave it a brief interlude during which it was not susceptible to international pressures and could pursue nuclear arms with relative impunity.

29. John W. Finney, "U.S. Aides Doubt That Israel Has Decided to Build A-bomb," *New York Times,* January 11, 1969; Smith, "Israelis Have A-bomb." A widely quoted account in *Time* magazine, however, states that Moshe Dayan, then the defense minister, issued a secret order in 1967 to construct the reprocessing facility, and the plant was completed in 1969 ("How Israel Got the Bomb").

30. This was precisely the result of Iraq's unusually large uranium purchases a decade later. See chapter on Iraq. Over the years, Israel reportedly obtained smaller quantities of uranium from a variety of foreign sources for the reactor. See note 4.

31. William Drozdiak, "Uranium Loss Is Admitted," *Washington Post,* May 3, 1977. When European Community officials first confirmed the loss of the material in 1977, press reports quoted unnamed American and European intelligence sources as being convinced that the diverted material was taken to Israel to fuel the Dimona reactor (Ibid). The episode is sometimes referred to as the "*Scheersberg* incident" after the ship involved or as the "Plumbat affair," since the drums containing the uranium were, reportedly, marked with this label (a reference to lead).

According to U.S. government sources, as another element of

its secret nuclear weapons program, in 1968 Israel diverted an unspecified amount of "fissionable material" from the Dimona reactor—presumably plutonium-bearing spent fuel. It is not known how the United States learned of the diversion or the amount of material involved, but U.S. authorities presumed the material had been taken for weapons use. The diverted material may then have been reprocessed in Israel or shipped to France for reprocessing there. Possibly, France retained the extracted plutonium in return for plutonium France may have supplied to Israel previously (Smith, "Israelis Have A-bomb").

32. *Israeli Nuclear Armament*, p. 16. Regarding Israel's other sources of uranium over the years, see note 4.

If the various accounts of Israel's acquisition of uranium are correct, it would have obtained a substantial stockpile of the material over the years, far more than needed to produce Israel's reported arsenal of twenty or so weapons. For, example one hundred metric tons yellowcake could yield over one hundred kilograms of high quality plutonium; at eight kilograms of plutonium per weapon this could allow construction of twelve bombs. The capacity of the Dimona reactor (eight to ten kilograms of plutonium per year or possibly twenty-five kilograms annually, of the reactor has been enlarged) would appear to restrict production of the material, however. This in turn, raises questions as to why Israel has sought to obtain such large quantities of uranium. Possibly larger-scale uranium enrichment activities are taking place than have been generally reported. One recent, unsubstantiated, report supports this hypothesis. It states that Israel is using the Becker jet nozzle enrichment process and possesses between eighty and two hundred weapons. (Russell Warren Howe, "Study Confirms Pakistan's Nuclear Bomb Know-How," *Washington Times*, July 25, 1984.

33. Smith, "Israelis Have A-bomb."

34. Warnke to Roger C. Molander, tape recorded interview at Roosevelt Center for American Policy Studies, 1984.   Israel has tied ratification of the Non-Proliferation Treaty to the prior attainment of peace in the Middle East. As the Israeli delegate stated in the United Nations debate on the text of the treaty in May 1968:
For obvious reasons my country has a special sensitivity to the security aspect. We are involved in an unresolved conflict in which our security is being threatened and which was thrice in two decades erupted into armed hostilities. That conflict is marked by a massive and unchecked arms race of conventional weapons which, by our standards, have a vast capacity to kill and destroy.

We cannot know what dangers and threats may confront us in the future. It is only natural that we should give earnest scrutiny to the security provisions intended to accompany and compensate for the restrictions that non-nuclear powers would voluntarily assume under the treaty. [Statement by the Israeli representative to the First Committee of the U.N. General Assembly, May 29, 1968, U.N. document A./C.1/PV.1576, cited in Stockholm International Peace Research Institute, *The Near-Nuclear Countries and the NPT* (New York: Humanities Press, 1972), p. 29.]

In a related area, since 1974 the United Nations General Assembly has annually adopted resolutions calling for all states in the Middle East to pledge not to produce or acquire nuclear arms and to accede to the Non-Proliferation Treaty *(Israeli Nuclear Armament,* p. 6, references collected). No progress has been made in advancing this proposal, however.

Beginning in 1975, Israel began to promote a Mideast nuclear-weapon-free-zone proposal of its own, abandoning its insistence that a general peace agreement was a precondition to talks on regional denuclearization. Inbar, "The Israeli Basement," p. 93. The Israeli proposal, first submitted to the United Nations in 1980, called upon all states in the region and all non-nuclear-weapon states adjacent to the region to convene a conference for negotiating a multilateral treaty establishing a Middle East denuclearized zone. The proposal was severely criticized by the Arab states since it implicitly entailed Arab recognition of Israel *(Israeli Nuclear Armament,* p. 7, citing draft resolution A/C.1/35/L.8, 1980). Israel withdrew the proposal but resubmitted it following the raid on Osirak. Nothing has come of this initiative, however.

In August 1981, U.S. Arms Control and Disarmament Agency Director Eugene Rostow stated in an interview that the United States had "started preliminary diplomatic talks" on establishing a nuclear free zone in the Middle East *(New York Times,* August 14, 1981). This initiative, too, is not known to have made any progress and has apparently been abandoned.

35. Pajak, *Nuclear Proliferation,* p. 38.

36. Shai Feldman, *Israeli Nuclear Deterrence* (New York: Columbia University Press, 1982), p. 211.

37. *Testimony of the Executive Director,* p. 178; Smith, "Israelis Have A-bomb."

38. National Security Decision Memorandum No. 6, cited in Seymour M. Hersh, *The Price of Power: Kissinger in the Nixon White House* (New York: Summit Books, 1983), p. 148. National Security Advisor Henry Kissinger's reported belief that nuclear weap-

ons would enhance Israel's security may have played a part in the reduction of U.S. pressures to forestall Israel's nuclear program (Ibid.).

39. According to a 1970 *New York Times* report, although U.S. inspectors visited the plant annually and never discovered any signs of nuclear weapons activities at the site, they were "somewhat dissatisfied" that their inspections were "hurried and limited." The article also reported that in 1969 the inspection team complained to Israeli authorities in writing "about the limitations on its inspections and reportedly stated that, for this reason, it could not guarantee that there was no weapons-related work at Dimona." The arrangements did not improve, however, and the visits ended (Smith, "Israelis Have A-bomb").

One reason the United States may have agreed to the cessation of the inspections was the concern that if Israel were engaging in nuclear weapons activities that went undetected by the United States' inspections, the United States might appear to be implicated if these activities subsequently came to light. Such concerns apparently troubled Johnson administration aides (Personal communication with informed former U.S. official).

40. Smith, "Israelis Have A-bomb." The CIA's 1968 estimate (noted earlier), which remained secret until 1978, concluded that Israel's nuclear capabilities relied upon highly enriched uranium from the U.S. NUMEC facility (*Testimony of the Executive Director*, p. 178). Possibly Israel obtained nuclear weapons material from both sources but the officials who briefed the Foreign Relations Committee chose not to mention the NUMEC matter to avoid the scandal that would have resulted were it known that Israel had circumvented U.S. security controls at the plant, and that the United States itself might bear some responsibility for equipping the world's next nuclear power.

Important corroboration for the conclusion that Israel had developed a nuclear weapons capability based on plutonium appears in the minutes of a January 1973 secret meeting of French nuclear officials that were revealed in 1982. The minutes reportedly summarized a statement by Andre Giraud, the head of France's nuclear program, who noted that Israel already had "appreciable quantities of plutonium," enough according to another meeting participant, to allow Israel "to fabricate several bombs" (Weissman and Krosney, *Islamic Bomb*, p. 118). The minutes reportedly do not specify whether the meeting participants believed that France supplied the plutonium directly—which Israeli sources denied—or whether Israel had obtained the plutonium by repro-

cessing Dimona spent fuel in an Israeli reprocessing plant built
with French aid (presumably sometime after the United States
stopped inspecting the site in 1969).

Israeli officials termed the 1970 *Times* story "speculative and
inaccurate" and reiterated their stock response, "Israel is not a
nuclear power and it will not be the first country to introduce
nuclear weapons into the Middle East" (Smith, "Israelis Have
A-bomb").

41. Feldman, *Israeli Nuclear Deterrence*, p. 215.

42. Central Intelligence Agency, "Prospects for Further Proliferation
of Nuclear Weapons," DCI NIO 1945/74, September 4, 1974, p. 1.
For Ford Administration statements, see House Subcommittee
on International Organizations and Movements and House Subcommittee on the Near East and South Asia, *U.S. Foreign Policy
and the Export of Nuclear Technology to the Middle East*, September 16, 1974, 93rd Congress, 1st Session (Washington, D.C.:
U.S. Government Printing Office, 1974); *Hearings on the International Security Assistance Act of 1976*, November 6, 1975, 94th
Congress, 1st Session (Washington, D.C.: U.S. Government
Printing Office, 1976). See also Feldman, *Israeli Nuclear Deterrence*, pp. 214-228. Concerns over the proposed sale and the
Indian test led Congress in 1974 to strengthen its authority to
oversee U.S. nuclear export policy by amending the Atomic Energy Act to permit new U.S. agreements for nuclear cooperation
to be rejected by a majority vote of both Houses of Congress.
Atomic Energy Act, section 123 (1974). Such agreements would
have been required for the Israeli and Egyptian reactor sales.

43. *Israeli Nuclear Armament*, p. 9, n. 3.

44. Acceptance of comprehensive safeguards became a legal requirement for any new or amended U.S. agreement for nuclear cooperation under the 1978 Nuclear Non-Proliferation Act.

45. Robert Gillette, "Uranium Enrichment: Rumors of Israeli Progress with Lasers," *Science*, March 22, 1974, p. 1172.

46. William Beecher, "U.S. Believes Israel Has More than 10 Nuclear Weapons," *Boston Globe*, July 31, 1975. According to this
account, Israeli military planners believed that nuclear arms could
achieve three ends: serve as a deterrent to protect against Israeli
cities becoming targets in a future Middle East war; discourage
Arab countries outside the immediate vicinity of Israel (e.g.,
Libya, Iraq, and Saudi Arabia) from participating in any such war;
and "put Arab states and the Soviet Union on notice that if some
future all-out war threatens the survival of Israel, it would be

prepared to employ nuclear arms against the cities of the attacker."

47. *Testimony of the Executive Director*, p. 178.

48. Feldman, *Israeli Nuclear Deterrence*, p. 215, citing Arthur Kranish, "CIA: Israel Has 10-20 A-Weapons," *Washington Post*, March 15, 1976.

49. "How Israel Got the Bomb," p. 39.

50. Ibid. These remarks, taken with President Katzir's comments in 1974, suggest that some Israeli statesmen may have been trying to augment the deterrent value of Israel's nuclear capabilities by hinting that Israel could retaliate with nuclear arms if the nation's existence were threatened.

51. Harkavy, *Middle Eastern Holocaust*, p. 15. Further evidence of U.S. leniency towards Israel's apparent development of nuclear arms, including the drafting of certain statutory provisions to avoid imposing sanctions on Israel, is compiled in Feldman, Israeli Nuclear Deterrence, pp. 215-228.

52. Inbar, "Israeli Basement," p. 90.

53. "The International Scope of IAEA Safeguards," *IAEA Bulletin*, October 1977, p. 2.

54. Weissman and Krosney, *Islamic Bomb*, p. 110.

55. Ibid., p. 113.

56. Bernard Gwertzman, "U.S. Monitors Signs of Atom Explosion Off South Africa," *New York Times*, October 25, 1979.

57. "Blowup," *Technology Review*, October 1980, p.78.

58. Eliot Marshall, "Navy Lab Concludes the Velo Saw a Bomb," *Science*, August 29, 1980, p. 996; Thomas O'Toole, "New Light Cast on Sky-Flash Mystery," *Washington Post*, January 30, 1980.

59. "Israel Reported Behind A-Blast Off South Africa," *Washington Post*, February 22, 1980. See Appendix G. for more details.

60. "Dayan Says Israelis Have the Capacity to Produce A-bombs," *New York Times*, June 25, 1981.

61. Judith Miller, "Three Nations Widening Nuclear Contacts," *New York Times*, June 28, 1981.

62. "The Middle East Nuclear Arms Race," *Foreign Report*, August 13, 1980, p. 6. At 25 megawatts, the Dimona reactor is said to be capable of producing eight to ten kilograms of plutonium per year, enough for one bomb (conservatively estimated to require eight kilograms of plutonium) or possible two (assuming a more sophisticated design requiring only five kilograms). At seventy megawatts, the reactor could produce about twenty-five kilograms of plutonium. U.N., *Israeli Nuclear Armament*, p. 16.

63. A group of experts convened by the secretary-general of the

United Nations to study the Israeli nuclear program has estimated that Israel might be able to produce two to three kilograms of highly enriched uranium per year in the laboratory-scale facilities it is thought to have. This would be enough for possibly one weapon every five years or so. *Israeli Nuclear Armament*, p. 20; but see Russell Warrèn Howe, "Study Confirms Pakistan's Nuclear Bomb Know-How," *Washington Times*, July 25, 1984 (Israel has 80 to 200 weapons; using Becker nozzle enrichment process to produce weapons-grade uranium).

64. "Prospects for Further Proliferation," p. 1; "How Israel Got the Bomb," p. 39.

65. Anthony H. Cordesman, *Jordanian Arms and the Middle East Balance* (Washington, D.C.: Middle East Institute, 1982), p. 85.

66. *Israeli Nuclear Armament*, p. 11.

67. See note 4, above, for references.

68. Christopher S. Raj, "Israel and Nuclear Weapons," pp. 114-118 (various reports collected); Yosi Melman, "Israel Aiding South Africa in Development of Nuclear Weapons in Exchange for Uranium," *Davar* (Tel Aviv), April 13, 1984, translated in FBIS/NDP, June 7, 1984, p. 30; see also, Judith Miller, "3 Nations Widening Nuclear Contacts," *New York Times*, June 28, 1981. An unsubstantiated press story in July 1984 stated that Israel is using the Becker jet nozzle technique to enrich uranium, a variant of which is also used by South Africa. If the account is correct, uranium enrichment may be an additional area of cooperation between the two nations. (Howe, "Study Confirms.")

69. Charles Hoffman, "Treasury to Back Up Investments in Nuclear Plant," *Jerusalem Post*, May 4, 1983, reprinted in Foreign Broadcast Information Service/Africa-Middle East (hereafter FBIS/AME), May 4, 1983, p. 15.

70. Padraic Sweeney, "Fearing Collapse, IAEA Retreats on Israel," *Baltimore Sun*, October 16, 1983.

71. "U.S. Scrutiny of Its Role in IAEA Jolted from Two Directions," *Nucleonics Week*, December 23, 1982, p. 3.

72. Diane Foulds, "U.S. to Resume Contributions to U.N. Energy Body," *Washington Post*, February 24, 1983.

73. Sweeney, "IAEA Retreats on Israel."

74. Ibid.

75. Ibid.

76. "Arens Threatens Bombing of Arab Nuclear Reactors," *Davar*, June 6, 1983, translated in FBIS/AME, June 6, 1983, p. 12. These remarks echo a similar, but less explicit, statement of Israeli intentions that Arens made in 1982, when he described the acqui-

sition of nuclear arms as a "red line" Israel would not allow any Arab state to cross. *Yedi'ot Aharonot,* translated in FBIS/AME, February 25, 1982, p. I3.

77. Neal Sandler, "Israel Will Spend $5 Million on Site Selection," *Nucleonics Week,* January 12, 1984, p. 11. Deuterium is short for deuterium oxide, or heavy water.

78. "Canadian-type Reactors Planned for Power Project," *Jerusalem Post,* July 14, 1981, p. 1, translated in Foreign Broadcast Information Service/Nuclear Development and Proliferation (hereafter FBIS/NDP), August 6, 1981, p. 11.

79. Yosi Melman, "Interest in Acquiring Nuclear Reactor from U.K. Reported," *Ha'aretz, May* 2, 1982, translated in FBIS/NDP, May 21, 1982 p. 9; "France to Negotiate Over Power Plant," *Jerusalem Domestic Service,* 1200 GMT, April 13, 1982, translated in FBIS/NDP, May 3, 1982, p. 27; "Independent Nuclear Power Developments Said Unlikely," *Har'aretz,* December 22, 1982, translated in FBIS/NDP, February 16, 1983, p. 33.

80. "Independent Nuclear Power Unlikely," *Har'aretz,* FBIS/NDP.

81. Ibid.

82. Ibid.

83. Ariel Cohen, "Nuclear Power Plants to Be Exported," *Yoman Hashavu'a,* December 17, 1982, translated in FBIS/NDP, March 25, 1983, p. 29.

84. Albert Wohlstetter, *Swords from Plowshares* (Chicago: University of Chicago Press, 1979), p. 184. Both heavy-water and light-water power reactors, the other type in wide use today, produce substantial quantities of plutonium in their spent fuel that can be used for weapons, although the former produce somewhat more. To avoid the risk of nuclear weapons yields being lower than expected, however, nuclear weapons normally use plutonium produced in spent fuel that has been irradiated in a reactor for a relatively brief time. Such "low burn-up" plutonium can be readily produced in heavy-water reactors because they are fueled continuously, without the need for shutting down; fuel can simply be moved more quickly than normal through the reactor to achieve low burn-up. In contrast, refueling a light-water reactor requires shutting down the reactor completely and performing a number of complicated tasks that usually take several weeks, making the repeated replacement of fuel after short periods of operation impractical.

85. Pending U.S. legislation would prohibit component exports even to safeguarded plants unless all other nuclear activities in the

recipient country were also under the IAEA system. This requirement has not been adopted by other suppliers, however.

86. For a more detailed discussion of possible Israeli motivations to
declare it possesses nuclear arms, see Feldman, *Israeli Nuclear
Deterrence,* ch. 1. Nuclear testing for Israel would also permit it to
build smaller, highly efficient atomic weapons or fusion bombs
(i.e., hydrogen and neutron bombs). These might require more
test data than Israel may have acquired previously through its
reported collaboration with France or through its possible participation in a test in the South Atlantic in 1979. Indeed, some press
reports have suggested that the South Atlantic test might have
been the detonation of a small atomic bomb of the type used as the
trigger on a neutron bomb.

87. Kenneth N. Waltz, *The Spread of Nuclear Weapons: More May
Be Better,* Adelphi Papers, No. 171 (London: International Institute for Strategic Studies, 1981).

Libya

1. Mohamed Heikal, *The Road to Ramadan* (New York: Quadrangle/The New York Times Book Co., 1975), pp. 76-77; see also Steve Weissman and Herbert Krosney, *The Islamic Bomb* (New York: Times Books, 1981), pp. 55-57; "Writer Reports Libya A-Bomb Bid," *Washington Post*, April 16, 1979, ("Writer" is Cord Meyer, a former CIA official); Joseph V. R. Micallef, "A Nuclear Bomb for Libya?" *Bulletin of the Atomic Scientists*, August-September 1981, p. 14.

2. Weissman and Krosney, *The Islamic Bomb*, p. 56.

3. Ibid., p. 60. Weissman and Krosney state they have confirmed this report through interviews with Pakistani and Libyan officials having direct knowledge of it.

4. Don Oberdorfer, "Pakistan: The Quest for the Atomic Bomb," *Washington Post*, August 27, 1979. Although France agreed to the sale, its contract with Pakistan was abandoned in 1978. See Pakistan chapter.

5. Congressional Research Service, *Analysis of Six Issues About Nuclear Capabilities of India, Iraq, Libya and Pakistan,* report prepared for the Subcommittee on Arms Control, Oceans, International Operations, and Environment of the Senate Foreign Relations Committee, 1982, p. 11.

6. Micallef, "Nuclear Bomb for Libya?" p. 14.

7. See Argentina chapter.

8. "Libya Reported Annexing Uranium-Rich Part of Chad," *Washington Post*, September 8, 1975.

9. Richard L. Homan, "Libya to Get Soviet-Built Nuclear Plant," *Washington Post*, June 3, 1975.

10. Senate Foreign Relations Commitee, *Hearings on the Israeli Air Strike,* June 18, 19, and 25, 1981, 97th Congress, 1st Session (Washington, D.C.: U.S. Government Printing Office, 1981), p. 50; Claudia Wright, "Libya's Nuclear Program," *The Middle East,* February 1982, p. 47.

11. "France Is to Build Libyan Atomic Plant," *New York Times,* March 23, 1976. According to the *Times* account, the French stated they would not provide Libya with "nuclear research facilities or the means to produce heavy water."

12. Thomas O'Toole, "Libya Said to Buy Soviet A-Power Plant," *Washington Post,* December 12, 1977.

13. "On-Again, Off-Again Libyan Nuclear Power Plant Surfaced Once More," *Nucleonics Week,* March 31, 1983, p. 11.

14. Weissman and Krosney, *Islamic Bomb*, pp. 211-212. Pakistan has

not ratified the Non-Proliferation Treaty and is under no similar obligation, although most yellowcake suppliers (including Niger) require exports to be placed on IAEA inventories. Niger reportedly believed this standard was satisfied in the case of Libya between 1978 and 1980 because the country was a Non-Proliferation Treaty party.

15. "Libya Presses India on Nuclear Technology," *Nuclear Engineering International,* November 1979, p. 7.

16. Ibid. See also "Libya Charged with Using Oil to Obtain Nuclear Technology," *Business Times* (Kuala Lumpur), August 30, 1979, (quoting from stories in the *Times of India* and the *Hindu),* translated in FBIS/NDP, October 31, 1979, p. 7.

17. Federation of American Scientists, *Public Interest Report,* December 1978, p. 1.

18. Ibid.

19. "An Interview with Gaddafi," *Time,* June 8, 1981, p. 31.

20. "Libya's Nuclear Dreams," *Foreign Report,* July 9, 1981.

21. "Libyan Leader Threatens to Hit U.S. Nuclear Depots," *Washington Post,* September 2, 1981.

22. Guy Duplat, "Possible Breakthrough in Belgian Nuclear Cooperation with Arab Countries," *Le Soir,* August 8, 1981, translated in FBIS/NDP, September 8, 1981, p. 2 ; "US Presses Belgians to Cut Libya Ties," *Nuclear Fuel,* April 26, 1982, p. 11.

23. "Libya Aided Argentina in War," *New York Times,* May 14, 1984.

24. "Brazilian Military Concern Over Argentine Talks with Libya," *Correio Braziliense,* May 24, 1983, translated in FBIS/NDP, June 30, 1983, p. 8.

25. Senate Committee on Foreign Relations and the Subcommittee on Energy, Nuclear Proliferation, and Government Processes, *Hearings on the Nuclear Non-Proliferation Act,* September 30, 1983, 98th Congress, 1st Session (Washington, D.C.: U.S. Government Printing Office, 1983), p. 50.

26. "Libya: Finnish N-Price Too High," *Helsingin Sanomat,* June 10, 1980, translated in FBIS/NDP, July 15, 1980, p. 4.

27. "Uranium Exports for First Six Months Given," *AFP,* 0859 GMT, August 27, 1981, translated in FBIS/NDP, September 24, 1981, p. 17.

28. Micallef, "Nuclear Bomb for Libya?" p. 15.

29. "U.S. Bans Libyans from Some Studies," *Washington Post,* March 11, 1983.

30. Judith Miller, "West German Concern Ends Libyan Rocket Project," *New York Times,* December 27, 1981; "Khadafi's Rocket,"

BBC Panorama broadcast, June 1, 1981, as summarized in U.S. State Department cable (unclassified) from U.S. Embassy, London, to Secretary of State, Washington, D.C., June 3, 1981, 1522 GMT.

31. "Belgium, Libya Reportedly Ready to Sign Nuclear Pact," *Wall Street Journal*, May 18, 1984.

32. Personal communication.

33. Uranium metal could also be placed around the core of Libya's Soviet-supplied research reactor, where part of the metal could be transformed into plutonium—a strategy similar to one that Iraq was apparently considering before Israel destroyed its research reactor in 1981. At ten megawatts, Libya's research reactor is one-fourth the size of Iraq's, however, and it is unlikely that significant amounts of plutonium could be produced in this way.

Iraq

1. The United States, for example, trained some twenty-four students between 1955 and 1976 [Congressional Research Service, *Analysis of Six Issues About Nuclear Capabilities of India, Iraq, Libya and Pakistan* (Washington, D.C.: U.S. Government Printing Office, 1982), report prepared for the Subcommitee on Arms Control, Oceans, International Operations, and Environment of the Senate Foreign Relations Committee, 1982, p. 8.

2. The IRT-2000 is located outside Baghdad [Senate Committee on Foreign Relations, *Hearings on the Israeli Air Strike*, June 18, 19, and 25, 1981, 97th Congress, 1st Session (Washington, D.C.: U.S. Government Printing Office, 1981)]. It is fueled with a small quantity of uranium that has varied over the years from 10 percent to 80 percent enriched. The reactor began to operate in 1968 and was upgraded from two- to five-megawatts in 1978 (Jed C. Snyder, "The Road to Osiraq: Baghdad's Quest for the Bomb," *Middle East Journal*, Autumn 1983, p. 1). At its original two-megawatt capacity, the reactor was capable of producing only thirty-eight grams of plutonium annually. One analyst has noted that by 1988, enough plutonium might be produced in the upgraded reactor's 80 percent enriched fuel for one atom bomb (CRS, *Analysis of Six Issues*, p. 7).

3. Shai Feldman, *Israeli Nuclear Deterrence* (New York: Columbia University Press, 1982), p. 74. By 1976, for example, the budget of Iraq's atomic energy commission increased from $5 million to $70 million ("What Israel Knew," *Newsweek*, June 22, 1981, p. 25).

4. The accord was signed in the wake of the Arab oil embargo, at a time when France depended on Iraq for from fifteen to twenty percent of its oil. *Foreign Report*, August 13, 1980; Steve Weissman and Herbert Krosney, *The Islamic Bomb* (New York: Times Books, 1981), p. 314, quoting Francis Perrin, former head of France's atomic energy commission.

5. *Israeli Air Strike Hearings*, p. 125.

6. Shai Feldman, "The Bombing of Osiraq Revisited," *International Security*, Fall 1982, p. 115.

7. Weissman and Krosney, *Islamic Bomb*, p. 92.

8. Ibid.

9. Ibid., p. 235.

10. CRS, *Analysis of Six Issues*, p. 7. The International Atomic Energy Agency considers twenty-five kilograms of highly enriched uranium to be a "significant quantity," i.e., sufficient for manufacturing a single nuclear device. As noted below, however,

a weapon can be made with fifteen kilograms of highly enriched uranium if widely published design improvements are used and even with 12.5. The smaller the amount used, however, the more sophisticated the design of the weapon must be. See Thomas B. Cochran, et al., *U.S. Nuclear Forces and Capabilities* (Cambridge, MA: Ballinger, 1984), pp. 24-25.

Throughout this book, twenty-five and fifteen kilograms are used in calculating rough estimates of the number of weapons that can be manufactured from a given amount of highly enriched uranium because these figures appear to be widely accepted. However, it would be possible, according to experts consulted by the author, to manufacture a weapon with 12.5 kilograms, an amount of particular importance in the case of Iraq.

11. In fact, Iraq would not necessarily have to violate IAEA safeguards to use the fuel for weapons, since Article X of the Non-Proliferation Treaty provides that a party may withdraw on ninety days' notice if it decides that "extraordinary events related to the subject matter of this Treaty have jeopardized the supreme interests of its country."

12. The IAEA considers eight kilograms of plutonium to be sufficient for a nuclear device; however, the core of an atomic weapon can be made with only five kilograms, or possibly less. See Cochran, *U.S. Nuclear Forces,* pp. 24-25. Because the eight and five kilograms figures are widely accepted, they are used herein to estimate the number of weapons that can be made from a given amount of plutonium.

13. The French Osiris reactor—the model for Osirak—had been modified to give it a seventy-megawatt capability. Reportedly, Iraq sought to have similar modifications made to Osirak, which would have increased the plant's plutonium production capabilities. It is not known if the French agreed (Synder, "Road to Osiraq," p. 570). The IAEA lists the reactor as having a forty-megawatt output.

14. Of the nearly 150 research reactors covered by IAEA safeguards in 1979, for example, only 16 had a capacity of more than ten-megawatts; and of these only 2 were outside the advanced industrial countries, one in Poland and one in Taiwan, both nations considerably more advanced than Iraq. India has a large unsafeguarded research reactor which it used to produce plutonium for its 1974 nuclear test, and Israel has a similar reactor thought to be used for its nuclear weapons program.

Indeed, Osirak was a materials-testing reactor, intended for qualifying components for new reactor prototypes, an activity well beyond Iraq's technical capabilities. However, developing nations have sometimes invested heavily in uneconomic undertakings, such as national airlines, for reasons of national prestige, and some have suggested this may have motivated Baghdad's acquisition of Osirak *(Israéli Air Strike Hearings,* p. 126). Nonetheless, as discussed below, the evidence suggests that Iraq's nuclear program decisions were motivated more strongly by a desire to gain access to nuclear weapons material.

15. Weissman and Krosney, *Islamic Bomb,* p. 236.

16. Milton Benjamin, "France Plans to Sell Iraq Weapons-Grade Uranium," *Washington Post,* February 28, 1980.

17. Weissman and Krosney, *Islamic Bomb,* p. 258.

18. Ronald Koven, "France Cites Nuclear Terms to Iraq," *Washington Post,* July 30, 1980.

19. "France-Iraqi Nuclear Deal: Core of a Dilemma," *Energy Daily,* July 28, 1980.

20. The first of these measures was not revealed until late July 1980, several weeks after France shipped the 12.5 kilograms of highly enriched uranium to Iraq. The understanding concerning the presence of French technicians at Osirak was contained in a 1978 agreement between the French government-owned nuclear firm Techniatome and Iraq; it was not publicly disclosed, however, until after Israel's bombing of the reactor. *Israeli Air Strike Hearings,* p. 143.

21. Richard Burt, "U.S. Says Italy Sells Iraq Atomic Bomb Technology," *New York Times,* March 18, 1980.

22. Ibid. When uranium is subjected to radiation, only part of it is actually transformed into plutonium, which remains amalgamated with the unchanged uranium and various radioactive residues after the uranium target or rod is removed from the reactor. The plutonium is then extracted by chemical means in a series of steps known as "reprocessing."

A number of analysts have challenged the estimate that the Italian hot cells would have been capable of extracting approximately eight kilograms of plutonium per year, arguing that while the hot cells could be used to separate plutonium, they had less than a tenth this capacity (Weissman and Krosney, *Islamic Bomb,* p. 101). The matter has never been definitively resolved in the published literature. Even a smaller reprocessing capability, it may be noted, would have permitted Iraq to train personnel in reprocessing techniques, an important first step for any long-range nuclear weapons development program. As noted below,

Iraq later entered into negotiations with Italy to acquire a larger reprocessing plant.

23. As in the case of the capacity of the hot cells, experts have disagreed as to the capacity of the fuel fabrication laboratory. Some imply that it could produce uranium targets in large enough quantities to permit maximum use of Osirak for plutonium production (Snyder, "Road to Osiraq," p. 575). Others, including the State Department, have stated that the laboratory was far too small for this. *Israeli Air Strike Hearings,* p. 157).

24. Weissman and Krosney, *Islamic Bomb,* p. 26.

25. Burt, "Italy Sells Atomic Bomb Technology." Interestingly, Italy needed U.S. approval to close its naval sale, since four frigates included in the transaction were to be powered by General Electric Company gas turbines for which the United States had to grant export licenses. The United States granted these export licenses—and thus did not exert maximum pressure on Italy to cancel its nuclear sale. Some have suggested that this action was taken to protect the sale of the gas turbines by the U.S. firm; Italy, apparently could have obtained them from other foreign sources if its U.S. export licenses had been denied.

26. Transcript of "Near Armageddon: The Spread of Nuclear Weapons in the Middle East," on *ABC News Close-up,* April 27, 1981, p. 29; Judith Miller, "Was Iraq Planning to Make the Bomb?" *New York Times,* June 19, 1981; Burt, "Italy Sells Atomic Bomb Technology."

27. "Near Armageddon," p. 29.

28. CRS, *Analysis of Six Issues,* p. 46. Iraq allegedly used Brazil's dependence on Iraqi oil—40 percent of Brazil's oil imports—to gain its acquiescence. Iraq's dealings with France and Italy had reportedly followed a similar pattern.

29. Ibid. Portugal also depended heavily on Iraqi oil imports.

30. David Fishlock, "IAEA Had Suspicions About Iraq," *Energy Daily,* July 17, 1981. In theory, Iraq could have legitimately had natural uranium enriched in France or the Soviet Union to the level needed to fuel Osirak and the IRT-2000, but much smaller quantities of natural uranium than those Iraq purchased would have been needed.

31. Miller, "Was Iraq Planning the Bomb?" Using the Italian laboratories, Iraq could purify the yellowcake and fabricate it into the necessary target specimens; again, using the hot cells, the targets after irradiation could be reprocessed to extract plutonium.

32. Depleted uranium is uranium containing less than the naturally occurring proportion of uranium-235 (0.7 percent), in effect the

opposite of enriched uranium. It is produced as a residue in the uranium enrichment process after the desired, but rare, isotope of uranium, U^{235}, has been partly culled out of some batches of natural uranium so that it can be added to other batches in order to increase their concentration of U^{235}.

33. "Italian Uranium Shuffle to Iraq Raises Concern in Bonn over Euratom Loopholes," *Nuclear Fuel*, May 12, 1980, p. 1.

34. Snyder, "Road to Osiraq," p. 578.

35. Ann MacLachlan, "Iraq Nuclear Export Vetoed," *Energy Daily*, October 2, 1980.

36. Weissman and Krosney, *Islamic Bomb*, p. 89. At the time of the Israeli raid, Israeli spokesmen cited a number of Iraqi statements which, they claimed, clearly indicated Iraq's intent to use Osirak to develop nuclear arms. A review by the Congressional Research Service (CRS) showed that several of these purported statements had not been made or were quoted out of context. See, *Israeli Air Strike Hearings*, pp. 58-68. None of the statements noted in the text, however, was invalidated by the CRS review.

37. Jonathan Kandell, "Iraq A-Bomb Ability Seen by '85," *International Herald Tribune*, June 27, 1980.

38. Robert Fisk, "President Husain Denies Iraq Has Atomic Bomb Programme," *Times* (London), July 22, 1980.

39. Ibid.

40. *Israeli Air Strike Hearings*, p. 62.

41. CRS, *Analysis of Six Issues*, pp. 21, 23.

42. Weissman and Krosney, *Islamic Bomb*, pp. 228-233. The equipment destroyed was not the fuel itself, but the grids and fittings, known as honeycombs, which hold the reactor's highly enriched fuel in place (Ann MacLachlan, "French-Iraqi Nuclear Deal: Core of a Dilemma," *Energy Daily*, July 28, 1980).

43. Koven, "France Cites Nuclear Terms;" Weissman and Krosney, *Islamic Bomb*, pp. 229, 259.

44. Weissman and Krosney, *Islamic Bomb*, pp. 239ff.

45. Ibid., pp. 243ff; "Islamic Terrorists Bomb Iraqi Nuclear Projects," *Washington Star*, August 8, 1980.

46. Richard L. Homan, "Iran Again Bombs Baghdad as Diplomatic Efforts Stall," *Washington Post*, October 1, 1980. At the time of the June 7, 1981, bombing raid, Israel claimed Osirak was about to begin operations; Iraq and others have suggested that it was unlikely this would have occurred before late 1981.

47. Weissman and Krosney, *Islamic Bomb*, p. 279; Homan, "Iran Again Bombs Baghdad." Eventually, France persuaded many to return. By the spring of 1981, some three hundred French techni-

cians had done so, but without their families ("French Staff Back at Iraqi Reactor," *Washington Post,* April 29, 1981).

48. "Baghdad Blocks Inspection of Its Nuclear Reactors," *Washington Post,* November 7, 1980.

49. H. Gruemm, "Safeguards and Tamuz: Setting the Record Straight," *IAEA Bulletin,* December 1981, p. 10.

50. Weissman and Krosney, *Islamic Bomb,* pp. 227ff; Edward Cody, "Israel Angered as French Send Uranium to Iraq," *Washington Post,* July 20, 1980; "Delivery of High-Enriched Fuel to Iraq Has Israelis Hinting Preemptive Action," *Nuclear Fuel,* July 21, 1980; Abraham Rabinovich, "Israel Hints Strong Action If Iraq Pursues Nuclear Quest," *Christian Science Monitor,* August 18, 1980.

51. Weissman and Krosney, *Islamic Bomb,* pp. 227ff.

52. Israel's initial claims that Iraq was on the verge of making nuclear weapons in a secret chamber 120 feet below Osirak and that Israel had to act before the reactor began operations to avoid spreading radioactive debris over Baghdad were quickly disproven. In fact, the chamber was for neutron beam experiments, an accepted part of Osirak's research program, and was 12 feet below ground. The radiological hazard from destruction of Osirak once it had commenced operating would have been limited to a small area near the reactor *(Israeli Air Strike Hearings,* p. 156).

   See also note 36.

53. "Iraq Asserts Arabs Must Acquire Atom Arms as a Balance to Israel," *New York Times,* June 24, 1981.

54. Though IAEA inspections were relatively infrequent at the time of the Israeli raid—three or four times per year—the Agency intended to increase their frequency to once every two weeks as soon as Iraq received a "significant quantity" (i.e., twenty-five kilograms) of highly enriched uranium from France. Although Iraq might have objected to this inspection schedule as more frequent than normal for research reactors, some increase in frequency from the three to four inspections per year would undoubtedly have been negotiated.

   Following the Israel raid, the IAEA accounted for all the highly enriched uranium France had supplied Iraq, 12.5 kilograms (H.Gruemm, "Safeguards and Tamuz," p. 11).

55. Since the insertions and rearrangements would have been relatively easy for the IAEA to observe, they would have had to be undertaken after each IAEA inspection and the reactor restored to normal before the next—possibly a month or even only two weeks later, depending on the final arrangements negotiated between Iraq and the Agency. In one year, some five hundred

natural or depleted uranium targets would have had to be placed in the reactor for irradiation—all on this rigid timetable. If the Agency were able to install videotape recording cameras, as it had planned, this activity would have been easily observed (Christopher Herzog, "Correspondence to the Editor, IAEA Safeguards," *International Security*, Spring 1983, p. 196). In any event, such movements would be extremely difficult to conceal from the French personnel who were continually at the site.

56. Herzog, "Correspondence to the Editor." At the Senate hearings on the Israeli raid, Roger Richter, a former IAEA inspector, pointed out that at the time of the Israeli raid the Agency was not, in fact, safeguarding the laboratories because its right to do so depended on Iraq's declaring that it had introduced nuclear materials into them—a declaration Iraq had not yet made. He also noted that since yellowcake is not normally inspected under IAEA rules (because it is so many steps away from being useful for nuclear explosives), Iraq's stores of this material were not subject to on-site IAEA verifications either. It was possible, therefore, that Iraq could have removed some of its uninspected yellowcake without detection and, as long as it did not declare it was doing so to the IAEA, could have used Italian laboratories to fabricate the uranium into targets for irradiation and later reprocessed the targets without the IAEA being the wiser (see *Israeli Air Strike Hearings*, pp. 108 ff). However, the presence of the French technicians at the Osirak site would seem to make the option of at least large-scale clandestine fabrication and reprocessing impracticable, especially given the fact that the hot cells were adjacent to the reactor.

57. "Israel's Raid in Iraq Ensnarls Diplomacy and Arms-Sale Plans," *Wall Street Journal*, June 9, 1981.

58. Based on conversations with Dr. Leonard Weiss, Minority Staff Director, Senate Subcommittee on Energy, Nuclear Proliferation, and Government Processes, June–July 1981.

59. "French Nuclear Aid to Iraq Stopped," *Washington Post*, June 27, 1981.

60. "Iraqi Says Nation Still Plans to Seek Nuclear Technology," *New York Times*, July 14, 1981; David B. Ottaway, "Saudis Offer Financing for Iraqi Reactor," *Washington Post*, July 17, 1981.

61. "France Gives Iraq One More Chance to Build a Reactor," *Energy Daily*, August 25, 1981.

62. Thomas O'Toole, "Paris Lists Terms for Rebuilding Reactor in Iraq," *Washington Post*, February 20, 1982.

63. Edward Cody, "France Asks Iraq to Include Other States in

Nuclear Project," *Washington Post*, March 19, 1982. Even as France was proposing these new controls, however, a team of senior French scientists at the National Centre for Scientific Research issued a report noting that even with the caramel fuel, Osirak could produce between 3.3 and 10 kilograms of plutonium by irradiating uranium targets ("French Scientists Say N-Reactor Could Produce Bomb," *AFP*, March 18, 1982, translated in Foreign Broadcast Information Service/Africa and the Middle East, March 22, 1982, p. E2).

64. Ann MacLachlan, "France-Iraqi Accord Makes No Provision for Rebuilding Reactor," *Nucleonics Week*, September 1, 1983, p. 1.
65. William Drozdiak, "Iraq to Get Soviet Nuclear Reactor," *Washington Post*, March 23, 1984.
66. "Italy Has No Intention of Selling Additional Nuclear Equipment to Iraq," *Nucleonics Week*, December 2, 1982, p. 5.
67. Michael J. Berlin, "UN Team Says Chemical Agents Used in Gulf War," *Washington Post*, March 27, 1984.
68. "Iran Claims to Push Back Iraqis," *Washington Post*, March 11, 1984.
69. Joseph T. Rom, "Poison Gas and the Death of Treaties," *Washington Post*, April 5, 1984.
70. Ibid.
71. Personal communication; see also Cochran, *U.S. Nuclear Forces*, pp. 24-25.
72. Drozdiak, "Iran to Get Reactor."
73. "Iraq's Bid for Plutonium Foiled," *Energy Daily*, June 15, 1984.

Chapter IV:
Argentina

1. For a thorough discussion of the early Argentine nuclear program, see Daniel Poneman, *Nuclear Power in the Developing World* (London: George Allen and Unwin, 1982), pp. 68-72. Many of these scientists, like Ronald Richter, were formerly associated with nuclear research under the Third Reich. Others were trained by the United States under the Atoms for Peace program. See U.S. General Accounting Office, *Difficulties in Determining if Nuclear Training of Foreigners Contributes to Weapons Proliferation*, ID-79-2 (1979).

2. Oscar A. Quihillalt, "Unconventional Exporting," *Realidad Energética*, April 1983, translated in Foreign Broadcast Information Service/Nuclear Development and Proliferation (hereafter FBIS/NDP), November 17, 1983, p. 24; personal communication with informed French official.

3. Quihillalt, "Unconventional Exporting," p. 24.

4. Poneman, *Nuclear Power*, p. 72; Douglas L. Tweedale, "Argentina," in James E. Katz and Onkar S. Marwah, eds., *Nuclear Power in Developing Countries* (Lexington, MA: Lexington Books, 1982), p. 88 and note 31. Pre-existing ties between the West German and Argentine nuclear communities also appear to have been a factor. See Poneman, p. 73; Tweedale, p. 84.

5. Norman Gall, "Atoms for Brazil," *Foreign Policy*, Summer 1976, p. 184; Albert Wohlstetter, ed., *Swords from Plowshares* (Chicago: University of Chicago Press, 1977), p. 40.

6. Thijs de la Court et al., *The Nuclear Fix* (Amsterdam: World Information Service on Energy, 1982), p. 22; Powell A. Moore, Assistant Secretary of State for Congressional Relations, to Senator Gary Hart, August 19, 1982; personal communication with informed West German officials.

7. International Atomic Energy Agency, "Agreement Between the Argentine Republic and the Federal Republic of Germany Concerning the Atucha I Nuclear Power Plant," IAEA Document INFCIRC/168 (1972); personal communication with informed U.S. officials.

8. William H. Courtney, "Nuclear Choices for Friendly Rivals," in Joseph A. Yager, ed., *Non-Proliferation and U.S. Foreign Policy* (Washington, D.C.: The Brookings Institution, 1980), p. 255.

9. U.N. General Assembly, 23rd Session, Official Records, Plenary Session, October 16, 1968, p. 13; International Atomic Ener-

gy Agency, 22nd General Conference, 1978 (Castro Madero statement to the conference).

10. Poneman, *Nuclear Power,* p. 74.

11. Powell A. Moore, Assistant Secretary of State for Congressional Relations, to Senator Gary Hart, August 19, 1982. Senator Hart did not inquire about possible West German assistance in development of the plant.

12. Ibid.

13. Ibid. In response to Senator Hart's inquiry into the validity of allegations in a BBC television broadcast that West Germany sent spent fuel to Argentina for reprocessing, resulting in greater quantities of plutonium becoming available, the State Department noted, "The German government has stated that it has never shipped irradiated nuclear material to Argentina and we know of no reason to question this statement or to accept the unsubstantiated BBC report, which we consider almost certainly erroneous." Regarding allegations that larger amounts of plutonium were obtained, see de la Court, *Nuclear Fix,* p. 23.

14. See Poneman, *Nuclear Power,* p. 76; Tweedale, "Argentina," p. 89; de la Court, *Nuclear Fix,* p. 22.

15. Poneman, *Nuclear Power,* p. 77; Tweedale, "Argentina," p. 89. The new IAEA guidelines are contained in International Atomic Energy Agency, Document Gov. 1621 (1983). The Argentine-IAEA agreement on the Embalse plant is International Atomic Energy Agency, Document INFCIRC/224 (1974).

16. Poneman, *Nuclear Power,* p. 78; Gall, "Atoms for Brazil," p. 188.

17. Burt Solomon, "Argentina Bent on Home-Grown Nuclear Program," *Energy Daily,* November 9, 1982, p. 3; Robert Laufer, "Argentina Looks to Reprocessing to Fill Its Own Needs Plus Plutonium Sales," *Nuclear Fuel,* November 8, 1982, p. 3; Milton Benjamin, "Argentina on Threshold of Nuclear Reprocessing," *Washington Post,* October 16, 1978.

18. Laufer, "Argentina Looks to Reprocessing," p. 3. Through mid-1984 all of Argentina's reactors were, in fact, under safeguards. However, Argentina has announced plans to build a large research reactor, designated RA-7, that would be unsafeguarded and might be able to produce fifteen kilograms of plutonium per year, enough for perhaps two atom bombs annually. Joseph Pilat, "An Analysis of Argentina's Nuclear Program and Its Closeness to Nuclear Weapons," Congressional Research Service, Library of Congress (1982), p. CRS-42.

19. Laufer, "Argentina Looks to Reprocessing," p. 3.

20. Benjamin, "Argentina on Threshold;" see also Ann MacLachlan, "Argentina: Tomorrow's Nuclear Exporter," *Energy Daily*, September 24, 1980, p. 4: "We want to be the exporter of nuclear technology in Latin America. We cannot appear in the market mutilated in one main part of the fuel cycle."

21. MacLachlan, "Tomorrow's Nuclear Exporter," p. 4; John J. Fialka and Gerald Seib, "Argentina's Nuclear Weapon Capability Is Estimated to Be Closer Than Thought," *Wall Street Journal*, April 29, 1982; "Germany and the Argentine Bomb," British Broadcasting Corporation, 1981.

22. Richard Kessler, "Panel Backs CNEA Nuclear Policy But Wants More Civilian Control," *Nucleonics Week*, February 23, 1984, p. 1; "Plutonium Export Capability, Other Issues Discussed," *Jornal do Brasil*, January 10, 1982, translated in FBIS/NDP, February 10, 1982, p. 33.

23. Personal communication with informed former U.S. official.

24. "Castro Madero Cites CNEA 1979 Accomplishments," *La Prensa*, January 7, 1980, translated in FBIS/NDP, February 1, 1980, p. 25; Argentine Nuclear Program, pp. 2-3. Apparently a separate, small indigenous UO_2 plant was also operating in Córdoba at this time, according to U.S. State Department sources.

25. "Heavy Water Project," *Realidad Energetica*, April 1983, translated in FBIS/NDP, November 17, 1983, p. 11.

26. John R. Redick, "Latin America: Policy Options After INFCE," paper prepared for the Center for Strategic and International Studies, Georgetown University (1979), p. 44. Argentina reiterated its intention to ratify the accord in a November 1977 joint U.S.-Argentine communiqué, and in statements before the International Atomic Energy Agency and the U.N. Special Session on Disarmament in 1978.

27. Redick, "Latin America," p. 44.

28. This cutoff, which was implemented informally by delaying reviews of pending export licenses was not required by the Nuclear Non-Proliferation Act, passed in March 1978. That statute's provisions required the cessation of nuclear fuel and reactor exports to nations not accepting safeguards on all of their nuclear installations only after March 1980. Nor was the cutoff absolute. Small amounts of 20 percent enriched uranium were exported to Argentina in February 1980.

29. Solomon, "Home-Grown Nuclear Program," p. 3. Outside aid for the heavy water plant has also been noted by an informed U.S. source. Personal communication.

30. See Poneman, *Nuclear Power*, pp. 78-81.

31. See Appendix F. Charles N. Van Doren, *Nuclear Supply and Non-Proliferation*, Congressional Research Service Report No. 83-2025 (1983), p. CRS-23.

32. "Canada, FRG Dispute Safety Standard on Reactor Sale to Argentina," *Der Spiegel,* November, 1979, translated in FBIS/NDP, December 10, 1979, p. 18; John M. Geddes, "Swiss, Germans Ignore U.S. Objections, Sell Nuclear Technology to Argentina," *Wall Street Journal,* June 16, 1980.

33. "Canada, FRG Dispute," *Der Spiegel,* FBIS/NDP, p. 18.

34. The combined cost of this bid was $1.6 billion, compared to Atomic Energy of Canada, Limited's $1.1 billion offer. "Argentina Figures Big Financial Penalty If It Buys German Reactor," *Nucleonics Week,* September 27, 1979, p. 13; Poneman, *Nuclear Power,* p. 80.

35. The views of the unnamed Argentine officials are reported in a careful analysis of the deal by Poneman, *Nuclear Power,* pp. 80-81. See also, Tweedale, "Argentina," pp. 88-90. Castro Madero defended the decision on the grounds that the German reactor was larger than the Canadian version and that Argentine experience with Germans in building the Atucha I reactor had been far superior to that with the Canadians in building the Embalse plant. The Swiss heavy-water plant—more expensive than one West Germany was offering—was selected to diversify sources of supply, he claimed. Poneman, pp. 80-81.

36. West Germany temporarily bowed to this pressure and to Canada's angry reaction by postponing its decision on the Atucha II reactor export license originally scheduled for early November. "Canada, FRG Dispute," *Der Spiegel,* FBIS/NDP, p. 18.

   See also Geddes, "Swiss, Germans Ignore U.S.;" Richard Burt, "U.S. Tries to Prevent Swiss Sale to Argentina for Atom Programs," *New York Times,* March 11, 1980; "U.S. Fails to Halt German Reactor for Argentina," *Washington Post,* April 4, 1980.

37. Josh Mosku, "Bonn Warned of Criticism from Canada on A-Sale," *Toronto Globe and Mail,* May 24, 1980. See also Geddes, "Swiss, Germans Ignore U.S."

   In a March 1984 interview conducted by the Roosevelt Center for American Policy Studies, Gerard C. Smith, former Ambassador-at-Large for Non-Proliferation, characterized the sales as "marginal exports" that would not be essential to a possible Argentine nuclear weapons effort and thus did not merit the United States' threatening trade or other sanctions against

West Germany and Switzerland.

West German approval was given in April 1980. See also Brad Graham, "U.S. Fails to Halt German Reactor for Argentina," *Washington Post*, April 4, 1980. Swiss approval came in June of that year. Geddes, "Swiss, Germans Ignore U.S."

38. See Senate Foreign Relations Committee and Subcommittee on Energy, Nuclear Proliferation, and Federal Services of the Governmental Affairs Committee, *Joint Hearing on the Nuclear Non-Proliferation Act*, 98th Congress, 1st Session, September 30, 1983; Milton R. Benjamin, "U.S. Is Allowing Argentina to Buy Critical A-System," *Washington Post*, July 19, 1982.

U.S. officials justified the sale—which, ironically, would help Argentina reap the benefit of the installation whose export had so concerned Washington in 1979-80—on three grounds: that such computers were used in non-nuclear settings, for which purposes they were not subject to U.S. export controls; that the computer was not on the Nuclear Suppliers list of controlled nuclear commodities; and that it was destined for a safeguarded facility. A prior export request for equipment for Argentina's unsafeguarded, indigenous heavy-water plant had been denied, U.S. officials noted. (Department of State, Press Guidance, "Export of Process Control Equipment for Argentina Heavy Water Plant," July 19, 1982.)

This export approval, which became publicly known only in mid-1982, along with proposed exports of nuclear components to South Africa in that year triggered a congressional outcry that the Reagan administration was circumventing the principle embodied in the 1978 U.S. Non-Proliferation Act that the United States would not engage in nuclear trade with nations refusing full-scope safeguards. Legislation to tighten the 1978 act to prohibit such exports had been introduced in 1981. See note 66, below.

39. Estrategía, No. 69, translated in FBIS/NDP, December 1, 1981, p. 10; "Castro Madero Asserts Nuclear Leadership," *Mercado*, July 30, 1981, translated in FBIS/NDP September 14, 1981, pp. 24-25; Carlos Castro Madero, "Argentina's Nuclear Energy Program," *Nuclear Europe*, July-August 1983, p. 33; Richard Kessler, "Argentina Softens Stance on 'Peaceful Nuclear Explosive,' " *Nucleonics Week*, April 28, 1983, p. 6.

40. Kessler, "Argentina Softens Stance," p. 1; ("Any Latin American country that begins an atomic energy buildup for belligerent purposes will be immediately imitated by the rest of the coun-

tries. I believe this would aggravate the problems of underdevelopment that the continent is experiencing,") *DYN* (Buenos Aires), 1827 GMT, Nov. 1, 1982, translated in FBIS/Latin America, November 3, 1982, p. B4; interview with Castro Madero, *O Globo,* February 28, 1982, translated in FBIS/Latin America, March 16, 1982, pp. B2-B5.

41. "Castro Madero Speaks on Future of Nuclear Program," *Convicción,* July 11, 1982, translated in FBIS/NDP, September 13, 1982, p. 27. "Castro Madero Cites Need to Review Nuclear Concepts," *Energeia,* No. 25, June 1982, translated in FBIS/NDP, July 23, 1982, p. 36.

42. See e.g., "Castro Madero Speaks," *Convicción,* FBIS/NDP, p. 27; AFP, 1259 GMT, June 24, 1984, translated in FBIS/Latin America, June 25, 1982, p. B7. Nonetheless, one observer has commented that the Falklands War has had "a profound effect on Argentina's thinking about the desirability of developing a 'small nuclear force,'" David J. Myers, "Brazil, Reluctant Pursuit of the Nuclear Option," *Orbis,* Winter 1984, p. 906.

43. Judith Miller, "U.S. Is Holding Up Peking Atom Talks," *New York Times,* September 19, 1982.

44. Robert Laufer, "Chinese Enriched Uranium Sale to Argentina Delayed by Money Problems," *Nucleonics Week,* November 11, 1982, p. 1.

45. Burt Solomon, "Home-Grown Nuclear Program," p. 3; "Argentina Purchases USSR Rolling Mills," *AFP,* 1230 GMT, November 3, 1979, translated in FBIS/NDP, January 17, 1980, p. 18.

At this juncture, other aspects of the Argentine nuclear program were also suffering substantial delays because of the nation's fiscal crisis. See Richard Kessler, "Economic Woes Plus Falklands Crisis Cloud Argentine Nuclear Program," *Nucleonics Week,* June 24, 1984, p. 3; Jackson Diehl, "Ambitious Argentine Nuclear Program Hits Snags," *Washington Post,* August 31, 1982; Carlos Castro Madero, "Argentina's Nuclear Program," p. 32.

46. "Embalse Fuel Loaded," *Nuclear Engineering International,* February 1982, p. 14. During 1984 Argentina hopes to become self-sufficient in producing fuel for the Atucha I plant. "Yriart Reviews Budget Cuts Effects on Major Nuclear Projects," *Energeia,* January 1984, translated in FBIS/NDP, May 14, 1984, p. 18.

47. The parts were to be made in Japan, sent to Brazil for finishing, and then shipped to Argentina for installation. "Castro Madero Asserts Nuclear Leadership," *Mercado,* FBIS/NDP, p. 28.

48. Ann MacLachlan, "Tomorrow's Nuclear Exporter," p. 3.

49. These are the zero-power KP-O reactor at the Peruvian Institute of Nuclear Energy, which began operating in July 1978 and the ten-megawatt RP-10 reactor at the Peruvian Nuclear Research Center in Huarangal. "Castro Madero Cites Accomplishments," La Prensa, FBIS/NDP, p. 25. U.S.-origin uranium was supplied in 1977 or 1978, to be returned in two years. Redick, "Latin America," p. 23.

50. Castro Madero, "Argentina's Nuclear Program," p. 33.

51. Ibid.

52. The exports to Israel probably occurred in the 1950s, according to a former U.S. official; John R. Redick, "Military Potential of Latin American Nuclear Energy Programs," (Beverly Hills, CA: Sage Publications, 1972), p. 13 ; MacLachlan, "Tomorrow's Nuclear Exporter," p. 3.

53. Robert Laufer, "Argentina Looks to Reprocessing," p. 3.

54. Pilat, "Argentina's Nuclear Program," p. CRS-7; Redick, "Latin America," pp. 29-33. The agreement with Chile was signed in 1976, but notes ratifying it were exchanged only in 1983. "Nuclear Cooperation between Chile, Argentina Ratified," TELAM, 1550 GMT, September 1, 1983, translated in FBIS/NDP, September 27, 1983, p. 8.

A number of Argentine nuclear experts, including a former president of the CNEA, served as advisors to the Iranian nuclear program in the late 1970s. Most, if not all, were refugees from the Peron government and obviously not part of an Argentine technical assistance program. Redick, p. 33 ; Federation of American Scientists, Public Interest Report, April 1984, p. 12.

55. Pilat, "Argentina's Nuclear Program," pp. 46-47; "Argentina Outlines Conditions for Signing Tlatelolco Pact," Nucleonics Week, March 1, 1984, p. 2.

56. "Castro Madero Asserts Leadership," Mercado, FBIS/NDP, p. 28; "Castro Madero Discusses Nuclear Plan, Tlatelolco Treaty," Estrategía, No. 69, translated in FBIS/NDP, December 1, 1981, p. 8.

57. "Castro Madero Asserts Leadership," Mercado, FBIS/NDP, p. 28.

58. Discussed above.

59. "Castro Madero Discusses Plan," Estrategía, FBIS/NDP, p. 8.

60. "Castro Madero Speaks," Convicción, FBIS/NDP, p. 28.

61. Federal Register, August 2, 1983, Section 4, p. 19.

62. Michael Knapik, "U.S.-Origin Heavy Water Approved for

Transfer to Argentina," *Nucleonics Week,* August 18, 1983, p. 1; personal communication with West German and U.S. officials.

63. These were the MZFR (prototype for Atucha I) and the FR-2: Knapik, "U.S.-Origin Heavy Water," p. 1.

64. Milton Benjamin, "U.S. to Allow Argentine Nuclear Aid," *Washington Post,* August 18, 1983; "Sale of Heavy Water to Argentina Rapped," *Washington Times,* August 23, 1983.

65. Section 109 of the act permits components to be exported if IAEA safeguards will be applied to them by the recipient country, if the country guarantees they will not be used for any nuclear explosive device, and if the recipient agrees not to transfer them to another nation without prior U.S. approval.

66. Other examples cited include approval of the export of the Foxboro process control computer for Argentina's industrial-scale heavy-water plant in 1981 (noted earlier); acquiescence in the efforts during 1981 of two U.S. uranium brokers, Edlow International and SWUCO, to obtain nuclear fuel from European sources for South Africa's Koeberg nuclear power plant—fuel whose export from the United States would have been prohibited by the Non-Proliferation Act; the decision to permit nuclear component sales to South Africa in 1982 (largely reversed through congressional opposition); arranging in 1982 for France to substitute for the United States as supplier of nuclear fuel for India's Tarapur reactors after further U.S. fuel shipments became legally prohibited; and the proposed sale of U.S. component parts for that reactor in 1983. See *Congressional Record,* May 18, 1983, p. S7002.

Largely in response to the heavy-water transfer approval, legislative efforts were intensified to tighten the 1978 act to prohibit nuclear component exports and retransfers to nations not accepting full-scope safeguards. These changes had been passed by both houses of Congress by early 1984 as riders to the Export Administration Act Amendments of 1983, H.R. 7781 and S. 979. As of July 1, 1984, however, this bill had not been enacted, pending action by a House-Senate conference committee. (See also Boschwitz-Glenn resolution, October 1983, calling on the president to "disapprove the export of and suspend or revoke approval for the export of any nuclear related equipment . . . including nuclear components and heavy water" to India,

Session.) U.S. negotiators were successful, however, in gaining Argentine agreement to place back on the IAEA safeguards inventory in Argentina seven metric tons of previously supplied heavy water inadvertently left off the list.

67. Department of State, Press Guidance, August 18, 1983. Administration officials did not supply details to back up the assertion concerning previous Carter administration component export approvals except to state the components were destined for the Canadian-supplied Embalse reactor. Personal communication.

68. Personal communication with knowledgable U.S. official; Richard Kessler, "U.S. Approval to Sell 143 Tonnes of Heavy Water," *Nucleonics Week,* August 25, 1983, p. 7. U.S. officials also noted that from a political and diplomatic standpoint, the United States needed particularly strong grounds to object to the transfer since the heavy water was owned by West Germany, making U.S. control over the material far more remote than in the case of an export directly from the United States itself. At the same time, the material would be subject to safeguards and would not, therefore, make any direct contribution to any possible Argentine nuclear weapons program, which made it harder to argue that the export was particularly sensitive. Personal communication.

69. Warren H. Donnelly, "Nuclear Non-Proliferation: Retransfer of German Heavy Water to Argentina," Congressional Research Service Issue Brief #IB-83-155, November 14, 1983, p. CRS-5. Miller, "U.S. Holding Up Peking Talks."

70. One press account reported CNEA president Castro Madero as commenting that "talks with the Soviet Union and China for heavy water have been slow and largely unproductive." Kessler, "Approval to Sell Heavy Water," p. 7. See also "After the War: Britain Backs Heavy Water Deal with Argentina," *Energy Daily,* August 19, 1983, p. 1 ("Argentina was having trouble lining up supplies for two heavy water reactors.") In any event, the USSR has traditionally required safeguards for heavy-water transfers, and, while China apparently offered Argentina five metric tons of the material without safeguards (Miller, "U.S. Holding Up Peking Talks"), it had by this point reportedly given the United States assurances that all future nuclear sales would be under safeguards.

71. It may also be noted that, assuming the material was destined largely for the Atucha II reactor, by authorizing the transfer the United States was facilitating Argentina's use of a plant whose export the United States had sought to block only three years earlier.

72. Embassy of West Germany, Press Guidance, August 18, 1983;

International Atomic Energy Agency, Annual Report for 1982, p. 62.

73. International Atomic Energy Agency, Annual Report for 1982, p. 62.

74. "After the War," *Energy Daily,* p. 1.

75. These Argentine positions had been publicly reaffirmed during the summer of 1983 by CNEA president Castro Madero in a major interview. See Castro Madero, "Argentina's Nuclear Program," p. 33.

76. "CNEA Chairman Makes Announcement," *TELAM,* 2102 GMT, November 18, 1983, translated in *FBIS/NDP,* Dec. 12, 1983, p. 7.

77. These were the United States, USSR, China, France, Great Britain, Japan, South Africa, and the Netherlands.

78. "Physicist Westerkamp Scores Nuclear Program," *Buenos Aires Herald,* November 29, 1983, translated in FBIS/NDP, December 20, 1983, p. 42. Jóse Westerkamp, an outside critic of the program, questioned whether more than a few grams of the material had actually been produced.

79. Personal communication. At this point, however, the plant had not yet apparently produced 20 percent enriched material. "Physicist Scores Program," *Buenos Aires Herald,* FBIS/NDP, p. 42.

80. "CNEA Chairman Makes Announcement," *TELAM,* FBIS/NDP, p. 7.

81. Richard Kessler, "More Details Emerge on Argentine Enrichment, As Speculation Heightens," *Nucleonics Week,* December 1, 1983, p. 1.

82. "CNEA Chairman Makes Announcement," *TELAM,* FBIS/NDP, p. 7. "Alfonsín Issues Statement," *DYN,* 1335 GMT, November 18, 1983, translated in FBIS/NDP, December 12, 1983, p. 10. Kessler, "More Details Emerge," p. 1.

On November 24, less than a week after the plant was announced, IAEA director-general Hans Blix, in the course of a previously scheduled trip to Argentina, was permitted to visit the facility briefly, a fact cited by Castro Madero as demonstrating Argentina's intention to use the plant only for peaceful purposes. Kessler, "More Details Emerge," p. 1.

83. "Castro Madero on Necessity of Nuclear Technology," *Televisora Color Network,* 0000 GMT, December 1, 1982, translated in FBIS/NDP, December 12, 1983, p. 47.

84. "CNEA Chairman Makes Announcement," *TELAM,* FBIS/NDP, p. 7; "Castro Madero on Necessity of Nuclear

Technology," *Televisora Color Network,* FBIS/NDP, p. 47. Jóse Westerkamp, a critic of the program, argued that CNEA did not, in fact, produce the needed isotopes domestically but purchased them abroad. "Physicist Scores Program," *Buenos Aires Herald,* FBIS/NDP, p. 44.

85. "CNEA Chairman Makes Announcement," *TELAM,* FBIS/NDP, p. 7; "Reasons for Adopting Decision," *DYN,* 2045 GMT, Nov. 18, 1983, FBIS/NDP, December 12, 1983, p. 9.

86. This, he claimed, would save 30 percent of the cost of fuel and 10 percent of the total costs of nuclear-generated electricity. "CNEA Chairman Makes Announcement," *TELAM,* FBIS/NDP, p. 7. Castro Madero also suggested that the enrichment project might make reuse of spent fuel elements at the Atucha I plant feasible, apparently referring to the concept of "re-enriching" the material up to the U-235 level of natural uranium (.7 percent) or higher (Ibid.). With Argentina's ample reserves of natural uranium, re-enrichment would appear, at first blush, to be highly uneconomical.

87. This amount was to be increased to twenty metric tons in 1988. Kessler, "More Details Emerge," p. 1.

88. Ibid. It may also be noted that Castro Madero had offered virtually the same justification of major savings through reductions in uranium usage to defend development of the Ezeiza reprocessing plant—like the Pilcaniyeu enrichment facility, a potential source of nuclear weapons material. In both instances the claim seems open to question, given Argentina's ample, competitively priced uranium reserves, whose exploitation to cover the needs of Argentina's nuclear power program had already been mandated by presidential decree and towards which substantial investment had already been made. Moreover, the justification for building *both* plants seems even more doubtful, since reductions in uranium usage achieved by either one would drive down the price of uranium and thus that of natural uranium fuel, reducing possible further savings from using the output of the other plant as a substitute fuel.

89. As noted earlier the planned Pilcaniyeu plant reportedly has the potential of producing 100 kilograms of highly enriched uranium per year—enough for four to six nuclear weapons.

90. "Castro Madero on Nuclear Technology," *Televisora Color Network,* FBIS/NDP, p. 47. In fact, in the mid-1970s, the United States had successfully urged France to terminate its sale of a large reprocessing plant to Pakistan, had pressured South Korea to drop its planned purchase of such a plant from France, and

had terminated military and economic aid to Pakistan (and promoted a global nuclear embargo of the country) to try to curtail its efforts to build a centrifuge enrichment facility.

91. Ibid. See also Kessler, "More Details Emerge," p. 1. Indeed, at least one critic in challenging Castro Madero's claims of success made this very comparison. "Physicist Scores Program," *Buenos Aires Herald,* FBIS/NDP, p. 44.

92. Although State Department sources in private conversations uniformly claimed that the announcement of the plant had caught them unaware, at least one Argentine press report suggested that the United States, had had advance notice and that high U.S. military officials visiting Argentina during the fall had confronted their Argentine counterparts with their knowledge, possibly leading to the revelation of the plant in December. "Commentator on Nuclear Policy," *La Prensa,* November 23, 1983, translated in FBIS/NDP December 20, 1983, p. 40.

93. One additional remaining question about the facility is where Argentina obtained uranium hexafluoride, the feedstock for enrichment. This gas is usually produced in the uranium purification process and, as noted earlier, Argentina has an unsafeguarded purification facility at Córdoba that may have been the source of the material.

94. "Figueiredo Messages Bignone on Nuclear Program," *O Estado de São Paulo,* November 19, 1983, translated in FBIS/Latin America, November 25, 1982, p. D1.

95. "Geo-political Significance of Enriched Uranium Report Viewed," *O Estado de São Paulo,* November 20, 1983, translated in FBIS/NDP, December 20, 1983, p. 31.

96. "Alfonsín Issues Nuclear Policy Communique," *Buenos Aires Domestic Service,* 1600 GMT, December 5, 1983, translated in FBIS/NDP, December 20, 1983, p. 30.

97. Jackson Diehl, "Nuclear Policy Shift Signaled in Argentina," *Washington Post,* December 9, 1983. Alfonsín also repudiated an earlier statement by his energy-secretary-designate that Argentina would strictly adhere to its existing nuclear policies, including its rejection of the Non-Proliferation and Tlatelolco treaties. See Jeremy Morgan, "Argentina Won't Sign Global Nuclear Treaties," *Journal of Commerce,* November 28, 1983.

98. Kessler, "Panel Backs CNEA Policy," p. 1. The commission intended to recommend, however, that construction of the unsafeguarded RA-7 research reactor and Argentina's fourth nuclear power plant be postponed. ("Constantini on Effects of Budget

Cuts in Nuclear Program," *Clarin*, April 24, 1984, translated in FBIS/NDP, June 7 1984, p. 22.)

99. "Clarín Interviews Foreign Minister Caputo," *Clarín*, February 19, 1984, translated in FBIS/Latin America, February 27, 1984, p. B1. Caputo also noted that the Alfonsín government would not abandon Argentina's "nuclear plan," although budgetary restrictions would necessitate some changes.

100. "Argentina Outlines Conditions for Signing Tlatelolco Pact," *Nucleonics Week*, March 1, 1984, p. 2. Other preconditions to Argentine ratification of the treaty were also noted in the letter, one of the most hard to satisfy being the desire to establish a back-up mechanism to ensure the safeguards under the treaty would continue to apply even if a new nuclear weapons state emerged that had failed to sign and ratify Protocol II.

101. Jackson Diehl, "Argentina Cuts Budget for Nuclear Program," *Washington Post*, April 5, 1984. The statement of the Argentine government was made in conjunction with a visit by the Mexican president to Buenos Aires within days of the successful conclusion of efforts, led by Mexico, to obtain interim financing for servicing Argentina's external debt so as to avoid a default.

102. "Argentina Cuts Budget for Nuclear Program;" Edward Schumacher, "Argentina Forges Warmer U.S. Ties," *New York Times*, April 19, 1983; "Nuclear Policy Support," *La Prensa*, November 19, 1983, translated in FBIS/NDP, December 12, 1983, p. 51.

103. Edward Schumacher, "Argentine Parties Sign a Peace Accord," *New York Times*, June 8, 1984.

104. "Castro Madero on Aid to Algeria, Nuclear Submarine," *DYN*, 1353 GMT, October 24, 1983, translated in FBIS/NDP, November 18, 1983, p. 20.

105. "Quihillalt on Technology Export," *La Prensa* January 9, 1984, translated in FBIS/NDP, February 9, 1984, p. 28.

106. See Poneman, "Nuclear Proliferation Prospects for Argentina," *Orbis*, Winter 1984, pp. 868-869.

107. Philip M. Boffey, "Experts Fear Argentina is Planning A-Bomb," *New York Times*, September 17, 1983.

108. Redick, "Latin America," p. 28.

Brazil

1. Norman Gall, "Atoms for Brazil, Dangers for All," *Foreign Policy,* Summer 1976, p. 181; David J. Meyers, "Brazil: Reluctant Pursuit of the Nuclear Option," *Orbis,* Winter 1984, p. 883.
2. Argentina is credited with winning the race (see e.g., Gall, "Atoms for Brazil," p. 182), but the IAEA shows Brazil's reactor starting up in 1957 and Argentina's in 1958 [Albert Wohlstetter et al., *Swords from Plowshares* (Chicago: University of Chicago, 1979), p. 203]. Argentina's was built in Argentina, using U.S. plans, while Brazil bought a finished plant. This may be the basis for Argentina's claim that its reactor was Latin America's "first."
3. Gall, "Atoms for Brazil," pp. 186-87.
4. Ibid.; Myers, "Brazil," pp. 885, 891.
5. John R. Redick, *Military Potential of Latin American Nuclear Energy Programs* (Beverly Hills, CA: Sage Publications, 1972), pp. 20, 24.
6. Ibid., pp. 27-28.
7. Ibid., p. 26.
8. *The Brazilian Nuclear Energy Program* (1977), cited in John R. Redick, "Latin America: Policy Options After INFCE," paper prepared for the Center for Strategic and International Studies, Georgetown University (1979), p. 42.
9. Brazil is believed by U.S. officials to have a small uranium purification plant and a small uranium hexafluoride plant at the Instituto des Pesquisas Energeticas e Nucleares (IPEN) in São Paulo that are unsafeguarded. In addition, an unsafeguarded laboratory-scale reprocessing unit is said to be located there, although it is not clear whether this has operated. See note 39 and accompanying text.
10. H. Jon Rosenbaum, "Brazil's Nuclear Aspirations," in *Nuclear Proliferation and the Near Nuclear Countries,* Onkar Marwah and Ann Schulz, eds, (Cambridge, MA: Ballinger Publishing Co., 1975), p. 266.
11. These concerns were fueled by reports at the time that Argentina might have diverted plutonium-bearing spent fuel from the Atucha I reactor. See Fay Willey, "Who's Going Nuclear?" *Newsweek,* July 7, 1975, p. 27. Although details of the episode are murky, the reports were apparently triggered by an accounting error that was subsequently rectified to the IAEA's satisfaction.
12. The two Brazilian contracts were among forty-five proposed fixed commitment contracts that were altered in this fashion when it

appeared that the United States' uranium enrichment capacity had been oversubscribed. (Gall, "Atoms for Brazil," p. 163.)

13. Ibid., pp. 169, 176.

14. For an example of the Argentine reaction, see Juan E. Gugliamelli, "The Brazilian-German Deal: A View from Argentina," *Survival*, Vol. 18, 1976.

15. Some U.S. officials were apparently aware of the deal as early as the spring of 1974, however. (Personal communication with former U.S. official.) It has also been suggested that the West German Ministry of Commerce tried to present a *fait accompli* to other elements of the West German government that might have been more sensitive to the proliferation consequences of the deal. (Edward Wonder, "Nuclear Commerce and Nuclear Proliferation: Germany and Brazil, 1975," *Orbis*, Summer 1977, pp. 289-299.)

16. Bonn's opposition to expanded nuclear export controls was not confined to the Brazilian deal, however. At the subsequent fall 1975 London Nuclear Suppliers Group talks, which the United States had initiated the year before in the wake of the Indian test, the United States sought to gain adoption of a total ban on reprocessing and enrichment plant sales and the withholding of major new nuclear exports of any kind from nations that had not accepted international safeguards on all of their nuclear activities. West Germany and France were the principal opponents of these positions.

17. Later, the Nuclear Suppliers' Guidelines would adopt such "replication" safeguards for the transfer of enrichment, reprocessing, and heavy water production technology. See International Atomic Energy Agency, "Nuclear Suppliers' Guidelines," INFCIRC/254.

18. Agreement of 26 February 1976 between the International Atomic Energy Agency, the Government of the Federative Republic of Brazil and the Government of the Federal Republic of Germany for the Application of Safeguards, IAEA Document INFCIRC/237.

19. Gall, "Atoms for Brazil," p. 159.

20. "Brazil Pot Boils as German Hold on Nuclear Technology Is Revealed," *Nucleonics Week*, August 30, 1979, p. 9; Alison Raphel, "German Role in N-Plant Stirs New Furor in Brazil," *Washington Star*, August 29, 1979.

21. *Facts on File*, 1977, p. 414 (June 4, 1977); personal communication with informed former U.S. official.

22. Charles N. Van Doren, "Toward an Effective International Pluto-

nium Storage System," Congressional Research Service, Library of Congress, CRS Report 81-255 (1981), p. CRS-20.

23. Under the 1973 U.S. contract, monetary penalties could be imposed against Brazil if it terminated the agreement. In 1981 the Reagan administration announced it would not impose the penalties if Brazil purchased fuel elsewhere. In effect this was a signal to the Western European uranium suppliers (France and the British-Dutch-West German consortium, URENCO) that the United States had no objection to their supplying Brazil even though it had not accepted full-scope safeguards. See Jim Brooke, "Bush In Brazil Announces Nuclear Cooperation Effort," *Washington Post,* October 17, 1981.

24. "More Enriched Uranium to be Purchased from URENCO," *NRC Handelsblad,* October 13, 1981, translated in *Foreign Broadcast and Information Service/Nuclear Development* and Proliferation (hereafter FBIS/NDP), December 11, 1981, p. 33; "British Firm to Supply Enriched Uranium," *O Estado de São Paulo,* April 2, 1981, translated in FBIS/NDP, June 10, 1981, p. 32.

25. Myers, "Brazil," p. 894; James Bruce, "Austerity Measures in Brazil Threaten Nuclear Development Program Cuts," *Journal of Commerce,* October 21, 1982.

26. Myers, "Brazil," p. 894. Angra II is scheduled to start at the end of 1988 and Angra III in 1989, but at least a year's additional delay is expected. ("NUCLEBRAS Decision to Suspend Several Projects Detailed," *O Estado de São Paulo,* July 3, 1983, translated FBIS/NDP, August 9, 1983, p. 23; "CNEN Expenditures to Increase by 203 Percent in 1983," *O Estado de São Paulo,* December 30, 1982, translated in FBIS/NDP, January 26, 1983, p. 14.)

27. "Critics See Brazil as Taken for a Ride on Its 'Last Train' to SWU Technology," *Nuclear Fuel,* April 26, 1982, p. 2; "Unfavorable Aspects of Nuclear Accord Come into Light," *O Estado de São Paulo,* April 1, 1982, translated in FBIS/NDP, May 3, 1982, p. 11. Costs have escalated for this demonstration plant from $950 million to nearly $1.5 billion. (Ibid.)

28. "Investment Cut to Delay Nuclear Plant Projects in 1983," *O Estado de São Paulo,* January 1, 1983, translated in FBIS/NDP, February 16, 1983, p. 23.

29. "Resende Site of Uranium Reprocessing Plant Confirmed," *O Estado de São Paulo,* March 30, 1983, translated in FBIS/NDP, May 10, 1983, p. 21.

30. OECD Nuclear Energy Agency and the International Atomic

Energy Agency, *Uranium Resources, Production, and Demand* (Paris: OECD, 1983), p. 98; George T. Kurian, *The New Book of World Rankings* (New York: Facts on File, 1984), p. 230.

31. Myers, "Brazil," p. 891.

32. IPEN had been operated independently by the São Paulo state government, but the elections of November 1982 gave control of the state government to the Brazilian Democratic Movement (PDMB), Brazil's major opposition political party. A desire to avoid opposition control over any nuclear research may also have motivated federalization of IPEN. (Myers, "Brazil," p. 896.)

33. Ibid.

34. Richard Fairbanks, Assistant Secretary of State for Congressional Relations, to Senator Charles H. Percy, November 27, 1981.

35. Personal communication with knowledgeable U.S. official.

36. Bernardo Kucinski, "Argentine Boasts Spur Brazil into Race for Bomb," *The Guardian* (London), December 29, 1981, reprinted in FBIS/NDP, February 19, 1982, p. 6. At least one congressional source has also characterized the plant as having a five-kilograms-per-year capacity. (Personal communication.) But see "Report on IPEN Reactor," *Jornal do Brasil,* February 4, 1983, translated in FBIS/NDP, February 19, 1982, p. 4.

37. Kucinski, "Argentine Boasts Spur Brazil;" personal communication with a knowledgeable U.S. official.

38. "Report on IPEN Reactor," *Jornal do Brasil,* FBIS/NDP, p. 4 (larger reprocessing plant); "IPEN Produces Uranium Hexafluoride on a Laboratory Scale," *Jornal do Brasil,* June 25, 1982, translated in FBIS/NDP, July 28, 1982, p.18 (hexafluoride plant).

39. Milton R. Benjamin, "Brazil Takes Step Toward Developing Nuclear Weapons Potential," *Washington Post,* February 3, 1983; Ambassador Azeredo da Silveira to the Editor, *Washington Post,* February 13, 1983.

40. Richard House, "Brazil's Nuclear Dream Falters," *Washington Post,* February 12, 1983.

41. Da Silveira to the Editor, *Washington Post,* quoting U.S. Ambassador Anthony Motley in Brasilia on February 4, 1983.

42. Senate Committee on Foreign Relations and the Subcommittee on Energy, Nuclear Proliferation, and Federal Services of the Governmental Affairs Committee, Joint Hearings on the Nuclear Non-Proliferation Act, 89th Congress, 1st Session, September 30, 1983, pp. 45-46. See below.

43. "Ten Billion Cruzeiros to Be Allocated for Nuclear Research," *Jornal do Brasil,* January 16, 1983, translated in FBIS/NDP, March 21, 1983, p. 28. The first step in the investigation of centri-

fuges, apparently, was to examine those that had been obtained from West Germany in the late 1950s. (Ibid.)

44. "IPEN Produces Uranium Hexafluoride on a Laboratory Scale," *Jornal do Brasil*; "Uranium Enrichment Plant in Itataia Confirmed," *O Estado de São Paulo*, December 12, 1981, translated in FBIS/NDP, January 28, 1982, p. 22.

45. "Ten Billion Cruzeiros," *Jornal do Brasil*, FBIS/NDP, p. 28.

46. Ibid.

47. Myers, "Brazil," p. 896. Myers characterizes the CTA as "among the most important . . . centers for nuclear weapons and related research."

48. Redick, *Military Potential*, pp. 25-26.

49. "CTA Director on Building of Rockets, Satellites," *Jornal do Brasil*, April 2, 1984, translated in FBIS/NDP, April 5, 1984.

50. Redick, *Military Potential*, p. 19; "Accord with Spain," *Brasilia Domestic Service*, 2200 GMT, May 12, 1983, translated in FBIS/NDP, May 25, 1983, p. 19.; "PRC-Brazil Nuclear Pact Prepared, *Jornal Do Brazil*, May 18, 1984, translated in FBIS/NDP, June 15, 1984, p. 6.

51. "Brazil's CNEN Has Opted to Delay Construction . . .," *Nucleonics Week*, December 2, 1982, p. 8.

52. See Argentina section on Brazil-Argentine nuclear cooperation.

53. Richard House, "Brazil's Nuclear Dream."

54. "Government to Sell Uranium," *AFP*, September 23, 1981, translated in FBIS/NDP, October 1981.

55. "Brazil Intends to Export Nuclear Technology, Says Energy Minister Cals," *Nucleonics Week*, May 31, 1979, p. 6. The joint West German-Brazil organization NUCLEP is producing the lower portion of the pressure vessel for Argentina's Atucha II reactor.

56. "Brazil and Iraq Signed a Nuclear Cooperation Agreement," *Nucleonics Week*, January 17, 1980, p. 10; John J. Fialka, "Iraq Reported Pressuring Brazil for Atom Data," *Washington Star*, December 1, 1979.

57. Paul Lewis, "Stockpiling of Uranium Reported by Iraq Before the Raid," New York Times, June 19, 1981.

58. "Construction of Reactor for Radioisotopes Announced," *Fôlha de São Paulo*, October 25, 1983, translated in FBIS/NDP, Dec 12, 1983, p. 13.

59. Israel had been concerned that Iraq was trying a similar method of producing plutonium when in 1976 it purchased a forty-megawatt research reactor from France along with significant supplies of natural uranium—some of it reportedly from Brazil. If the natural uranium had been placed around the reactor's core, it would have

been partially transformed into plutonium during the reactor's operation.

60. Personal communication with informed U.S. officials.

61. "Brasilian Army Undisturbed Over Argentine Nuclear Advances," *AFP*, 1912 GMT, November 19, 1983, translated in FBIS/NDP, Dec. 12, 1983, p. 5; "Figueiredo Messages Bignone on Nuclear Program," *O Estado de São Paulo*, November 19, 1983, translated in FBIS/NDP, December 12, 1983. The Figueiredo letter went on to state, "I know that Argentina's nuclear policy pursues peaceful purposes as does Brazil's policy. Our two countries have attained an excellent level of cooperation in the nuclear field, and I am certain that the two countries will continue to seek mutual benefits and to promote the economic and social development of Latin America."

62. "Atomic Policy," *O Estado de São Paulo*, November 22, 1983, translated in FBIS/NDP, December 20, 1983, p. 54.

63. "Brazilian-Argentine Nuclear Exchange," *O Estado de São Paulo*, November 26, 1983, translated in FBIS/NDP, December 20, 1983, p. 56.

64. "Debate on the Behind-Schedule Nuclear Program," *O Globo*, November 27, 1983, translated in FBIS/NDP, December 12, 1983.

65. *São Paulo Radio Bandeirantes Network*, 1000 GMT, Nov. 29, 1983, translated in FBIS/NDP, December 12, 1983, p. 19.

66. "Possibility of Producing Bomb by 1990 Discussed; Reaction," *O Estado de São Paulo*, December 9, 1983, translated in FBIS/NDP, January 11, 1984, p. 30. The use of a breeder reactor seems an unlikely choice to produce plutonium for weapons, since breeder reactors themselves require substantial amounts of plutonium for fuel. If Brazil could get such plutonium, it could use it for weapons directly, making the breeder unnecessary.

67. "Potential Confirmed," *O Estado de São Paulo*, Dec. 10, 1983, translated in FBIS/NDP, January 11, 1984, p. 38.

68. "Cals Cites Manufacture of Bomb as Priority, Clarification," *Correio Braziliense*, December 14, 1983, translated in FBIS/NDP, January 11, 1984, p. 45.

69. Ibid.

70. "Navy Minister on Nuclear Submarine Program," *Jornal do Brasil*, January 22, 1984, translated in FBIS/Latin America, January 25, 1984, p. D1. Maximiano contended that while using material from the Resende plant for nuclear weapons would be forbidden under IAEA safeguards, this did not necessarily rule out using highly enriched uranium fuel for the military purpose of operating a nuclear submarine. (Ibid.)

71. Ibid.

72. "Nuclear Program Delayed; Priorities Established," *Fôlha de São Paulo,* January 5, 1984, translated in FBIS/Latin America, January 9, 1984, p. D1.

73. "Uranium Enrichment Production to Begin in 1985," *AFP,* 2333 GMT, March 11, 1984, translated in FBIS/Latin America, March 13, 1984, p. D3.

74. David Marsh, "Brazil N-plant Worries France," *Financial Times,* January 3, 1984; personal communication with a knowledgeable French spokesman.

75. Marsh, "Brazil N-Plant."

76. "Bar on Brazil Uranium Plant," *Financial Times,* January 4, 1984.

77. "Military Cooperation with the U.S. to Be Expanded," *O Estado de São Paulo,* December 27, 1983; translated in FBIS/Latin America, December 29, 1983, p. D1.

78. Foreign Assistance Act of 1961, Sections 669, 670, 22 U.S.C. 2429, 2429a (1981).

79. "French Mull Supply of Compressors for Resende Enrichment Plant," *Nucleonics Week,* February 16, 1984, p. 1. Brazil had been advised in August 1983 that the U.S. contract would be suspended. Secretary Shultz signed an agreement formalizing the arrangement.

80. "NUCLEP Submits Bids for Plant Construction in Turkey," *Jornal do Brasil,* Dec. 1, 1983, translated in FBIS/NDP, February 9, 1984, p. 36.

81. "Memorandum Signed with PRC on Nuclear Matters," *Folha de São Paulo,* May 30, 1984, translated in FBIS/Latin America, June 1, 1984, p. D1.

82. "Brazilian-Venezuelan Nuclear Agreement," *Gazeta Mercantil,* January 25, 1984, translated in FBIS/NDP, March 15, 1984, p. 19.

83. "Navy Minister," *Jornal do Brasil,* FBIS/Latin America, p. D1.

84. How much might be allowed to accumulate in this intermediate status before being placed in international storage is one of the many details yet to be worked out to implement this arrangement.

Chapter V:
Africa Introduction

1. Department of Political and Security Council Affairs, United Nations Centre for Disarmament, Report of the Secretary General, *South Africa's Plan and Capability in the Nuclear Field,* Report A/35/402 (New York: United Nations, 1981), p. 20. Although 25 kilograms of highly enriched uranium are normally considered the minimum for a crude nuclear device, more sophisticated designs can produce nuclear weapons with a yield of approximately 20 kilotons using 15 kilograms of the material (or possibly even less). Estimates here are based on the 15 to 25 kilogram range. If South Africa has been running its small enrichment plant, described below, to maximize the production of weapons-grade uranium, 375 kilograms of the material may have been produced.

2. Jonathan Kwitny, "Nigeria Considers Nuclear Armament Due To South Africa," *Wall Street Journal,* October 6, 1980.

3. "Africans Are Advised To Develop Atom Arms," *New York Times,* June 10, 1983.

South Africa

1. Department of Political and Security Council Affairs, United Nations Centre for Disarmament, Report of the Secretary General, *South Africa's Plan and Capability in the Nuclear Field,* Report A/35/402 (New York: United Nations, 1981), p. 4.

2. C. Raja Mohan, "Atomic Teeth to Apartheid: South Africa and Nuclear Weapons," in K. Subrahmanyam, ed., *Nuclear Myths and Realities: India's Dilemma* (New Delhi: ABC Press, 1981), p. 123. The Combined Development Agency was the successor to the wartime Combined Development Trust established by the United States, Canada, and Great Britain as a means for attempting to monopolize world supplies of uranium.

3. Ibid., p. 124.

4. A. R. Newby-Fraser, *Chain Reaction: Twenty Years of Nuclear Research and Development in South Africa* (Pretoria: Atomic Energy Board, 1979), pp. 22-25, as cited in U.N., *South Africa's Plan,* p. 4.

5. Peter Pringle and James Spigelman, *The Nuclear Barons* (New York: Holt, Rinehart and Winston, 1981), pp. 203-204.

6. U.N., *South Africa's Plan,* p. 15.

7. Ibid.

8. Ibid., p. 12.

9. Personal communication with knowledgeable U.S. officials; Warren H. Donnelly and William N. Raiford, *U.S. Foreign Policy Towards South Africa: The Case for Nuclear Cooperation,* Congressional Research Service, Report No. 82-24S-F, January 26, 1981, p. CRS-5, n. 2.

10. Robert S. Jaster, "Politics and the 'Afrikaner' Bomb," *Orbis,* Winter 1984, p. 826. Jaster notes, "An example would be experiments involving the generation and control of neutrons and the properties of material under neutron bombardment, which would be critially important to the development of a clean tactical weapon."

11. Jim Hoagland, "South Africa, With U.S. Aid, Near A-Bomb," *Washington Post,* February 16, 1977. Regarding name change of Atomic Energy Institute, see note 13.

12. Department of State Telegram to U.S. Consul-General, Capetown, February 10, 1965 (LBJ Library), as cited in Richard E. Bissell, *South Africa and the United States: The Erosion of an Influence Relationship* (New York: Praeger, 1982), pp. 107-108; personal communication with knowledgeable former U.S. official. See U.S.-IAEA-South Africa agreement for the application

of IAEA safeguards, October 8, 1965, 16 U.S.T.5880.

3. J. E. Spence, "The Republic of South Africa: Proliferation and the Politics of an 'Outward Movement,' " in Robert M. Lawrence and Joel Larus, eds., *Nuclear Proliferation Phase II* (Lawrence, Kansas: University Press of Kansas, 1974), p. 215. The Atomic Energy Institute was renamed the Atomic Energy Board in 1957 and its powers expanded to include overseeing of South Africa's nuclear research program.

14. Ibid.

15. Ibid.

16. Ibid.

17. United Nations, General Assembly, A/C.1/PV.1571, May 20, 1968, as cited in Spence, "Proliferation and Politics," pp. 222-223. In fact, over the years, developing effective safeguards for enrichment facilities that also protect industrial secrets has been an ongoing problem for the IAEA. Only in 1983, for example, did a group of nations with uranium enrichment plants, including Japan, the Netherlands, France, and the United States, agree on IAEA measures that would allow adequate safeguarding without compromising enrichment processes. It has also been suggested that South Africa may have hoped to extract political concessions in the form of warmer ties with the United States and other Western governments in return for its signature on the treaty. Spence, "Proliferation and Politics," p. 220.

18. Edouard Bustin, "South Africa's Foreign Policy Alternatives and Deterrence Needs," in Onkar Marwah and Ann Schulz, eds., *Nuclear Proliferation and the Near Nuclear Countries* (Cambridge, MA: Ballinger, 1975), p. 207.

19. Mohan, "Atomic Teeth," p. 126. Roux and other senior scientists of the South African Atomic Energy Board initiated work on uranium enrichment as early as 1960.

20. Spence, "Proliferation and Politics," p. 221. In contrast to South Africa's nominal support for the treaty, Argentina and Brazil, for example, opposed the U.N. resolution endorsing the accord.

21. Christopher S. Raj, "Israel and Nuclear Weapons," in K. Subrahmanyam, ed., *Nuclear Myths and Realities* (New Delhi: ABC Press, 1981), p. 115; Thijs de la Court et al., *The Nuclear Fix* (Amsterdam: World Information Service on Energy, 1982), p. 95. If such a transaction took place, it may have constituted a violation of the guidelines of the Western Suppliers Group.

22. J. E. Spence, "South Africa: The Nuclear Option," *African Affairs,* October 1981, p. 441.

23. Richard K. Betts, "A Diplomatic Bomb? South Africa's Nuclear

Potential," Joseph A. Yager, ed., *Nonproliferation and U.S. Foreign Policy,* (Washington, D.C.: Brookings Institution, 1980), p. 289.

24. Raimo Vayrynen, *South Africa: A Coming Nuclear-Weapon Power?* (Tampere, Finland: Tampere Peace Research Institute, 1977), p. 37; "Germany, S. Africa Hold Uranium Talks," *Washington Post,* August 23, 1973.

25. The relationship is described at considerable length in Zdnek Cervenka and Barbara Rogers, *The Nuclear Axis: Secret Collaboration Between West Germany and South Africa* (London: J. Friedmann, 1978). See also Murray Seeger, "Trial Testimony in S. Africa Indicates W. German A-Link," *International Herald Tribune,* November 26, 1975; *Facts on File* (1975), p. 789. Cervenka and Rogers also point out that through a complicated corporate structure, the West German government itself owned a substantial portion of STEAG.

26. U.N., *South Africa's Plan,* pp. 8-10, 16-17.

27. In contrast, when West Germany sold Brazil jet-nozzle uranium enrichment technology in 1975, Brazil was required to accept safeguards on any installation it built using that process. See Brazil chapter.

28. Spence, "Proliferation and Politics, pp. 217-218.

29. Mohan, "Atomic Teeth," p. 128.

30. Senate Committee on Government Operations, *Hearings on the Export Reorganization Act,* 94th Congress, 1st Session, April 30 and May 1, 1975 (Washington, D.C.: U.S. Government Printing Office, 1975), pp. 68-69. The Foxboro sale did not become publicly known until 1976, when it was brought to light in the course of congressional investigations of U.S. non-proliferation policy.

31. Personal communication with knowledgeable former U.S. official.

32. 25 U.S.T. 1158, Article IX. The annual requirements of the two nuclear power plants would be about fifty tons of three-percent enriched uranium; the capacity of the Valindaba pilot plant could meet only a small fraction of that demand.

33. "S. Africa Cites A-bomb Capacity," *Washington Post,* July 12, 1984.

34. Energy Research and Development Administration, *U.S. Nuclear Power Export Activities, Final Environmental Statement,* ERDA-1542, (Springfield, VA: National Technical Information Service, 1976), p. 3-56.

35. Central Intelligence Agency, "Prospects for Further Proliferation of Nuclear Weapons," DCI NIO 1945/74, September 4, 1974, p. 3.

36. Bissell, *South Africa and the U.S.*, pp. 11-13. With the approval of National Security Study Memorandum 39, Nixon endorsed the policy of "benign neglect" towards South Africa's racial practices.

37. The lack of congressional interest in South African nuclear developments went back to the 1950s. A 1981 Congressional Research Service study found that although the 1957 U.S. agreement for nuclear cooperation with South Africa was amended three times (in 1962, 1969, and 1974), "the initial agreement and each of its amendments were submitted to the Joint Committee on Atomic Energy where they remained for 30 days before taking effect as was required by the Atomic Energy Act of 1954. On none of these occasions did the Committee hold hearings nor does the *Congressional Record* indicate other congressional interest in them" (Donnelly and Raiford, *U.S. Policy Towards South Africa*, p. CRS-4).

38. An interesting comparison is provided by the U.S. response in 1983 to Argentina's announcement that it had mastered the enrichment process when the United States immediately urged that the plant be put under safeguards. Although for the moment U.S. pressure on the newly inaugurated Alfonsin government is being applied sparingly, there is no question that Argentina's continued construction of the plant without safeguards will be viewed with alarm and that a concerted international effort will be made to impede its progress. As another example, France recently refused to supply pumps for the Resende enrichment plant in Brazil. Even though this will be a safeguarded installation, the potential for misuse of enrichment technology is now well recognized, and few governments are likely to be cooperative in assisting nuclear threshold states develop such new capabilities.

39. David Fishlock, "The South African Nuclear Weapons Scare," paper prepared for the Congressional Research Service, December 1977, p. CRS-5.

40. "I Won't Call You a Liar," *Newsweek,* May 17, 1976, p. 53.

41. Jaster, "The 'Afrikaner' Bomb," p. 28.

42. Bissell, *South Africa and the U.S.*, pp. 109, 115.

43. Ibid., p. 108.

44. Thomas O'Toole, "French Get S. Africa A-Plant Sale," *Washington Post,* May 29, 1976. Senator Dick Clark, chairman of the Senate Subcommittee on African Affairs, stated that black African leaders would view the sale as a "signal that the U.S. hasn't really changed its African policy at all and has no intention of doing so. I think this will only increase the potential for violence

and bloodshed in Southern Africa.'' (Ibid.)

45. Jim Hoagland, "Paris Warns South Africa on A-Testing," *Washington Post,* August 23, 1977.

46. International Institute for Strategic Studies, The Military Balance: 1971-72 through 1978-79 (London, 1972-1979), as cited in Mohan, "Atomic Teeth," p. 133.

47. Jim Hoagland, "S. Africa with U.S. Aid, Near A-Bomb," *Washington Post,* February 16, 1977.

48. Murray Marder and Don Oberdorfer, "How West, Soviets Moved to Head Off S. Africa A-Test," *Washington Post,* August 28, 1977; Bissell, *South Africa and the U.S.,* pp. 110-111; John F. Burns, "South Africa Stirs New A-Arms Flurry," *New York Times,* August 31, 1977.

49. "U.S. Disagrees with Vorster on A-Weapon," *Washington Post,* October 25, 1977.

50. Burns, "New Flurry."

51. Jaster, "The 'Afrikaner' Bomb," p. 831.

52. Personal communication with knowledgeable former U.S. official.

53. See, Richard Betts, "Diplomatic Bomb?" p. 106, ("A nuclear shock may have seemed the appropriate counter to mounting pressure, a way of highlighting Afrikaner power and determination, a demonstration that apartheid is here to stay and that the world would have to deal gingerly with Pretoria.")

54. U.N., *South Africa's Plan,* pp. 30-31.

55. Atomic Energy Act (as amended by the Nuclear Non-Proliferation Act), Section 128, 42 U.S.C. 2157 (1978).

56. Spence, "Nuclear Option," p. 450.

57. Caryle Murphy, "Embargo Slows South African A-Plants," *Washington Post,* September 12, 1980.

58. Caryle Murphy, "South Africa Powers Reactor with Uranium It Enriched," *Washington Post,* April 30, 1981.

59. Caryle Murphy, "S. Africa Skirts U.S. Efforts to Bar Nuclear Fuel Supply," *Washington Post,* November 13, 1981.

60. Ann MacLachlan, "U.S. Firm Plays Role in South Africa Purchase of Uranium," *Energy Daily,* December 10, 1981.

61. Ibid.; see also Thomas O'Toole, "U.S. Firms Help South Africa Get Uranium," *Washington Post,* April 13, 1982.

62. House Subcommittee on Africa and House Subcommittee on Economic Policy and Trade, *Hearings on Control of Exports to South Africa,* 97th Congress, 2nd Session, February 9 and December 2, 1982 (Washington, D.C.: U.S. Government Printing Office, 1983), pp. 251-256.

63. Senate Foreign Relations Committee and Subcommittee on Energy, Nuclear Proliferation, and Government Processes of the Committee on Governmental Affairs, *Joint Hearings on Nuclear Non-Proliferation*, 98th Congress, 1st Session, September 30, 1983 (Washington, D.C.: U.S. Government Printing Office, 1983), p. 47.

64. Malcolm Baldrige, Secretary of Commerce, to Senator Charles H. Percy, Chairman, Subcommittee on Energy, Nuclear Proliferation, and Government Processes, May 12, 1982; Milton R. Benjamin, "Administration Reconsidering South Africa Equipment Ban," *Washington Post*, September 15, 1982. The particular items at issue included helium-3, material South Africa hoped to use in testing nuclear fuel of its own manufacture for the Koeberg reactor, and hot isostatic presses for shaping metals, which are potentially useful in shaping material for nuclear weapons.

65. Rob Laufer, "Reactor Components Struck In Bombings At South Africa's Koeberg Station," *Nucleonics Week*, December 23, 1982, p. 1.

66. George Lardner, Jr., and Don Oberdorfer, "China Was Source of Atomic Fuel for South Africa, U.S. Believes," *Washington Post*, November 18, 1981.

67. "China Says Study Shows It Wasn't Uranium Source," *Washington Post*, December 8, 1981; Rob Laufer, "Interview With Malone," *Nucleonics Week*, August, 1982, p.1; Judith Miller, "U.S. Is Holding Up Peking Atom Talks," *Washington Post*, September 19, 1982. Characterization of administration views based on personal communications with informed officials. Regarding the possible enrichment of low-enriched uranium to weapons-grade, see China section, note 13 and appendices.

68. Bernard Gwertzman, "U.S. Monitors Signs of Atom Explosion Off South Africa," *New York Times*, October 25, 1979.

69. "Blowup," *Technology Review*, October 1980, p. 78.

70. "Israel Reported Behind A-Blast Off South Africa," *Washington Post*, February 22, 1980.

71. Arnold Kramish, "Nuclear Flashes in the Night," *Washington Quarterly*, Summer 1980, p. 3; personal communication.

72. U.N., *South Africa's Plan*, p. 17.

73. Ibid.

74. In the early 1970s, South Africa's major nongovernmental uranium producer, Rio Tinto Zinc, joined other major uranium producers in Canada, Australia, Britain, and France to establish a uranium supply cartel. The cartel's activities contributed significantly to the sharp rise in uranium prices during the mid-1970s—from $8

per pound in 1972 to \$20 per pound in 1976, and subsequently higher. One impact of these price increases was to make the use of plutonium as a nuclear power reactor fuel appear more economical than would otherwise have been the case, stimulating interest in reprocessing. The cartel no longer appears to be functioning.

75. Christopher S. Raj, "Israel and Nuclear Weapons: A Case of Clandestine Proliferation," in K. Subrahmanyam, ed., *Nuclear Myths and Realities* (New Delhi: ABC Publishing House, 1981), p. 114-118; de la Court, *The Nuclear Fix*, p. 95.

76. Yosi Melman, "Israel Aiding South Africa in Development of Nuclear Weapons in Exchange for Uranium," *Davar* (Tel Aviv), April 13, 1984, translated in FBIS/NDP, June 7, 1984, p. 30; Judith Miller, "3 Nations Widening Nuclear Contacts," *New York Times*, June 28, 1981. One recent unsubstantiated report on the Israeli nuclear program states that Israel has employed the Becker jet-nozzle enrichment process, similar to South Africa's. If correct, this may be an additional area of cooperation between the two nations. Russell Warren Howe, "Study Confirms Pakistan's Nuclear Know-How," *Washington Times*, July 25, 1984.

77. Milton R. Benjamin, "Bid to Service Nuclear Plant in S. Africa Mulled," *Washington Post*, September 20, 1983.

78. The Export Administration Act Amendments, H.R. 7781 and S. 979, 98th Congress, 2nd Session (1984). As of July 1, 1984, however, these provisions, which were attached as riders to the reauthorization of the Export Administration Act, were still tied up in a House-Senate conference committee and their future was uncertain. Despite U.S. Department of Energy authorization, however, the ten-year, \$50 million contract was won by a competing French firm.

79. Simon Barber, "S.A. Atomic Energy Development Detailed," *Rand Daily Mail*, March 18, 1983, reprinted in *Foreign Broadcast Information Service/Nuclear Development and Proliferation*, April 21, 1983, p. 39.

80. Quoted in Allister Sparks, "S. Africa Pledges to Abide by Nuclear Treaty," *Washington Post*, February 10, 1984.

81. Ibid.

82. U.N., *South Africa's Plan*, p. 20.

83. Thomas B. Cochran, *U.S. Nuclear Forces and Capabilities* (Cambridge, MA: Ballinger, 1984), p. 15.

84. Jaster, "The 'Afrikaner' Bomb," pp. 834ff; Betts, "Diplomatic Bomb?" pp. 100ff.

China

1. International Institute for Strategic Studies, *The Military Balance: 1983-1984* (London, 1984), p. 82.

2. Colina MacDougall, "China Chooses the Nuclear Solution," *Financial Times*, June 12, 1984.

3. Christopher S. Wren, "China Is Building Atom Power Plant," *New York Times*, September 30, 1982.

4. "Zhao Says China May Purchase French Reactor," *Washington Post*, May 5, 1983; "Hong Kong-China N-Plant," *Financial Times*, December 8, 1983.

5. Milton R. Benjamin, "Westinghouse Seeks Nuclear Sale To China," *Washington Post*, December 16, 1982.

6. "World: Dollar Falls Sharply Abroad; Gold Closes Higher; Atomic Pact," *Washington Post*, September 4, 1981; "Italian Nuclear Sources Believe They Have A Good Chance of Winning Contracts . . . ," *Nucleonics Week*, December 23, 1982.

7. "U.S.-French Reactor Deal Blessed," *Energy Daily*, January 26, 1981, p. 1. In addition, the coordinating committee of Western nations implementing export controls on sales to Communist-bloc nations (COCOM) had to approve the sales; here, too, U.S. consent was required.

8. Personal communication with informed former U.S. official. The decision to allow the French sale, it may be noted, was at odds with previous U.S. policy under which Washington in the late 1960s had required Great Britain, a nuclear weapon state like China and also a close ally, to accept safeguards on U.S. exports of enriched uranium.

9. A. D. Horne, "U.S., China Open Nuclear Talks; Weinberger to Go to Peking," *Washington Post*, July 12, 1983.

10. Jack Anderson, "CIA Says China Has Sent A-Fuel to South Africa," *Washington Post*, July 23, 1981; Judith Miller, "U.S. Is Holding Up Peking Atom Talks," *New York Times*, September 19, 1982.

11. Christopher S. Wren, "China Denies Selling Uranium to South Africa," *New York Times*, September 26, 1982. Some U.S. officials believed that China had sold low-enriched uranium to intermediaries without realizing that it would wind up in South Africa, although others believed Peking was aware of the ultimate destination of the material from the beginning. Miller, "U.S. Holding Up Peking Talks."

12. Rob Laufer, "Chinese Enriched Uranium Sale Delayed By Money Problems," *Nucleonics Week*, November 11, 1982, p. 1.

13. Weapons-grade uranium is made up of 90 percent or more uranium-235, a rare isotope that is found in natural uranium in a concentration of less than 1 percent. South Africa's small Valindaba uranium enrichment facility is capable of increasing the concentration of uranium-235 to weapons-grade, but using natural uranium as a feedstock, it can produce only enough weapons-grade material for two or possibly three nuclear weapons per year. Because of the peculiarities of the uranium enrichment process, a large proportion of the work (and hence of plant capacity) involved in reaching the highly enriched level needed for weapons is expended in upgrading natural uranium to the low-enriched stage (3 percent uranium-235); considerably less effort (and plant capacity) is required to increase the low-enriched material to weapons-grade levels. The Valindaba plant, which uses the jet-nozzle process, is thought to be composed of thousands of nozzle units, each of which incrementally increases the concentration of the material passed through it. After each slight concentration, the improved material is fed into another nozzle for further slight enhancement, a process that is repeated until the desired enrichment level is obtained. To produce highly enriched uranium from natural uranium, a large proportion of the available nozzle units must, therefore, be devoted to reaching the low-enriched stage. If the enrichment process begins with low-enriched material, however, a larger proportion of the facility can, in principle, be devoted to the task of reaching the higher enrichment level needed for weapons.

Even if any material received from China were not used in a South African nuclear weapons program, Peking's reported uranium sale may have aided Pretoria circumvent the nuclear fuel embargo imposed by the United States, which was threatening to delay the start-up of the Koeberg nuclear power plants. Although South Africa was able to obtain safeguarded low-enriched uranium fuel for those plants from European sources during 1981, the material reportedly obtained from China would nevertheless be useful as a reserve against shortages that might arise at a later time before South Africa's own semi-industrial-scale enrichment plant at Valindaba was operating and able to supply the twin reactors.

14. Rob Laufer, "Interview With Malone: Defense Of Policy and Assessment of 'Hot Spots,' " *Nucleonics Week,* August 19, 1982, p. 1; Miller, "U.S. Holding Up Peking Talks;" Milton R. Benjamin, "China Aids Pakistan On A-Weapons," *Washington Post,* February 28, 1983; Leslie H. Gelb, "Pakistan Link Perils U.S.-China Nuclear Pact," *New York Times,* June 22, 1984.

15. Mike Knapik, "U.S.-China Nuclear Accord Now Faces Congres-

sional Scrutiny," *Nucleonics Week*, May 3, 1984, p. 9.

16. "U.S. and China Sign Technology Pacts," *New York Times*, January 13, 1984.

17. Ibid.

18. Some coordination of policy among the Western suppliers in initiating nuclear trade with China is said to be taking place (personal communication with knowledgeable U.S. officials; but see "No Cooperation Exists Between West Germany, Japan, and the United States On Negotiations With China," *Arms Control Reporter*, p. 602.B.43, 1984). Moreover, whatever coordination is occurring among the Western suppliers, a joint nuclear embargo has not been adopted (see note 36 and accompanying text).

19. Horne, "U.S., China Open Nuclear Talks."

20. Knapik, "U.S. China Accord Faces Scrutiny." France, West Germany, and possibly Japan have signed nuclear trade pacts with China. Some reports indicate they do not contain any safeguards provisions (*Arms Control Reporter*, pp. 602.B.40, 602.B.41, 602.B.44, 1984); but see, text accompanying note 8, above.

21. Hedrick Smith, "U.S. Assumes the Israelis Have A-Bomb Or Its Parts," *New York Times*, July 18, 1970.

22. Atomic Energy Act of 1954, Section 123 (a)(7), 42 U.S.C. 2153 (a)(7) (1978). The Non-Proliferation Act amended section 123 of the Atomic Energy Act to incorporate this requirement.

23. Don Oberdorfer, "China Pact On A-Arms Is Oral One," *Washington Post*, May 5, 1984.

24. Atomic Energy Act, Section 129, 42 U.S.C. 2158 (1978).

25. "China Becomes Newest Member of International Nuclear Agency," *Washington Post*, January 7, 1984.

26. Warren H. Donnelly and Carol A. Eberhard, Congressional Research Service, "Nuclear Energy: Congressional Consideration of the Proposed Agreement for U.S. Nuclear Cooperation with China," Issue Brief Number IB84102, updated May 9, 1984, p. 4.

27. *Facts on File*, Vol. 44, January 13, 1984, p. 23.

28. Donnelly and Eberhard, "Nuclear Energy," p. 4. Zhao's statement was reiterated during a visit by Australian prime minister Hawke to Peking in February 1984.

29. Oberdorfer, "China Pact On A-Arms."

30. Knapik, "U.S.-China Accord Faces Scrutiny;" Michael Weisskopf, "Zhao's Nonproliferation Stand Seen As Path To U.S. Aid Pact," *Washington Post*, January 13, 1984.

31. The key Supreme Court decision invalidating the congressional veto is *Immigration and Naturalization Service v. Chadha*,

103 S. Ct. 2764 (1983). The existing congressional veto mechanism is set out in Atomic Energy Act of 1954, Section 123, 42 U.S.C. 2153 (1978). Senator Proxmire's amendment, discussed below, is Section 27 of S. 979 (98th Cong. 2d sess.) (1984).

32. Knapik, "U.S.-China Accord Faces Scrutiny;" Oberdorfer, "China Pact On A-Arms."

33. Gelb, "Pakistan Link Perils U.S.-China Pact."

34. Ibid.; Leslie H. Gelb, "Peking Said To Balk At Nuclear Pledges," *New York Times*, June 23, 1984.

35. Gelb, "Peking Said To Balk."

36. "Germany Approves N-Deal With China," *Financial Times*, May 1984; MacDougall, "China Chooses Nuclear Solution;" E.J. Dionne, Jr., "China and France Near Nuclear Accord," *New York Times*, June 30, 1984; "PRC-Japanese Nuclear Power Deal," *Kyodo*, March 2, 1984, translated in Foreign Broadcast Information Service/Nuclear Development and Proliferation, March 29, 1984, p. 3.

37. "China Turns To West Germany For Cooling and Injection Pumps," *Nucleonics Week*, January 12, 1984, p. 4.

38. "Japan, China Recess Talks on N-Energy," *Washington Post*, July 29, 1984.

39. Paul Lewis, "China Bids to Store Radioactive Waste," *New York Times*, February 8, 1984.

40. Ann MacLachlan, "Chinese Offer Spent Fuel Disposal Services to European Utilities," *Nucleonics Week*, February 9, 1984, p. 1. During the above-ground storage phase, the spent fuel would be "retrievable," i.e., customers could take back the material for commercial reprocessing to extract unused uranium and plutonium for fuel should this prove economical.

41. It may be noted, however, that plutonium from nuclear power reactors, though usable for nuclear arms, is of lower quality than that used by the nuclear weapon states in manufacturing nuclear arms. For this reason, the material would presumably be less attractive to China for this purpose. On the other hand, the quantity of spent fuel obtained might be so great that its plutonium content would significantly overshadow anything producible in China through its nuclear weapons program.

42. MacLachlan, "Chinese Offer Spent Fuel Disposal."

43. Ann MacLachlan, "Austria May be China's First Spent Fuel Customer," *Nucleonics Week*, March 1, 1981, p. 9. Austria had previously held discussions with Egypt and the prerevolutionary Iranian government, along with some small island nations and some countries in South America, about the possibility of export-

ing spent fuel to those locations for permanent disposal (Ibid.). "West German Consortium and China Near Agreement on Spent Fuel," *Nucleonics Week,* May 31, 1984, p. 1.

44. MacLachlan, "Chinese Offer Spent Fuel Disposal."

45. The Carter proposal was announced in October 1977 (U.S. Department of Energy, "DOE Announces New Spent Fuel Policy," Press Release R-77-017, October 18, 1977). It called for the U.S. government to accept spent fuel from domestic utilities, and in some limited cases from foreign nations, in return for the payment of a one-time charge that would cover the costs of continued interim storage at government-owned away-from-reactor spent fuel storage facilities as well as the permanent disposal of this material once its geological repository began operation. The Department of Energy submitted legislation to authorize these activities in 1979 (Spent Nuclear Fuel Act of 1979, H.R. 2586, S.797, 96th Cong., 1st Session, 1979); concerning domestic opposition, see "Committee Tells DOE to Avoid Building AFR [away-from-reactor spent fuel storage facility] but to Prepare to React to India's Threats," *Nuclear Fuel,* July 9, 1979, p. 11; on U.S. policies during this period see Leonard S. Spector and Geoffrey B. Shields, "Nuclear Waste Disposal: An International Legal Perspective," *Northwestern Journal of International Law and Business,* Autumn 1979, p. 569.

Controls & Safeguards Section

1. "21 Members of The So-Called Zangger Committee Exchange Notes," *Nucleonics Week*, February 2, 1984; see also *Federal Register*, January 24, 1984, p. 2881.
2. Leslie H. Gelb, "Nuclear Nations Agree to Tighten Export Controls," *New York Times*, July 16, 1984; Joanne Omang, "Nuclear Suppliers Seek Tighter Export Controls," *Washington Post*, July 17, 1984.
3. "Belgians Awaiting Government Approval to Complete Pakistani Reprocessing Lab," *Nuclear Fuel*, March 16, 1984, p. 9. See Libya section.
4. Omang, "Suppliers Seek Controls;" personal communication with knowledgeable U.S. official.
5. Ibid.
6. International Financial Institutions Act, Section 701 (b)(3), 22 U.S.C. 262g (b)(3)(1977).
7. Amendment by Congressman Leon Panetta to H.R. 2957 (1983); Supplemental Appropriations Act for 1984, P.L. 98-181 (1983).
8. See China section, note 31 and accompanying text.
9. This section based on IAEA Press Release, 84/14, "Safeguards Implementation in 1984."

Appendices

It is generally accepted today that designing an atomic bomb—drawing the blueprint—is within the capabilities of most nations. Indeed, a number of American college students have come up with workable designs based on unclassified sources.

The major technical barrier to making a nuclear device is obtaining the nuclear material for its core. Twenty-five kilograms (fifty-five pounds) of highly enriched uranium, or eight kilograms (about eighteen pounds) of plutonium are generally considered the necessary minimum, although in both cases more sophisticated designs relying on high compression of the core material, neutron reflecting "tampers," or both, enable a bomb to be built with considerably less material—perhaps 15 kilograms of highly enriched uranium and 5 kilograms of plutonium, and even smaller amounts can apparently be used. Neither of these materials occurs in nature, however, and highly complex and expensive facilities must be built and operated in order to make them—an undertaking of considerable difficulty for developing nations without assistance from more advanced nuclear supplier countries.

Highly enriched uranium. To make a weapon from uranium, the unstable "isotope" of uranium having a total of 235 protons and neutrons in its nucleus (U^{235}) is used. Since natural uranium consists of less than one percent U^{235}, while nuclear weapons use material that is made up of 90 percent or more U^{235}, natural uranium must be upgraded at an enrichment plant to achieve this concentration.   Uranium enrichment is an extremely complex process and requires considerable investment. For this reason, the uranium enrichment route is generally considered a less likely path to proliferation than the plutonium option. However, South Africa, Argentina, and (with extensive outside aid obtained mostly by clandestine means) Pakistan have all developed independent uranium enrichment capabilities, and Israel, Brazil, and India are known to be conducting research in the field.

Enriched uranium can also be used as a fuel in nuclear power or research reactors. The power reactors used in the United States and most other countries (called "light water reactors") use *low-enriched uranium* fuel, i.e., uranium that has been enriched to 3 percent U^{235}. Thus a country can have entirely legitimate, non-weapons-related reasons for developing uranium enrichment technology even though the same technology can be used to upgrade uranium to the high enrichment level useful for nuclear weapons. On the other hand, developing a sizable independent uranium enrichment capability is economically justifiable only for nations with large domestic nuclear power programs or significant potential export markets.

Because highly enriched uranium is sometimes used to fuel research reactors, a nation can have legitimate reasons for obtaining small quantities of this material, despite its usefulness in nuclear explosives. In recent years the United States and France have developed lower-enriched uranium fuels that can be used in lieu of highly enriched material in most of these reactors, however, considerably reducing the proliferation risks they pose.

Producing highly enriched uranium entails many steps apart from the enrichment process itself, and many other installations and capabilities are necessary. For nations wishing to obtain highly enriched uranium without international restrictions prohibiting its use for nuclear explosives, all of these would have to be developed independently, or obtained illegally, since virtually all nuclear exporter states are unwilling to sell nuclear equipment and materials unless recipients pledge not to use them for nuclear explosives purposes and place them under the inspection system of the International Atomic Energy Agency. (See Appendix C). For illustrative purposes the basic nuclear resources and facilities that would be needed include

- uranium deposits;
- a uranium mine;
- a uranium mill (for processing uranium ore containing less than 1 percent uranium into uranium oxide concentrate, or yellowcake);
- a conversion plant (for purifying yellowcake and converting it into uranium hexafluoride gas, the material processed in the enrichment plant);
- an enrichment plant (for enriching the uranium hexafluoride gas in the isotope U^{235}); and

- a capability for converting the enriched uranium hexafluoride gas into solid uranium oxide or metal (usually associated with a yellowcake-to-hexafluoride conversion plant).

Plutonium. To obtain plutonium a country needs a *nuclear reactor.* This can be one designed specifically to maximize plutonium production (a "production reactor"), a large research reactor, or a power reactor for producing electricity. *Uranium fuel,* usually in the form of uranium-filled tubes (fuel rods) made of zirconium alloy (zircaloy), is placed in the reactor. For most production, power, and for a number of large research reactors, the fuel itself is either natural or low-enriched uranium, which is not usable for nuclear weapons at this point. As the reactor operates, the uranium fuel is partly transformed into plutonium. This is amalgamated in the fuel rods with unused uranium and highly radioactive waste products, however, and must then be extracted. To do this, "spent" fuel rods are taken to a *reprocessing plant* where they are dissolved in nitric acid and the plutonium is separated from the solution in a series of chemical processing steps. Since the spent fuel rods are highly radioactive, heavy lead casks must be used to transport them, and the rooms at the reprocessing plant where the chemical extraction of the plutonium occurs must have thick walls, lead shielding, and special ventilation to prevent radiation hazards.

Although detailed information about reprocessing was declassified by the United States and France in the 1950s and is generally available, it is still a complex procedure from an engineering point of view, and virtually every nation at the nuclear-weapons threshold that has attempted it, has sought outside help from the advanced nuclear supplier countries.

Like enrichment facilities, however, reprocessing plants can also be used for legitimate civilian purposes, because plutonium can be used as fuel in nuclear power reactors. Indeed, through the 1970s it was generally assumed that as the use of nuclear power grew, worldwide uranium resources would be depleted and plutonium extracted from spent fuel would have to be "recycled" as a substitute fuel in conventional power reactors.

In addition, research and development is underway in many advanced nations on a new generation of reactors known as breeder reactors. These use plutonium as fuel surrounded with a "blanket" of natural uranium; as the reactor operates, slightly more plutonium is created in the blanket than is consumed in the core, thereby "breeding" new fuel.

Like plutonium recycle, the economic advantages of breeders depend on natural uranium becoming scarce and expensive. But over the past decade new uranium reserves have been discovered, nuclear power has reached only a fraction of its expected growth levels, and reprocessing spent fuel to extract plutonium (a critical step in both cases) has proven far more expensive and complex than anticipated. Moreover, concern over the proliferation risks of widescale use of plutonium as a fuel has grown. These factors have led one advanced nation, the United States, to abandon its plans to use plutonium fuel, although Japan, France, Britain, and West Germany are continuing to develop this technology actively. Nevertheless, the advanced nuclear-supplier countries are strongly discouraging plutonuim use in nations of proliferation concern.

The long-standing view that plutonium is a legitimate and anticipated part of civilian nuclear programs, however, has allowed India, Pakistan, Argentina, and Brazil, to justify their reprocessing programs—even though they currently provide these nations with a nuclear-weapons capability, or may soon do so.

Like the production of enriched uranium, the production of plutonium entails many steps and many installations and capabilities apart from the reactor and reprocessing plant are needed. For illustrative purposes, the following facilities and resources would be required for an independent plutonium production capability assuming a heavy-water research or power reactor is used:

- uranium deposits;
- a uranium mine;
- a uranium mill (for processing uranium ore containing less than one percent uranium into uranium oxide concentrate, or yellowcake);
- a uranium purification plant (to further improve the yellowcake into reactor grade uranium dioxide);
- a fuel fabrication plant (to manufacture the fuel elements placed in the reactor), including a capability to fabricate zircaloy tubing;
- a heavy-water research or power reactor;
- a heavy water production plant; and
- a reprocessing plant.

If the option of building a natural-uranium/graphite reactor is used, the needs would be the same although reactor-grade graphite would have to be produced instead of heavy water. A light water reactor would necessitate use of low-enriched uranium, implying an enrichment capability was available; if so, highly enriched uranium could be produced, obviating the need for plutonium as a weapons material.

Appendix B: Typical Nuclear Material Requirements and Production Rates

Nuclear Weapons—Amounts of highly enriched uranium or plutonium needed for core of multi-kiloton atomic bomb.

Plutonium
5 to 8 kilograms (11 to 17.6 pounds)

Highly Enriched Uranium
15 to 25 kilograms (33 to 55 pounds)

(Note: Rough estimates; no allowance made for losses in fabrication. Smaller quantities can apparently be used if more sophisticated designs are employed. Eight kilograms of plutonium and 25 kilograms of highly enriched uranium are used by the IAEA as the minimum amounts of material necessary for nuclear weapons. The smaller figures, however, appear to be conservative, widely accepted benchmarks. See Thomas B. Cochran, et al., *U.S. Nuclear Forces and Capabilities,* (Cambridge, MA: Ballinger, 1984, pp. 24-25); U.S. Congress, Office of Technology Assessment, *Nuclear Proliferation and Safeguards* (Washington, D.C.: Office of Technology Assessment, 1977), pp. 154-158; John Kerry King, ed., *International Political Effects of the Spread of Nuclear Weapons* (Washington, D.C.: U.S. Central Intelligence Agency, 1979), p. 7.

Nuclear Power Plants

1,000 MW low-enriched-uranium/light-water reactor (PWR type)[a]

Fueled by uranium enriched to about 3%, requires:

	Start-up	Annual	30-year life
U_3O_8[b]	324 tons	140 tons	4,350 tons (approx.)
SWUs[c]	227,000	110,000	3,500,000 (approx.)

Produces about 168 kg fissile plutonium per year

1,000 MW natural uranium/heavy-water[5] (CANDU) reactor [a]

Fueled by natural uranium moderated by heavy water (D_2O), requires:

	Start-up	Annual[d]	30-year life
U_3O_8[b]	130 tons	120 tons	3,600 tons
D_2O	800 tons	10-20 tons	1,200 tons

Produces about 300 kg fissile plutonium per year

a. Data on U_3O_8 and SWUs derived from International Nuclear Fuel Cycle Evaluation, Report of Working Group 8 (1980); data on D_2O from Non-Proliferation Alternative Systems Assessment Program, Vol. 3 (Department of Energy, 1980).
b. Uranium oxide. Yellowcake (uranium concentrate) is about 80% U_3O_8. Uranium ore when mined typically contains about .1% U_3O_8, though both lower and higher concentrations occur.
c. Separative work units (a measure of enrichment effort), in kilograms. South Africa's semi-commercial enrichment plant at Valindaba, for example, is expected have a capacity of about 300,000 SWU's, enough for annual reloads for the two 922-megawatt Koeberg reactors.
d. CANDU reactors are continuously refueled, but this is the approximate aggregate of fresh fuel required per year.

Appendix C: International Atomic Energy Agency Safeguards

The International Atomic Energy Agency, a Vienna-based U.N.-affiliated organization now having over 110 members, was founded in 1957. By the mid-1960s, it had established a program of on-site inspections, audits, and inventory controls know collectively as "safeguards." Today, the IAEA monitors some seven hundred installations in over fifty nations and is widely regarded as a principal bulwark against the spread of nuclear arms.

The basic purpose of IAEA safeguards is to deter the diversion of nuclear materials from peaceful uses to military purposes through the risk of timely detection. In simplified terms, the Agency monitors the flow of nuclear materials at nuclear installations by auditing plant records and conducting physical inventories. Seals and cameras are used to ensure materials are not diverted while IAEA inspectors are not present.

To date, the IAEA has never concluded that material under safeguards has been diverted. In September 1981, however, the Agency stated that it was unable to determine whether material being diverted from Pakistan's KANUPP reactor or from a similarly designed reactor in India because the Agency had not been permitted to apply all of the monitoring apparatus needed at these installations. The Indian deficiency was quickly corrected, but it was nearly a year and a half before the safeguards at the KANUPP reactor were declared adequate. It is possible that during this period plutonium-bearing spent fuel was removed from the reactor without detection.

Apart from these unusual cases, the IAEA safeguards system has some well-recognized limitations.

First, and most important, key installations in countries of proliferation concern including enrichment and reprocessing facilities, are not under the IAEA system. Thus, Argentina, Brazil, India, Israel, Pakistan, and South Africa all remain free to use unsafeguarded installations to manufacture material for nuclear weapons. (Even in all these countries, however, some installations are subject to the IAEA system, and nuclear materials produced in them cannot, therefore, be used for this purpose.) Nations that have ratified the Non-Proliferation Treaty or for which the Treaty of Tlatelolco is in force have accepted safeguards on all their nuclear facilities.

Secondly, certain types of facilities, such as fuel fabrication, reprocessing, and enrichment installations, handle nuclear materials in bulk form, i.e. as powders, liquids, or gasses. Such materials are particularly difficult to safeguard since measurement techniques are not accurate enough to keep track of 100 percent of these substances as they move through the facilities processing them. This makes it theoretically possible to divert a certain small percentage of material for military purposes without detection since this could appear to be a normal operating discrepancy. The problem is especially dangerous at fuel fabrication plants handling plutonium or highly enriched uranium in powdered form, at reprocessing plants where plutonium is dissolved in various liquids for processing, and at enrichment plants, which use uranium hexafluoride gas as feed.

Low IAEA budgets and manpower have also meant that far fewer inspections are conducted at safeguarded installations than needed to meet the IAEA's safeguards objectives fully. Other problems include the fact that it is virtually impossible for Agency inspectors to make unannounced visits to safeguarded installations. Nations subject to IAEA safeguards are also permitted to reject particular IAEA inspectors.

It must be stressed, however, that even if safeguards as applied are imperfect, their deterrent value remains strong since would-be diverters could not have confidence that their misuse of nuclear materials would go undetected.

Finally, even assuming that IAEA safeguards functioned perfectly, their usefulness may be limited when applied to highly enriched uranium and plutonium, materials directly usable for nuclear weapons. Here, even if the IAEA system reacted instantaneously to diversion, it might still be possible for the nation appropriating this material to manufacture nuclear weapons within a matter of weeks if all the non-nuclear components had been prepared in advance, presenting the world community with a *fait accompli*. In such a setting, safeguards cannot provide "timely warning" sufficient to allow the international community to react before the nation diverting the material had achieved its objective. For this reason, the United States has worked actively to curtail commerce with nations of proliferation concern involving plutonium, highly enriched uranium, or enrichment and reprocessing facilities—whether or not safeguards would be applied. With the apparent exception of China, virtually all other nuclear supplier nations have adopted the cautious approach of the United States in transferring such items.

In the event of a safeguards violation, the Agency's Board of Governors has the authority to notify the United Nations Security Council, but not to impose sanctions of any kind.

Appendix D: The Treaty on the Non-Proliferation of Nuclear Weapons (NPT)

The treaty divides the countries of the world into two categories, "nuclear-weapon states" (those which had detonated a nuclear weapon before 1967, i.e., the United States, the Soviet Union, Great Britain, France, and China) and "non-nuclear-weapon states" (those which had not). Under this pact:

- Non-nuclear-weapon states ratifying the treaty pledge not to manufacture or receive nuclear explosives. (Both nuclear weapons and peaceful nuclear explosives are prohibited.)

- To verify that they are living up to this pledge, non-nuclear-weapon states also agree to accept International Atomic Energy Agency safeguards on all their peaceful nuclear activities (an arrangement known as "full-scope" safeguards).

- All countries accepting the treaty agree not to export nuclear equipment or material to non-nuclear-weapon states except under IAEA safeguards and nuclear weapon states agree not to assist non-nuclear weapon states in obtaining nuclear arms.

- All countries accepting the treaty agree to facilitate the fullest possible sharing of peaceful nuclear technology. (In practice this is a pledge by the advanced nations to help less developed countries build peaceful nuclear programs).

- All countries accepting the treaty agree to pursue negotiations in good faith to end the nuclear arms race, and achieve nuclear disarmament under international control. (In practice, this applies to the United States and the Soviet Union.)

- A party to the treaty may withdraw on 90-days notice if "extraordinary events" related to the subject matter of the treaty have "jeopardized" its "supreme interests."

In effect, the treaty is an agreement among countries with differing interests. The less developed countries, for example, give up their right to develop nuclear arms and accept full-scope safeguards. In return, the advanced countries agree to share peaceful nuclear technology, and those with nuclear arsenals agree to pursue arms control negotiations.

The treaty does *not* prohibit parties from accumulating nuclear weapons material (highly enriched uranium or plutonium) as part of their peaceful nuclear energy or research programs as long as the material is subject to IAEA inspection. This means parties to the pact can come dangerously close to possessing nuclear arms without violating the terms of the treaty.

The treaty has also been interpreted to permit parties to make nuclear sales to countries that are not parties, such as India or Argentina, even if these countries have unsafeguarded nuclear facilities. However, the items exported (and nuclear materials produced through their use), must themselves be placed under IAEA safeguards. Thus, for example, U.S. sales of nuclear fuel to South Africa, which has at least one unsafeguarded nuclear installation, are permissible under the treaty as long as the fuel were placed under safeguards in South Africa. (However, U.S. law, the 1978 Nuclear Non-Proliferation Act, prohibited sales to countries with unsafeguarded facilities after March 1980, absent a special presidential waiver. Canada, Sweden, and Australia have also adopted this policy.)

Negotiations devoted specifically to the Non-Proliferation Treaty began in earnest in 1965, when the United States, and later the Soviet Union, submitted draft treaties to the Eighteen-Nation Disarmament Committee. After overcoming a number of potential stumbling-blocks—including disagreement over the form and extent of the proposed safeguards and demands for security assurances by the non-nuclear-weapon states—the treaty was opened for signature on July 1, 1968, and signed on that date by the United States, the United Kingdom, and the Soviet Union, along with fifty-nine non-nuclear-weapon states. The U.S. Senate ratified the treaty in 1970. A total of 121 non-weapon states have ratified the treaty, along with the three nuclear-weapon states, mentioned earlier.

France, though not a party, has pledged to behave as though it were. However, China, also not a party, is believed to have taken actions that would be prohibited by the treaty. In the late 1970s and early 1980s, it sold nuclear materials to Argentina and reportedly to India, Pakistan, and South Africa without requiring the application of IAEA safeguards, and it may have directly assisted Pakistan in designing nuclear weapons. In 1983, however, China advised the United States that it would require safeguards on all its future nuclear exports.

Six non-nuclear-weapon states of proliferation concern—Argentina, Brazil, India, Israel, Pakistan, and South Africa—have not ratified the treaty. All have unsafeguarded nuclear activities. Libya and Iraq, two additional potential nuclear weapon states, are parties to the accord.

Two review conferences on the implementation of the treaty have been held since it was signed, one in 1975 and one in 1980; another is scheduled for 1985.*

---

* See, generally *Arms Control and Disarmament Agreements, Text and Histories of Negotiations,* United States Arms Control and Disarmament Agency, 1982 edition, pp. 82-95.

A. Parties to the Non-Proliferation Treaty

Afghanistan	1970	Indonesia	1979
Antigua and Barbuda	1981	Iran	1970
Australia	1973	Iraq	1969
Austria	1969	Ireland	1968
Bahamas, The	1976	Italy	1975
Bangladesh	1979	Ivory Coast	1973
Barbados	1980	Jamaica	1970
Belgium	1975	Japan	1976
Benin	1972	Jordan	1970
Bolivia	1970	Kampuchea	1972
Botswana	1969	Kenya	1970
Bulgaria	1969	Korea (South)	1975
Burundi	1971	Laos	1970
Cameroon	1969	Lebanon	1970
Canada	1969	Lesotho	1970
Cape Verde	1979	Liberia	1970
Central African Rep.	1970	Libya	1975
Chad	1971	Liechtenstein	1978
Congo	1978	Luxembourg	1975
Costa Rica	1970	Madagascar	1970
Cyprus	1970	Malaysia	1970
Czechoslovakia	1969	Maldives	1980
Denmark	1969	Mali	1971
Dominica	1968	Malta	1970
Dominican Republic	1971	Mauritius	1969
Ecuador	1969	Mexico	1969
Egypt	1981	Mongolia	1969
El Salvador	1972	Morocco	1970
Ethiopia	1970	Nauru	1982
Fiji	1972	Nepal	1970
Finland	1969	Netherlands	1975
Gabon	1974	New Zealand	1969
Gambia, The	1975	Nicaragua	1973
Germany (East)	1969	Nigeria	1968
Germany (West)	1975	Norway	1969
Ghana	1970	Panama	1977
Greece	1970	Papua New Guinea	1982
Grenada	1975	Paraguay	1970
Guatemala	1970	Peru	1970
Guinea-Bissau	1976	Philippines	1972
Haiti	1970	Poland	1969
Holy See	1971	Portugal	1977

Honduras	1973	Romania	1970
Hungary	1969	Rwanda	1975
Iceland	1968	St. Kitts & Nevis	1983
St. Lucia	1979	Togo	1970
San Marino	1970	Tonga	1971
Sao Tome & Principe	1983	Tunisia	1970
Senegal	1970	Turkey	1980
Sierra Leone	1975	Tuvalu	1979
Singapore	1976	Uganda	1982
Solomon Islands	1981	USSR*	1970
Somalia	1970	United Kingdom*	1968
Sri Lanka	1979	United States*	1970
Sudan	1973	Upper Volta	1970
Suriname	1976	Uruguay	1970
Swaziland	1969	Venezuela	1975
Sweden	1970	Vietnam	1982
Switzerland	1977	Western Samoa	1975
Syria	1969	Yemen, (Aden)	1979
Taiwan	1970	Yugoslavia	1970
Thailand	1972	Zaire	1970

B. Countries that have signed but not ratified the Treaty

Colombia   Trinidad & Tobago
Kuwait   Yemen (Sana)

C. Countries that have neither signed nor ratified the Treaty

Albania, Algeria, Angola, Argentina, Bahrain, Belize, Brazil, Burma, Chile, Comoros, China*, Cuba, Djibouti, Equatorial Guinea, France*, Guinea, Guyana, India**, Israel, Kiribati, Korea (North), Malawi, Mauritania, Monaco, Mozambique, Niger, Oman, Pakistan, Portugal, Qatar, St. Vincent & Grenadine, Saudi Arabia, Seychelles, South Africa, Spain, Tanzania, United Arab Emirates, Vanuatu, Zambia, Zimbabwe

* Nuclear weapon state
** India has detonated a "peaceful nuclear device."

Appendix E: The Treaty of Tlatelolco

The international non-proliferation regime is strengthened in Latin America by the Treaty on the Prohibition of Nuclear Weapons in Latin America (the Treaty of Tlatelolco), which establishes a nuclear weapons free zone in the region. Parties to the treaty agree not to manufacture, test, or acquire nuclear weapons or to accept weapons on their territory deployed by others. To verify that these pledges are kept, adherents agree to accept "full-scope" International Atomic Energy Agency (IAEA) safeguards (i.e., IAEA accounting and inspection measures on all of a nation's nuclear activities). In addition, the treaty establishes the Agency for the Prohibition of Nuclear Weapons in Latin America (OPANAL). OPANAL will undertake special inspections at the request of members who have reason to believe that another party is engaging in prohibited activity, a unique investigatory function not available under the IAEA system.

Under its entry-into-force provisions, the treaty becomes effective once it has been ratified by all eligible countries in the region. However, twenty-two nations have ratified the accord and waived this provision so that the treaty has become effective for these countries. Only four countries have yet to make the treaty operative. Part way there, but avoiding the full-scope safeguards requirements entirely are Brazil and Chile, which have ratified the pact, but not waived the entry-into-force requirement. Further away are Argentina, which has signed but not ratified, and Cuba, which has neither signed nor ratified the accord. Because Cuba has made approval of the treaty contingent upon U.S. withdrawal from the Guantanamo naval base, progress toward full effectiveness has been stymied.

The treaty is supplemented by two Protocols that

apply to countries outside the region. Protocol I requires that outside nations with territories in Latin America respect the treaty's denuclearization requirements with respect to those territories. Protocol II prohibits nuclear weapon states from using or threatening to use nuclear arms against treaty parties. All nations with territories in the region, the U.S., U.K., France, and the Netherlands have signed Protocol I, and all but France have ratified it. All nuclear weapon states have ratified Protocol II.

One highly controversial issue arises from the treaty's definition in Article 5 of a nuclear weapon as a nuclear explosive "which has a group of characteristics that are appropriate for use for warlike purposes." When the United States and the Soviet Union ratified Protocol II, they formally stated that in their view this phrase meant that the treaty's prohibitions applied to *all* nuclear explosives, including so-called "peaceful nuclear explosives" since there was no technological difference between them and nuclear weapons. Argentina and Brazil have objected to this interpretation and cited Article 18 of the treaty which states that parties "may carry out explosions for peaceful purposes—including explosions which involve devices similar to those used in nuclear weapons"—under IAEA supervision. Virtually all other treaty parties, however, have accepted the U.S.-Soviet view since they are also parties to the Non-Proliferation Treaty which expressly prohibits the manufacture of any nuclear explosive.

Treaty for the Prohibition of Nuclear Weapons in Latin America

Country	Year of Signature	Year of Ratification
Argentina	1967	—
Antigua and Barbuda	1983	1983
Bahamas, The	1967	1976
Barbados	1968	1969
Bolivia	1967	1969
Brazil	1967	1968*
Chile	1967	1974*
Colombia	1967	1972
Costa Rica	1967	1969
Dominican Republic	1967	1968
Ecuador	1967	1969
El Salvador	1967	1968
Grenada	1975	1975
Guatemala	1967	1970
Haiti	1967	1969
Honduras	1967	1968
Jamaica	1967	1969
Mexico	1967	1967
Nicaragua	1967	1968
Panama	1967	1971
Paraguay	1967	1969
Peru	1967	1969
Suriname	1976	1977
Trinidad and Tobago	1967	1975
Uruguay	1967	1968
Venezuela	1967	1970

Protocol I to the Treaty

Country	Year of Signature	Year of Ratification
France	1979	—
Netherlands	1968	1971
United Kingdom	1967	1969
United States	1977	1981

Protocol II to the Treaty

Country	Year of Signature	Year of Ratification
China (PRC)	1973	1974
France	1973	1974
U.S.S.R.	1978	1979
United Kingdom	1967	1969
United States	1968	1971

* Not in force because entry-into-force provision not waived.

(Source: U.S. Arms Control and Disarmament Agency) *Control and Disarmament Agreements: Texts and Histories of Negotiations* (Washington, D.C.: U.S. Arms Control and Disarmament Agency, 1982), and U.S. Department of State.

Appendix F: Nuclear Suppliers Organizations

Non-Proliferation Treaty Exporters Committee (Zangger Committee)

Shortly after the Non-Proliferation Treaty came into force in 1970, a number of countries entered into consultations concerning the procedures and standards they would apply to nuclear fuel and equipment exports to non-nuclear-weapon states in order to implement the requirement in the pact that such exports and any enriched uranium or plutonium produced through their use be subject to IAEA safeguards. The countries engaged in those consultations, which were chaired by the Swiss expert, Claude Zangger, were parties to the Non-Proliferation Treaty (or have since become parties) and were also exporters or potential exporters of material and equipment for peaceful uses of nuclear energy.

In August 1974, the governments of Australia, Denmark, Canada, Finland, West Germany, the Netherlands, Norway, the Soviet Union, the United Kingdom, and the United States each informed the Director General of the IAEA, by individual letters, of their intentions to require IAEA safeguards on their nuclear exports in accordance with certain procedures described in memoranda enclosed with their letters. Those memoranda were identical in the case of each letter and included a "Trigger List" of materials and items of equipment which would be exported only under such safeguards. (The individual letters and the identical memoranda were published by the IAEA in September 1974 in document INFCIRC/209).

Subsequently, Austria, Czechoslovakia, East Germany, Ireland, Japan, Luxembourg, Poland and Sweden sent individual letters to the Director General, referring to and enclosing memoranda identical to those transmitted by the initial groups of governments.

The agreed procedures and Trigger List represented the first major agreement on uniform regulation of nuclear exports by actual and potential nuclear suppliers. It had great significance for several reasons. It was an attempt to strictly and uniformly enforce the obligations of Article III, paragraph 2, of the Non-Proliferation Treaty requiring safeguards on nuclear exports. It was intended to reduce the likelihood that states would be tempted to cut corners on safeguard requirements, because of competition in the sale of nuclear equipment and fuel-cycle services. In addition, and very important in the light of subsequent events, it established the principle that nuclear supplier nations should consult and agree among themselves on procedures to regulate the international market for nuclear materials and equipment in the interest of non-proliferation. Notably absent from the list of actual participants or potential suppliers, as from the list of parties to the Non-Proliferation Treaty, were France, India, and the People's Republic of China.

Nuclear Suppliers Group

In November 1974, within months of the delivery of these memoranda a second series of supplier negotiations were underway. This round, convened largely at the initiative of the United States, was a response to three developments 1) the Indian nuclear test of May 1974, 2) mounting evidence that the pricing actions of the Organization of Oil Exporting Countries were stimulating Third World and other non-nuclear states to initiate or accelerate their nuclear power programs, and 3) recent contracts or continuing negotiations on the part of France and West Germany for the supply of enrichment or reprocessing facilities to Third World states.

The initial participants in these discussions, conducted in London were Canada, the Federal Republic of Germany, France, Japan, the Soviet Union, the United Kingdom, and the United States. One of the Group's chief accomplishments was to induce France to join in such efforts, since France (which had not joined the Non-Proliferation Treaty or the Zangger Committee) could have undercut reforms of nuclear supply. The French, hesitant about becoming involved and uncertain as to where the effort might lead, insisted that any meetings be kept confidential—which was also the preference of some other participants. So the meetings in London were held in secret. But it soon became known that such meetings were taking place, and this led to suspicion and exaggerated fears of what they were about. The group was inaccurately referred to as a "cartel." Instead, one of its purposes was to foster genuine commercial competition based on quality and prices, untainted by bargaining away proliferation controls.

Two major issues were discussed in the series of meetings which led to a new agreement in late 1975. The first was if, and under what conditions, technology and equipment for enrichment and reprocessing, the most sensitive parts of the nuclear fuel cycle from a weapons proliferation perspective, should be transferred to non-nuclear states. The United States, with support from several other participants, was reported to argue in favor of both a prohibition on such transfer and a commitment to reprocessing in multinational facilities. France had already signed contracts to sell reprocessing plants to Pakistan and South Korea, and West Germany had agreed to sell technology and facilities for the full fuel cycle (including enrichment and reprocessing) to Brazil. They successfully resisted the prohibition proposed by others.

The second issue was whether transfers should be made to states unwilling to submit all nonmilitary nuclear facilities to IAEA safeguards, or whether total industry ("full-scope") safeguards should become a condition of sales. The Nuclear Suppliers Group came close to reaching consensus on requiring full-scope safeguards in recipient countries as a condition of future supply commitments, but was unable to persuade the French and the West Germans, though they did not rule out later reconsideration and possible changes by unanimous consent. The group did act to expand safeguards coverage by adopting a "Trigger List" of exports, similar to that of the Zangger Committee, that would be made only if covered by IAEA safeguards in the recipient state.

On January 27, 1976, the seven participants in the negotiations exchanged letters endorsing a uniform code for conducting international nuclear sales. The major provisions of the agreement require that before nuclear materials, equipment, or technology are transferred the recipient state must:

1. pledge not to use the transferred materials, equipment, or technology in the manufacture of nuclear explosives of any kind;

2. accept, with no provision for termination, international safeguards on all transferred materials and facilities employing transferred equipment or technology, including any enrichment, reprocessing, or heavy water production facility that replicates or otherwise employs transferred technology;

3. provide adequate physical security for transferred nuclear facilities and materials to prevent theft and sabotage; and

4. agree not to retransfer the materials, equipment, or technology to third countries unless they too accept the constraints on use, replication, security, and transfer, and unless the original supplier nation concurs in the transactions.

5. The participants also agreed to: employ "restraint" regarding the possible export of "sensitive" items (relating to uranium enrichment, spent fuel reprocessing, and heavy water production); and

6. encourage the concept of multilateral regional facilities for reprocessing and enrichment.

The guidelines have now been adopted by the United States, Great Britain, France, West Germany, Japan, Canada, the Soviet Union, Belgium, Italy, the Netherlands, Sweden, Switzerland, Czechoslovakia, East Germany, Poland, Australia, and Finland.

The Nuclear Supplier's Guidelines extended the Zangger Committee's requirements in several respects. First, France (which had not participated in the Zangger group) agreed to key points adopted by that Committee, such as the requirement that nuclear export recipients pledge not to use transferred items for nuclear explosives of any kind and that safeguards on transferred items would continue indefinitely. Secondly, the Suppliers Group went beyond the Non-Proliferation Treaty and the Zangger Committee requirements, by imposing safeguards not only on the export of nuclear materials and equipment, but also on nuclear technology exports. India had demonstrated the existence of this serious loophole by building its own unsafeguarded replica of a safeguarded power reactor imported from Canada. The Suppliers Group was unable to reach agreement on the application of this reform to reactor technology, however, and so confined its recommended application to "sensitive" facilities—i.e., reprocessing, enrichment, and heavy water production plants built with the use of exported technology. The Group's acceptance of this limited reform was facilitated by the fact that such a condition was incorporated by West Germany in its safeguards agreements for sale of enrichment and reprocessing facilities to Brazil, and the French in their safeguards agreements covering their proposed sale of reprocessing plants to the Republic of Korea and Pakistan.

Third, the Suppliers' Guidelines, while not prohibiting the export of these sensitive facilities do embody the participants' agreement to "exercise restraint" in transferring them, and where enrichment plants are involved, to seek recipient country commitments that such facilities will be designed and operated to produce only low-enriched uranium not suitable for weapons.

Several supplier countries subsequently announced policies stricter that those in the Guidelines. France, the West Germany, and the United States all made separate public announcements that they did not, at least for the time being, contemplate any further new commitments to export reprocessing technology. In addition, the United States, Canada, Australia, and Sweden have all made recipient country acceptance of full-scope safeguards a condition for nuclear transfer.

* * *

Excerpted and adapted from, Charles N. Van Doren, "Nuclear Supply and Non-Proliferation: The IAEA Committee on Assurances of Supply," A Report for the Congressional Research Service (Rep. No. 83-202-8) October 1983, pp. 61-64; U.S. Congress, Office of

Technology Assessment, *Nuclear Proliferation and Safeguards*, (Washington, D.C.: OTA, 1977) pp. 220-221; U.S Department of State, "Report to the Congress Pursuant to Section 601 of the Nuclear Non-Proliferation Act of 1978" (January 1979), pp. 25-27.

Appendix G: The September 22, 1979 "Flash" in the South Atlantic Observed by U.S. Satellite

(Excerpt from *South Africa's Plan and Capability in the Nuclear Field,* Report of the Secretary General, United Nations, General Assembly, A/35/402, September 9, 1980, pp. 33-35.)

Following a disclosure on ABC-TV—a private American television network—the United States Department of State issued on 25 October 1979 the following statement:

"The United States Government has an indication suggesting the possibility that a low yield nuclear explosion occurred on September 22 in the area of the Indian Ocean and South Atlantic including portions of the Antarctic continent and the southern part of Africa. No corroborating evidence has been received to date. We are continuing to assess whether such an event took place." *(The Department of State Bulletin,* 25 October 1979.)

Nearly one year later, what actually occurred on 22 September has yet to be conclusively established. The indication of a possible nuclear explosion was provided by two "bhangmeters" on a United States VELA satellite placed in orbit in 1970 to monitor compliance with the 1963 partial nuclear-test-ban. At 3 a.m. (local time) on 22 September 1979, these sensors observed a flash of light consistent with that caused by a nuclear explosion on or near the earth's surface. The VELA's sensors at that instant had been watching an area about 3,000 miles in diameter, encompassing, as the preceding statement notes, southern Africa, the Indian Ocean, the South Atlantic, and some of Antarctica. (Eliot Marshall, "Flash Not

Missed by VELA Still Veiled in Mist," *Science*, vol. 206, 30 November 1979, p. 1051; "U.S. Officials Uncertain about that Event near South Africa," *Washington Post*, 27 October 1979.) Consequently, the initial presumption of many United States officials and scientists was that a nuclear explosive device with a yield of about two to four kilotons had been detonated by South Africa in the Southern Hemisphere. ("U.S. Monitors Signs of Atomic Explosion near South Africa," *New York Times*, 26 October 1979.)

In late 1979 an *ad hoc* panel of non-government scientists was convened by Dr. Frank Press, Science Adviser to President Carter, to assist in determining the likelihood that the light signal was from a nuclear explosion. Based on thorough study, the report of this *ad hoc* panel (A/35/358, appendix) concluded:

"1. The light signal from the September 22 event strongly resembles those previously observed from nuclear explosions, but it was different from the others in a very significant way. The discrepancy suggests that the origin of the signal was close to the satellite rather than near the surface of the earth. In order to account for the September 22 VELA signal as coming from a nuclear explosion, one must hypothesize particularly anomalous functioning of the instruments (bhangmeters) that observed the event.

"2. The bhangmeters on the VELA satellites have been triggered by and have recorded many previous nuclear explosions. They have also recorded hundreds of thousands of other signals, mostly from lightning and cosmic ray particles striking the light sensors. In addition they have been triggered several hundred times by signals of unknown origin, 'zoo events.' A few of these zoo events had some of the characteristics associated with signals from nuclear explosions, although they could be distinguished clearly from nuclear explosion signals upon examination of their complete time histories.

"3. The search for nuclear debris and for geophysical evidence that might support the hypothesis that a nuclear explosion was the source of the September 22 event has so far only produced data that is ambiguous and 'noisy.' At this date, there is no persuasive evidence to corroborate the occurrence of a nuclear explosion on September 22.

"4. Based on the lack of persuasive corroborative evidence, the existence of other unexplained zoo events which have some of the characteristics of signals from nuclear explosions, and the discrepancies observed in the September 22 signal, the panel concludes that the signal was probably not from a nuclear explosion. Although we cannot rule out the possibility that this signal was of nuclear origin, the panel considers it more likely that the signal was one of the zoo events, possibly a consequence of the impact of a small meteoroid on the satellite."

In reaching its conclusion that there is no persuasive corroborative evidence of a nuclear explosion, the *ad hoc* panel took into account, for example, the fact that other United States monitoring systems for detecting the seismic, airborne or waterborne acoustic signals linked with the shock wave of a nuclear explosive either were negative or recorded very weak signals which could not be clearly ascribed to the 22 September event. It also noted that an initial report (A/34/674/Add.1) in mid-November from the Institute of Nuclear Science at Wellington, New Zealand that it had found traces of fall-out in rainwater was not borne out of additional examination, while other attempts to find nuclear debris proved unavailing. Also evaluated as possible corroborative evidence was the occurrence of a traveling ionospheric disturbance, observed by the Arecibo radar in Puerto Rico, moving from south-east to north-west during the early morning of 22 September. But, on the grounds that up until the sighting of this disturbance, there had been only limited observation on which to base an estimate of the frequency of natural occurrence of such a disturbance, the presence of a tropical storm near Arecibo which could have generated an ionospheric disturbance, and uncertainty about the velocity—and thus the origin—of the signal, the *ad hoc* panel rejected this disturbance as evidence.

Similarly, the requests of the Secretary-General and the Special Committee Against Apartheid immediately following the announcement of the 22 September event that Member States provide any information that they might have about that event also failed to turn up corroborative evidence . . . .

Nevertheless, some questions still remain, particularly since the details regarding the recorded signals and the monitoring equipment, American or other, have not been fully disclosed. According to some experts with experience in nuclear-weapon testing, there are conditions under which a very low yield nuclear explosion could result in no observable radio-active fall-out after 24 hours. If such a device were detonated at a low altitude, for example, its fall-out might not be carried into the higher atmosphere and could quickly come down to earth with local winds and rains. ("Officials Hotly Debate Whether African Event Was Atom Blast," *Washington Post,* 17 January 1980.) In fact, it has been reported that instances of nuclear explosions without confirmation by nuclear debris detectors have occurred; these explosions were confirmed by other, not necessarily geophysical, means. (Marshall, "Flash Not Missed by VELA Still Veiled in Mist," p. 1051.)

Moreover, other more speculative information, such as reports of a South African naval task force in the region, have yet to be discredited ("South African Ships in Zone of Suspected N-Blast," *The Guardian*, 31 January 1980), and, as the *ad hoc* panel report notes, the explanation provided in the report of the 22 September event itself is not fully credible. Further, the *ad hoc* panel report does not discuss the possiblity that the lack of persuasive corroborative evidence may reflect not that no explosion occurred but that some country tested a nuclear device but went to great pains to cover its tracks.

Finally, there is so far no undisputed scientific explanation of the light signal recorded by the VELA satellite on 22 September 1979. The initial presumption that there had been a nuclear explosion by South Africa or any other country in the South Atlantic area has not been substantiated; nor has it been fully disproved.

Glossary

atomic bomb A bomb whose energy comes from the fission of uranium or plutonium.

blanket A layer of fertile material, such as uranium-238 or thorium-232, placed around the core of a reactor. During operation of the reactor, additional fissile material is produced in the blanket.

breeder reactor A nuclear reactor that produces somewhat more fissile material than it consumes. The fissile material is produced both in the reactor's core and when neutrons are captured in fertile material placed around the core (blanket). This process is known as breeding. Breeder reactors have not yet reached commercialization, although active research and development programs are being pursued by a number of countries.

CANDU (Canadian deuterium-uranium reactor.) The most widely used type of heavy-water reactor. The

CANDU reactor uses natural uranium as a fuel and heavy water as a moderator and a coolant. Recovery of plutonium from its spent fuel is not at present economical. Hence, the CANDU fuel cycle excludes both the enrichment and reprocessing steps.

centrifuge See ultracentrifuge.

chain reaction The continuing process of nuclear fissioning in which the neutrons released from a fission trigger at least one other nuclear fission. In a nuclear weapon an extremely rapid, multiplying chain reaction causes the explosive release of energy. In a reactor, the pace of the chain reaction is controlled to produce heat (in a power reactor) or large quantities of neutrons (in a research reactor).

chemical processing Chemical treatment of materials to separate specific usable constituents.

coolant A substance circulated through a nuclear reactor to remove or transfer heat. The most common coolants are water and heavy water.

core The central portion of a nuclear reactor containing the fuel elements and, usually, the moderator. Also the central portion of a nuclear weapon containing highly enriched uranium or plutonium.

critical mass The miniumum amount of fissionable material required to sustain a chain reaction. The exact mass varies with many factors such as the particular fissionable isotope present, its concentration and chemical form, the geometrical arrangement of the material, and its density. When fissile materials are compressed, for example, by high explosives in implosion-type atomic weapons, the critical mass needed for a nuclear explosion is reduced.

depleted uranium Uranium having a smaller percentage of uranium-235 than the 0.7 percent found in natural uranium. It is a by-product of the uranium enrichment process, during which uranium-235 is culled from one batch of uranium, depleting it, and then added to another batch to increase its concentration of uranium-235.

enrichment The process of increasing the concentration of one isotope of a given element (in the case of uranium, increasing the concentration of uranium-235).

feed stock Material introduced into a facility for processing.

fertile Material composed of atoms which easily absorb neutrons to produce fissile materials. One such element is uranium-238, which becomes plutonium-239 after it absorbs a neutron. Fertile material alone cannot sustain a chain reaction.

fission The process by which a neutron strikes a nucleus and splits it into fragments. During the process of nuclear fission, several neutrons are emitted at high speed, and heat and radiation are released.

fissile material Material composed of atoms which readily fission when struck by a neutron. Uranium-235 and plutonium-239 are examples of fissile materials.

fusion The formation of a heavier nucleus from two lighter ones (such as hydrogen isotopes), with the attendant release of energy (as in a hydrogen bomb).

gas centrifuge process A method of isotope separation in which slightly heavier gaseous atoms or molecules are separated from lighter ones by centrifugal force. See ultracentrifuge.

gaseous diffusion A method of isotope separation based

on the fact that gas atoms or molecules with different masses will diffuse through a porous barrier (or membrane) at different rates. The method is used to separate uranium-235 from uranium-238. It generally requires large plants and significant amounts of electric power.

gas-graphite reactor A nuclear reactor in which a gas is the coolant and graphite is the moderator.

heavy water Water containing significantly more than the natural proportion (1 in 6,500) of heavy hydrogen (deuterium) atoms to ordinary hydrogen atoms. (Hydrogen atoms have one proton and one neutron; deuterium atoms have one proton and two neutrons.) Heavy water is used as a moderator in some reactors because it slows down neutrons effectively and does not absorb them (unlike light, or normal, water) making it possible to fission natural uranium and sustain a chain reaction.

heavy-water reactor A reactor that uses heavy water as its moderator and natural uranium as fuel. See CANDU.

highly enriched uranium Uranium in which the percentage of uranium-235 nuclei has been increased from the natural level of 0.7 percent to some level greater than 20 percent, usually around 90 percent.

hot cells Lead-shielded rooms with remote handling equipment for examining and processing radioactive materials. In particular, hot cells can be used for reprocessing spent reactor fuel.

hydrogen bomb A nuclear weapon that derives its energy largely from fusion. Also known as a thermonuclear bomb.

irradiation Exposure to a radioactive source; for example, being placed in an operating nuclear reactor.

isotopes Atoms of the same element having the same number of protons, but a different number of neutrons. Two isotopes of the same element are very similar and difficult to separate by ordinary chemical means. Isotopes can have very different nuclear properties, however. For example, one isotope may fission readily, while another isotope of the same atom may not fission at all. An isotope is specified by its atomic mass number (the number of protons plus neutrons) following the symbol denoting the chemical element (e.g., U^{235} is an isotope of uranium).

jet-nozzle enrichment method A process of uranium enrichment that uses both uranium hexafluoride and a light gas flowing at high speed through a nozzle along curved walls.

kilogram A metric weight equivalent to 2.2 pounds.

kiloton The energy of a nuclear explosion that is equivalent to an explosion of 1,000 tons of TNT.

laser enrichment method A still experimental process of uranium enrichment in which a finely tuned, high-power carbon dioxide laser is used to differentially excite molecules of various atomic weights. This differential excitation makes it possible to separate uranium-235 from uranium-238.

light water Ordinary water (H_2O), as distinguished from heavy water (D_2O).

light-water reactor A reactor that uses ordinary water as moderator and coolant and low-enriched uranium as fuel.

low-enriched uranium Uranium in which the percentage

of uranium-235 nuclei has been increased from the natural level of 0.7 percent to less than 20 percent, usually 3 to 6 percent. With the increased level of fissile material, low-enriched uranium can sustain a chain reaction when immersed in light-water and is used as fuel in light-water reactors.

medium-enriched uranium Uranium in which the percentage of uranium-235 nuclei has been increased from the natural level of 0.7 percent to between 20 and 50 percent. (Potentially usable for nuclear weapons, but very large quantities are needed.)

megawatt One million watts. Used in reference to a nuclear power plant, one million watts of electricity. Used in reference to a research reactor, one million watts of thermal energy. (Roughly three thermal megawatts are needed to produce one megawatt of electricity). Also equal to 1000 kilowatts.

metric ton One thousand kilograms. A metric weight equivalent to 2200 pounds or 1.1 tons.

milling A process in the uranium fuel cycle by which ore containing only a very small percentage of uranium oxide (U_3O_8) is converted into material containing a high percentage (80 percent) of U_3O_8, often referred to as yellowcake.

moderator A component (usually water, heavy water, or graphite) of some nuclear reactors that surrounds the core and slows neutrons, thereby increasing their chances of fissioning by fissile material.

natural uranium Uranium as found in nature, containing 0.7 percent of uranium-235, 99.3 percent of uranium-238, and a trace of uranium-234.

neutron An uncharged elementary particle, with a mass slightly greater than that of a proton, found in the nucleus of every atom heavier than hydrogen.

nuclear energy The energy liberated by a nuclear reaction (fission or fusion) or by spontaneous radioactivity.

nuclear fuel Basic chain-reacting material, including both fissile and fertile materials. Commonly used nuclear fuels are natural uranium, and low-enriched uranium; high-enriched uranium and plutonium are used in some reactors.

nuclear fuel cycle The set of chemical and physical operations needed to prepare nuclear material for use in reactors and to dispose of or recycle the material after its removal from the reactor. Existing fuel cycles begin with uranium as the natural resource and create plutonium as a by-product. Some future fuel cycles may rely on thorium and produce the fissile isotope uranium-233.

nuclear fuel element A rod, tube, plate, or other mechanical shape or form into which nuclear fuel is fabricated for use in a reactor.

nuclear fuel fabrication plant A facility where the nuclear material (e.g., enriched or natural uranium) is fabricated into fuel elements to be inserted into a reactor.

nuclear power plant Any device or assembly that converts nuclear energy into useful power. In a nuclear electric power plant, heat produced by a reactor is used to produce steam to drive a turbine that in turn drives an electricity generator.

nuclear reactor A mechanism fueled by fissionable materials that give off neutrons, thereby inducing heat.

Reactors are of three general types: power reactors, production reactors, and research reactors.

nuclear waste The radioactive by-products formed by fission and other nuclear processes in a reactor. Most nuclear waste is initially contained spent fuel. If this material is reprocessed, new categories of waste result.

nuclear weapons A collective term for atomic bombs and hydrogen bombs. Weapons based on a nuclear explosion. Generally used throughout the text to mean atomic bombs, only, unless used with reference to nuclear weapon states, (all five of which have both atomic and hydrogen weapons).

plutonium-239 A fissile isotope occurring naturally in only minute quantities, which is manufactured artificially when uranium-238, through irradiation, captures an extra neutron. It is one of the two materials that have been used for the core of nuclear weapons, the other being highly enriched uranium.

plutonium-240 A fissile isotope produced in reactors when a plutonium-239 atom absorbs a neutron instead of fissioning. Its presence complicates the construction of nuclear explosives because of its high rate of spontaneous fission.

power reactor A reactor designed to produce electricity as distinguished from reactors used primarily for research or for producing radiation or fissionable materials.

production reactor A reactor designed primarily for large-scale production of plutonium-239 by neutron irradiation of uranium-238.

radioactivity The spontaneous disintegration of an unstable atomic nucleus resulting in the emission of subatomic particles.

radioisotope A radioactive isotope.

recycle To reuse the remaining uranium and plutonium found in spent fuel after they have been separated at a reprocessing plant from unwanted radioactive waste products also in the spent fuel.

reprocessing Chemical treatment of spent reactor fuel to separate the plutonium and uranium from the unwanted radioactive waste by-products and (under present plans) from each other.

research reactor A reactor primarily designed to supply neutrons for experimental purposes. It may also be used for training, materials testing, and production of radioisotopes.

spent fuel Fuel elements that have been removed from the reactor after use because they contain too little fissile and fertile material and too high a concentration of unwanted radioactive by-products to sustain reactor operation. Spent fuel is both physically and radioactively hot.

thermonuclear bomb A hydrogen bomb.

thorium-232 A fertile material.

ultracentrifuge A rotating vessel that can be used for enrichment of uranium. The heavier isotopes of uranium hexafluoride gas concentrate at the walls of the rotating centrifuge and are drawn off.

uranium A radioactive element with the atomic number 92 and, as found in natural ores, an average atomic weight of 238. The two principal natural isotopes are uranium-235 (0.7 percent of natural uranium), which is fissionable, and uranium-238 (99.3 percent of natural uranium), which is fertile.

uranium-233 (U^{233}) A fissile isotope bred in fertile thorium-232. Like plutonium-239 it is theoretically an excellent material for nuclear weapons, but is not known to have been used for this purpose. Can be used as reactor fuel.

uranium-235 (U^{235}) The only naturally occurring fissile isotope. Natural uranium contains 0.7 percent U^{235}; light-water reactors use about 3 percent and weapons grade, highly enriched uranium normally consists of 93 percent of this isotope.

uranium-238 A fertile material. Natural uranium is composed of approximately 99.3 percent U^{238}

uranium dioxide (UO_2) Purified uranium. The form of natural uranium used in heavy water reactors. Also the form of uranium that remains after the fluorine is removed from enriched uranium hexafluoride (UF_6). Produced as a powder, uranium dioxide is, in turn, fabricated into fuel elements.

uranium oxide (U_3O_8) The most common oxide of uranium found in typical ores. U_3O_8 is extracted from the ore during the milling process. The ore typically contains only 0.1 percent U_3O_8; yellowcake, the product of the milling process, contains about 80 percent U_3O_8.

uranium hexafluoride (UF_6) A volatile compound of uranium and fluorine. UF_6 is a solid at atmospheric pressure and room temperature, but can be transformed into gas by heating. UF_6 gas (alone, or in combination with hydrogen or helium) is the feed stock in all uranium enrichment processes and is sometimes produced as an intermediate product in the process of purifying yellowcake to produce uranium oxide.

vessel The part of a reactor that contains the nuclear fuel.

weapons grade Nuclear material of the type most suitable for nuclear weapons, i.e., uranium enriched to 90 percent U^{235} or plutonium that is primarily Pu^{239}.

weapons-usable Fissile material that is weapons-grade or, though less than ideal for weapons, that can still be used to make a nuclear explosive.

yellowcake A concentrate produced during the milling process that contains about 80 percent uranium oxide (U_3O_8). In preparation for uranium enrichment, the yellowcake is converted to uranium hexafluoride gas (UF_6). In the preparation of natural uranium reactor fuel, yellowcake is processed into purified uranium dioxide. Sometimes uranium hexaflouride is produced as an intermediate step in the purification process.

yield The total energy released in a nuclear explosion. It is usually expressed in equivalent tons of TNT (the quantity of TNT required to produce a corresponding amount of energy).

Sources

1. Congressional Research Service, *Nuclear Proliferation Factbook* (Washington, DC: U.S. Govt. Printing Office, 1977).
2. Energy Research & Development Administration, *U.S. Nuclear Power Export Activities* (Springfield, VA: National Technical Information Service, 1976).
3. Nuclear Energy Policy Study Group, *Nuclear Power: Issues and Choices* (Cambridge, MA: Ballinger Publishing Co., 1977).
4. Office of Technology Assessment, *Nuclear Proliferation and Safeguards* (Washington, D.C.: Office of Technology Assessment, 1977); *Nuclear Power in an Age of Uncertainty* (Washington, D.C.: Office of Technology Assessment, 1984).
5. Wohlstetter, Albert, *Swords from Plowshares: The Military Potential of Civilian Nuclear Energy* (Chicago· The University of Chicago Press, 1977).
6. United Nations Association of the USA, *Nuclear Proliferation: A Citizen's Guide to Policy Choices* (N.Y.: UNA-USA, 1983).

Index